ISBN 978-1-331-22226-2
PIBN 10160324

Similar Books Are Available from
www.forgottenbooks.com

Correction of Errors:

Volume I, page xv, The title of illustration, "Breaking Prairie,"
&c., the cut was lost and does not appear.
" I, page 267, fourth line from the bottom, October, 1863,
should be October, 1853.

Volume II, page 39, line 25 from the top, the word fourteen
should be eight; and in line 26 the words
ten and twenty-two should be three and
thirteen.
" II, page 78, line 17 from top, F. H. Pierpont should be
Frederick Holbrook.

Volume III, page ix, "List of Illustrations," after "Frontispiece"
should be Frederick E. Bissell, page 12.
" III, page 274, 9th line from the bottom, Sixth General
Assembly should be Sixteenth General As-
sembly.
" III, page x, "List of Illustrations," "Lead Mining near
Dubuque" should be page 438, instead of
page 443.

Some of the cuts used in this work were made from old and faded
photographs and are imperfect, but the best attainable.

In the case of Colonel Asbury B. Porter. Vol. II, page 387, and Vol.
IV, page 214, appears the statement that he was dismissed from the
service. This statement made in the published official reports of the
Adjutant-General's office was incorrect.

Colonel Porter resigned for disability, and his resignation was accepted by General Grant, then department commander, March 19, 1863, and
he was honorably discharged from the service. Some person reported
him absent without leave, and under a misapprehension of the facts, the
President ordered his dismissal, April 30.

Instead of entering his honorable discharge on the records, dating
from March 8, 1863, the Adjutant-General's Department erroneously
made the entry "Dismissed." This error has never been corrected in the
public Reports of that office: hence writers of war history have been misled and great injustice done a gallant Iowa officer.

MOUTH OF THE WISCONSIN RIVER

Where Marquette Discovered Iowa. Iowa Shore in the Distance Beyond the Mississippi River

FROM THE EARLIEST TIMES
TO THE BEGINNING OF THE TWENTIETH CENTURY

FOUR VOLUMES

By BENJAMIN F. GUE

*Illustrated with Photographic Views of the Natural Scenery of
the State, Public Buildings, Pioneer Life, Etc.*

WITH PORTRAITS AND BIOGRAPHIES OF NOTABLE MEN AND WOMEN OF IOWA

VOLUME I

THE PIONEER PERIOD

1903

THE CENTURY HISTORY COMPANY
136 LIBERTY STREET
NEW YORK CITY

Publication Office
136 Liberty Street
New York, N. Y., U. S. A.

TABLE OF CONTENTS

VOLUME ONE

CHAPTER V

CHAPTER VI

CHAPTER VII

CHAPTER VIII

CHAPTER XVIII

CHAPTER XIX

CHAPTER XX

CHAPTER XXI

CHAPTER XXX

LIST OF ILLUSTRATIONS

GENERAL INTRODUCTION

WHILE Iowa is one of the younger states of the Republic, as compared with the Thirteen Colonies which won independence from Great Britain through the War of the Revolution, it has a history which may be traced with some degree of certainty for a period of more than two hundred years. From the time of its discovery in 1673, by Marquette and Joliet, investigation has brought to the knowledge of civilized people many facts relating to the prehistoric period during which it was occupied by the aboriginal races who preserve no history. Through traditions handed down from one generation to another by the Indian tribes, and recorded observations of the earliest explorers who ventured among them, much of the history of the Red Men who made their homes in Iowa has been gathered. The story of the first explorers of our rivers who gave them names, is incomplete, and even the origin and signification of the beautiful name of our State is involved in obscurity and uncertainty.

No connected history of Iowa from the earliest period down to the close of the Nineteenth Century is in existence and the time has arrived when the growing prominence of our State among the members of the Union would seem to justify the presentation of a narrative of the important events of the past. The approaching centennial anniversary of the acquisition of Louisiana, a vast region west of the Mississippi River of which Iowa is one of the greatest states, renders it especially appropriate that its written history should now be given to the public.

In preparing this work the utmost care has been exercised in the investigation of authorities examined, and in all cases of conflict the evidence has been sifted with the sole purpose of discovering the truth. These conflicts of opinion, which are not uncommon, compel the writer to act as a judge in the trial of causes, giving due considera-

tion to the preponderance of evidence and the credibility
of witnesses.

Having been a citizen of Iowa for more than half a
century, and for a large portion of that period an active
participant in political and other conflicts as an editor
and legislator, I am well aware that it is difficult to exercise strict impartiality in recording events which, in
times of great excitement during the Civil War and numerous heated political campaigns, aroused the passions
and prejudices of the active participants. But the lapse of
time and the cooler judgment coming with mature years
has, I trust, eliminated prejudice and enabled me to deal
justly with all.

Believing that one who has lived in the State during
the period of development from a frontier region of wild
prairies, stretching almost unbroken from the Mississippi
to the Missouri, who has witnessed settlement from scattered log cabins along its water courses and among its
native groves, with a population of less than two hundred thousand to more than two million two hundred
thousand, who has known personally most of the public
men who have framed its laws, founded its public institutions and shaped its policy—can better tell the story of
the " building of the State," than the profound scholar
or deeply learned historian who has lived apart from its
life, struggles, and conflicts, through which growth and
development come to people or countries.

The pioneers who closely followed the retreating Indians laid the first foundations upon which the fabric of
our commonwealth has been slowly reared. These rugged settlers led the way through hardships and privations, creating from nature's resources new homes where
the rude log cabins crowded the vanishing wigwams farther westward. They first ventured upon the unsheltered
prairies and turned over the sod of countless years' formation, which carpeted with grass and flowers a soil of un-

surpassed fertility. They brought from distant states and countries habits, customs, religions, prejudices, and virtues of widely separated communities and nationalities. It was through compromising and harmonizing these diverse elements that our first laws were evolved, schools established, and churches organized.

Among the earliest educators and civilizers were the pioneer newspapers which made their appearance soon after the first civil government was extended over the land acquired by treaty with the Indians. The files of the first weekly journal printed on Iowa soil, before it became a separate Territory, bear unmistakable evidence of the spirit of progress which even then characterized the newspaper, long before the advent of regular mails, railroads, or telegraphs. It was the leader in local enterprises, public opinion and the policy of the earliest forms of government. The files of early newspapers, wisely preserved by Theodore S. Parvin, and Chandler Childs of Dubuque, and the State Historical Society of Iowa City, contain much of the current history from 1836 to 1850 that would otherwise have been lost. Many of these ancient Iowa newspapers are now accessible to the public in the fireproof rooms of the Historical Department at Des Moines. While newspaper history is not always reliable, it leads the investigator to the fixing of dates, examination of additional authorities and the resurrection of many forgotten events which might have been lost to the historian.

The "Annals of Iowa," established in 1863 by the State Historical Society, and now published by the Historical Department, the "Historical Record" of Iowa City, the publication by the State of the valuable papers and addresses of the "Pioneer Lawmakers' Association"—furnished a large amount of material of inestimable value which has been liberally drawn upon in the preparation of this history.

Among the authorities consulted relating to the earliest

period of which any knowledge can be obtained of Iowa and its ancient inhabitants may be mentioned " The Ice Age of North America " by G. F. Wright; Foster's " Prehistoric Races of the United States "; Geological Reports of Iowa by Owen, Hall, McGee, White and Calvin; Monett's " History of the Mississippi Valley "; De Soto's Expedition, Parkman's Historical Works on the French occupation of America; " Expedition of Marquette and Joliet "; Voyages and Travels of La Salle and Hennepin in the Mississippi Valley; Reports of the Expeditions of Captains Lewis and Clark, of Lieutenant Zebulon M. Pike, of Major S. H. Long; " Notes on the Iowa District of Wisconsin Territory " by Lieutenant Albert M. Lea; Gayarre's " History of Louisiana "; Galland's " Iowa Emigrant of 1840 "; Newhall's " Glimpse of Iowa in 1846.'

The history of Iowa Indians has been compiled from the following works: Schoolcraft's " Indians of the United States," Catlin's " North American Indians," Thatchers's " Indian Biographies," Drake's " Indians of North America," Fulton's " Red Men of Iowa," the " Life of Black Hawk " and writings of numerous pioneers.

The facts relating to the Sioux Indian hostilities in northwestern Iowa, the causes leading thereto, the massacre at the lakes, captivity of four young women, the march and sufferings of the Relief Expedition have been gathered from " Historical Sketches of Northwestern Iowa " by Major William Williams, " History of the Spirit Massacre " by Abbie Gardner Sharp, one of the captives, addresses by members of the Relief Expedition delivered at Webster City upon the occasion of the erection of a tablet to the memory of Captain Johnson's Hamilton County Company and R. A. Smith's " History of Dickinson County."

Among the authorities used in the preparation of the

political and statistical records were the following: Hildreth's, Bancroft's and Bryant's Histories of the United States; Appleton's Cyclopedia Annuals; the Whig, Tribune and World Almanacs; the " Iowa Political Register "; Cleveland's " Political Text Book "; Fairall's " Manual of Iowa Politics "; Official Registers of Iowa from 1886 to 1902; Official Registers of the United States from 1846 to 1901; United States and Iowa Census Reports and hundreds of volumes of State Documents.

The record of Iowa in the Civil War from 1861 to 1865, inclusive, has been gathered from nine volumes of the Reports of Adjutant-General Nathaniel B. Baker; numerous histories of Iowa regiments; Ingersoll's " Iowa and the Rebellion "; Stuart's " Iowa Colonels and Regiments "; Lathrop's " Life and Times of Samuel J. Kirkwood "; Greeley's " American Conflict "; Personal Memoirs of Generals Grant and Sherman.

In compiling a history of the causes and events leading to the Civil War the following authorities have been consulted: " Garrison and the Antislavery Movement "; Halloway's " History of Kansas "; " John Brown and Mis Men " by Hinton; Sanborn's " Life and Letters of John Brown "; " Life of Abraham Lincoln " by Nicholay and Hay.

The historical sketches of Iowa counties have been gleaned from more than one hundred county histories· " Andrea's Historical Atlas of Iowa "; Fulton's " Sketches of Iowa Counties " and personal recollections of early settlers.

The biographical sketches have been prepared from data procured from the subjects of the sketches, or from those who knew them intimately where the facts desired could not be found in some of the numerous biographical publications of notable Iowa men and women.

A number of the illustrations in the several volumes were obtained from the " Annals of Iowa," the " Iowa

Geological Survey," the " Midland Monthly," the " Overland Stage to California," by Root and the " Progres-
sive Men of Iowa." These acknowledgments are made
here in preference to quoting authorities in foot notes
through the body of the work.

It will be observed that the general plan of this history
embraces the following distinctive features:

First.—A connected narrative of the most important
events relating to Iowa, shown by scientific investigations
to have transpired before the historic period.

Second.—Reasonably authenticated history of the Indian tribes known to have occupied Iowa.

Third.—Brief records of the exploring expeditions
which discovered the Mississippi River and valley. The
western trend of settlements towards the prairie regions.
The acquisition of Louisiana, a country larger than the
entire Republic east of the Mississippi River. Discoveries made by the various exploring expeditions which
examined portions of the Mississippi Valley and Iowa
from 1673 to 1836.

Fourth.—The first white adventurers and pioneer settlers who entered the region which became Iowa. The
evolution of civil government from claim regulations to
written constitutions. Early political parties, nominating conventions and elections.

Fifth.—Progress of slavery agitation and legislation
leading to civil war and emancipation. The part taken
by Iowa citizens and lawmakers in these critical times.

Sixth.—Iowa statesmen, citizens and soldiers during
the Civil War. History of Iowa Volunteer Regiments.

Seventh.—The period of development in settlement.
education, transportation, labor-saving inventions, man-
ufactures, mining and civil government from the close
of the war to the beginning of the Twentieth Century.

Eighth.—Historical sketches of Iowa counties; the
naming and changing of boundaries; establishing of

county-seats; the first settlers, county officials and newspapers.

Ninth.—A complete Directory of Iowa public officials,
Territorial, State, and National from the establishment
of the first civil government over the " Black Hawk Purchase " to the beginning of the Twentieth Century.

Tenth.—Biographical sketches of more than four hundred notable Iowa men and women who were prominent
in some work of public interest during the Nineteenth
Century.

It has been my purpose, so far as practicable in a work
of this size, to make it a cyclopedia of general information
pertaining to Iowa, that will render it indispensable as a
work of reference to all who are interested in the found-
ing, development, government, and resources of the fore-
most State of the Louisiana Purchase as well as in the
character and achievements of its people.

A distinguished citizen of Iowa has said, " Of all that
is good Iowa affords the best." I have endeavored to
show in these volumes wherein this claim has solid foundation and that this classic phrase is not an extravagant
statement as applied to the progress made by our people
in education, general intelligence, good government, and
exemplary citizenship.

Des Moines, Iowa.

March Third, 1902.

CHAPTER I

NATURE'S supreme laws of never ending change from one degree of development to another, seem to pervade the universe. Man in all ages has been slowly reading these immutable statutes, unwritten, and only to be known through careful observation and patient investigation.

A little gained by one generation handed down to another, since the first appearance of man upon the earth, has made the sum of human knowledge. For how many ages on some other far off planet human intellect has been slowly pursuing the same great study we have no means of knowing.

Here the astronomer has discovered the existence of other worlds, has carefully computed their size, has measured their distance from the earth and each other, has observed their motion, their satellites, and learned some of the laws which govern them. He has even constructed a plausible theory as to how these planets were formed from the original elements.

As to the comparative antiquity of the eastern and western continents of our own earth, recent investigation brings evidence to reverse the old belief that Asia and Africa were earlier formations than America. Agassiz says:

" First born among the continents, though so much later in culture and civilization than some of more recent birth, America, so far as her physical history is concerned, has been falsely denominated the ' new world.' Hers was the first dry land lifted out of the waters; hers the first shores washed by the ocean that enveloped all the earth besides; and while Europe was represented only by islands rising here and there above the sea, America already stretched one unbroken line of land from Nova Scotia to the far west."

In our limited world the investigators have explored the beds of ancient rivers, lakes and seas; the caverns of rocks and mountains, and penetrated deep into the earth in search of knowledge that may be derived from rock formations, animal and vegetable fossils. These to the scientist reveal much of the story of earth's growth; its stages of development; its desolations and changes through the agencies of fire, water and air. In these reservoirs have been found keys to earth's prehistoric changes. They reveal to the student a history of its geological growth, vegetable and animal development for millions of years before written history begins. Scientists explore every known country, every island of the ocean, examine rocks, clays, gravels and fossils in pursuit of knowledge of the past. From these they read much of the story of the earliest formations, convulsions, growth and population of the earth with almost as much certainty as though the events had been inscribed in legible characters on imperishable tablets. It is from these evidences that we learn some of the history of the remote past, relating to the land we live in, which men have named Iowa.

Professor Samuel Calvin has well said:

"The finding of a single genuine prehistoric arrow-point may enable us to write up an important chapter in the history of a people that no historian ever saw, and concerning whose existence there is not even the shadow of a human tradition. When, as is often possible, we may add the knowledge gained by exploring their homes, their shrines and sepulchers, we are in a position to write up somewhat more fully the portion of their history which deals with their daily occupations and their domestic life. Many records tell of other facts than the mere presence of human occupants in a region such as Iowa. Vegetable remains preserved in peat bogs in the mud that accumulated at the bottom of ancient ponds and lakes enable us to reconstruct the prehistoric forests. With such vegetable remains are usually found bones of the animals that lived in the forests. Human weapons or human skeletons are often there too. So in records preserved in the peat bog or in the lake bed, science may rehabilitate in a general way the prehistoric landscapes, and may see them enlivened with multitudes of struggling creatures, man among the rest; all bent on accomplishing the two great objects for which living things below the higher planes

of humanity seem to strive,—' to eat and to escape being eaten.' Not only
may we restore the forests in the shadow of which prehistoric man lived,
we may know the size and habits of the animals that roamed through the
forest; those that man chased and those from which he in turn fled; we
may even go farther and determine the climatic conditions under which all
this assemblage of animal and plant life existed."

Geology unfolds to us a wonderful history of the most
remote periods of time, which reduced to language reads
like a fairy tale. It tells us nearly all we know of the
countless years that passed away while the continent, of
which Iowa is a part, was in the process of formation.
Professor Calvin continues:

" These geologic records, untampered with, and unimpeachable, declare
that for uncounted years Iowa, together with the great valley of the
Mississippi, lay beneath the level of the sea. So far as it was inhabited at
all, marine forms of animals and plants were its only occupants."

During the ages of submergence, the sedimentary strata
of Iowa, as well as of all the adjacent States, was being
formed on the sea bottom. This formation contains a
record of a period of duration altogether incomprehensi-
ble. Centuries pass while the light colored limestones so
well represented at Anamosa are slowly forming by an
imperceptible sedimentary accumulation. Other ages
come and go while the limestones represented in Johnson
County are forming. About this time a small portion of
northeastern Iowa rises above the sea, while all the vast
region south and west is still buried deep beneath the all
pervading water. Odd shaped fishes and a species of
ferns mark the highest point reached in the evolution of
animal and plant life at this time.

Ages again go by while the sediment of the sea is forming beds of rock which appear in Marshall, Des Moines
and Lee counties. Then slowly come the Coal Measures
and rocks above them. Ferns and air-breathing creatures
have made their appearance. The sea gradually recedes
to the southward and the surface of our whole State is
visible. Later forests and other forms of vegetation cover

portions of the land; birds appear in the woods and a
few small rat-like animals are found, as well as reptiles.

But another great change comes; the waters again cover
the northwestern portion of the State and ages come and
go before the sea recedes, never to return. Iowa has finally
been raised above the sea level and the waters drain
toward the ocean, forming great rivers, and plowing
deep channels through the oozing sediment. The sun and
wind finally dry the surface; forests and rank vegetation
again make their appearance; animals come forth from
Nature's nurseries and spread themselves over the land,
and roam through the jungles, preying upon each other
in their struggle for food. The climate is that of the
tropics, and myriads of forms of life are evolved.

All of the conditions are now favorable for the advent
of man, but no evidence is found of his existence on any
portion of the earth at this period. The rivers, which
ages later were named the Mississippi and Missouri, were
then carrying the inland waters to the sea which reached
as far north as the Ohio river.

Where the upper Missouri now flows through the prairies of Nebraska, the Dakotas and Montana, were lakes
spreading over a large portion of these States. Remains
of forests and strange species of animals, long since ex-
tinct, have been found in the sediment that was formed
in these lakes. Tropical trees such as the cypress, mag-
nolia, cinnamon, fig and palm flourished in Iowa, Dakota,
and far northward into British America; tropical birds
sang in the forests; huge reptiles crawled about in the
rank vegetation and swamps.

Then came the Tertiary period. Iowa was a part of the
land area which then made up the half formed continent
of North America. The drainage of the State must have
been much the same as now, although the altitude above
sea level was several hundred feet lower.

In the beds of Tertiary lakes were entombed animals and
plant remains which man in these late generations has

found. The sediment exposed to the action of the atmosphere has been converted into vast plains and prairies. In many cases the lakes have been gradually filled and converted into dry land. Modern streams, such as the Yellowstone, Missouri and the Platte rivers cut their way through these old lake beds. The surface of the sediment underwent continual changes through erosion. The remains of plants and animals were thus slowly laid bare, and the scientist was able to read the story of their lives. Such beds are believed to be the only places of importance where the records of Tertiary plants and animals have been preserved. While none of these lake beds have been found within the limits of our State, it cannot be doubted that the conditions which prevailed upon our western and northern boundaries were not unlike those which obtained here.

The animal inhabitants of this period consisted of opossums, a strange species of squirrel, beavers and gophers. There were large hoofed animals not unlike the rhinoceros; others bore resemblance to the tapir and the swine family. There were creatures with three hoofs to each foot and three toes on each hoof, of a species related to the horse. There were others resembling camels, oxen and cud-chewing animals that seemed to be a combination of the deer, the camel and the hog. There was a family of short jawed animals resembling the panther with sharp, knife-like teeth. There were saber-toothed tigers more powerful and cruel than the Asiatic species; there were monkeys, foxes and wolves. Huge snakes, lizards and turtles infested the swamps. Bright winged birds flitted among the forests and open glades. Bats and myriads of strange insects were present preying upon others.

Throughout the Tertiary period the climatic conditions appear to have been remarkably uniform over regions extending north to Greenland and westward to Montana. Iowa, and all adjacent regions far north and westward reveled in the luxuriance of a tropical climate. The air was balmy and laden with the odor of flowers and fruits. The bright summer days seemed never ending. A listless languor sent the birds and beasts into the shade at midday. Tropical vegetation grew spontaneously; brilliant foliage and flowers, luxuriant ferns and clinging vines mingled with the forests and open vistas in landscapes of surpassing beauty.

But in the course of time a change was perceptible. The intense heat of the long summer days was tempered by refreshing breezes, and the nights became delightfully cool. The winters were slowly growing colder. Snow storms came and piercing winds swept over plain and forest. Tropical plants were stricken with early frosts; ice formed in lakes and streams where it had never before appeared. The more hardy animals sought the shelter of wooded ravines and deep gorges. Snow fell to unusual depths; year after year it came earlier, and winter continued later. The earth became frozen to great depths; fruits and trees disappeared. As the snow piled higher each succeeding year, and the summers were too short and cold to melt it, all animal life perished. The pressure of mountains of snow and the percolating rains converted the mass into a solid sheet of glacier ice that not only covered nearly all of Iowa, but reached out over the northern half of North America.

The ice sheet of this period had its southern margin south of the latitude of St. Louis. The ice was slowly moving outward from the center of accumulation, grinding over the underlying rocks, crushing them into the finest powder. Fragments of enormous size were frequently caught in the lower portion of the flowing ice and carried forward bodily, grinding the rock strata into rock flour, and being themselves planed and grooved on the lower surface. All bowlders of crystalline rock which we find strewn over our State were carried from their native ledges in British America by these ice sheets of what geologists call the Quaternary period.

BOWLDER IN BUCHANAN COUNTY

KS IN DES MOINES COUNTY.

Another climatic change slowly came, and the ice began to melt. Rivers were gradually formed, carrying on their turbid waters the soil made by the grinding ice. This was deposited over the surface of the State, forming yellow clay.

Professor Samuel Calvin, State Geologist for Iowa, has told how the soils of the State were produced by the action of the ice in the glacial period. He says:

" Glaciers and glacial action have contributed in a very large degree to the making of our magnificent State. What Iowa would have been had it never suffered from the effects of the ponderous ice sheets that successively overflowed its surface, is illustrated, but not perfectly, in the driftless area. Here we have an area that was not invaded by glaciers. Allamakee, parts of Jackson, Dubuque, Clayton, Fayette and Winneshiek counties belong to the driftless area. During the last two decades numerous deep wells have been bored through the loose surface deposit, and down into the underlying rocks. The record of these wells shows that the rock surface is very uneven. Before the glacial drift which now mantles nearly the whole of Iowa was deposited, the surface had been carved into an intricate system of hills and valleys. There were narrow gorges hundreds of feet in depth, and there were rugged, rocky cliffs and isolated buttes corresponding in height with the depth of the valleys.

" To a person passing from the drift-covered to the driftless part of the State, the topography presents a series of surprises. The principal drainage streams flow in valleys that measure, from the summits of the divides, six hundred feet or more in depth. The Oneota, or Upper Iowa River, in Allamakee County, for example, flows between picturesque cliffs that rise almost vertically from three to four hundred feet, while from the summit of the cliffs the land rises gradually to the crest of the divide, three, four, or five miles back from the stream. Tributary streams cut the lateral slopes and canyon walls at intervals. These again have tributaries of the second order. In such a region a quarter section of level land would be a curiosity. This is a fair sample of what Iowa would have been had it not been planed down by the leveling effects of the glaciers. Soils of uniform excellence would have been impossible in a non-glacial Iowa. The soils of Iowa have a value equal to all of the silver and gold mines of the world combined.

" And for this rich heritage of soils we are indebted to great rivers of ice that overflowed Iowa from the north and northwest. The glaciers in their long journey ground up the rocks over which they moved and mingled the fresh rock flour from granites of British America and northern Minnesota with pulverized limestones and shales of more southern regions, and used these rich materials in covering up the bald rocks and leveling the irregular surface of preglacial Iowa. The materials are in places hundreds of feet in depth. They are not oxidized or leached, but retain the carbonates and other soluble constituents that contribute so largely to the growth of plants. The physical condition of the materials is ideal, rendering the soil porous, facilitating the distribution of moisture, and offering unmatched opportunities for the employment of improved machinery in all of the processes connected with cultivation. Even the driftless area received great benefit from the action of glaciers, for although the area was not invaded by ice, it was yet to a large extent covered by a peculiar deposit called loess, which is generally connected with one of the later sheets of drift. The loess is a porous clay, rich in carbonate of lime. Throughout the drift-less area it has covered up many spots that would otherwise have been bare rocks. It covered the stiff intractable clays that would otherwise have been the only soils of the region. It in itself constitutes a soil of great fertility. Every part of Iowa is debtor in some way to the great ice sheets of the glacial period."

*   *   *   *   *

" Soils are everywhere the product of rock disintegration, and so the quality of the soils in a given locality must necessarily be determined in large measure by the kind of rock from which they were derived.

" From this point of view, therefore, the history of Iowa's superb soils begins with first steps in rock making. The very oldest rocks of the Mis-sissippi Valley have contributed something to making our soils what they are, and every later formation laid down over the surface of Iowa, or regions north of it, has furnished its quota of materials to the same end. The history of Iowa's soils, therefore, embraces the whole sweep of geologic times.

" The chief agents concerned in modifying the surface throughout most of Iowa since the disappearance of the latest glaciers have been organic, al-though the physical and chemical influences of air and water have not been without marked effect. The growth and decay of a long series of genera-tions of plants have contributed certain organic constituents to the soil. Earth worms bring up fine material from considerable depths and place it in position to be spread out upon the surface. They drag leaves and any manageable portion of plants into their burrows, and much of the material so taken down into the ground decays and enriches the ground to a depth of several inches. The pocket gopher has done much to furnish a surface layer of loose, mellow, easily cultivated and highly productive soil. Like the earth worm, the gopher for century after century has been bringing up to the surface fine material, to the amount of several tons annually to the acre, avoiding necessarily the pebbles, cobbles and coarser constituents. The burrows collapse, the undermined bowlders and large fragments sink downwards, rains and winds spread out the gopher hills and worm castings, and the next year, and the next, the process is repeated; and so it has been for all the years making up the centuries since the close of the glacial epoch. Organic agents in the form of plants and burrowing animals have worked unremittingly through many centuries, and accomplished a work of incalculable value in pulverizing, mellowing and enriching the superficial stratum, and bringing it to the ideal condition in which it was found by the explorers and pioneers from whose advent dates the historical period of our matchless Iowa."

It is estimated that the last invasion of Iowa by the glaciers was from 100,000 to 170,000 years ago. For many years scientists have been investigating the causes which have produced the great treeless plains of the Mississippi Valley. East of Ohio prairies are unknown, but as we go westward they increase in number and size. In western Indiana, and from there to the Rocky Mountains west and north the vast prairies* prevail, although groves are often found, and the margins of lakes, rivers and creeks are generally bordered to some extent with trees. From 98° of longitude west and treeless plains become almost a desert.

The soil of the prairies varies in formation and quality to almost as great an extent as in the timbered regions. In Michigan, Indiana and Illinois the prairies are inclined to be quite level, the surface soil is a black vegetable formation from six inches to five feet or more in depth. In Iowa the prairies are more rolling, affording better surface drainage.

In southern Wisconsin, Minnesota, the Dakotas, western Nebraska, northern Missouri and western Kansas, the vegetable formation is lighter, sand and gravel being quite common on the surface.

Along the first river bottoms, the soil is generally a deep rich alluvium. The second bench often presents a mixture of sand and gravel while the bluffs show soil of a lighter color, with clay near the surface. Large bodies of

---

*Prairie is a French word signifying meadow. It was the name first applied to the great treeless plains of North America by the French missionaries who were the discoverers of the prairie regions of the west.

broken land, cut up into steep hills, generally extend back
from the water courses, through which deep ravines have
been cut in all directions. This land is generally covered
to some extent with growth of stunted oak and hickory
trees, among which are thickets of wild plum, crab apple
and hazel bushes. These lands were called " barrens " by
the early settlers. The soil of this hill land is productive,
producing grain, grass and fruit of excellent quality. The
" Missouri Slope " is the name given to that portion of
Iowa which is drained into the Missouri River. The soil
is a bluff deposit, generally destitute of surface stone and
gravel, or rock strata beneath, and produces excellent
crops of grain, grass, vegetables and fruit. The bluffs
along the Missouri River rise to a height of from one to
two hundred feet, everywhere intersected with deep ravines. They are generally treeless, but in some places
small timber is found. Northern Iowa is but gently rolling fifty miles west of the Mississippi, while the southern
half of the State is more broken into hills and valleys, and
has large tracts of woodland.

Although essentially a prairie State, almost every
variety of surface soil is found, showing conclusively that
it is not the peculiar soil formation which causes forests
to grow in one locality and prairies to be found inter-
mingled with them.

After more than half a century of investigation of the
causes which have produced the prairies, the problem is
yet unsettled. No theory yet advanced explains satisfactorily why the treeless plains begin in certain sections
of Michigan, Indiana, Wisconsin, Missouri, Kansas and
Louisiana, without any noticeable difference in soil or
surface. In many places in the States where the prairies
predominate, remains of forests are found that show evidences of having existed for hundreds of years, and among
them are prairies which furnish no indications of ever
having been covered with trees.

The origin of the prairies is one of the most interesting

problems that has engaged the attention of all thoughtful people who have seen them before they were touched by the plow. Scientists have sought carefully for evidences to sustain the different theories advanced. Professors Whitney and Hall, who made early geological surveys and examinations of portions of Iowa, gave considerable attention to the origin of prairies. Whitney says

" The cause of the absence of trees on the prairies, is the physical character of the soil, and especially its exceeding fineness, which is prejudicial to the growth of anything but a superficial vegetation. The smallness of the particles of soil being an insuperable barrier to the necessary access of air to the roots of deeply rooted vegetation. Wherever, in the midst of the extraordinary fine soil of the prairies, coarse and gravelly patches exist, there dense forests occur. The theory that fineness of soil is fatal to tree growth finds its most remarkable support in the fact that in southeast Russia the limits of the black earth and the treeless regions are almost exactly identical. The black soil of Russia is an earth of exceeding fineness, so fine indeed that it is with the greatest difficulty that the air can penetrate it so as to oxidize the organic matter which it contains. It is easy to see why plains are likelier than mountain slopes to be treeless, it being toward the plains that the finer particles of the material which is abraded from the higher regions is being constantly carried. The more distant the region from the mountains, and the broader its area, the more likely it is that a considerable portion of it will be covered with a fine detritus, whether this be of sub-aerial origin, or deposited at the bottom of the sea.

" The exceedingly fine soil of the typical prairie region consists in large part of the residual materials left after the removal by percolation of rain and other atmospheric agencies of the calcareous portion of the undisturbed stratified deposits, chiefly of the Paleozoic age, which underlies so large a portion of the Mississippi Valley. The finer portions of the formations of more recent age in the Gulf States have also over considerable areas remained treeless."

Professor James Hall says:

" Throughout the prairie regions the underlying rocks are soft sedimentary strata, especially shales and impure limestones. Most of these on exposure disintegrate readily and crumble to soil. The whole soil of the prairies appears to have been produced from such materials, not far removed from their present beds. The valley soil, containing a larger portion of coarse materials than that of the uplands, seems to have been adapted to the growth of forest vegetation. In consequence of this we find such localities covered with an abundant growth of timber. We sometimes meet with ridges of coarse material, apparently drift deposit, on which from some cause there has never been an accumulation of fine sediment; in such localities we invariably find a growth of timber. This is the origin of the groves scattered over the prairies, for whose isolated position and peculiar circumstances of growth we are unable to account in any other way."

Dr. Charles A. White, who made a later geological survey of Iowa, in discussing this subject, says:

"It is estimated that seven-eighths of the surface of Iowa was prairie when the State was first settled. They are not confined to the level surface, but sometimes are quite hilly and broken; and it has been shown that they are not confined to any particular variety of soil, for they prevail equally upon alluvial, drift and lacustral. Indeed we sometimes find a single prairie whose surface includes all of these varieties, portions of which may be sandy, gravelly, clayey, or loamy. Neither are they confined to the regions of, nor does their character seem at all dependent upon the formation which underlies them; for within the State of Iowa they rest upon all formations from those of the Azoic to those of the Cretaceous age inclusive, which embraces almost all kinds of rocks. Southwestern Minnesota is almost one continuous prairie upon the drift which rests directly upon not only the hard Sioux quartzite, but also directly upon the granite.

"Thus whatever the origin of the prairies might have been, we have positive assurance that their present existence in Iowa and the immediate vicinity is not due to the influence of the climate, the character or composition of the soil, nor to the character of any of the underlying formations. The cause of the present existence of prairies in Iowa is the presence of autumnal fires. We have no evidence to show or to suggest that any of the prairies ever had a growth of trees upon them. There seems to be no good reason why we should regard the forests as any more natural or normal condition of the surface than the prairies are. Indeed it seems the more natural inference that the occupation of the surface by the forests has taken place by dispersion from original centers, and that they encroached upon the unoccupied surface until they were met and checked by the destructive power of fires. The prairies doubtless existed as such almost immediately after the close of the Glacial epoch."

The International Cyclopedia, in an elaborate article on the prairies, says:

"The origin of the very fertile prairies of the valley of the Mississippi River proper has been the subject of many theories. How a soil so rich upon which most of the trees of neighboring forests flourish luxuriantly when protected should have failed to have been covered with them in a state of nature, is the question. It is answered by some vegetable physiologists thus:

" ' The excrements of vegetable growth from the roots of trees and plants, and even the annual accumulation of their own leaves after a continuous growth of the same species, become poisonous to the genera which emit them, though perfectly nutritious to plants of different families. It is claimed that the long continuance of forest growth on a rich soil made constantly richer by its own annual deposits of leaves, dead wood and excretions from the roots, finally makes it unfit for their growth. Sickliness and decay produce more dead wood so that fires finally destroy utterly what the soil refuses to nourish. Rank weeds and grasses follow, which in their turn ripen and dry in autumn, make food for new flames that destroy the remnant of tree vegetation, and even the young wood of new species which might otherwise hold their ground. Tree roots cannot live when their tops are destroyed. Perennials, on the other hand, have an extraordinary power to preserve life in their roots under the action of prairie fires. Once in possession of the soil it is easy to see that annual autumn fires, where there are not animals enough to feed down the summer growth, will not only preserve the ground won from the forest by grasses, but will singe the surrounding forests, and wherever they are sickly from the cause first named will finally consume them. Ages of the continuous growth of grasses and other perennials have assimilated those qualities of the soil that become noxious to trees; and in nature's rotation of crops, the soil has again become fitted for their growth. It is only necessary to check the prairie fires for a new crop of forest to dominate the grasses. Trees were beginning to resume possession of the prairies when the settlements began. The increase of the buffalo decreased the food for autumn fires by so much as they pastured upon the grasses. The moisture of the ground contiguous to streams, and the sweetness of the late summer grasses in those places, would naturally make spots where the trees could have time to get rooted in the absence of fires."

It will be seen from these quotations that the subject of the origin of the prairies is by no means settled. Little, if anything new, has been developed during the last quarter of a century by scientific investigation to throw new light upon a subject that will always be of interest in the Mississippi Valley. The fact that prairie and forest conditions have been found on all of the continents, and among the islands, when first seen by men, show clearly that the solution of the problem cannot be found in local or

climatic conditions. Some of the treeless plains are the
most fertile lands known; some are level as the lakes;
some are barren deserts of drifting sands; others are lofty
elevations rising into hills and mountains; they exist in
the Arctic regions, in the temperate latitudes and in the
torrid zones; some are entirely destitute of sand, gravel
or rocks of any description. Others are thickly strewn
with granite bowlders, and in others arise enormous ledges
of rocks. In some places in Kansas the prairies are covered with flat limestone, in sufficient quantities to fence
the land into fields with walls, as in New England and
Pennsylvania with cobble stones.

CHAPTER II

D URING the period of melting glaciers the surface of the earth was again occupied by plants and animals. Soon after these appeared we find the first evidences of man's advent upon this portion of the earth. Professor Aughey's discovery of arrow points in undisturbed beds of loess at various places in Iowa and Nebraska, indicates with certainty the presence of man soon after the melting of the glaciers. Horses appeared about this time and were used for food, as is clearly shown by the finding of skulls crushed in a manner that could only come from the blows of an implement similar to the stone ax. These axes are found in the same deposit with the skulls, both in this country and Europe, showing that man appeared on both continents during the same geological period.

What sort of people were the first inhabitants of Iowa is a question that must ever be of interest. It is generally believed by archæologists that remains of two distinct prehistoric races have been found in the Valley of the Mississippi.

The first human skulls discovered resemble those of the gorilla, having thick ridges over the eyes and an almost total absence of forehead, indicating a low degree of intelligence. Similar skulls have been found throughout the different countries of Europe, indicating that the first inhabitants of the earth known to ethnologists were low-browed, brute-like, small-bodied beings, who were but a grade above the lower animals. Skulls of this type have been found in Illinois, Wisconsin, as well as in Johnson, Floyd, Chickasaw and Dubuque counties of Iowa.

---

* Several skulls of this low type may be seen in the collection of the Academy of Science at Davenport.

The first inhabitants of Iowa and the Mississippi Valley of which we have any evidence are called the " Mound Builders." Stone and copper implements found indicate that they had made progress in the scale of intelligence. Whether they cultivated the soil, erected comfortable dwellings and built towns is not known; but that they made cloth is proven by samples found in mounds, strangely preserved through the innumerable ages that have elapsed. The numbers, color, habits, customs and forms of government of these people, as well as the manner in which their mounds were constructed, the purpose for which these enduring earthworks of various forms

FIG. 2—MOUND OPENED ON THE BANK OF THE IOWA RIVER IN WHICH WAS FOUND A STONE VAULT CONTAINING THE SKELETON OF A "MOUND BUILDER" WITH A POTTERY VESSEL BY HIM

were used, and a thousand interesting details of the history of these inhabitants of Iowa must forever remain unknown. Whence they came, how long they possessed the land, from what cause they were exterminated, are problems that will never cease to have an absorbing interest to succeeding races and generations. We can only call them the " Mound Builders," in absence of almost all knowledge of their history.

Evidences of the work of these people are found in many of the eastern states and as far south as Tennessee in great abundance. The mounds are numerous along the Mississippi Valley in Iowa, extending from Dubuque at intervals through Jackson, Clinton, Scott, Muscatine, Louisa and other counties. Many of these when opened are found to contain skeletons partially preserved, with various implements, vessels, pipes and ornaments. One opened near Dubuque disclosed a vault divided into three cells. In the central cell was found eight skeletons sitting in a circle, while in the centre of the group was a drinking vessel made of a sea shell. The whole chamber was covered with logs preserved in cement.

Some very interesting mounds were found on the Cook

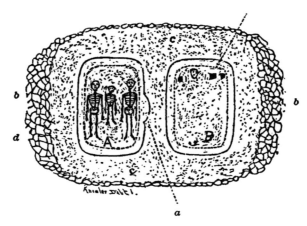

FIG. 3—MOUND OPENED ON THE COOK FARM NEAR DAVENPORT

farm, near Davenport, which were opened by Rev. Mr. Gass in 1874. There were ten mounds in the group, about two hundred and fifty feet back from the river. Several of them were opened and found to contain sea shells, copper axes, hemispheres of copper, stone knives, pieces of galena, mica, pottery and copper spools. Many of the axes were wrapped with coarse cloth, which had been preserved by the copper. The pipes were of the Mound-Builders' pattern, some of which were carved with effigies of birds and animals. One bird had eyes of copper, another had eyes of pearl, showing much delicacy of manipulation and skill in carving. Twenty copper pipes **and** eleven copper awls were taken from these mounds.

All of the mounds contained skeletons and ashes; two contained altars of stone. In one, tablets were found upon which were hieroglyphics representing letters and figures of people, trees and animals.

In the mound represented in the accompanying illustration, not far below the surface, two skeletons were found. Below these were layers of river shells and ashes several feet in thickness. Beneath this three mature skeletons were lying in a horizontal position, and between them was the skeleton of a child. Near them were five copper

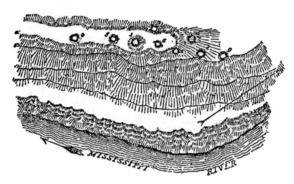

FIG. 4—MAP OF SECTION OF COOK FARM

axes wrapped in cloth, stones forming a star, carved pipes, several bears' teeth and a broken lump of ochre.

In a mound opened by Rev. Mr. Gass west of Muscatine slough, in 1880, there was found a carved stone pipe, a carved bird, a small copper ax and a pipe carved in the shape of an elephant. Another pipe was discovered in that vicinity shaped to represent a mastodon.

The section of a map here presented shows the location of the mounds on the Cook farm where these interesting relics were discovered.

Similar evidences of the ingenious and skillful work of that prehistoric race have been found over a wide range

MAP OF MOUNDS IN EASTERN IOWA
(Work of the Ancient Mound Builders.)

of country, showing conclusively that these first inhabitants of Iowa, of which anything is known, must have made considerable progress in some of the arts of civilized people.

Their mounds extend as far west as the Little Sioux River, and the Des Moines Valley is especially rich in these evidences of occupation by the '' Mound Builders.'' At one point a few miles above the city of Des Moines, on a bold bluff of the river, are many acres covered with their mounds. At other points are found well preserved earthworks laid out on high bluffs, evidently for defense. There is, near Lehigh, in Webster County, an elaborate system of these earthworks commanding a view of great extent.

The lines of these works can be easily traced and in many places huge trees have grown up in them. There are evidences that these people cleared forests, graded roads, wove cloth, made stone and copper implements, exhibiting great skill in these works which have survived them. If they were of the same race with the inhabitants of Central America, who erected the massive structures found in ruins on that portion of the continent, their civilization must have become well advanced. It is not improbable that as these antiquities are further explored, additional light will be thrown upon the history of this race of people who preceded the Indians in America. That they existed in great numbers, and through a period of many thousand years, cannot be doubted. That they were assailed by warlike invaders coming upon them from the north and west is generally believed. That the earthworks found along the rivers were erected as protection against enemies there can be little doubt.

How long they resisted the invaders can never be known. The terrible conflicts may have lasted through several generations, as they were gradually dislodged from their strongholds and forced southward. They may have slowly perished before the resistless onslaught of the invaders until the remnants of the once numerous race

became the hunted " cliff dwellers," who sought a last
refuge in the sides of the deep gorges where some of the
cliff houses have been preserved. It is generally believed
that the remote ancestors of the North American Indians
were the conquerors of the " Mound Builders."

The discovery of America by Columbus was followed
by an era of adventure, and successive expeditions for con-
quests in the new world, in which the nations of Europe
vied with each other for supremacy. Visions of rich gold
fields, vast empires of fertile lands for planting colonies
and enlarging the domain of the nations of the old world,
stimulated the spirit of adventure and opened unlimited
fields for the acquisition of wealth and official rank and
power. No scheme was too visionary to enlist men and
money to launch it. Spain was at this time one of the
powerful nations of Europe. Her countrymen led in
all of the most daring expeditions. Her navigators were
the most courageous of that period. Her armies were
renowned for their valor. Her religious leaders were as
zealous as they were cruel and unscrupulous. Her noble-
men were ambitious for wealth and increased power.

All of these elements now united in race for discovery
and conquest in the unexplored regions of the far West.
Then followed an era of cruelty that rivaled the most in-
human raids of the Dark Ages. As new lands were discovered, they were overrun by reckless adventurers, the
inhabitants were robbed and enslaved with as little restraint as though they had been wild beasts. Spain, by
virtue of discovery, claimed all of the region lying south
of a line running west from Manhattan Island. It was
held under the name of Florida, and extended south to
include Mexico. The West India Islands and all south of
Mexico to Brazil was also claimed by Spain. But north of
the Gulf of Mexico and in the far West was a vast region
yet wholly unexplored.

In 1528 Panfilo Narvaez, a Spanish nobleman, was
appointed by Charles V Governor of Florida. He was

given authority to wrest it from the Indian inhabitants and rule over it. He fitted out an expedition with five ships and four hundred soldiers, with implements to found a colony. On the 12th of April his fleet anchored in a bay on the coast of Florida, and he took formal possession of the country by proclamation in the name of the Spanish king. Leaving his fleet with instructions to its commander to find a good harbor and then return to Havana for supplies for the colony, Narvaez, with three hundred selected officers and soldiers, plunged into the wilderness to conquer the Indians and seize their possessions. He began war upon them, burning their villages, killing the inhabitants and carrying off their provisions. The natives soon discovered that they must exterminate the invaders, or themselves be exterminated. The tribes turned upon the Spanish army, lurked in ambush among the tangled underbrush by day and made fierce attacks by night, giving their enemies no rest. For more than five months the Spanish army wandered through the forests amid dismal swamps, subsisting upon fish and game, with such corn as they could find in the deserted fields. The Indians retreated before the invaders, burning their own villages and destroying their provisions.

Narvaez now realized the desperation of his situation, and followed a large river southward hoping to reach the sea and open communication with his fleet. The Spanish were on the verge of starvation, and in this extremity, some clumsy boats were built, by means of which they hoped to reach the Gulf of Mexico. From battle and disease, one-third of the army had perished. Narvaez, in his desperation, took the best boat, and, deserting his army, lost his own life in a storm. The survivors were now reduced to five men, of whom Alvar Nunez was the leader. They returned to the main land, and for years wandered about subsisting upon fish, game and wild fruit. They searched in vain for a settlement. They passed the mouth of the Mississippi River, were captured by the Indians and enslaved. They were traded from one tribe to another and carried almost to the foot of the Rocky Mountains. They were the first white men who ever saw the great prairies of the West. After ten years spent in the wilds of the interior, Nunez reached a Spanish settlement, the only survivor of the expedition. Alvar Nunez Cabeza de Vaca was the full name of this first white man who traversed the future territory of Louisiana.

The fate of Narvaez and his companions did not discourage other adventurers. Hernando de Soto was one of the most daring of Pizarro's officers in the conquest of Peru. Upon hearing the story of Nunez, and the strange lands he had traversed in his ten years' wanderings, he determined to lead an expedition into that region, which he believed to be rich in gold. He hoped to rival Pizarro's achievements and win fortune and fame. He was a favorite of the king and easily secured the appointment of Governor of Cuba, with a grant of an indefinite amount of land in eastern Florida.

He soon raised an army of more than one thousand men. It was made up largely of nobles, cavaliers, soldiers of fortune and ambitious young men. He embarked his army in ten vessels which he had purchased and equipped. Priests, scientists, artisans and miners were secured, and three hundred and fifty of the best drilled soldiers of Spain were added to the expedition. Live stock and farm implements were taken to found a colony. Chains, fetters and bloodhounds were provided to be used in enslaving the Indians. The soldiers were equipped with helmets, shields and coats of mail for protection in battle. The expedition sailed from Havana on the 12th of May, 1539, amid the booming of cannon and a profusion of gay flags. All were in high spirits in anticipation of wealth, glory and the easy conquest of Florida. Monette, in his history of the Mississippi Valley, says:

"They were a band of gallant freebooters in quest of plunder and fortune; an army rendered cruel and ferocious by avarice, ready to march to

any point with slaughter where they might plunder Indian villages supposed to be stored with gold and other riches."

Upon landing they at once entered into the forest, and
for a year wandered among the trackless woods and
swamps of eastern Florida and southern Georgia. They
encountered savage resistance from the fierce Seminoles,
who made a desperate struggle for their homes and freedom. The captives who were forced to act as guides
craftily led the Spaniards through tangled forests and
amid impassable swamps, where by day and night the
Indian warriors assailed them.

The first winter was spent in the Appalachee country;
and early in the spring De Soto pressed on through northern Georgia and Alabama, encountering the Cherokees.
In the lower Alabama Valley the Indians had gathered a
large army to resist the advance of the Spaniards. During
the battle which was here fought, De Soto lost heavily,
and most of his baggage was burned. He turned northward into upper Mississippi and encountered severe
winter storms while camped on the Tallahatchee. The
Indians harassed the army, killing men and horses, capturing clothing, armor and other property. The Spaniards had slaughtered men, women and children, tearing
them with savage bloodhounds, burning their villages and
seizing all provisions. Now the time of retribution was
at hand. The Indians gave the invaders no rest. In a
battle fought in April, 1541, the Spaniards lost heavily,
and retreated westward through an uninhabited region
of forests and swamps. They finally reached the banks of
a large river, where they found an Indian village named
Chisca. They stood on the low shore and gazed upon the
largest river they had ever seen. Its swift current was
sweeping southward with irresistible power, bearing upon
its turbid water great trees. They named it the "Rio
Grande" and encamped upon its eastern shore, to rest
and better care for the sick and wounded. The nights
were made hideous with the war-whoop and unceasing at-

tacks. The invaders were now on the defensive and fighting for existence. After several days of continuous battle, De Soto ordered a retreat northward along the river banks, followed by the ever present foe. Reaching a prairie country, where a better defense could be made, it was decided that the only hope was to cross the river beyond the attacks of the Indians. The order was given to the mechanics to build boats sufficient to carry the army across.

Their situation was still full of perils. De Soto now seemed to realize it. The search for gold had brought no results, and all energies were now concentrated upon extricating the survivors. To retreat meant financial ruin to all who had embarked their fortunes in the expedition. The order was given to resume the march westward. The point where the army crossed the river is supposed to have been near the northwest corner of the State of Mississippi. The route led through trackless forests, swamps, deep ravines, over rocky hills, among thorns and tangled thickets so dense as to obscure the sunlight.

They at length emerged upon a vast treeless plain stretching westward as far as the eye could reach. Game was found for food, but there was no appearance of gold or inhabitants. But still they pushed on westward in sheer desperation, until the barren plains were finally reached, and here, for the first time, De Soto abandoned hope. He saw that further search for gold in that direction was useless. His men were exhausted with their long marches, scarcity of food, continuous warfare with the Indians and increasing sickness. Of the thirteen hundred men who started out in his command, less than six hundred survived. The bones of seven hundred of their comrades were bleaching along the line of their march. Nearly all of their horses had perished and their riders were struggling along on foot. The sick and wounded were daily dying for want of suitable care and medical attendance. He no longer commanded a conquering army, but was conducting a hopeless band of fugitives to escape from an avenging and relentless enemy.

The only plan that seemed to offer a chance for extrication from the perils which encompassed them was to return to the " Rio Grande," as they called it, and construct some buildings to better care for the disabled, build boats, send a portion of the command down the river to the Gulf of Mexico in search of aid, while the others defended themselves, in rude fortifications, from the Indians. They followed down the valley of the Arkansas River to its junction with the Mississippi, selected a site for the army, and began at once the building of boats. The difficulties encountered in constructing vessels from green trees were almost insurmountable. The Indians assailed them day and night, while disease was rapidly thinning their ranks.

De Soto was finally prostrated with fever, and in his delirium raved wildly over the failure of all of his plans. Death came and forever ended all his schemes of ambition. His followers gathered sadly about his silent form, while the priests chanted a solemn requiem—the first ever heard in the valley of the Mississippi—over the remains of the departed commander. In order to conceal his death from the Indians, the body was inclosed in a cavity hewn in a green oak log. He was wrapped in his military cloak, and the rude coffin rowed into the middle of the river and sunk beneath its waters. Thus his last resting place became the great river of the continent, and for all time he will live in history as its discoverer.

When the vessels were completed the army had become reduced to three hundred and fifty, including the sick. They descended the river, the first white men to navigate its waters. Reaching the gulf, they landed on an unsettled coast and wandered for months on the verge of starvation. Finally the survivors, two hundred and fifty in number, reached a Spanish settlement in Mexico.

Spain was entitled to hold all of the region which the armies under Narvaez, Nunez and De Soto had traversed.

It embraced territory which has since formed eight States of the American Union. But so disastrous had been the fate of the explorers that no considerable portion of it was ever occupied by Spanish colonists.

In 1564 Admiral Coligny, of France, sent three ships to Florida to established a colony. A settlement was made near St. Mary's River, and no effort was spared by kind treatment to win the friendship of the natives. Members of the colony in 1565 explored the country westward in search of gold as far as the Mississippi River, but no permanent settlement was made in its valley. Through the missionary zeal of the Jesuits, the French had extended a chain of posts up the St. Lawrence River far westward and around the great lakes. Bancroft says of this brotherhood:

" The history of their labors is connected with the origin of every celebrated town in the annals of French America. Not a river was entered, not a cape turned, but a Jesuit led the way. Although certain privation and suffering were their lot, and martyrdom might be the crown of their labors, they ventured into the remotest regions and among the most warlike tribes."

In 1634 Jean Nicolet, a French explorer in the Northwest, penetrated the forests beyond Lake Superior and about the Fox River. It was thought by some that he descended the Wisconsin River to its confluence with the Mississippi, and was the first discoverer of its headwaters. But a careful tracing of his account of the country through which he traveled, by recent historians, satisfies them that Nicolet never penetrated the country as far westward as to reach the Mississippi River.

In 1669 Father Claude Allouez, a French missionary, explored the Canadian forests west to Lake Superior. Here he learned from some remote Indian tribe that there was a great river in the distant west called by them the " Mes-a-sip-pi," or " Great River." They said no white man had been seen in the valley through which it flowed. The country westward extending to the river was described by the Indians as beautiful meadows covered with grass, and abounding in wild game. In the Indian language " Mis-sis " signifies meadow, and the word " se-pe " a river; hence we have " Mississippi," as some early French explorers wrote it, signifying " River of the Meadows."

The French at first supposed that the " River of the Meadows " flowed toward the Pacific Ocean and would afford the long sought direct route to China and India. The people of western Europe had for nearly a hundred and fifty years been hoping to find a direct route by water across the new continent, and it was long believed that it would be reached through this " Great River," often mentioned by explorers.

The Jesuit revelations given by Father Claude Dablon in 1670, in an account of the Illinois Indians, says:

"These people were the first to come to Green Bay to trade with the French. They are settled in the midst of a beautiful country away southwest toward a great river named Mis-sis-se-pi. It takes its rise far in the north, flowing toward the south, discharging its waters into the sea. All of the vast country through which it flows is of prairie without trees. It is beyond this river that the Illinois live, and from which are detached the ' Mus-co-tins,' which signifies a land bare of trees."

It does not appear to have been suspected by any of the early French explorers that this river, so often told of by the Indians, was a part of the " Great River " discovered by De Soto more than one hundred and thirty years before.

CHAPTER III

FATHER JACQUES MARQUETTE, a French Jesuit, who had long lived on the frontier, in 1669 determined to explore the far west to the great river. He enlisted the coöperation of M. Talon, the Intendant, to aid him in fitting out an expedition. Father Marquette was one of the most devoted of missionaries, who had for years spent his life among the Indians in the French possessions. He had built up churches among them, learned their language, and endeared himself to the Indians by devoted friendship and kindly intercourse.

An intelligent French explorer and Indian trader, at Quebec, Louis Joliet, was selected by M. Talon to accompany Marquette on this expedition. On the 13th day of May, 1673, Marquette and Joliet, with five experienced voyagers, embarked from Michilimacinac in two birch canoes. When they arrived at Green Bay, the Indians, who had a warm affection and great veneration for the good missionary, who had devoted the best years of his life to their welfare, implored him to abandon the dangerous enterprise. They told him fearful stories of the Mes-as-se-pi country, and besought him with tears to give up such a hazardous expedition and remain with them. But his religious zeal, and the love of adventure, prompted him to make light of the apprehended dangers, and eager to go forward into the unexplored valley of the great river which it was believed no white man had seen, he pressed on. The party sailed up Green Bay to the mouth of Fox River and ascending this stream some distance, came to a village of the Miami and Kickapoo Indians. This was the extreme western limit of French explorations, and here Marquette engaged Miami guides to pilot his company to the Wisconsin River. Upon reaching this river, the guides returned to their tribe, leaving the fearless leaders of the expedition to find their way as best they could through the unknown region they had now entered.

Floating down the Wisconsin, they finally saw before them the broad waters of the Mississippi. In was on the 17th day of June, 1673, that Marquette and Joliet looked out on the bold bluffs of the western shore a few miles below where McGregor now stands. They were the first white men who ever saw Iowa. Pushing out into the current they beheld a wild, beautiful landscape. On the Wisconsin side was a level prairie shore stretching northward for many miles, covered with tall grass waving in the June breeze. Deer and elk were grazing on the meadow. Eastward were the bluffs which in prehistoric times had been washed by a torrent to which the Mississippi of modern days is but a little remnant. Westward, coming down to the water's edge were lofty, wooded, rocky hills and deep gorges fringed with rich foliage and flowers. Once out upon the waters of the largest river of the continent, they felt the inspiration of a great discovery. All about them was an unknown region. Not a human being was seen. The solitude of an uninhabited country surrounded them. They landed from time to time, made camps, killed game, and caught fish. They ascended the bluffs and saw in the distance boundless prairies upon which herds of buffalo and elk could be seen. Fringes of trees and bushes in the distance marked the course of creeks winding through the meadows. Here and there were beautiful groves, rising up like islands in the sea. The atmosphere was laden with the perfume of flowers. The air was soft and balmy as the breezes were wafted over the luxuriant vegetation. The woods were vocal with the music of birds. Squirrels, quail, prairie chickens, wild turkeys, and other game, were found in great abundance. The explorers passed between shores of unsurpassed beauty, where Dubuque, Clinton, Davenport, Rock Island, Muscatine, Bur-

FATHER MARQUETTE DISCOVERS IOWA, JUNE 17, 1673
(From Photo Owned by Dr. John R. Bailey)

lingtou, and other flourishing cities were to be built more than one hundred and fifty years later.

On the 25th day of June they landed on the west shore, and discovered human footprints in the sand. They followed them to a path which led up the bluff to the westward. Leaving their boats in care of their companions, Marquette and Joliet ascended an elevation, and standing upon the bluff, gazed westward over an ocean of green grass waving in the breeze like the long swell of the sea. As far as the eye could reach were elevations covered with miniature groves, serving as guides to the natives in their wanderings. The stillness of a desert pervaded the beautiful landscape, which had a charm of wildness unsurpassed.

Following a path for several miles in a westerly direction, they saw a fringe of woods extending from the north, southeasterly. Columns of smoke were ascending in the distance, sure indications of human beings. Soon they came in sight of wigwams erected in a grove which they discovered to be a part of an Indian village. It was built on the banks of another river much smaller than the Mississippi. Its shores were shaded by a wide belt of oak, elm, walnut, maple and sycamore.

The natives were greatly astonished at the sight of the visitors, but no hostile demonstrations were made, while they gazed with wonder upon the white men who had so suddenly come among them. It is likely that few, if any of these Indians, had ever before seen a European. The Indians made signs of friendship and offered the Frenchmen the pipe of peace. The natives proved to be a band of the Illinois tribe, and had two other villages a few miles distant. The river upon whose banks they were living, was called by them the Mon-in-go-na. Marquette was well enough acquainted with the language of the Illinois nation to be able to converse with the villagers. When he had explained to them who their visitors were, the object of their voyage, and his pleasure at meeting some of the

inhabitants of this beautiful country, the Indians gave the
strangers a most cordial welcome. One of the chiefs addressed them in the following terms:

"I thank the Black Gown Chief (Father Marquette) and his friend
(Joliet) for taking so much pains to come and visit us. Never before has
the earth been so beautiful, nor the sun so bright as now. Never has the
river been so calm or free from rocks which your canoes have removed as
they passed down. Never has the tobacco had so fine a flavor, nor our corn
appeared so beautiful as we behold it to-day. Ask the Great Spirit to give
us life and health, and come ye and dwell with us."

At the close of the chief's address, the visitors were invited to a feast which the squaws had prepared, a description of which is given by Marquette:

"It consisted of four courses. First there was a large wooden bowl
filled with a preparation of corn meal boiled in water and seasoned with
oil. The Indian conducting the ceremonies had a large wooden spoon with
which he dipped up the mixture (called by the Indians *tagamity)*, passing
it in turn into the mouths of the different members of the party. The
second course consisted of fish nicely cooked, which was separated from
the bones and placed in the mouths of the guests. The third course was a
roasted dog, which our explorers declined with thanks, when it was at once
removed from sight. The last course was a roast of buffalo, the fattest
pieces of which were passed to the Frenchmen, who found it to be most
excellent meat."

Marquette and Joliet were charmed with the beauty of
the country, the fertile prairies with their mantles of luxuriant grass and wild flowers stretching away westward;
the fish and game most plentiful, and their friendly reception by the Indians. This was Iowa, as it was first seen
by white men, and no more enchanting land ever met the
gaze of explorers. For six days the Frenchmen remained
with their Indian friends, traversing the valley of the
river, hunting elk, buffalo and prairie chickens, fishing and
bathing in the pure waters, feasting on the choicest of
the products of the fields, forests and streams. The natives exerted themselves to provide every entertainment
possible for their white visitors, and urged them to pro-
long their stay. When Marquette and his party could not

A TYPICAL IOWA PRAIRIE

be prevailed upon to remain longer, more than six hundred Indians escorted them back to the Mississippi where their canoes were anchored, and regretfully bade them good-bye. The Indians watched the white men, waving their farewells, until they disappeared in the bend of the river.

The exact location of the point on the Mississippi where Marquette and his party landed is not known; but from the meager description that was given, nearly all investigators agree that it must have been near where the town of Montrose now stands, in Lee County, at the head of the lower rapids. The village at which the explorers were entertained was called by the Indians Mon-in-go-na. Whether the same name was given to the river along which their villages were built, is not certain. Nicolet gives the following version of the matter, and of the origin and meaning of the name "Des Moines," which was given to the river by the earliest white settlers in its valley. He writes:

"The name which they gave to their settlement was Monin-gouinas (or Moingona, as laid down in the ancient maps of the country), and is a corruption of the Algonkin word Mikouaug, signifying at the road. The Indians, by their customary elliptical manner of designating localities, alluding, in this instance, to the well-known road in this section of the country, which they used to follow as a communication between the head of the lower rapids and their settlement on the river that empties itself into the Mississippi to avoid the rapids. This is still the practice of the present inhabitants of the country.

"After the French had established themselves on the Mississippi they adopted this name; but with their custom (to this day that of the Creoles of only pronouncing the first syllable, and applying it to the river, as well as to the Indians who dwelt upon it, they would say 'la riviere des Moins'—'the river of the Moins'; 'allez chez les Moins'—'to go to the Moins' (people). But, in later times the inhabitants associated this name with that of the Trappist monks (Moines de la Trappe), who resided with the Indians of the American bottom.

"It was then concluded that the true reading of the riviere des Moins was the 'Riviere des Moins,' or river of monks, by which it is designated on all the modern maps.

"The Sioux or Dakotah Indians call the Des Moines Inyan-sha-sha-watpa, or Redstone River, from inyan, stone; sha-sha, reduplication of sha, red; and watpa, river. They call the upper east fork Inyan-sha-sha-watpa sunkaku, the brother of Redstone River."

This discovery of the valley and river of the upper Mississippi, and the beautiful prairie country, which has since been named Iowa, attracted but little attention in European countries at that time. Another great river had been added to the list of discoveries in the far west, hundreds of miles beyond the farthest frontier posts, and that was all. It is greatly to be regretted that the elaborate report made by Joliet of this discovery of the upper Mississippi and the exploration of its valley was lost. Father Marquette's chief interest, in all of his daring expeditions into unknown regions, was the conversion of the Indians to Christianity. He has not given especial attention in his writings to many facts relating to the country through which he traveled. We gather enough from the imperfect records, however, to draw a picture of the " beautiful land " as it was when he first looked upon it.

Tribes of red men who roamed over its boundless prairies, camped in its valleys and paddled their canoes along rivers and lakes, made no substantial improvements. Their houses were of the most temporary character; their villages could be moved at a day's notice. They had no roads, farms, or orchards. A few years effaced every mark of their occupancy. In a country abounding in game, fish and wild fruit, they found enough to satisfy their wants with very little labor.

Generations of Indians had grown up and passed away, leaving no monument or record of their existence. Their predecessors, the Mound Builders, when they possessed Iowa, had constructed enduring works which gave a key to their history; but the buffalo has left as many and enduring marks of its occupancy as the Indian.

Fierce feuds and savage warfare had prevailed among various tribes of the natives, but the first white men who came among them met with a warm welcome and substantial tokens of friendship. The French had, in America, treated the Indians with kindness, and respected their rights. The people of nearly all other nations had regarded them as savages, "having no rights that a white man was bound to respect." The French lived in peace and security with them, while the English, Spaniards, and Portuguese made war upon them that brought retaliation in massacres of men, women and children.

Father Marquette won their confidence, esteem and veneration. When he and his party bade farewell to the Illinois chief, the latter presented to him the pipe of peace—the sacred calumet—ornamented with brilliant feathers. This, suspended from his neck, was to be a safeguard among all the strange tribes that he might encounter in his voyage.

He and his party continued their journey down the river, floating with the current by day and landing at night. They often made excursions into the country, exploring woods and prairie, and paddling up many rivers flowing into the Mississippi. They passed the mouth of a large river, the waters of which were of a muddy hue, discoloring the water for miles below the junction. They learned that the Indian name of this river was Pe-ki-ta-no-ni, afterward called by the French Missouri. Passing between heavily timbered banks, the explorers occasionally saw immense prairies to the eastward covered with a growth of grass as high as a man's shoulders. In the distance rose hills almost mountain high. Next they came to a broad stream of clearer water which the Indians had named the "Beautiful River." This was the Ohio.

The journey was continued along low swampy shores shut in by forests and canebrakes until the heat became intolerable. Swarms of insects tormented the travelers. Herds of buffalo were frequently seen in the open country, and game was found in great abundance and variety.

In latitude 33° they encountered a fierce tribe of Indians of the Michigamie nation. These natives had learned by tradition of the invasion by De Soto's army a hundred and thirty-five years before, and of the atrocities perpetrated upon their ancestors. At the first sight of the canoes manned by white men, the alarm was sounded. A large band of warriors assembled, and embarking, armed with bows, arrows, tomahawks and war clubs, and with yells of defiance, advanced upon the seven Frenchmen. The fearless Marquette, unawed by the impending danger, held aloft the sacred calumet. Seeing the token of peace, the Indian chief restrained his braves, and in return made signs of peace. He invited Marquette and his companions to the village, where for several days they were entertained with hospitality.

Again embarking with a fresh supply of provisions, the explorers floated down to a village named Ak-an-sea. Through an interpreter, Marquette learned from the Indians that the course of the river was southward to the sea. They had now descended nearly to the mouth of the Arkansas River, a distance of more than eleven hundred miles. They had learned that the river they had discovered emptied into the Gulf of Mexico at a distance of about six hundred miles from where they were camped. The object of the expedition had been accomplished. The party had entered a region where the Algonquin dialect was unknown, and it was very difficult to communicate with, or procure information from the natives. The Indians were hostile, and might at any time attack the little company. Should these men be killed, all of their valuable discoveries would be lost to France. They were liable to come upon Spanish settlements or armed freebooters, of whom they were as much in fear as of the Indians.

After considering the situation, Marquette and Joliet agreed that it was their duty to return to Canada and report the results of their long and interesting journey. It was midsummer when it was decided to return. The heat was becoming intense. Slowly the oarsmen propelled the light canoes against the river's powerful flow.

For weeks they ascended the river until they reached the mouth of the Illinois. Here they learned from the Indians that this river afforded a much shorter route to the great lakes than the Wisconsin. They ascended it for two weeks, and then crossed the Illinois prairies from its head waters to the Chicago River, and followed that stream to the shore of Lake Michigan.

Here the two leaders parted company; Father Marquette returning to his mission among the Huron Indians; Joliet going on to Quebec to report to his government the magnitude of the discoveries made by the expedition. The story of finding the great river and its large navigable tributaries, their broad and fertile valleys, the forests and boundless prairies, filled all of New France with rejoicing. The discovery gave France the right to occupy this entire region. Its resources of fertile soil, valuable timber, navigable rivers, natural meadows, fur-bearing animals and game, mineral wealth and genial climate, were unsurpassed by any country yet explored in America.

This territory embraced parts of what are now the States of Wisconsin, Illinois, Iowa, Missouri, Kentucky, Tennessee, and Arkansas. It was found to be occupied by Indians in all respects similar to those living along the St. Lawrence and the great lakes. They spoke a variety of dialects, but careful observation showed but eight radically different languages. The Algonquin tongue, spoken along the St. Lawrence, the upper Mississippi, the Des Moines and the Illinois, was most widely diffused. It was heard from Cape Fear to the land of the Esquimaux, a thousand miles north of the sources of the Mississippi.

The Illinois Indians were kindred to the Miamis, and their country lay between the Wabash, the Ohio and Mississippi rivers. Marquette found a village of them within the limits of Iowa on the lower banks of the Des Moines River. At this time (1673) the entire tract embraced in Illinois contained only five or six Indian villages, so far as known. Marquette saw but one village along the Iowa shore of the Mississippi from the mouth of the Wisconsin to that of the Des Moines.

Bancroft estimates that at the time of the discovery of America, the entire Indian population of the region now embraced in the States of Ohio, Kentucky, Indiana, Michigan, Illinois, Wisconsin and Iowa, was but little more than twenty-five thousand. And all of this land was still sparsely occupied one hundred and eighty years later. The extent and importance of the discoveries made by these energetic pioneers was not realized by France, and no effort was made by the government to occupy or further explore the new empire.

Joliet was but twenty-seven years old at this time. He was an expert draughtsman, and had carefully prepared maps and notes descriptive of their joint discoveries. But he met with a great misfortune in descending the St. Lawrence River, where his canoe was capsized and all of his valuable papers and maps lost. No complete history of the expedition was now in existence, and the only report he was able to make to the French Government was an imperfect narrative, from memory, of the results of the discoveries. Some years later he gathered all the data obtainable and reproduced the lost maps from memory as accurately as was possible, with a chart of the general course of the river. He added to it such proximate draught as he was able to make from information obtained from the Indians, of that portion of the lower valley and river beyond which their voyage extended.*

---

* Illinois has given the name of this young explorer to one of its large towns

CHAPTER IV

THE next expedition sent to the valley of the Mississippi was led by Cavalier de La Salle. He was a young and ambitious Frenchman who had recently come to New France; a man of great courage and robust constitution. He was highly educated and well equipped for the work. Governor Frontenac heartily coöperated with La Salle in his plans to explore the river to its mouth.

The expedition embarked on Lake Frontenac (Ontario) on the 18th of November, 1678. When it reached Niagara Falls the weather had become so cold that it was necessary to go into winter quarters. In the spring reinforcements came, and among them was Father Louis Hennepin, a daring Franciscan friar, who had been a missionary among the Indians. As the vessel could not proceed beyond the falls, another had to be built, detaining the explorer for six months. On the 7th of August, 1679, they reëmbarked and reached Green Bay on the 8th of October.

Collecting a load of furs, La Salle sent his vessel back with them and set out with thirty-five men for the Illinois River. Sixty miles below he erected a fort and opened trade with the Indians. Here the party remained until March, 1680, when a company of seven, led by Father Hennepin, was sent down the Illinois River to explore the upper Mississippi Valley. These men ascended the river in a canoe for 800 miles, past the eastern shore of Clayton and Allamakee counties in Iowa as well as the States of Wisconsin and Minnesota. They reached the falls above the present site of St. Paul. and gave them the name of St. Anthony.

Father Hennepin with five men then started down the river intending to explore to its mouth, passing along the entire eastern borders of Iowa. Arriving at the mouth of the Arkansas, and learning that it was still a long distance to the Gulf, he returned to the posts on the Illinois, and soon after sailed for France. There he published a glowing account of the regions he had visited, naming the country Louisiana. Hennepin and his party traveled in all a distance of more than three thousand miles and discovered a large tract north of the Wisconsin, but he did not explore the Mississippi to its mouth as he claimed after the death of La Salle, who completed this enterprise in 1682.

The river had been named by Marquette ''Conception''; by Hennepin the '' St. Louis,'' and by La Salle '' Colbert,'' for the French minister.

On the 27th of March the party reached the mouth of Red River, and on the 6th of April arrived at the Mississippi delta. Sending D'Antray down the east, Touly down the middle, La Salle followed the west channel, all in time reaching the Gulf of Mexico. He here took formal possession of the great valley in the name of his sovereign, Louis XIV, thus securing to France Louisiana.*

The fate of this first explorer of the lower Mississippi was a sad one. In 1685 he organized a party of two hundred and eighty persons to found a colony near the mouth of the Mississippi, to hold the territory of Louisiana for France. Not knowing the longitude of the mouth of the river, the fleet sailed too far west and landed the colonists near the Colorado in the present limits of Texas. The fleet then returned to France. After two years of hardship, sickness and suffering La Salle started with a small party to try to reach the nearest settlements in Illinois, and while in the wilderness was treacherously assassinated by some members of his own company. His body

---

* Near the mouth of the river, La Salle erected a column and a cross upon which the following inscription was made: *Louis the Great, King of France and Navarre, reigning April 9th,* 1682.

was left unburied in the forest. A few of his devoted
friends hunted down and killed the murderers and finally
reached the Illinois settlements.

The colonists thus left to their fate nearly all died from
disease and Indian raids. Finally the survivors were
overcome by the natives, captured and reduced to slavery.
In 1690 the few who were alive were rescued by a Spanish
expedition sent out to destroy the French colony. In 1682
La Salle wrote a lengthy account of Father Hennepin's exploration of the upper valley, and in it makes the first
mention of the Ai-o-un-on-ia (Iowa) Indians, and from
this tribe our State takes its name.

In 1684 Louis Franguelin published the best map that,
up to that time, had been made of Louisiana, which comprised all of the French possessions south, and west, and
northwest of the great lakes. On this map first appeared
the two rivers bearing their present names, "Mississippi"
and "Missouri."

The Ontavus Indians living along the valley of the
great river, called it the Mis-cha-si-pi, and posterity has
united in preserving the beautiful Indian name, with a
slight change in the orthography.

For forty years French settlers were slowly entering
the Mississippi Valley, while trappers, fur traders and
missionaries penetrated remote regions exploring the
rivers of the territory lying west of the Mississippi. It
was from these pioneers that many of our Iowa water
courses received their first names, several of which have
been retained.

Twelve years elapsed after the disastrous attempt of
La Salle to plant a colony in the lower Mississippi Valley,
before another movement was made by the French to
establish settlements in that region. In 1699 D'Iberville,
a distinguished French naval officer, collected a colony at
San Domingo for settlement in Louisiana. The company
landed west of Mobile Bay, where the ships and most of
the settlers remained. D'Iberville, with a party of sailors,

started in small boats westward along the coast in search
of the mouth of the Mississippi. Ascending one of the
channels, they met a band of Indians, among whom they
found various articles which had been given them by La
Salle in 1682. Some time later a letter was found in
possession of the Indians written April 20, 1685, to La
Salle by De Tonti, who was searching at that time for the
lost French colony. They also found a Spanish coat-of-
mail that must have been taken from De Soto's army one
hundred and sixty years before.

After exploring the country along the river for some
distance, D'Iberville selected a place for his colony eighty
miles east of where New Orleans stands, on the north
coast of Biloxi Bay. This was the first permanent settlement established in the lower Mississippi Valley.

From here D'Iberville and his younger brother, Bienville, examined the valley of the Mississippi as far north
as Natchez. On the bluff where that city now stands the
commander selected a site for the future capital of the
French possessions. The Natchez Indians, a powerful nation, had made some progress toward civilization. Fire
was the emblem of their divinity, and the sun was their
god. In their principal temple a fire was kept continually
burning by their priests. D'Iberville concluded a treaty
of peace with the Natchez chief, with permission to found
a colony and erect a fort. From this place the French
commander explored the Red River Valley for more than
a thousand miles.

In 1702 Lesueur, a French explorer, with a party of
adventurers ascended the Mississippi River, past the entire eastern boundary of Iowa. They went northward to
the mouth of the St. Peter River and up that stream to
the Blue Earth, and there erected a fort. This was
probably the first attempt to take formal possession of
the region now embraced in the States of Minnesota, Iowa
and the Dakotas.

In 1705 Frenchmen traversed the Missouri to the Kansas River and built a fort at the mouth of the Osage. In 1710 the first African negroes were taken into the new French colony and slavery was established in Louisiana.

After the death of D'Iberville, his brother, Bienville, became Governor of Louisiana. In 1717 the entire trade of the Mississippi Valley was granted by a charter from the French king to the "Western Company" for twenty-five years. The absolute control of the French possession was by this grant turned over to the corporation, even to the selection of its Governor and all military officers, the command of its forts, vessels and armies. The company was bound to introduce into Louisiana, during the period of its charter, six thousand white settlers and three thousand negro slaves. Bienville was chosen Governor of the whole province. He at once founded a city and established a colony on the banks of the Mississippi.

The shores were low, flat and swampy for more than a hundred miles from its mouth, but the Governor selected a site where New Orleans now stands for the capital, and proceeded to clear the dense forest that covered it. He laid out the city and gave it the name it now bears. The first cargo of slaves, direct from Africa, was landed on the west bank of the river opposite the new city in 1719. It consisted of five hundred men, women and children, forcibly torn from their homes, transported in a slave ship, and sold out to the colonists at an average price of one hundred and fifty dollars each.

From 1756 to 1762 war was waged by England against France for the conquest of Canada, and all of the French possessions in the Mississippi Valley. After a conflict in which the colonists and many tribes of Indians took part, the English armies succeeded in wresting Canada from the French, and in 1763 a treaty of peace was concluded by which England secured all of the French territory east of the Mississippi River, except a region east of New Orleans. The king of France at the same time, by a secret treaty, ceded to Spain all of the remainder of Louisiana, embracing the entire country west of the Mississippi to its remotest tributaries, including Iowa and all north to the source of the river.

Thus after nearly a century from the time France became the owner of Louisiana, its entire possessions were surrendered and its French inhabitants became the unwilling subjects of England and Spain.

The French settlers in the Mississippi Valley were, for the most part, small farmers, supplying nearly all of their wants by the products of the fertile soil. They were simple in their habits and lived in peace with the Indians. In religion they were devoted Catholics. There were no public houses, as every house entertained travelers. Lawyers, courts, prisons and instruments for punishment were unknown, as were crimes and quarrels for which they are maintained. In village schools the children acquired a limited education, but sufficient for their simple lives. Priests were almost the only well educated men among them. They did not enter into political contests, but cheerfully accepted the government of the King, as one that must not be questioned. Worldly honors were troubles they never desired. Without commerce, they knew nothing of the luxuries or refinement of European countries. There were no distinctions of rank and wealth. They were free from envy, avarice and ambition. The wives of the household had entire control of all domestic affairs, and were the supreme umpires in settling all disputes. They exercised a greater influence than in any other civilized country. Agriculture was almost the only occupation, where every man had his herd of cattle, ponies, sheep and swine; and each was his own mechanic.

Thus lived the first settlers in the Mississippi Valley for more than a hundred years. But when their country was surrendered to English rule, many left their peaceful homes along the Illinois, the Mississippi and Wisconsin, so strong was their affection for France and its government.

During the time that Iowa had been under the dominion
of France, no towns had been laid out or permanent colonies established. Fur traders, within its limits, hunters,
trappers and missionaries had ascended the Des Moines,
the Iowa, the Cedar, Wapsipinicon and the Missouri.
Their cabins had been built in the beautiful groves; but
the Indian nations that occupied the State when Columbus discovered America still held undisputed possession.
No record has been left of the French traders and missionaries who for a century visited the " beautiful land "
and named many of its water courses. They made no war
on the natives, but mingled with them in friendly intercourse. Little can ever be known of the history of the
inhabitants during all the years which elapsed from 1492
up to 1800.

One consideration which led to the early exploration
of the valleys of the Mississippi and Missouri and their
tributaries, was the importance of the fur trade in all of
that region. As early as 1667 the Hudson's Bay Company
had been organized by English capitalists. The principal
business was dealing in buffalo, elk, bear and deer skins
and furs in the British possessions of North America.
The company sent its hunters, trappers and traders far
north into the Arctic regions, as well as south through
Canada, and westward to the Pacific Coast. Its operations grew to such magnitude, and its profits became so
large, that the stock of the company was sold at a premium
of two thousand per cent. The visions of rich gold mines
that had lured the first Spanish adventurers into the far
west, had gradually faded away. New sources of wealth
were sought by those who were yearly penetrating the
wilderness of America.

A strong rivalry grew up between the English and
French over the fur trade, and it was one of the chief
causes leading to the war with French and Indians on the
frontier. French traders had pushed their traffic up the
rivers of Missouri, Kansas, Iowa, Nebraska and Minne-

sota, more than a hundred years before these States had an existence on the map. These pioneers acquired their first knowledge of the lakes and rivers from the Indians with whom they traded. Rude maps were made from the information thus gained.

In 1762 a fur company was organized in New Orleans for the purpose of extending the profitable traffic among the Indians of the region lying between the upper Mississippi and the Rocky Mountains. Pierre Laclede was one of the projectors and took charge of establishing trading posts. He stopped at St. Genevieve, where a French colony settled in 1755. He also landed on the west shore of the Mississippi, about eighteen miles below the mouth of the Missouri, to establish a trading station. While here he was impressed with the spot as a favorable site for a town, and on the 15th of February, 1764, he caused a plat to be made, naming it St. Louis in honor of Louis XV, then king of France, little suspecting that his trading post was destined to become one of the great cities of America.

Louisiana had already been ceded to Spain by that weak monarch for whom the new town was named, but the disgraceful act had not been made public. England was extending its settlements in the Illinois country lately wrested from the French. The French settlements in that region were largely confined to the east side of the upper Mississippi, and the Illinois rivers.

The acquisition of this country by the English was very distasteful to its French inhabitants. When Captain Stirling of the British army took command of Fort Chartres in 1765, in order to extend the government of Great Britain over the country, many of the citizens abandoned their homes and moved to the French settlements of St. Genevieve and St. Louis. The French population of the whole Illinois country at the time it passed under English rule, was about five thousand. Nearly one-half of this number refused to become British subjects and joined their own countrymen on the west side of the Mississippi. Ten years later the population of Kaskaskia had become reduced to about one hundred families, and Kahokia to fifty. This region received but few immigrants from the English provinces while it was under British rule, but remained an isolated French settlement in the heart of a wild country surrounded by Indians, and unreconciled to the hated English Government. Its only means of communication with the civilized world was by canoes or bateaux to Detroit or New Orleans. The military government that was arbitrarily extended over these people, who had braved every danger and endured all the hardships inseparable from making homes in that remote but beautiful and fertile territory, was despotic and oppressive.

When the English colonies in America united in the determination to free themselves from British rule, the people of the Mississippi Valley were not slow to make common cause with them.

In 1777 George Rogers Clark, a gallant young Kentuckian, projected a military expedition to aid the patriots of the far west. Thomas Jefferson and Patrick Henry, of Virginia, secured authority for young Clark to raise troops and seize the British frontier posts. Speedily enlisting one hundred and eighty young backwoodsmen, who were expert riflemen, fearless and inured to hardships, he embarked on the " Ohio " and finally arrived at Kaskaskia. This town was on the west bank of Kaskaskia River, five miles from its mouth, about sixty-five miles south of St. Louis and was the oldest settlement in Illinois.

Colonel Clark surprised the English garrison occupying the town and seized the place. He followed up his brilliant success by capturing Kahokia and Vincennes. The French population of these places was greatly rejoiced over the expulsion of the English and cordially cooperated with Colonel Clark.

When Lieutenant-Governor Hamilton, the English commander at Detroit, heard of the capture of these places, he started with an army of British and Indians to " punish the rebels.'' He determined to recover the Illinois towns, and carry the war into Kentucky. He recaptured Vincennes* and sent a force to destroy Colonel Clark's little army. But that young officer was on the alert, made a bold dash upon Fort Vincennes, where General Hamilton was in command, and captured the post, taking the British general prisoner, seizing his stores, baggage and army equipments.

But the English made yet another effort to recover possession of the Mississippi Valley. An army of fourteen hundred was speedily equipped with Indian allies to march on St. Louis. The citizens sent a special messenger to Colonel Clark for aid. The fearless young commander did not hesitate, but selecting five hundred of his best men hastened to the relief of the besieged town. The citizens were making a gallant defense against overwhelming numbers and anxiously watching for the arrival of their friends. Suddenly the sharp report of hundreds of rifles smote the British army in the rear. The Indian allies, who had a wholesome fear of the young American commander, were panic stricken and fled in terror, soon followed by the British, and St. Louis was saved.

Colonel Clark had a fort erected at the '' Falls of the Ohio,'' where Louisville was subsequently built. In the spring of 1780 he built Fort Jefferson on the Mississippi below the mouth of the Ohio. Natchez had been taken from the British and Colonel Clark now held the entire upper Mississippi Valley, from Illinois to the Spanish boundary. If he could have been reinforced by two thousand men, he was confident that he could have captured Detroit and expelled the British from the entire northwest. But the American armies were so hard pressed by the British in the Atlantic colonies, that it was impossible to reinforce him. But he had by his foresight, skill and

---

.* Fort Vincennes, or St. Vincent as the French named it, was on the Wabash River, one hundred and fifty miles from its mouth. It was on a direct line from Detroit to Kashkashis. The entire region northwest of Ohio was commanded by these posts.

courage already wrested the West from the English, never again to pass under the dominion of a foreign nation.

The Virginia Legislature inscribed a memorial of Colonel Clark's brilliant achievements upon its records and granted to each soldier of his army two hundred acres of land.*

The first English adventurers found their way into the upper Mississippi Valley in about 1766. They were lawless hunters and trappers and there is little doubt that they extended their traffic with the Indians up several of the Iowa rivers. From this crude beginning developed finally the great Northwest Fur Company, which in 1806 had extended its trade from the St. Lawrence to Hudson's Bay; and from headquarters on the west shore of Lake Superior, their hunters, trappers and traders penetrated the west as far as the Rocky Mountains, embracing Iowa and Minnesota in their range.

At the close of the war of the Revolution, Great Britain relinquished to the United States its possessions east of the Mississippi River, from its sources to the 31st parallel of latitude, and with it free navigation of the river to its mouth as derived by previous treaties with France and Spain.

---

* George Rogers Clark was a brother of Captain William Clark who was one of the commanders of the Lewis and Clark exploring expedition of 1804; and who was appointed by President Jefferson Governor of Missouri Territory. One of Col. Clark's soldiers in his western campaign was John Todd who became a prominent citizen of Kentucky and was the great uncle of Mary Todd, wife of Abraham Lincoln.

CHAPTER V

B Y the cession to Spain in 1762 of that portion of Louisiana lying west of the Mississippi River the French, who had slowly extended their settlements into that region, were, against their will, made subjects of an alien government. When Spain undertook to extend its dominion over its newly acquired possessions, the Acadians and Creoles resisted and drove the Spanish officials from the country.

In 1768 Governor Don O'Reilly, the new Spanish ruler, landed at New Orleans with a strong force, suppressed the insurrection, and inaugurated Spanish rule. The population of Louisiana, at this time, was but about 13,500, although more than seventy years had elapsed since the first French colony had been established. But few settlements had been made west of the Mississippi, the most important of which were at St. Genevieve and St. Louis.

The use of Spanish courts, laws and language was decreed in the province to the intense disgust of its French population. Spain at this time claimed the region on both sides of the Mississippi River for the first three hundred miles above its mouth, and west to the Pacific Ocean. Spain was endeavoring to strengthen her grasp on American territory along the Gulf of Mexico and throughout the country lying north and west. The free navigation of the river to its mouth became of vital importance to the United States, as it was the only commercial outlet for its possessions in that valley.

As the great prairies were yearly attracting settlers from the eastern States, Spain realized that before long she would be compelled to yield the free navigation of the lower river unless the inhabitants of the upper valley could be alienated from their allegiance to the United

States. To permit the free navigation of the river appeared to Spain like laying the foundation for the ultimate loss of her American possessions.

The settlements in the valley were separated by wide stretches of wilderness, with no prospect of markets or access to the commerce of the world, save through the Spanish dominions. These settlements were surrounded by hostile Indians and remote from protection of the home government. Their navigable rivers all led to the Mississippi. Spain saw the necessity and used all of these arguments to persuade settlers to unite with the Spanish possessions and separate themselves from the United States. The pressure was increased by levying heavy duties upon all imports the settlers received by way of the lower Mississippi. These duties were arbitrary. Every boat passing up or down the lower river was required to land and submit to these exactions under penalty of seizure, confiscation and imprisonment of the crew. The Spanish officers enriched themselves from these exorbitant taxes.

The pioneers of the valley were poor, and endured all the hardships and privations inseparable from settlement in a wild country. They were wholly dependent upon their own ingenuity and toil for the common necessaries of life and they felt keenly the merciless taxation that was levied upon a traffic which brought them a scanty supply of groceries and hardware in exchange for their products. Spain insolently refused to even grant them the free navigation of the river, unless they would unite their fortunes with Spanish Louisiana and separate from their own kindred and country.

In 1786 John Jay, the American minister to Spain, having failed to procure concessions from the government on this point, in compliance with instructions from Washington, almost consented to waive the right of free navigation for twenty years, provided Spain would concede that right at the expiration of that period.

A knowledge of this timid policy aroused intense indignation among the settlers in the upper valley, who determined to assert their rights by force if abandoned by their own government. They proposed to organize an army and seize the Spanish posts, capture New Orleans and compel the recognition of their claims.

The Spanish governor, Muro, realized that some concessions must be made or his province might be invaded by an army of backwoodsmen whose fame as expert riflemen was a terror to the Spanish authorities. He therefore granted the privilege of free trade to James Wilkinson and certain other Americans in tobacco, flour and other products. Spanish emissaries were sent into the settlements with promises of great commercial advantages if the people would declare their independence of the Federal Government. Spain in this event proposed to forever guarantee the free navigation of the Mississippi. Many citizens who had waited long years for relief through their own government were disposed to enter into the scheme that promised such great and immediate benefits. They would establish an independent government. But a large majority of the settlers were loyal to their country.

In 1788, after years of fruitless negotiations with Spain, Congress declared "that the free navigation of the Mississippi River is a clear and essential right of the United States and that it ought to be enforced." The western people rejoiced greatly over this declaration and became convinced that the government would protect their interests. Spain finally realized its danger. A war would almost certainly result in the loss of Louisiana and probably Florida.

General Washington, who was President, began to prepare for a conflict which seemed likely to come. Spain still delayed making any concessions, hoping the western people might be won over to separation from the Union. Untiring efforts were made, through secret emissaries

traveling among the settlements, to bring on a movement
for independence. In order to embarrass the Government of the United States and alienate the western people,
Spanish emissaries were sent among the Indian tribes in
the south and British emissaries, co-operating in the
northwest, endeavored to bring on a general Indian war.
The ''Whisky Rebellion'' in Pennsylvania and an Indian
war in the west conspired to encourage Spain to postpone
any substantial concession.

About this time it was proposed by the American minister at Madrid that if Spain would cede to the United
States her possessions east of the Mississippi, including
the island and city of New Orleans, that the United States
would make no claim to the vast territory west of the
river. as her real interest would then require that Spain
should retain her possessions west of it. Since the free
navigation of the river was of such absolute necessity to
the United States, it must sooner or later be conceded.
The minister said:

    ''This is the decree of Providence written on every map of the continent
and it cannot be prevented by any human agency. Would it not be the part
of wisdom to anticipate an irresistible event peaceably and cement a lasting
friendship with the United States on this basis of mutual interests and
benefits?''

But Spain still procrastinated. She seemed to realize
that the only security she had in her American possessions was in holding her vantage ground and checking the
onward tide of emigration that was menacing Louisiana.

And thus for more than twelve years were the American settlers in the Mississippi Valley kept in suspense and
subjection to Spanish cupidity. General Carondelet of
Louisiana now made a final effort to detach the western
territory from the American Union. He sent Lieutenant-
Governor Gayoso of Natchez as a special agent to the
mouth of the Ohio River to meet four of the most prominent of the American conspirators—Sebastian, Innis,
Murray and Nicholas—to arrange the terms of an alliance

between Kentucky, Tennessee and adjacent territory, and
Louisiana under the Spanish government. But General
Wayne had defeated the hostile Indians; the rebellion in
Pennsylvania had been suppressed, and the American
army was now free to attend to this incipient revolution.
The conspirators became timid and Judge Sebastian of
Kentucky was the only one who ventured to meet the
Spanish commissioner. The United States officers were
on the alert, and Judge Sebastian, fearing arrest, fled to
New Orleans. Spain was now becoming deeply involved
in European wars, and fearing an invasion of Louisiana
by the long suffering pioneers, finally proposed a settlement of the controversy.

A treaty was concluded on the 20th of October, 1795, by
which the middle of the Mississippi River was made the
western boundary of the United States from the thirty-first
degree of latitude to its source, and navigation made free to
its mouth. Spanish rule in Louisiana was drawing to a
close. The French nation had never become reconciled to
the loss of its possessions in America, which had been
surrendered by a weak king. Under the brilliant young
first consul, Napoleon, France had become the most powerful nation of Europe. Spain had been compelled to bow
to his iron will. Napoleon resolved to restore to France
her former possessions in the Valley of the Mississippi.
On the first of October, 1801, a treaty was made with
Spain by which she ceded to France all of the province of
Louisiana; but before Napoleon could take possession of
the newly acquired American province, England and her
allies were pressing the French armies so hard that Napoleon feared the powerful British navy would seize and
blockade the ports of Louisiana, thus cutting France off
from her new acquisitions. The French and Americans
were traditional friends and, in order to save Louisiana
from England, Napoleon determined to transfer it to a
friendly power able to defend and hold it. This acquisition by the American Republic would greatly strengthen

that rising nation, make it a formidable rival of Great Britain and enable it to check the rapacious policy of British power in America.

Confidential negotiations were opened with the American minister to France and the scheme was at once communicated to President Jefferson. He was rejoiced at the prospect of being able to secure, by peaceable means, such a vast and important addition to the territory of the new Republic. On the 30th of April, 1803, this treaty was concluded by which Louisiana was ceded to the United States for $15,000,000.

When this treaty negotiated by Jefferson's administration came before the Senate for ratification, constitutional objections were made; but in view of the national, commercial and financial benefits to be derived, opposition soon disappeared. All came to see the wisdom and broad statesmanship of the great author of the immortal Declaration of Independence. This act extended our dominion from the Mississippi River to the Pacific Ocean and gave to the growing young nation the vast empire out of which the Indian and Oklahoma territories and the States of Louisiana, Arkansas, Missouri, Minnesota, North and South Dakota, Nebraska, Kansas, Colorado, Montana, Washington, Oregon and Iowa have been organized. Louisiana embraced an area greater than all of our possessions at that time lying east of the Mississippi River.

A secret clause had been inserted in the treaty of 1801, between France and Spain, which provided that if France should ever permit Louisiana to pass out of her possession, Spain should have the exclusive right to re-purchase it. But so great had become the power and influence of Napoleon through his invincible armies in Spain, that he now readily coerced that kingdom to waive all rights under this secret provision and permit the sale to the United States.

The extent of the territory, then known as Louisiana, had never been realized by any of its possessors. Louis

XIV of France had at one time actually granted that unexplored region to a private citizen, M. Crosat, who, in
consideration of the grant, was to pay to the king one-
fifth of the gold and silver annually which it should yield.
This was by far the most munificent grant of public domain ever made by a sovereign to a subject; but after a
few years search for the precious metals Crosat, dis-
couraged by failure, regarded the possessions worthless
and relinquished them to the crown. A few years later
the same tract was granted to the famous John Law, who
used it to inaugurate one of the most gigantic real estate
speculations ever devised. After its collapse, the grant
was again relinquished.

The treaty, which had been negotiated on the part of
the United States by Robert R. Livingston, minister pleni-
potentiary, and James Monroe, envoy extraordinary, was
ratified by the Senate on the 19th of October, 1803, and, by
act of the 31st of October, President Jefferson was authorized by Congress to take possession of and occupy the
country. On the 20th of December possession was taken
by the Government at New Orleans through Governor
William C. C. Claiborne, who had been appointed by the
President.

Our new possessions proved to be of greater value than
all the territory conquered and held by Napoleon during
his brilliant and unscrupulous wars of conquest in Europe and Africa. No such acquisition of valuable territory was ever before made peaceably by any nation in the
world's history. The industrial, commercial, political and
geographical importance of this region were colossal and
inestimable. It rounded out our territorial possessions,
opened up the inland water route to the sea and at one
step lifted the young Republic into rank and power with
the first nations of the earth.

The accompanying map shows on the extreme east the
territory embraced in the thirteen original States which
in 1776 declared their independence from British rule

and in the war of the Revolution won the right to self-government. The area of the thirteen original colonies embraced 420,892 square miles, and the region lying between these States and the Mississippi River claimed and held by the Republic embraced an area of 406,952 square miles, making the entire area of the United States after the close of the Revolution 827,844 square miles.

The Louisiana Purchase secured by treaty with France contained an area of 1,171,931 square miles, exceeding in size by 344,087 square miles all of the former territory of the United States.

Florida, which was acquired from Spain in 1819, contained 59,268 square miles; and the territory acquired from Mexico, including Texas, covered an area of 967,451 square miles. But this last acquisition was only won by an aggressive war upon a neighbor greatly inferior in strength and reflected no credit upon the powerful Republic which was founded upon the right of people to self-government.

The almost unexplored province of Louisiana had been discovered by Spanish adventurers in 1542, but abandoned by them for one hundred and thirty years before French explorers took possession if it in the name of their king. It was held by France for eighty-two years, from 1681 to 1763, when it was ceded to Spain. During this period of more than two and a half centuries the entire white population of this immense fertile territory had only reached about fifty thousand, while the exports amounted to but $2,158,000, and the imports to $2,500,000.

Up to the close of the Revolutionary War Virginia claimed all of the tract lying north and west of the Ohio River in the United States, as well as Kentucky. In 1784 Virginia ceded to the United States all of its claim to the region north of the Ohio River and west to the Mississippi. In the same year a treaty was made with the Sioux Indians, who claimed a large portion of this territory, by which they relinquished their claim to all west of the

State of New York. By another treaty made with other
western tribes, a large portion of Ohio was relinquished
and opened to settlement by whites.

On the 20th of May, 1785, Congress passed an act providing for the survey of public lands. These lands were
divided into townships six miles square, the ranges of
townships to be numbered from the Pennsylvania boundary west, and the townships themselves to be numbered
north from a point on the Ohio River due north of the
western termination of the southern boundary of Pennsylvania. The townships were divided into thirty-six sections each one mile square. This was the origin of our
excellent system of surveying, dividing and describing of
public lands. Some changes have been made by subsequent legislation, but the system remains substantially as
it was originated at that time.*

After the surveys were made and recorded, the lands
within certain limits were offered for sale at not less than
one dollar and a quarter per acre. It was a part of the
plan of Congress at the session of 1784 to have the Northwest Territory divided by parallels of latitude and meridian lines into ten States. They were to be named, beginning at the northwest corner and going south: Sylvania, Michigania, Chersonisus, Assenispia, Metropotamia,
Illinoia, Saratoga, Washington, Plypotamia and Peli-
sipia.† Fortunately the people of the future great States
of that region were spared the infliction of such inap-
propriate names as were some of these.

On the 7th of July, 1786, the subject was again considered by Congress, and a joint resolution adopted providing that not less than three, nor more than five States,
should be organized out of the territory. On the 13th
day of July, 1787, Congress passed an act known as the
" Ordinance of 1787," by which all of the country lying
north and west of the Ohio River and east of the Missis-

* Colonel James Mansfield, then Surveyor-General of the Northwestern Territory, was the author of this system.
† Sparks' " Life of Washington."

sippi, was organized into the Northwest Territory. This embraced what has since become the States of Ohio, Indiana, Illinois, Michigan and Wisconsin. Seventeen million acres of land had been acquired by treaties with the various tribes of Indians. The ordinance providing for its organization had forever prohibited the introduction of slavery within its limits.*

Within a year from the time of its organization, more than 20,000 men, women and children had settled in the new territory. One thirty-sixth of all the public lands was reserved and the proceeds of the sales appropriated to the support of public schools. These two acts of Congress, viz.: the prohibition of slavery, and the grant of lands for public schools, were measures of the broadest statesmanship, which were destined to eventually work out the emancipation of our great republic from the crime and curse of human slavery and provide a comprehensive free public school system. Thus we see how from our eastern neighbors we inherited our simple system of land surveying, our method of providing a common school education and our exemption from African slavery.

---

* This prohibition was proposed and introduced by Thomas Jefferson, author of the Declaration of Independence and afterwards President of the United States.

CHAPTER VI

MORE than four hundred years have passed since Europeans began the invasion of America, and the savages whose ancestors exterminated the Mound Builders are rapidly meeting a similar fate. When the Twentieth Century shall have passed away, the American Indians will have almost, if not quite, disappeared from the face of the earth. They seem to be incapable of civilization and consequently their complete extinction is probably near at hand. Whatever of the history of the Indian nations and tribes of Iowa can be found must be of interest to the civilized millions who now occupy the State.

The wresting of Iowa from its Indian inhabitants was attended with little of the cruelty of war which followed the advent of the Spanish, English and Portuguese invaders in other portions of America. Three hundred years of sturdy but unavailing resistance to the advance of the European races had exhausted the original fierce and unyielding courage of the Indians and impressed them with the gloomy conviction that resistance was unavailing. Nation after nation of their ancestors had been vanquished in the unequal contest. Slowly but surely they had been dispossessed of their homes and hunting grounds. The most powerful Indian tribes of America had disappeared in the warfare. Their lands had long been peopled by the white men who had forced the savages step by step westward. Their conquerors must be their historians, and justice demands that we shall record their virtues as well as their vices.

If they were cruel, treacherous, revengeful and merciless as enemies, it is no less true that they were brave warriors, hospitable, devoted and loyal friends. They were as ready to risk life in defense of their benefactors and allies as they were to tomahawk, scalp and burn their enemies and prisoners. Their torture of captives was no more merciless than that exhibited by the so-called civilized people and governments of England, France, Spain and Italy in crushing out religious freedom during the same centuries. The Indians used the tomahawk, scalping knife and fire no more fiendishly than did the white bigots the rack, the thumbscrew and the blazing fagot.

The Indians resisted the invaders of their country with a stern and relentless ferocity born of ages of barbarism; torturing and exterminating their white enemies, the despoilers of their homes. Their conquerors, many of whom had fled from persecution and oppression in the civilized countries of Europe, turned upon the natives, robbing them of their lands, killing men, women and children. It was an age of disregard of human rights and human life, in which Christians vied with barbarians in the infliction of merciless cruelties.

When Iowa was first explored by the whites the Dakota Indians were found in possession of Minnesota and northern Iowa. This family consisted of the following tribes: Iowas, Omahas, Winnebagoes, Osages, Sissetons, Missouris and Otoes. The Algonquin family, consisting of the Illinois, Sauks, Foxes, Chippewas, Attouays and Pottawattamies, occupied northern Missouri and southern Iowa.

THE ILLINOIS INDIANS

The Indians seen by Marquette and Joliet in the valley of the Des Moines River were of the Illini or Illinois tribe. Illinois seems to have been the name of a confederacy embracing the five sub-tribes—Peorias, Cahokias, Kaskaskias, Michigamies and Tamaroas. These being of the Algonquin race were hereditary enemies of the warlike Iroquois, or Six Nations, whose seat of government was in the Mohawk Valley of New York. During the generations through which their wars had extended the Illinois had been gradually driven into the region between Lake Michigan and the Wabash River and extending thence west across the Mississippi River. More than two hundred years ago, when visited by Marquette, they had become greatly reduced in numbers and strength from wars with the Iroquois on the east and the Chickasaws on the south. When Iowa was next visited by white men the once powerful Illinois Indians had been nearly exterminated by the Sacs and Foxes. In 1803 a few Iowas were found who were friendly with the Sacs and Foxes, with whom they made an alliance which lasted about twenty years.

THE MASCOUTINES

A tribe called Mascoutines, first mentioned by Father Allouez in 1670, then found in the valley of the Wisconsin River, had moved into Iowa. These Indians were on friendly terms with the Illinois and occupied a portion of Iowa west of Muscatine Island, where they located, having been driven out of their former lands by hostile tribes. The Algonquin word " Mascoutenck " means a place having no woods or prairie. The Mascoutines built a village on the island of that name, which was a level prairie embracing about twenty thousand acres.

In 1673 when Marquette and Joliet first penetrated the Mississippi Valley they found the Mascoutines living near the Fox River where they had a village near the Miamis and Kickapoos, who were friendly with them. They were a fierce tribe and usually at war with some other nation. Long before the advent of the first French explorers the Mascoutines fought a great battle with the Sacs and Foxes on Iowa waters. These nations in large numbers descended the Mississippi in canoes. When near the mouth of the Iowa River, they were attacked by the Mascoutines. A desperate conflict ensued lasting an entire day. The Sacs and Foxes found themselves outnumbered and unable to force a passage through the enemy's country. As night was approaching, their losses being heavy, the command was given to retreat. As the fleet turned back and attempted to ascend the river, the Mascoutines left the shelter of the woods and from the water's edge sent a shower of arrows into the disordered enemy. Pushing their canoes out into the river, the Mascoutines continued the conflict. Beset on all sides by superior numbers, the invaders made a heroic fight for their lives; but one by one they fell before the enraged Mascoutines, who seized their canoes and capsized them, tomahawking the occupants as they struggled in the water. In the darkness that ensued a few of the Sacs and Foxes escaped in their canoes; but three-quarters of the army was sunk beneath the Mississippi.

When La Salle descended the Mississippi Valley in 1680, he found this tribe still in that vicinity. The Mascoutines, displeased with the presence of the white men, sent emissaries to the Illinois to influence them to join in resistance. Ninety-eight years later they are mentioned as attending a council when Colonel George Rogers Clark led a party into that region. Little more is known of the Mascoutines in later times, save that they lived near where Muscatine now stands and that the city derives its name from them.

It is supposed that as they became weakened by frequent wars, the remnants of the once powerful tribe were merged with some other nation, as they had disappeared before the first white settlers came to Iowa.

THE IOWAS

We first hear of the Iowa Indians in 1690 when they were found in the vicinity of the great lakes. Their noted chief, Man-haw-gaw, was then at the head of the tribe and under his leadership they migrated westward. They crossed the Mississippi and occupied the country about the lower valley of the Iowa River, giving to that stream its present name, although it was for a long time called the Ayouas by the earliest French explorers. Lewis and Clark in the journal of their explorations, in 1804, refer to this tribe of Indians as the Ayouways. In later years the orthography became changed to Ioway and finally the *y* was dropped and we have the beautiful name Iowa, with the accent on the I.

Antoine Le Claire, a half-breed of French and Indian parentage, who was familiar with several of the Indian languages, defines the word Iowa as '' This is the place.'' Theodore S. Parvin, a high authority, relates an Indian legend as follows:

"This tribe separated from the Sacs and Foxes and wandered off westward in search of a new home. Crossing the Mississippi River they turned southward, reaching a high bluff near the mouth of the Iowa River. Looking off over the beautiful valley spread out before them they halted, exclaiming ' Ioway ! ' or ' This is the place ! ' "

As far back as the history of the Iowa nation has been traced by Schoolcraft and others, it is found that this tribe migrated fifteen times. It appears to have moved in about 1693 from the vicinity of the great lakes to near the mouth of Rock River and some years later to the Iowa. The next move was to the Des Moines Valley in the vicinity of Van Buren, Wapello and Davis counties. Many years later the Iowas journeyed through southern and western Iowa, up the Missouri Valley, into Dakota. For several years they lived near the red pipestone quarries in the valley of the Big Sioux River, roaming over into northwestern Iowa as far as Spirit Lake and the upper valleys of the Little Sioux and Des Moines rivers. Leaving these regions they descended the Missouri into southeastern Nebraska in the Platte Valley. They next wandered into northern Missouri and from there into southern Iowa in the region of the Chariton and Grand rivers.

They engaged in frequent wars with the Sioux and Osages.
In 1807 they had a battle with the Osages. After a fierce
conflict they captured the village, destroying thirty lodges
and massacring all the inhabitants. A few years later the
smallpox ravaged their settlement, destroying more than
a hundred of their warriors and nearly two hundred wom-
en and children. Twelve years later they lost nearly two
hundred more of the tribe by the same disease. In 1819
they were attacked by a superior force of Sioux and a
desperate battle was fought. In the end the Iowas were
defeated, losing scores of their best warriors. The Sioux
captured and carried into captivity many of their women
and children.

One of the most noted chiefs after the death of Man-
haw-yaw was his son Ma-has-kah. His home was in the
Des Moines Valley, near where the town of Eldon now
stands, at the old village of Iowaville. He had seven
wives; the favorite one was a beautiful woman named
Rant-che-wai-me (Female Flying Pigeon). In 1824, when
Ma-has-kah, with a party of warriors, went to Washington to have an interview with President Monroe, this favorite wife joined the party the third day after their departure and announced her intention to accompany her
husband and shake hands with the President. She was
permitted to go with him and attracted marked attention
in Washington from her great beauty and intelligence.
Her portrait was painted by an artist at the Capital and
for a long time adorned his studio. She was a kind and
generous woman, devoting much of her time to minister-
ing to the sick and unfortunate. General Hughes, the Indian agent, who was well acquainted with her, spoke in
the highest terms of her excellent qualities. She returned
from Washington with new views of life and tried to im-
press upon the young women of her race useful lessons
from her observations of civilized people. Ma-has-kah
was deeply attached to her and was greatly depressed at
her tragic death, which was the result of a fall from a

MAHASKA
Chief of the Iowa Indians

horse soon after her return from Washington. He never ceased to extol her many virtues and beautiful character.

Soon after Ma-has-kah became the Iowa chief, he determined to avenge the assassination of his father. He selected a party of daring young warriors and led them on a secret raid against the Sioux. They met a party of their enemies and, after a battle, killed and scalped ten Sioux warriors, among them the chief in whose lodge his father had been slain. Ma-has-kah was one of the most famous war chiefs of the tribe of Iowas.

The last battle between the Iowas and Sacs and Foxes was fought near the old town of Iowaville. Here in 1824 the Iowas had assembled in great numbers to witness a horse race on the river bottom about two miles from their village. Most of their warriors were present, unarmed and unsuspicious of the impending danger. The Sacs and Foxes were led by their chief, Pash-e-pa-ho, assisted by Black Hawk, who was then a young man unknown to fame. Their spies had watched the assembling of the Iowas and reported to Pash-e-pa-ho the numbers of the enemy. He secreted his warriors in the forest not far distant. The old chief led two divisions in the stealthy attack, while young Black Hawk was sent with the third division to capture and burn the village. In the midst of an exciting race, when all eyes were fixed upon the rival horses, the terrible war whoop burst upon their ears and the fierce Sacs and Foxes rushed like a whirlwind upon the unarmed and panic-stricken crowd. The Iowa warriors made a dash for the village, where their arms had been left, only to find it in flames. Shrieks of agony from their wives and children mingled with the yells of young Black Hawk's band. as the cruel tomahawk fell upon the defenseless villagers, nerved the Iowa braves to superhuman resistance. But few of their arms could be found in the confusion and they were massacred by scores in a hopeless effort to rescue their families. They fought with clubs and stones, until seeing the utter hopelessness of further resistance, the remnant of the band finally surrendered. Their power was broken, their proud spirit crushed by this disaster and the survivors never recovered from the blow. They lingered in despair about the ruins of their village and the graves of their kindred, gloomy and hopeless. The renown of their once powerful tribe had departed. They moved from place to place, through southern Iowa and northern Missouri. They ceased, as an independent tribe, to hold any considerable portion of the State to which their name has been given.

When Ma-has-kah was about fifty years of age members of his tribe made an incursion into the country of the Omahas to avenge the assassination of a son of one of their subordinate chiefs. They returned with the scalps of six Omahas. General Clark, at St. Louis, was notified of the bloody reprisal and sent General Hughes to arrest the Iowa'braves. Ma-has-kah surrendered the young men to the military authorities and they were imprisoned at Fort Leavenworth. They felt the disgrace keenly and determined to be revenged upon their chief. Two of the number, escaping from prison and learning that Ma-has-kah was camped on the Nodaway, sixty miles from the village, stealthily approached his camp at midnight and killed him while asleep in his tepee. One of his murderers sought refuge among the Otoes, but when they learned of his cowardly deed they executed him. The other assassin was killed by his own tribe.

The Iowas in 1825 sold their undivided interest in their Iowa lands to the United States. At this time their numbers were estimated to be one thousand and their principal village was in the valley of the Little Platte River. In 1838 they ceded their interest in Iowa to the United States for $157,500, which was kept as a trust fund; the interest at five per cent. is paid annually to the tribe. The remnant of the Iowas accepted lands west of the Missouri River, with the Sacs and Foxes, their former conquerors. They soon after outnumbered the tribes that subdued them and had become in some degree civilized. During the Civil War the Iowas were loyal to the Union and many of them enlisted in the National Army, making good soldiers. In October, 1891, they finally surrendered their tribal organization and accepted lands in severalty.

At the time of the removal of the tribe from Iowa, the second Ma-has-kah, son of the great Ma-has-kah and his favorite wife, Rant-che-wai-me, was the ruling chief. He was a quarrelsome, drunken fellow, inheriting none of the virtues of his mother, nor the administrative ability or military genius of his father.

The Iowas were worshipers of a Great Spirit, the creator and ruler of the universe. They had a tradition that a very long time ago a month's rain came and drowned all living animals and people, excepting a few who escaped in a great canoe. The Great Spirit then made from red clay another man and woman and from them all Indians descended. They regarded rattlesnakes and a certain species of hawks with veneration. Unlike most other Indian tribes, they are chaste in their social relations; illegitimate children are never found among them. Among themselves the Iowas were called Pa-hu-cha, which in English means "dusty nose." Their tradition is that when they separated from the original tribe, they settled near the mouth of a river having large sandbars along the shore. The sand and dust from these were blown into their faces, giving them dusty noses and their name Pa-hu-chas. Their language was that of the Dakota group, of which they were a part. They were divided into eight clans, known as Eagle, Pigeon, Buffalo, Elk, Bear, Wolf, Beaver and Snake; each clan having a totem of the bird or animal they represented. Each clan had a particular method of cutting and wearing the hair. The name of the greatest of the Iowa war chiefs, Mahaska, has been given to one of the counties in the Des Moines Valley, embracing a portion of our State over which this once powerful tribe held dominion.

CHAPTER VII

THE SACS AND FOXES

THERE is evidence to show that early in the seventeenth century the Foxes occupied the country along the Atlantic coast now embraced in the State of Rhode Island. Later they moved to the valley of the St. Lawrence River and thence to the vicinity of Green Bay, where they were found by Jean Nicolet in 1634. In 1667 Claude Allouez, a French Jesuit, found on the Wolf River in Wisconsin, a village of Musquakies, which contained a thousand warriors, and nearly five thousand persons. The Musquakies seemed to realize that the invasion of the west by French trappers and missionaries threatened the eventual occupation of their lands by the whites, and from the first they waged war against the French intruders and were nearly the only tribe with whom the French could not live in peace. The English and Dutch were seeking to gain possession of the far west, and they bribed some of the Indian tribes to assist them. They succeeded in forming an alliance with the Musquakies and other tribes, for the purpose of exterminating the French. The French, on the other hand, formed an alliance embracing the Hurons, Ottawas, Pottawattamies, Sacs, Illinois, Ojibwas and other tribes who greatly outnumbered the Musquakies and their allies and a long war followed.

In 1712 the Foxes joined the Iroquois in an attack upon the French fort at Detroit but were defeated with heavy loss. They were driven by the French out of that part of the country and settled on Fox River in the vicinity of Green Bay. They continued their war on the fur traders and explorers, but met with a disastrous defeat on a battle field which was given the name of "Hill of the Dead." The Foxes lost hundreds of their bravest warriors at this place and the remnant of them retreated to the valley of the Wisconsin River.

In the early years of this war the Kickapoos and Mascoutines were allies of the Foxes, but they were finally won over by the French, and in 1732 joined the Hurons, Iroquois and Ottawas against their former friends. In this unequal conflict the Foxes were nearly exterminated, so that in 1736 their warriors were reduced to little more than one hundred. The Foxes now formed a close alliance with the Sacs, in the nature of a confederacy; each tribe, however, reserved the right to make war or peace without the consent of the other. The headquarters of the Foxes was at Prairie du Chien and the Sacs at Prairie du Sac, in Wisconsin. The Foxes had villages on the west side of the Mississippi, while the Sacs remained on the east side. The Sacs could muster about three hundred warriors, and the Foxes about three hundred and twenty. The Sacs had long before occupied the region about Saginaw, in Michigan, calling it Sauk-i-nong, from which came Saginaw. They called themselves Sau-kies, signifying " Man with a red badge." Red was the favorite color used by them in personal adornment. The Indian name of the Foxes was Mus-qua-kies, signifying " Man with a yellow badge." The name Fox originated with the French, who called them Reynors. The river in Wisconsin where these Indians had their home, was called by the French " Rio Reynor," as will be seen on the early French maps. When the English wrested the country from France, they gave the river its English translation Fox. The early English writers called the tribe Reynards. In the latter part of the eighteenth century the Sacs joined the Miamis in an attack upon St. Louis. The Foxes appear to have remained in the vicinity of the lead mines of Galena and Dubuque, for in 1788 they ceded to Julien

Dubuque for mining purposes the right to a strip of land northward from the Little Maquoketa in Iowa.

The first treaty made by the United States with the Indians of the Northwest was on the 9th of January, 1789, at Fort Harmar on the Muskingum River in Ohio. It was conducted by Arthur St. Claire, then Governor of Northwest Territory, on part of the government. The Indian tribes represented were the Pottawattamies, Chippewas, Wyandots, Delawares, Ottawas and Sacs.

The territory embracing Iowa was represented by two Sac chiefs. The objects of the treaty were to fix the boundary between the United States and the several Indian tribes. It was agreed that the Indians should not sell their lands to any person or nation other than the United States; that persons of either party who should commit robbery or murder, should be delivered up to the proper tribunal for trial and punishment. By this treaty the United States extended protection and friendship to the Pottawattamies and Sacs.

When Lieutenant Zebulon M. Pike ascended the Mississippi River with his exploring party in 1805, he found four Sac villages. The first was at the head of the Des Moines rapids on the Iowa side and contained thirteen lodges; the second was on the Illinois side about sixty miles above; the third was near the mouth of Rock River; and the fourth was on the lower Iowa River. The Foxes had three villages: one on the west shore of the Mississippi River above Rock Rapids, one twelve miles west of the Dubuque lead mines and another near the mouth of Turkey River. Lieutenant Pike reported their numbers as follows: The Foxes, 1,750, of which 400 were warriors, 500 women and 850 children; Sacs, 700 warriors, 750 women and 1,400 children; making a population of 2,850.

The Sac village on Rock River was one of the oldest in the upper Mississippi Valley. Black Hawk, in his autobiography, says it was built in 1731; it was named

Saukenuk. This was for more than fifty years the largest
village of the Sacs and contained in 1825 a population of
not less than eight thousand. The houses were substantially built, and were from thirty to one hundred feet in
length and from sixteen to forty feet in width. They
were made with a frame of poles covered with sheathing
of elm bark fastened on with thongs of buckskin. The
doorways were three feet by six and before them were
suspended buffalo skins. These houses were divided into
rooms separated by a hall extending the length of the
building. Fire-pits were provided with openings for the
smoke. The beds were made of skins of animals thrown
over elevated frames of elastic poles. Half a mile east of
the town is a bold promontory rising two hundred feet
from the bed of Rock River. This was known as " Black
Hawk's Watch Tower," and was the favorite resort of
the great Sac chieftain. Here he would sit smoking his
pipe, enjoying the grand scenery spread out before him;
the beautiful valley of Rock River, the mighty current of
the Mississippi and the bluffs of the Iowa shore fringed
with forests. Here he was born and it was the home of
his father, Py-e-sa, one of the great Sac chiefs. It is to
his credit that he clung to his old home and fought his
last hopeless battles against overwhelming numbers of
well-equipped white troops in defense of his native land.

On the 27th of June, 1804, William H. Harrison, governor of Indiana Territory and of the Louisiana District,
being also superintendent of Indian affairs, was instructed
by President Jefferson to negotiate with the Sacs and
Foxes for a portion of their lands. In November Harrison met five Sac and Fox chiefs at St. Louis, and obtained
their signatures to a treaty which granted to the United
States fifty-one million acres of their land, embracing a
region east of the Mississippi River extending from a
point nearly opposite St. Louis to the Wisconsin River,
for the insignificant sum of $2,234 worth of goods and one
thousand dollars in money a year.

Black Hawk and several other chiefs repudiated this treaty and claimed that the chiefs making it had no authority to dispose of this immense tract of land, including the site of the principal and oldest village of the Sac nation. The chiefs were sent to St. Louis to secure the release of a prominent member of their tribe and Black Hawk always asserted that they had no right to thus dispose of their choicest lands. When it was claimed that he had subsequently ratified the treaty of 1804 with his own signature he asserted that he had been deceived, and did not intend to dispose of their lands. There can be no doubt that the whites violated the terms of the treaty which stipulated that the Sacs should remain in undisturbed possession of the lands until they were surveyed and sold to white settlers.

In 1808 adventurers began to enter the Indian country attracted by reports of rich mines of lead, and frequent collisions occurred between them and the Indians. In order to protect the whites a fort was built, which was named in honor of the President. The building of this fort without their consent, in undisputed Indian territory on the west-side of the Mississippi River, was a clear violation of the treaty and could only be regarded as an act of hostility. The Indians resented its occupation as a violation of the treaty of 1804 and young Black Hawk led a party of Sac and Fox warriors in an assault upon it, which was repulsed by the garrison. When the war of 1812 against Great Britain began, the Sacs and Foxes were sent into Missouri to be out of reach of British influence. But they soon crossed the river and became allies of the English army. In 1813 a stockade was built near the present town of Bellevue, in Jackson County, Iowa, in order to hold the country from the hostile Winnebagoes, Sacs and Foxes.

In 1814 Major Zachary Taylor was sent with a detachment of 334 soldiers up the Mississippi River by boats, with orders to destroy the corn fields of the Sacs and

Foxes and burn their villages on the Rock River. The Indians were located on both sides of the Mississippi in the vicinity of Rock Island and Davenport. They rallied from all points to the attack. A detachment of British soldiers from Prairie du Chien joined them and the battle lasted three hours. The Indians led by Black Hawk fought with great courage to save their homes and Taylor was driven back with heavy loss and compelled to retreat. Black Hawk had become an ally of the British upon a promise that they would aid him to drive the Americans out of the valley which he claimed and refused to abandon. But when the war closed and the British were unable to aid him farther, he returned to his old home on Rock River and found that Keokuk had become a chief of the party friendly to the Americans.

In 1815 a large council of Sacs and Foxes assembled near the mouth of the Missouri River at which the treaty of 1804 was ratified, but Black Hawk refused his assent to it and withheld his signature, as did many of the minor Fox chiefs. They would not consent to the barter of their country and ultimate removal from it. Black Hawk made no resistance to the erection of Fort Armstrong in 1816 as a portion of his tribe under Keokuk had determined to give up their lands on the east side of the river and move to the Iowa side. Settlers now began to come in under the protection of the soldiers and open farms in the Rock River Valley and vicinity. But the old war chief, Black Hawk, with about 500 followers, held his village and lands on Rock River.

In 1824 the Sacs and Foxes ceded to the United States all lands lying between the Mississippi and Des Moines rivers south of the north line of Missouri, excepting a small portion lying at the junction of these rivers afterward known as the " half-breed tract," which they reserved for the families of the whites who had married Indian wives. In 1825 an agreement was reached in council held at Prairie du Chien fixing the southern boundary of the Sioux country, separating their hunting grounds from those of the Sac, Fox and Iowa Indians, on the south. It began at the mouth of the Upper Iowa River, extending westward to its fork in Winneshiek County, thence west to the Red Cedar in Black Hawk County, thence west to the east fork of the Des Moines in Humboldt County, then in a direct line west to the lower fork of the Big Sioux in Plymouth County, following that river to its junction with the Missouri.

In 1828 the Sioux and Winnebagoes, then in alliance, sent an invitation to the Sac and Fox chiefs near Dubuque to meet them in council and forever bury the hatchet. The Fox chiefs, unsuspicious of treachery, started toward the place of meeting. On the second evening as they were in camp for the night on the east shore of the Mississippi near the mouth of the Wisconsin River, they were fired upon by more than a thousand Sioux warriors. Rushing from their hiding place, the treacherous Sioux killed all but two of the Foxes, who plunged into the Mississippi and swam to the west shore, carrying news of the massacre to their village. Stung to desperation by the act of treachery, the Foxes prepared to avenge the murder of their chiefs. A war party was organized, led by the newly elected chief, Ma-que-pra-um. They embarked in canoes and stealthily landed in the vicinity of their enemies, concealed by the dense underbrush. Toward midnight they swam the river and crept up silently upon the' sleeping foe. Nerved with the spirit of vengeance, they silently buried their tomahawks in the heads of seventeen Sioux chiefs and warriors and escaped to their canoes without loss of a man. The war between the Sioux and Sacs and Foxes was waged for many years.

THE BLACK HAWK WAR

The followers of Black Hawk always repudiated the treaty of 1804, feeling that they had been wronged; but the white settlers who were swarming around them, fearing hostilities, demanded their removal. Collisions took place and, in 1830, when Black Hawk and his tribe returned from their annual hunting excursion, they found their lands had been surveyed and sold to white settlers. Their cabins had been seized and occupied and their own women and children were shelterless on the banks of the river. Black Hawk drove the white intruders out of the village and restored the wigwams to their owners. The whites called upon Governor Reynolds of Illinois for assistance and he called upon General Gaines to bring an army strong enough to expel the Indians.

On the 25th of June, 1831, General Gaines with sixteen hundred mounted soldiers took possession of the Sac village, driving the Indians from their homes to the west side of the Mississippi River. On the 30th Governor Reynolds and General Gaines, at the point of the bayonet, dictated terms with the Sac chiefs by which the Indians were prohibited from returning to the east side of the river without permission of the United States authorities. It was now too late to plant corn again and autumn found the Indians without food for winter.

In April, 1832, Black Hawk with his followers, including women and children, crossed to the east side of the Mississippi, near the mouth of Rock River. He declared the purpose of his journey was to join the Winnebagoes in raising a crop of corn. As they were proceeding toward the country occupied by their friends, the Winnebagoes, General Atkinson, in command at Fort Armstrong, on Rock Island, sent a messenger to Black Hawk, commanding him to return immediately to the west side of the river. Black Hawk refused to comply with the order, stating that his people were suffering greatly for food. He sent word to General Atkinson that they were on a peaceable journey to visit the Winnebagoes who had invited them to come and help raise a crop of corn. Governor Reynolds, upon hearing of the return of the Sacs, called out the militia to aid the regulars at Fort Arm-

BLACK HAWK
Sac Chief

strong in driving them out of the State. General Samuel Whiteside was placed in command of the Illinois militia, numbering about two thousand. One of the captains serving under him was Abraham Lincoln, afterward President of the United States. Serving under General Atkinson were Lieutenant-Colonel Zachary Taylor, who was elected President in 1848, Lieutenant Jefferson Davis, afterward President of the Southern Confederacy, and Captain W. S. Harney, afterward a distinguished general. The militia burned the Indian village at Prophetstown and then joined the regulars under General Atkinson. The combined army numbered about two thousand four hundred, while Black Hawk had less than five hundred warriors.

Black Hawk's little band was now near Dixon's Ferry, about forty miles from Kishwacokee. Major Stillman, with two hundred and seventy-five mounted volunteers, was anxious for a fight and General Whiteside sent him out in the direction of the Sac camp to make observations. Black Hawk hearing of Stillman's approach sent three young men with a flag of truce to conduct Major Stillman into camp, that they might hold a conference. Five more young warriors were sent by the Sac chief to watch the reception of his messengers. When the messengers bearing the flag of truce reached Major Stillman's camp, they were taken prisoners and one of them was shot. As the second party of five approached the camp, they were fired upon and two of them killed. The others escaped and reported to Black Hawk the slaughter of his messengers. The Sac chief had but forty warriors with him, the main body was in camp ten miles distant. The three Indians who escaped were pursued by the militia into Black Hawk's camp. The fearless old chief concealed his forty warriors in the brush and prepared for battle. As Major Stillman approached with his entire force, the Indians in hiding opened fire upon them and gave their terrific war whoop. The volunteers fired one volley and then fled in a wild panic as the forty Sac warriors poured hot shot into their broken ranks. Eleven of the volunteers were killed. As they fled, their provisions and camp equipage were abandoned. The fugitives scattered into little parties and never ceased their wild flight until thirty miles were placed between them and the enemy. Fifty of them kept on until they found shelter in their homes, spreading alarm as they ran their horses, reporting an overwhelming force of Indians in close pursuit. The wanton murder of his messengers and the attack upon his camp enraged Black Hawk, and he prepared as best he could to defend his people to the last.

After several battles against greatly superior numbers, the Indians were gradually driven to the Wisconsin River. General Henry Dodge, with two brigades of mounted men, now came upon the remnant of the tribe and killed sixty-eight. The Indians fought with great bravery, and when driven to the river bank, made a heroic stand against overwhelming odds, checking for several hours the pursuit.

While the warriors were inspired to the most determined resistance by their undaunted old chief, the squaws stripped bark from the trees, making frail boats of it in which they placed the small children and household goods. Swimming in the deep waters, guiding their precious freight and leading their ponies, they reached a sheltered island. When the women, children, ponies and baggage were thus sheltered from the enemy, one-half of the warriors held their foes in check, while the other half plunged into the current, each holding his gun above his head with one hand, swimming with the other, until they reached the opposite shore. They then opened fire upon their pursuers, until those on the other shore could cross in the same manner. Black Hawk stood calmly on the river bank next to the enemy directing this retreat, which was accomplished in the most skillful manner. Jefferson Davis, who was serving under General Dodge and witnessed this heroic defense by Black Hawk's little band, was greatly impressed with the skill of the old chief in holding the pursuing army in check while his women and children crossed the river. A few years before his death Mr. Davis wrote as follows:

"This was the most brilliant exhibition of military tactics that I ever witnessed; a feat of most consummate management and bravery in face of an enemy of greatly superior numbers. I never read of anything that could be compared with it. Had it been performed by white men it would have been immortalized as one of the most splendid achievements in military history."

Black Hawk modestly says of this desperate struggle at the river:

"In this skirmish, with fifty braves, I defended and accomplished my passage over the Wisconsin, with a loss of only six men, though assailed by a host of mounted militia. I would not have fought there, but to gain time for our women and children to cross to an island. A warrior will duly appreciate the disadvantage I labored under."

Sixty-eight of the Sacs fell in this brilliant retreat and battle; but the remnant of the tribe was saved for the time. An attempt was made to escape on rafts and canoes down the Wisconsin River, but the white soldiers from safe shelter on the shore killed men, women and children in their flight. Many were drowned and others sought shelter in the woods and died of starvation.

On the first of August, Black Hawk had gathered the shattered remnants of his band on the banks of the Mississippi and offered to surrender. But the soldiers who crowded the steamer "Warrior" were ordered to fire upon the white flag Black Hawk had raised in token of surrender. Twenty-three of his people were thus killed while offering no resistance. The next day the Indians were attacked by the combined forces of Generals Dodge, Henry, Alexander and Posey and shot down again without mercy. Men, women and children were killed like wild animals as they sought to escape by swimming the river. More than three hundred Indians were thus massacred and the slaughter was dignified by the name of the "battle of Bad Axe." Black Hawk and a few of his people escaped but were captured by treacherous Indians, delivered up to Colonel Zachary Taylor and by him sent to Jefferson Barracks near St. Louis. Thus ended the Black Hawk war in which the whites lost about two hundred killed, the Indians about five hundred men, women and children. The cost to our government was about $2,000,000.

Black Hawk was taken by his captors to Washington in 1833, and when presented to General Jackson, he stood unawed before the President, remarking, " I am a man, you are only another." He then addressed the President as follows:

"We did not expect to conquer the whites. They had too many men. I took up the hatchet to avenge injuries my people could no longer endure. Had I borne them longer without striking my people would have said Black Hawk is a squaw; he is too old to be our chief; he is no Sac. These reflections caused me to raise the war-whoop. The result is known to you. I say no more."

The prisoners were taken to Fortress Monroe where they were kept until the 4th of June, when they were released by order of the President. They were then conducted by Major Garland, of the United States Army, through several of the large cities to have impressed upon them the great power of the nation. Crowds of people gathered to see the famous Sac chieftain and his braves. As they were conveyed down the Mississippi River to Fort Armstrong and along the shores of their old homes and hunting grounds, the dauntless old chief sat with bowed head. The memory of the power and possessions of his race in former years came over him as he looked for the last time upon the familiar shores, woods and bluffs. Here he had reigned over the most powerful tribes of the west. Here his father had ruled before him. Here he had dwelt in happiness from boyhood. Here he had

taken his one young wife to his cabin and lived faithful to
her all the years of his life. Here for half a century he
had led his warriors to scores of victories. He was returning a prisoner shorn of his power, to be humiliated
before his hated rival, Keokuk.

Upon landing at Fort Armstrong, Keokuk was seen
gayly decorated as the chief of the Sacs and Foxes, surrounded by his chosen band of personal attendants.
Black Hawk was required to make a formal surrender of
his authority as chief of his nation, to his triumphant rival
and enemy. It was the bitterest moment of his life and he
only bowed to the humiliation at the command of his conquerors, when powerless to resist. He retired with his
faithful wife, two sons and a beautiful daughter to the
banks of the Des Moines River near Iowaville. There
he lived a quiet life, furnishing his home in the style of
white people. He cultivated a small farm, raising corn
and vegetables for his family. His cabin stood near the
banks of the river shaded by two majestic trees. He saw
his once proud and warlike nation dwindling away year by
year. Under his despised rival they were selling their
lands to the whites and spending the money in drunken-
ness and degradation.

Here on the old battle field, where years before he had
wrested the country from the powerful Iowas, the proud
Sac chieftain now brooded over his fallen fortunes. His
last appearance in public was at a celebration at Fort
Madison, on the 4th of July, 1838, where the following
toast was given in his honor: '' OUR ILLUSTRIOUS
GUEST, BLACK HAWK—May his declining years be
as calm and serene as his previous life has been boisterous
and warlike.'' In responding the old chief said:

"It has pleased the Great Spirit that I am here to-day. I have eaten
with my white friends. It is good. A few summers ago I was fighting
you. I may have done wrong. But that is past. Let it be forgotten. Rock
River Valley was a beautiful country. I loved my villages, my corn fields
and my people. I fought for them. They are now yours. I was once a

great warrior. Now I am old and poor. Keokuk has been the cause of my downfall. I have looked upon the Mississippi since I was a child. I love the great river. I have always dwelt upon its banks. I look upon it now and am sad. I shake hands with you. We are now friends. I may not see you again. Farewell."

He died on the third day of October following, and was buried on a spot long before selected by himself on the banks of the Des Moines River near the northeast corner of Davis County. His age was about seventy-two.

Mrs. Maria Peck, of Davenport, who made a careful study of the famous Sac chieftain, writes in the "Annals of Iowa" as follows:

" In Black Hawk was incarnated the very spirit of justice. He was as inflexible as steel in all matters of right and wrong, as he understood them. Expediency formed no part of his creed, and his conduct in the trying emergency that ended in the fatal conflict was eminently consistent with his character. No thought of malice or revenge entered his great soul. The contest was waged with no other purpose in mind than to protect his people in what he believed was their inalienable right to the wide domain that was being wrested from them. It matters not whether his skin was copper-colored or white, the man who has the courage of his convictions always challenges the admiration of the world, and as such pre-eminently the noble old Sac war chief will ever stand as an admirable figure."

CHAPTER VIII

ON the 21st of September, 1832, General Winfield Scott and Governor Reynolds, of Illinois, negotiated a treaty with the Sacs, Foxes and Winnebagoes, by which there was acquired from these tribes six million acres of land on the west side of the Mississippi, known as the "Black Hawk Purchase." The treaty was made on the west bank of the river in the present limits of the city of Davenport. The tract thus ceded extended from the northern boundary of Missouri, to the mouth of the Upper Iowa River, and had an average width of fifty miles, westward of the Mississippi.

The consideration to be paid for this grant was an annual sum of twenty thousand dollars for a period of thirty years; and a further sum of fifty thousand dollars to be applied to the payment of debts due from the Indians to traders Davenport and Farnam, at Rock Island. Six thousand bushels of corn, fifty barrels of flour, thirty barrels of pork, thirty-five beef cattle and twelve bushels of salt were also appropriated for the support of the Indian women and children whose husbands and fathers had been killed in the war just closed. It was estimated that the United States paid in money and provisions about nine cents an acre for this munificent grant of lands.

Black Hawk being a prisoner, the treaty was agreed to on part of the Indians by Keokuk, Pashepaho and about thirty other chiefs and warriors of the Sac and Fox nation. There was reserved to the Sacs and Foxes within the limits of this grant, four hundred square miles of land on the Iowa River, including Keokuk's village. This tract was called "Keokuk's Reserve," and was occupied by the Indians until 1836, when by a treaty negotiated by Governor Henry Dodge, of Wisconsin Territory, it was

ceded to the United States. The Sacs and Foxes then
moved to a reservation on the Des Moines River, where
an agency was established for them on the site where
Agency City has been built. Here Keokuk, Appanoose
and Wapello, chiefs of the united tribes, had each a large
farm under cultivation. The farms belonging to Keokuk
and Wapello were on what is known as Keokuk Prairie,
lying back from the right bank of the Des Moines River.
Appanoose's farm included a portion of the present site
of the city of Ottumwa. The memory of these chiefs has
been perpetuated in our State by three counties and two
cities, which bear their names, while a county in northern
Iowa bears the name of the famous old war chief, Black
Hawk.

On the 11th of October, 1842, another treaty was made
with the Sac and Fox Indians, in which they conveyed all
of their remaining lands in Iowa to the United States.
They were to vacate the eastern portion of the lands ceded,
to a line running on the west side of the present counties
of Appanoose and Lucas and north through Marion, Jasper, Marshall and Hardin counties, to the north limit of
the grant, on May 1, 1843, and the remainder on October
11, 1845.

When the time came for the departure of the Indians,
they were sad and sorrowful. They lingered around
their old homes reluctant to leave them forever. The
women were weeping as they gathered their children and
household goods together for the long journey to a strange
and distant country. The warriors could hardly suppress their emotion as they looked for the last time
upon the beautiful rivers, groves and prairies that they
had owned so long and were so reluctant to surrender.
As the long line of the retreating red men silently and
sorrowfully took its way westward, the booming of guns
and the light of a hundred bonfires gave evidence of the
advancing hosts of white settlers who hastened in to occupy the vacant places. In the progress of years these

KEOKUK
Sac Chief

once powerful and warlike tribes became listless and ener-
vated, losing the energetic characteristics which distinguished them in former times. The excitement of war
and the chase having long ago died out in their changed
environment, they became degenerate, intemperate and
lazy.

Keokuk, or " the Watchful Fox," was born in the Rock
River Valley in 1780. He was not a hereditary chief of
the Sacs, but attained that position by bravery in battle
with the Sioux, when a young man. When Black Hawk
had determined to resist the occupation of the lands which
certain chiefs had sold to the United States without his
consent in 1804, Keokuk was the leader of the peace party.
He was wily, shrewd, ambitious, selfish and avaricious.
He knew that his race could not successfully war with the
United States and he determined to submit to the demands,
surrender the homes on the east side of the river and
make the best terms possible for himself. He saw the opportunity to eventually supplant Black Hawk by becoming the leader of a peace party and thus secure influence
and assistance of the whites in his ambitious plans. He
was a most eloquent public speaker and used his oratory
with great effect. While the warriors of the united tribes
were disposed to fight for their homes under Black Hawk,
Keokuk by shrewd diplomacy won a majority to his
peace policy. Upon one occasion when the war spirit was
running high he called his followers together and addressed them thus:

" Warriors: I am your chief. It is my duty to lead you to war if you
are determined to go. The United States is a great nation and unless we
conquer them we must perish. I will lead you against the whites on one
condition, that is that we shall first put all our women and children to
death, and then resolve that when we cross the Mississippi we will never
retreat, but perish among the graves of our fathers rather than yield to
the white men."

His warriors after listening to the desperate proposal,
hesitated and finally determined to yield to the greatly

superior power of the whites. When the war of 1832 was
ended and Black Hawk was defeated and a prisoner, Keokuk's day of triumph came. Black Hawk was deposed by
his conquerors and, amid great pomp and ceremony, Keokuk arrayed in all his gaudy trappings was installed in
his place. " Keokuk's Reserve " was on the Iowa River,
and his village was for several years about six miles below where the city of Muscatine stands. In 1836 this
reserve was sold to the United States and Keokuk removed to the Des Moines River near Iowaville.

The followers of Black Hawk hated and despised Keokuk and never became reconciled to his accession to power
by the bayonets of the United States. Their leader was
Wish-e-co-ma-que, called by the whites Hard Fish. In
1845, having sold all of their lands in Iowa to the whites,
Keokuk led the remnant of the once powerful Sac and
Fox nation to a new home in Kansas. Here Keokuk, once
the gaudily dressed chief, in his old age became a confirmed inebriate. He was avaricious in the extreme and
was believed by his people to have dishonestly appropriated to his own use large sums of money received from
our government for his tribe. He had four wives and
upon all public occasions adorned his person with gay
trappings and was attended by a band of forty or fifty
favorites. In June, 1848, he died from poison administered by a member of his tribe.

Pashepaho, which signifies " The Stabber," was the
head chief of the Sacs at the beginning of the nineteenth
century. He was an old man when first known by the
whites. He was the leader of the five chiefs who went to
St. Louis in 1804 to meet William H. Harrison to negotiate the release of a member of his tribe accused of killing
a white man. While there he and his companions became
intoxicated and were persuaded to agree to a treaty conveying to the United States an immense tract of land on
the east side of the Mississippi River, including that upon
which their ancient village of Saukenuk stood. They re-

WAPELLO
Fox Chief

turned loaded with presents and it was a long time before their tribe knew that they had conveyed to the whites more than fifty-one million acres of their choicest lands, including their homes of more than a hundred years. Pashepaho had won great fame as a warrior, having been the leader of the Sacs and Foxes in their long war with the Iowas. He was the commander in the last great battle in the Des Moines Valley, which nearly annihilated their old-time enemies. He led an unsuccessful attack upon Fort Madison soon after its establishment. He was easily won over to the peace party by the wily Keokuk and joined the "Sly Fox" in the treaty of 1832, by which they sold the "Black Hawk Purchase" to the United States. He, like Keokuk, became a drunkard and moved with his tribe to Kansas.

Poweshiek, whose name signified "Roused Bear," was, after the Black Hawk war, head chief of the Fox tribe. His rank was superior to that of either Appanoose or Wapello. His village in 1837 was near the Iowa River, not far from where Iowa City stands. He was born on Iowa soil about the year 1797. He was a large, powerful man, weighing more than two hundred and fifty pounds. He was a noble specimen of his race, a man of great energy, a wise counselor and the soul of honor. He was grateful for favors and always truthful. In 1838 he led a party to select a location for a Sac and Fox agency on the Des Moines, in company with General Joseph M. Street, the Indian agent. When his tribe moved west he made his home near the mouth of the Raccoon River, in the vicinity of the future capital of Iowa. From there he went south with his people to Grand River and in 1846 reluctantly conducted them to their distant reservation in Kansas. A remnant of his tribe, dissatisfied with the Kansas reservation, after a short time returned to their old homes in Iowa. An Iowa county perpetuates the memory of Poweshiek.

Wapello, which signifies "prince," was a head chief of

the Fox tribe. He was born at Prairie du Chien in 1787, and at the time of the erection of Fort Armstrong, on Rock Island, his principal village was on the east side of the Mississippi, where the city of Rock Island was subsequently laid out. In 1829 he moved his village to the west shore of the river opposite Muscatine Island. A few years later he had a village built where the town of Wapello now stands. He belonged to the " peace party," and supported Keokuk and Pashepaho in adhering to the treaty of 1804. He signed numerous treaties with the United States, ceding lands to the government. He appears to have been easily influenced by Keokuk to part with their lands. It is related of Wapello that when one of his sons was slain by a Sioux warrior, in 1836, instead of avenging the murder, he purchased a barrel of whisky and, inviting his people to partake, they appeased their sorrow by indulging in a drunken debauch. His favorite hunting grounds were along the Skunk River, but he finally moved his village to the Des Moines Valley where Ottumwa now stands. He died in 1842 and was buried at Agency City, near the grave of General Street, who had been his friend.

Kiskkckosh, which signifies " The man with one leg," was a Fox chief. He was a daring warrior and won his fame in battle with the Sioux. He was an orator; tall, straight and perfect in figure. His village was at one time on Skunk River in Jasper County. He sought to bring about a reform with his tribe by changing the long established custom of his race which required Indian women to perform all of the labor, while the warriors, young and old, refrained from work as degrading. He was very much attached to his beautiful wife and was unwilling to leave all of the toil for her to perform. It was a hopeless effort, but this independent chieftain, though unsuccessful in overcoming an unjust and oppressive requirement, exhibited his convictions of right by aiding his wife in her labor. From 1843 to 1845 his tribe lived

KISHKEKOSH
A Chief of the Fox Indians

APPANOOSE
Sac Chief

at various times in Jasper County on the Skunk River, in Marion County, in the valley of the Des Moines and later near old Fort Des Moines. He was reluctant to give up his Iowa home and remove to the Kansas reservation. Monroe County was, when first organized, named Kishkekosh, but it was afterward changed by act of the Legislature.

Appanoose, which signifies '' A chief when a child,'' presided over a band of Sacs. Little is known of his early life, but during the Black Hawk war he belonged to the peace party. He was tall, straight as an arrow, finely formed and intelligent. After the removal of the tribes to the Des Moines Valley the village over which he presided stood near where Ottumwa has been built. Appanoose was one of the chiefs who accompanied Keokuk to Washington in 1837. At Boston he made a speech which made him famous. He had four wives and lived a very quiet life, seldom going far from his village. The exact date of his death is not known.

Taimah, '' The man who makes the rocks tremble,'' was a Fox chief. In 1820 his village stood on the Flint Hills, where Burlington was built. It was called Shock-o-con. Taimah was the head of a secret society of Indians noted for their courage and good character. Women of the best class were eligible to membership. It was known by the name of '' Great Medicine,'' and its secrets were never divulged. Taimah was one of the chiefs who went to Washington in 1824 and signed the treaty made at that time. Tama County was named in honor of this chief.

THE MUSQUAKIES

These are a remnant of the Pottawattamies and Foxes who returned from the Kansas reservation in about 1850, and stopped on the Iowa River to hunt and fish. They were so attached to Iowa that they persisted in staying in the State that had so long been their home.

Che-me-use (Johney Green) was the chief of the Pottawattamies, who first returned to the Iowa River. In 1859
Maw-nae-wah-ne-kah, a Fox chief with some of his tribe
joined the Pottawattamies on the Iowa River. Here they
lived peaceably, cultivating small patches of land, hunting, fishing and trapping for several years. In 1866 a
special agent was appointed by the government who paid
them a share of the annuities due their tribes. Two thousand dollars of the annuity fund was invested in the purchase of land, and additions to it were made from time to
time until several hundred acres were acquired. These
lands lie in Tama County, within a few miles of Toledo,
in the valley of the Iowa River and on the line of the Chicago and Northwestern railroad. In 1880 the tribe numbered three hundred and thirty-five people and they had
accumulated personal property to the value of about $20,-
000. They make frequent excursions into other portions
of the State in small parties for the purpose of hunting,
fishing and begging. They have made very little improvement in erecting their dwellings and in their cos-
tumes, adhering to the customs of their ancestors.

THE WINNEBAGOES

This tribe belongs to the Dakota group and is mentioned by French writers as early as 1669. They appear
to have been the first of the Dakotas to migrate eastward,
crossing the Mississippi River from Iowa at a remote
period. When first known to the French they were a
powerful tribe and hostile to the Algonquins. Early in
the seventeenth century the tribes of the Northwest formed
an alliance against the Winnebagoes and in a battle five
hundred of the latter were slain. In 1766 Carver found
them on the Rock River. They and the Iowas are thought
to be the only Dakotas that migrated to the east. Meeting the Algonquin tribes of Pottawattamies, Chippeways,
Sacs, Foxes, Mascoutines and Ottawas, they finally formed

an alliance, which lasted for more than one hundred and fifty years. They were reluctant to come under English rule after the expulsion of the French, but finally became reconciled and fought with the British through the war of the American Revolution.

In 1794, in alliance with other hostile tribes, they met General Anthony Wayne in battle and were defeated with heavy loss. In 1811 they are found fighting under Tecumseh at Tippecanoe, where they were again defeated by General Harrison. They joined the Pottawattamies in the massacre at Fort Dearborn in 1812 and were, with Black Hawk, allies of the British throughout the war. In 1816 they entered into a treaty of peace with the United States. In 1832 they joined Black Hawk in his war and at its termination were required to relinquish their lands in Wisconsin in exchange for a tract in Iowa known as the "Neutral Ground." They were not compelled to remove to their new home until 1841. By the terms of this treaty the Winnebagoes were to be paid $10,000 annually for twenty-seven years, beginning in September, 1833. The government agreed also to supply them with certain farm implements and teams and establish schools for the Indian children, maintaining them also for twenty-seven years. The "Neutral Ground" was a tract forty miles wide extending from the Mississippi River to the Des Moines. The boundary line which had been established between the Sioux on the north and the Sacs and Foxes on the south in 1825, was agreed to by a council held at Prairie du Chien on the 19th of August of that year, in which William Clark and Lewis Cass were the commissioners on part of the United States, and the following tribes of Indians: The Sacs and Foxes, Sioux, Chippeways, Winnebagoes, Pottawattamies, Ottawas and Menomonies. The principal object of the treaty was to establish peace between contending tribes as to the limits of their respective hunting grounds in Iowa. In this treaty the line is described as follows: Beginning at the mouth

of the Upper Iowa River on the west bank of the Mississippi, and ascending said Iowa River to its west fork;
thence up the fork to its source; thence crossing the fork
of the Red Cedar in a direct line to the second or upper
fork of the Des Moines River; thence in a direct line to
the lower fork of the Calumet (Big Sioux) River, and
down that to its junction with the Missouri River.

On the 15th of July, 1830, at a council held at Prairie du
Chien, the Sacs and Foxes ceded to the United States a
strip of land twenty miles in width lying immediately
south of the above named line and extending from the Mississippi to the Des Moines River.

At the same time the Sioux ceded to the United States
a strip of the same width lying immediately north of the
line. Thus the United States came into possession of a
belt of land forty miles wide, extending from the Mississippi to the Des Moines River. This tract was known as
the "Neutral Ground," and the tribes on either side
were allowed to hunt and fish on it unmolested until it
was ceded to the Winnebagoes in exchange for their lands
on the east side of the Mississippi River.

While occupying the "Neutral Ground" of Iowa, the
Winnebagoes found themselves between the hostile Sioux
on the north and the friendly Sacs and Foxes on the south.
Their hunting grounds were along the Upper Iowa,
Turkey, Wapsipinicon and Cedar rivers. On the 16th
day of October, 1846, they were induced to cede their Iowa
lands for a tract in Minnesota, north of St. Peter River,
to which they soon after removed. For many years parties of them returned to hunt and trap along their favorite Iowa rivers until most of the game had disappeared.

One of their most noted chiefs was Wee-no-shiek, or
Winneshiek, as now written, in whose memory an Iowa
county is named. In the Winnebago war of 1827 young
Winneshiek, who was but fifteen years of age, took an active part. He was captured by Colonel Dodge, but refused

FORT ATKINSON
Erected in 1840

to surrender until forcibly disarmed. He fought bravely
with Black Hawk in 1832, but was again taken prisoner
by General Dodge. In 1845 he was made head chief of his
tribe. He is described as one of the finest specimens, both
physically and intellectually, of his race. Tall, well-pro-
portioned and of dignified bearing, graceful in manners,
and of undaunted courage, he was always popular with
his tribe. He never became reconciled to the fate of his
race in being dispossessed of their homes by the whites,
and he regarded them as implacable foes to the end of his
life.

Waukon-Decorah, signifying "White Snake," was another of the most noted of Winnebago chiefs. He was inclined to keep peace with the whites, as he realized that
war upon that powerful race was useless. His influence
with his tribe often prevented acts of hostility on part of
the impulsive young warriors. His village was located
on the Upper Iowa River near the site of the town of Decorah, which bears his name. After his death the citizens
of that village gave his remains a final resting place in
the public square.

Two treacherous members of this tribe captured the
leader of their allies, Black Hawk, when he had taken refuge among them after the massacre of Bad Axe and delivered him over to his enemies. Their names were
Chasta and One-eyed Decorah.

In 1829 the Winnebagoes numbered five thousand eight
hundred. In 1836 the smallpox destroyed one-fourth of
their people. In 1855 they had become reduced to two
thousand seven hundred and fifty-four. When they were
first seen by the French they were of good stature, strong,
athletic and dignified, with straight black hair, piercing
black eyes and superior mental capacity. But after generations of contact with the whites, they degenerated rapidly, acquiring a strong appetite for intoxicating liquors.
They were not a quarrelsome people and only made war
to avenge the killing of members of their tribe. Their

[Vol. 1]

warriors were always volunteers who furnished their own
equipments. The war chief commanded in campaigns and
battles and decided the fate of prisoners. They usually
killed and scalped wounded prisoners and left their own
dead on the field of battle. The dead of their tribe were
dressed in a new suit before burial and the arms of warriors were buried with them. The graves of their chiefs
and noted warriors were protected with poles or pickets.
In winter their dead were deposited on scaffolds. Their
cabins were built by setting posts in the ground and covering them with bark. In winter skins of animals were
stretched over them. They were kind to old people and
carefully nursed the sick.

CHAPTER IX

THE POTTAWATTAMIES

THIS tribe belonged to the Algonquin group and was first seen by French missionaries near the northern limits of the Michigan peninsula, extending east to Lake Erie and southward into northern Indiana. They were allies of the French in the war with England. They joined Pontiac in his war against the English colonies in 1763. At the council of 1789 they formed a part of the Pontiac Confederacy. During the Revolutionary War they were the allies of the British and in the War of 1812 they were a part of Tecumseh's Confederacy against the United States. They occupied Fort Dearborn after the United States troops left it and made no opposition to the massacre by the Winnebagoes which followed.

By a treaty made August 24, 1816, the United States ceded a portion of the lands acquired from the Sacs and Foxes, in 1804, to the Pottawattamies and other tribes, in exchange for lands lying on the west shore of Lake Michigan, including the site of Chicago. Afterward the ceded lands (the boundary line of which passed just north of Black Hawk's village on Rock River, near Rock Island) were repurchased from the Pottawattamies, Ottawas and Chippeways, in two treaties dated September 20, 1828, and July 29, 1829. In the latter treaty the Indians were to be paid $16,000 a year forever, for a small portion of the lands originally purchased of the Sacs and Foxes in 1804 for $2,000 per annum. Black Hawk, who never recognized the treaty of 1804, well said: " If a small portion of our lands are worth $16,000 per annum, how was it that more than 50,000,000 of acres were sold for the insignificant sum of $2,000 per year?'' The question could never be satisfactorily answered.

In 1825 they were parties to the treaty negotiated by Governor William Clark on part of the United States to settle the dispute among the Chippeways, Sacs and Foxes, Winnebagoes and other tribes as to the limits of their respective hunting grounds in Iowa. In 1829 by a treaty they ceded to the United States a portion of their lands in southern Wisconsin and northern Illinois. In 1833 they also ceded all of their remaining lands along the west shore of Lake Michigan in exchange for 5,000,000 acres in southwestern Iowa.

In 1835 they moved to the lands thus acquired, which were also occupied in part by some of the Ottawas and Chippeways, who owned an interest in them. An agency known as Traders' Point was established in what is now Mills County. At this place Colonel Peter A. Sarpy, a French trader from St. Louis, for many years supplied the Indians with powder, lead, tobacco, blankets and other goods. Colonel Sarpy became a prominent man in the early history of Nebraska, which named one of its counties for him.

In 1838, while the Pottawattamies were occupying the country along the east shores of the Missouri River, now embraced in the counties of Mills and Pottawattamie, Davis Hardin was one of their agents. He opened a farm and built a mill in the vicinity of Council Bluffs. The Indians in that region numbered about three thousand. The following year two companies of United States troops were sent there to preserve peace. They selected a camp on the side of the bluffs descending into the valley of Indian Creek, near which was found a large spring. Here they proceeded to erect a blockhouse of logs. Its walls were pierced with holes for musket firing and from a pole floated the American flag. Barracks and tents were erected in the vicinity of the parade ground. With the

BLOCKHOUSE AT COUNCIL BLUFFS
Erected in 1838

Indians came Fathers De Smet and Verreydt, two Catholic priests, who established a mission, erecting a rude building for religious services. A cemetery was prepared where the dead were buried up to 1846 when the Indians removed to their Kansas reservation. One of the Pottawattamie villages was on the Nishnabotna River, near where the old county seat, Lewis, was built in Cass County. Its Indian name was Mi-au-mise (" The Young Miami "), after one of their chiefs, and here was located one of their largest burial grounds. Pottawattamie County was named to perpetuate the memory of this tribe whose lands embraced its territory.

On the 5th of June, 1846, a treaty was made with the Pottawattamies by which they exchanged their Iowa lands for a reservation thirty miles square within the limits of Kansas, to which they removed. The Pottawattamies were called by the French *Pouks*, and by this name they were designated on the early maps. The word Pottawattamie means "makers of fire" and was to the tribe expressive of the fact that they had become an independent people. Their relations with the Ottawas and Chippeways were intimate, as the language of the three tribes was substantially the same. In the transaction of important business their chiefs assembled around one council fire.

THE DAKOTAS

By careful examination of the records of the earliest explorers of the Northwest, it is ascertained that three great Indian nations occupied the upper Mississippi Valley in the sixteenth century. The most powerful and populous of these was the Dakota nation. The wanderings of these Indians extended northward to latitude 55° in the Rocky Mountains, east to the Red River of the north, southward along the headwaters of the Minnesota River, thence east to the shores of Green Bay. In the Rocky Mountains they were found as far south as the headwaters of the Arkansas and down to the Canadian and Red rivers of Louisiana, and eastward to the Mississippi. Thus it will be seen that this great Indian nation early in the sixteenth century occupied a large portion of British America, Montana, Wyoming, all of the Dakotas, more than half of Iowa, Missouri and Arkansas, all of Kansas and Nebraska, the greater part of Minnesota, and the north half of Wisconsin.

The Mahas, or Omahas, who speak a language similar to the Dakotas, occupied, at this period, the west side of the Missouri River from the Kansas to the James River of Dakota. It was an offshoot of the Omahas known as the Oc-to-ta-toes, or Otoes, who occupied the east side of the Missouri in what is now Iowa. Their hunting grounds extended from near Council Bluffs to the Des Moines River.

THE SIOUX

The Sioux Indians belonged to the Dakota nation and were first known to the French in 1640. In 1680 when Hennepin was sent to explore the valley of the upper Mississippi and was encamped with his party on the banks of one of the tributaries of the river, he was captured by a band of Sioux. They took him with them in their wanderings over Minnesota from April until September. The explorers were finally rescued by DuLuth, a French adventurer who had penetrated that region to the St. Peter River.

When the French took possession of that country in 1685 the Dakotas were divided into seven eastern and nine western tribes. During the wars between the French and various Indian tribes, the Sioux were forced southward into northern Iowa about the headwaters of the Des Moines River and Okoboji and Spirit Lakes. The branch of the Dakotas known as Sioux was divided into five bands, the Tetons, Yanktons, Sissetons, Mendawakantons

PILOT ROCK
In Cherokee County

and Wahpakootas. These bands called themselves Dakota, meaning a confederacy.

When Lewis and Clark explored the Missouri Valley in 1804, the Yankton Sioux occupied the country along the upper Des Moines and Little Sioux valleys and about the group of lakes in northern Iowa and southern Minnesota. They had for many generations roamed over that region and eastern Dakota and had named the rivers and lakes. Their principal villages were along the shores of Okoboji and Spirit Lake. Their name for the latter was Minne-Mecoehe-Waukon, or " Lake of the Spirits." Its name was derived from an old tradition among the Sioux that " a very long time ago there was an island in the lake; that the first Indians who sailed to it in their canoes, were seized and drowned by demons. No Indian again ventured near its shores, and it finally disappeared beneath the waters."

The Little Sioux River was called by the Indians Ea-ne-ah-wad-e-pon, signifying stone river. It was so named from the fact that near its bank in the southern part of Cherokee County is an immense red granite bowlder projecting above the surface twenty feet, being about sixty feet long and forty feet wide. It is flat at the top with a basin near the middle. It was called by the early settlers in that region Pilot Rock. From its summit could be seen a vast expanse of beautiful undulating prairie, through which winds the Little Sioux River, fringed with a narrow belt of woods.

In 1805 Lieutenant Pike estimated the number of Sioux at more than twenty-one thousand. One of their most noted chiefs in the first half of the nineteenth century was Wa-ne-ta of the Yanktons. When but eighteen years old he distinguished himself in the War of 1812, fighting with his tribe for the British at the. battle of Sandusky. He was instrumental in organizing a union of all of the Sioux tribes and became the chief of the confederacy of Sioux, often leading them in battle and victory against the

Iowas and Chippeways. In 1830 the Sioux ceded to the United States a strip of land twenty miles north of the line of 1825, from the Des Moines River to the Mississippi, receiving in part payment a tract on Lake Pepin, fifteen by thirty-two miles in extent. Seven years later the Sioux ceded to the United States all of their lands east of the Mississippi River. They were always more or less hostile to the Americans and only restrained from open hostilities by the wholesome fear of troops stationed in the frontier forts. They were also deadly enemies of the Sac and Fox nation.

In 1841 a party of Sioux surprised a hunting camp of twenty-four Delawares on the Raccoon River, killing all but one of them. The Delawares, led by their chief, Neo-wa-ge, made a heroic fight against overwhelming numbers, killing twenty-six of their enemies, four of whom fell beneath the terrific blows of the Delaware chief. But one escaped to carry the tidings to their Sac and Fox friends, who were camped on the east bank of the Des Moines River, near where the State House now stands. Pashepaho, the chief, who was then eighty years of age, mounted his pony and, selecting five hundred of his bravest warriors, started in pursuit of the Sioux. He followed the trail from where the bodies of the Delawares lay unburied, for more than a hundred miles up the valley of the Raccoon River, where the Sioux were overtaken. Raising their fierce war cry and led by their old chieftain, the Sacs and Foxes charged on the enemy's camp. The battle was one of the bloodiest ever fought on Iowa soil. Hand to hand the savages fought with a desperation never surpassed in Indian warfare. The Sioux were fighting for life and their assailants to revenge the slaughter of their friends. The conflict lasted for many hours. The defeat of the Sioux was overwhelming. More than three hundred of their dead were left on the field of battle. The Sacs and Foxes lost but seven killed.

In 1852 a band of Musquakies from Tama County, un-

WANATA
A Sioux Indian Chief

der the leadership of Ko-ko-wah, made an incursion into the " Neutral Grounds," and camped near Clear Lake. Learning that a party of Sioux were hunting on the east fork of the Des Moines River, six miles north of the present town of Algona, Ko-ko-wah with sixty warriors started out to attack the enemy. The Musquakies reached the river bank in the night a mile above the Sioux camp. Secreting themselves in the underbrush, they watched the enemy until most of the warriors had started off in the morning for a hunt. Ko-ko-wah then led his band silently into the Sioux camp, taking it by surprise. But the handful of warriors rallied and made a most desperate defense, the women seizing weapons and fighting fiercely for their homes and children. One squaw killed a noted Fox warrior named Pa-tak-a-py with an arrow at a distance of twenty rods. The Sioux had sixteen slain while the Musquakies lost but four of their number. This was the last battle between the Sioux and Foxes in Iowa.

A band of Sioux, under Si-dom-i-na-do-ta, engaged in two battles with the Pottawattamies in northwestern Iowa. One was fought near Twin Lakes in Calhoun County and the other on the South Lizard in Webster County. The Sioux were both times the victors. These were the last Indian battles in Iowa as the various tribes soon after left the State for their western reservations. The Sioux were the most warlike and treacherous of all of the tribes which have at any time had homes in this State. It was a band of Sioux who massacred nearly the entire settlement at Spirit Lake, Okoboji and Springfield in March, 1857. It was an uprising of the Sioux that in 1862 murdered nearly two thousand unarmed men, women and children in Minnesota. The cruelties perpetrated by the Sioux upon helpless women and children in this greatest of all Indian massacres, were never surpassed in atrocity by savages in any period of the world's history.

The tribes here mentioned are the principal ones that are known to have had a bona fide residence in the limits of the State of Iowa since it became known to the whites. All of these tribes occupying Iowa and claiming portions of it, either moved away or ceded their lands by treaty to the United States, as white settlers crowded upon them from the east. All, with the exception of the Mascoutins, Dakotas and Sioux, were finally provided with lands in Kansas or the Indian Territory.

This Territory was created by act of Congress June 30, 1834, and solemnly dedicated by that and subsequent acts as a final home for the Indians. It has since been reduced in size by successive formation of territories and states until its area has been diminished to sixty-nine thousand square miles. Subsequent acts of Congress have provided that no states or territories shall ever have a right to pass laws for the government of the tribes occupying this Territory and that no part of the lands granted to the Indians shall ever be embraced in any state or territory. The lands occupied by each tribe are the absolute property of such tribe and the unoccupied lands are held in reserve for other Indian tribes who may in the future agree to settle in the Territory. White settlers are not permitted to occupy any portion of the Territory without the consent of its Indian owners. It has been set aside for the exclusive use and permanent homes of the Indians for all time to come, where they shall be unmolested and protected by the general Government.

By terms of the treaty negotiated by Governor Chambers at Agency City, October 11, 1842, the Sac and Fox Indians ceded to the United States all of the remainder of their lands in Iowa, but retained possession until October 11, 1845. It was feared that hostilities might arise between these Indians and the Sioux or Pottawattamies on the north and west, who still held lands in that portion of the State.

A band of outlaws also had penetrated the upper Des Moines Valley, built rude cabins in the woods along the river, traded and sold whisky to the Indians in defiance of law, stolen horses from them and also from the nearest white settlers. To preserve peace and protect the country from their depredations, an order was issued in 1842 for the establishment of a fort at the forks of the Raccoon and Des Moines rivers. Captain James Allen, of the First United States Dragoons, at Fort Sanford, had in November, 1842, ascended to the forks of the rivers in the Indian reservation for the purpose of selecting a suitable site for a fort whenever the Government should determine to establish one farther up the river. He had reported in favor of a point at the junction of the two rivers. His reasons for this selection are given as follows:

" The soil is rich; wood, stone, water and grass are all abundant. It will be high enough up the river to protect these Indians against the Sioux, and is in the heart of the best part of the country, where the greatest efforts of the squatters will be made to get in. It is about equi-distant from the Missouri and Mississippi rivers and offers a good route to both. It will be within twenty-five miles of the new line, about the right distance from the settlements, and above all of the Indian villages and trading houses. All of the Sacs have determined to make their villages on a larger prairie bottom that commences about two miles below, and the traders have selected their sites there also. It will be about the head of keel-boat navigation on the Des Moines. I think it will be better than any point farther up, because it will be harder to get supplies farther up, and no point or post that may be established on this river need be kept up more than three years, or until these Indians shall leave. A post for the northern boundary of future Ioway will go far above the sources of the Des Moines.

" I would build but common log cabins for both men and officers, giving them good floors, windows and doors; stables very common. Pine lumber for the most necessary parts of the buildings ought to be sent up in keel boats in the spring rise of the river. One of their agents has told me that the American Fur Company would send a steamboat up to the Raccoon on the early spring rise. If they do it would be a good time to send up army supplies. Such is the desire of people to get a footing in the country that I believe I could hire corn raised here for twenty-five cents a bushel. The rise in the Des Moines will occur in March."

The establishment of the post was delayed until March, 1843, when Captain Allen was selected to build the fort. He left Fort Sanford on the 29th of April with a small detachment and supplies, took passage on a steamer which had been sent up from St. Louis and, selecting a site near the forks, returned to Fort Sanford for additional supplies. The water had become so low by the last of May that steamers could not go up and he was obliged to use keel boats and wagons. His nearest post-office was at Fairfield. He named the fort " Raccoon." General Scott did not approve of the name fortunately and ordered it changed to " Fort Des Moines." The camp was laid out along the west bank of the Des Moines River, in a belt of timber near the present line of Second Street. Twenty log buildings were erected for barracks and other purposes. There were two companies of soldiers; the infantry under command of Lieutenant John H. King, who was adjutant of the post; the cavalry under command of Lieutenant William N. Grier.

The Indian agent was Major Beach whose interpreter was Josiah Smart and, in addition to the garrison, there were several Indian traders and mechanics most of whom became permanent citizens after the fort was vacated. Settlers were not permitted by the treaty to occupy the lands recently acquired until October, 1845. The Government established a reservation one mile square around the fort, which was maintained until after the post was abandoned in 1846.

FIRST LOG CABIN AT FORT DES MOINES

AS early as 1690 it was known that lead ore existed in the upper Mississippi Valley. Nicholas Perrot was one of the early explorers of that region where he for several years carried on a profitable trade with the Indians in furs and skins of elk, deer and buffalo.

On the 8th of April, 1689, he took formal possession of the upper Mississippi Valley for the kingdom of France. His trading post was on the banks of the river and he built a fort for protection against hostile Indians, which he named " St. Nicholas." The exact location of this post and fort is not known. In 1690 a Miami chief with whom he was trading gave Perrot a specimen of lead ore taken from a creek that flows into the Mississippi which was undoubtedly " Catfish," the stream that empties into the river near the site of the original Dubuque mines. Perrot visited the place where the ore was found at that early day.

In 1700 the French explorer, Le Sueur, ascended the Mississippi River in search of valuable minerals. He explored as far north as the St. Peter River. In 1752 we find the lead region of the upper Mississippi located on a map published by Phillip Bouche. The mines are mentioned in an article by M. Guetard in a volume of the French Academy of Rheims in 1752. No effort seems to have been made to work or develop the mines in all of these years that lead ore was known to exist in that region.

The first white man who settled within the limits of the State of Iowa was Julien Dubuque. He was a French Canadian, born in the province of Quebec, January 10,

1762. He was well educated, an accomplished writer and conversationalist. He had given particular attention to mineralogy and mining. He went to the then far west in 1784, when but twenty-two years of age, settling in the province of Louisiana, near Prairie du Chien. Lead mines had been discovered several years before near the Mississippi River and young Dubuque determined to procure an interest in some portion of the mineral region. The Fox Indians then occupied a portion of northeastern Iowa. Dubuque, who was a shrewd, plausible man, succeeded in gaining the confidence of the Kettle Chief and his tribe and explored the country in that vicinity for lead ore, soon finding that it existed in considerable quantities.

The wife of a prominent Fox warrior, named Peosta, had in 1780 discovered lead within the limits of the present city of Dubuque and the shrewd Canadian soon succeeded in persuading the Indians to grant him the exclusive privilege of lead mining on a tract of land extending along the river from the mouth of the Little Maquoketa to the Tete des Morts, a distance of seven leagues, and running westward about three leagues. In drawing up the papers making this grant Dubuque had written, "We sell and abandon to Dubuque all the coast and the contents of the mines discovered by the wife of Peosta, so that no white man or Indian shall make any pretentions to it without the consent of Sieur Julien Dubuque." The grant was dated at Prairie du Chien, September 22, 1788.

As soon as he had secured the lease, he brought from Prairie du Chien ten Canadians to assist him as overseers, smelters, wood choppers and boatmen. There was a Fox village near where the city of Dubuque now stands, called the village of the Kettle Chief. It consisted of Indian lodges extending back from the river, sufficient to shelter about four hundred people, one hundred of whom were warriors. Dubuque had secured the friendship of the Indians who permitted him and his companions to make

their homes in this village. He employed Indian women
and old men of the tribe to work in the mines. He learned
the habits, superstitions and traditions of the Fox nation
and in the course of a few years had acquired great influence with them. They gave him the name of '' Little
Cloud.''

He opened farms, built fences, erected houses and a
horse mill. He put up a smelting furnace on a point now
known as Dubuque Bluff. He opened stores, bought furs,
sold goods and Indian trinkets, carrying on a large business, including the preparation of ore for market. Twice
a year he took boatloads of ore, furs and hides to St. Louis,
exchanging them for goods, supplies and money.

He became well known in that city as the largest trader
of the upper Mississippi Valley and his semi-annual trips
were events of importance to that frontier town. Dubuque
is described as a man of medium size, wiry and well built,
with black hair and eyes, very courteous and affable, with
all the grace of the typical Frenchman. He was an accomplished diplomat but was not successful in making
money. After eight years in mining and trading he made
an effort to secure a title to his leased lands, the only
title he held being the permit granted by a council of Fox
Indians. The instrument executed was a concession or
permit from the Indians to Dubuque to mine for lead ore
on the lands described. He now claimed that he had paid
for the lands in goods and in October, 1796, he presented
to the Spanish Governor of Louisiana a petition asking
a title to the lands.

Dubuque fully realized the value which time and development must bring to his munificent possessions and
took every precaution to perfect his title to the grant.
The petition was referred by Governor Carondelet to Don
Andrew Todd, a prominent merchant who had secured a
monopoly of the Indian trade with the tribes of the Mississippi Valley. Todd was requested to examine into the
nature of Dubuque's claim and report to the Governor.

In his report Todd stated that he saw no reason why
the land claimed by Dubuque should not be granted to him,
provided Dubuque should be prohibited from trading with
the Indians, unless with the written consent of Mr. Todd
upon such terms as he should require. Governor Carondelet, on the 10th of November, 1796, made the grant to
Dubuque as requested in his petition and indorsed upon
it these words: " Granted as asked for under the restrictions mentioned by the merchant, Don Andrew Todd, in
his report." Monuments were erected· by the Fox chiefs
and Dubuque to mark the boundaries on the three sides
from the river front, soon after the grant was made.

The right of the Indians to sell their lands had always
been recognized by Spain and Dubuque now considered
his title secure. As the years passed he carried on a
large trade with Auguste Chouteau of St. Louis and became heavily indebted to him. In October, 1804, he conveyed to Chouteau in settlement of his indebtedness, an
undivided seven-sixteenths interest of his land, estimated
to consist of seventy-three thousand three hundred and
twenty-four acres. It was also provided that at the death
of Dubuque all of the remainder of his interest in the
lands should belong to Chouteau or his heirs. In 1807
Chouteau sold one-half of his interest in the lands to John
Mullanphy, of St. Louis, for $15,000.

Dubuque and his little white colony lived among the
Indians, worked the mines, carried on trade for twenty-
two years, in the limits of the future State of Iowa. Many
of the French Canadians married Indian wives and in a
measure adopted the Indian mode of living. Families of
half-breed children were growing up and the place became widely known as the " Mines of Spain."

On the 24th of March, 1810, Dubuque was attacked with
pneumonia and died after a short illness. The highest
honors were bestowed by the Indians upon their dead
friend. The entire population followed him to the grave
and his virtues were eloquently set forth by the Indian

chiefs. His death brought a great change to the village, the mines and the white colony.

John T. Smith, a famous Indian fighter and western pioneer, bought an interest in Dubuque's grant, after his death, and took possession of some of the lead works. He attempted to carry on mining and smelting but the Indians refused to recognize his title. They claimed that the grant to Dubuque was a permit or lease to him personally and conveyed no absolute title to the lands and could not be used by other parties. The Fox chief, Pia-no-sky, gathered his warriors and destroyed the buildings, driving all of the whites out of the village and across to the east side of the river.

In 1805 Dubuque and Chouteau had filed a claim with the United States for title to all of the land which Dubuque had originally leased of the Indians, embracing a tract nine miles wide west from the Mississippi and extending twenty-one miles up and down the river. It included all of the then known lead mines and all of the present city of Dubuque. For nearly half a century this claim was pending before various tribunals. Finally, by agreement, in order to settle the titles to a vast amount of valuable property, a suit of ejectment was instituted by the heirs of the claimants of the grant, against a farmer in Dubuque County, Patrick Molony, who held a United States patent for his farm. The suit was tried in the United States District Court, John J. Dyer, judge, and judgment was rendered in favor of Molony. An appeal was taken to the United States Supreme Court and in March, 1853, the judgment of the lower court was confirmed.

The Chouteau heirs employed several able St. Louis attorneys, assisted by Reverdy Johnson, the great Maryland lawyer, while the Dubuque settlers were represented by Caleb Cushing, of Massachusetts, Judge T. S. Wilson and Platt Smith of Dubuque. It was one of the most important and closely contested law cases in Iowa litigation.

The titles to hundreds of farms and thousands of city lots and homes, and all of the lead mines in Dubuque County and vicinity, were involved. The decision turned largely upon the legal construction given to the original grant made by the Indian council to Dubuque, in 1788, and also upon the nature of the Spanish grant made by Governor Carondelet to Dubuque in 1796. The courts held that both grants were in the nature of permits or leases to mine lead on the lands described and were not intended to convey actual title to the land. From a statement made by Dubuque to Lieutenant Pike, in September, 1805, it is learned that at that time the Dubuque mines yielded but from twenty to forty thousand pounds of lead and that traces of copper were also found.

During the twenty-two years that Dubuque and his Canadian assistants lived in Iowa, from 1788 to 1810, the territory was owned by three different nations, viz.: Spain, France and the United States. The mines and the village which were first named by Dubuque the "Mines of Spain" were, after his death, called "Dubuque Lead Mines." The burial place of the pioneer was on a high bluff two hundred feet above the river and close to it, near the site of the old Indian village of Kettle Chief. Inscribed on a cedar cross in large letters was, " JULIEN DUBUQUE, Miner of the MINES OF SPAIN, died March 24th, 1810, aged 45 years and 6 months." His friend, the Fox chief, was buried near his grave. For ten years after the death of Dubuque little was known of the lead mines, as the Indians had undisputed possession.

In 1820 Henry R. Schoolcraft, in company with Hon. Lewis Cass. who was then Governor of Michigan Territory, went on a journey to the sources of the Mississippi River. Schoolcraft was a distinguished scientist and had spent many years studying the habits, customs and history of the North American Indians. It was on this voyage that Mr. Schoolcraft visited the Dubuque Lead Mines. He writes as follows of that locality:

" I left Prairie du Chien in a canoe manned by eight voyageurs, including a guide, at half-past eleven, a. m., August 6, 1820. Opposite the entrance of the Wisconsin River is Pike's Hill, the high elevation (near where the city of McGregor stands) which Pike recommended to be occupied as a military post. His advice was not adopted. * * * I camped at seven p. m. on the site of a Fox village on the east bank, a mile below the Turkey River from the west. The village, consisting of twelve lodges, was deserted, not even a dog left behind. My guide informed me that the cause of the desertion was the fear of an attack from the Sioux in retaliation for a massacre lately perpetrated by a party of Fox Indians of their people on the head waters of the St. Peter. I embarked on the 7th at half-past three a. m. and landed at the Fox village of the Kettle Chief, at the site of Dubuque's house, which had been burned down. The village is situated fifteen miles below the entrance of the Little Makokety River, consisting of nineteen lodges built in two rows, pretty compact, having a population of two hundred and fifty souls.

" There is a large island in the Mississippi directly opposite this village which is occupied by traders. I first landed there to get an interpreter of the Fox language, and obtained some information about the location of the mines. I succeeded in getting Mr. Gates as interpreter, and was accompanied by Dr. Muir, a trader, who politely offered to go with me.*

" On entering the lodge of Aquoqua, the chief, and stating the object of my visit, some objections were made by the chiefs who surrounded him, and they required time to consider. In the meantime I learned from another source that since the death of Dubuque, to whom the Indians had formerly granted the privilege of working the mines, that they had manifested great jealousy of the whites, were afraid they would encroach on their rights, denied all former grants, and did not make it a practice even to allow strangers to view their diggings. I had provided some presents, and directed one of my voyageurs to bring in some tobacco and whisky; and in a few moments I received their assent and two guides were furnished. They led me up the cliff where Peosta, the Indian woman, first found lead ore. After reaching the level of the bluffs we pursued a path of undulating hills, exhibiting a half prairie and a picturesque aspect. On reaching the diggings the most striking part of them exhibited excavations such as Indians only do not seem persevering enough in labor to have made.

" The principal mines are situated on a tract of one square league, beginning at the Fox village of Kettle Chief, and extending west. This is the seat of the mining operations carried on by Dubuque, as well as of what are called the Indian diggings. The ore is now exclusively dug by Indian women. Old and superannuated men also partake of the labor, but the warriors hold themselves above it.

" In this labor the persons engaged in it employ the hoe, shovel, pickax

---

* This Dr. Muir was an army surgeon, and was the first white settler at Keokuk.

and crowbar. These implements are supplied by the traders at the island, who are the purchasers of the crude ore. They dig trenches until they are arrested by the solid rock. There are no shafts and the windlass, buckets and the use of gunpowder in mining operations are unknown to them. Their mode of going down into the deepest pits is by digging an inclined way, which permits the women to keep erect in walking. I descended into one of these inclined excavations, which had been probably carried down forty feet at the perpendicular angle. When a quantity of ore has been taken out it is carried in baskets to the bank of the Mississippi and ferried over to the island. The Indians receive at the rate of two dollars for a hundred and twenty pounds, payable in goods. At the rate these are sold the ore may cost the traders at the rate of seventy-five cents or a dollar, cash value, per hundred weight. The traders smelt the ore in furnaces on the island. Formerly the Indians were in the habit of smelting the ore themselves on log heaps, by which an unusual proportion was converted in lead ashes and lost. They are now induced to collect these lead ashes, for which they receive a dollar a bushel. There are three mines in addition upon the upper Misissippi which are worked by the Indians: Sinsinaway mines, fifteen miles below the Fox village, on the east shore; Mine Au Fevre, on the River Au Fevre, which enters the Mississippi on its east bank below the Dubuque mines—the lead ore is found ten miles from its mouth; Mine of the Makokety, fifteen miles above Dubuque's mine. The mineral character and value of the country has been but little explored.

"After the death of Dubuque in March, 1810, the Indians burnt down his house and fences, he leaving no family. He had lived with a Musquakee squaw. There is I believe no instance in America where the Indians have annulled grants or privileges to persons settling among them and leaving families founded on the Indian element. They have erased every vestige of civilized life, and revoked or at least denied the grant, and appear to set a very high value on the mines.

"Having examined the mines with as much minuteness as the time allowed me would permit, and obtained specimens of its ores and minerals, I returned to Prairie du Chien."

The next white settlement attempted in the limits of Iowa was by Basil Giard, a French American who obtained from the Lieutenant-Governor of Louisiana, in 1795, a grant to a tract of land in the limits of Clayton County, known as the "Giard Tract." It contained five thousand eight hundred and sixty acres and was occupied several years. When Louisiana was acquired by the United States, a patent was issued to Giard by the Gov-

ernment, which was the first legal title obtained by a white
man to land in the limits of Iowa.

The third settlement was made by Louis Honore Tesson, a French Canadian, in 1799. He procured authority
from the Lieutenant-Governor of upper Louisiana to establish a trading post at the head of the Des Moines
Rapids of the Mississippi River. His selection was made
in Lee County, where Montrose now stands. Tesson at
once proceeded to erect a trading post and other buildings.
He inclosed a farm with a rail fence, raising corn, potatoes and other crops. He brought from St. Charles, Missouri, upon a mule, a hundred small seedling apple trees,
which were planted on his farm. This was the first
orchard planted upon the soil of Iowa. The trees grew
and proved to be well adapted to the country and some
of them were living in 1876. In 1803 the property was
sold on execution to Thomas F. Reddick. The sale was
confirmed to Reddick by an act of Congress. Attorney-
General Felix Grundy gave an opinion confirming the
title to the Reddick heirs and a patent was accordingly issued to them for six hundred and forty acres, February 7,
1839.

An act of Congress of October 3, 1803, authorized the
President to take possession of the Territory of Louisiana,
lately ceded by France, and establish a temporary government. On the 26th of March, 1804, an act was passed
organizing the Territory of Orleans, which embraced what
subsequently became the State of Louisiana, while the
remainder of the purchase was made the District of
Louisiana and placed under the jurisdiction of the Governor of Indiana Territory. This District of Louisiana
was an immense country, the boundaries of which were not
clearly defined. It embraced all of the region lying north
of the present State of Louisiana, including that State, to
the British possessions and west of the Mississippi River
into some uncertain portion of the Rocky Mountain region and the Pacific Ocean. On the 3d of March, 1805,

Louisiana was organized into a separate territory, with General James Wilkinson as Governor. The white population at this time did not exceed one thousand and the capital was St. Louis.

Soon after the purchase of Louisiana, the Government fitted out expeditions to explore the upper Mississippi and Missouri rivers, their tributaries and the regions through which they flowed. The one sent up the Missouri was under the joint command of Captain Meriwether Lewis and Captain William Clark. Captain Lewis was the private secretary of President Jefferson when selected for this important command and was well qualified for the work. His associate, Captain Clark, who was selected at his request, was a brother of the famous General George Rogers Clark. The forty-three men chosen to accompany them were mostly young, vigorous and experienced frontiersmen, well equipped for the important work. The boats which were to convey them were fitted expressly for the expedition. One of them was fifty-five feet long and half-decked. The others were strongly built, open boats.

The expedition embarked at St. Louis on the 14th of May, 1804, to explore a vast unknown region inhabited by tribes of Indians of which almost nothing was known. All felt that it was a hazardous undertaking for so small a body of men; but they were courageous spirits, accustomed to the perils and hardships of pioneer life and entered upon the long, uncertain journey with enthusiasm and undaunted courage.

They pulled out into the great river, depending upon oars to propel their boats against the powerful current for thousands of miles. When they reached the Missouri the waters were gray and muddy with the soil washed from its shores by a resistless, grinding flood that bore great numbers of uprooted trees upon its swift current. Sandbars were continually being formed, holding huge trees in their grasp, then undermined by the wash, quickly crumbled away from the volume of swift waters that ground them to atoms. The channel and shores were daily changing.

The progress of the party was slow as the men toiled at the oars through the day and went into camp at night in the dense forests along the shores. It was the 8th of July when they reached the mouth of the Nodaway River which they found navigable for several miles. As they passed up along the west shore of Iowa they describe the country as a vast prairie, the great valley of the Missouri broadening out on the Iowa side into immense meadows, many miles in width, and level as a floor, covered with a dense growth of tall waving grass. Beyond could be seen a high range of steep bluffs, often treeless, broken into sharp points and deep ravines. Roaming over the prairies were large herds of buffalo, elk and deer. Their record says:

" The greatest river merging its waters with the Missouri from the west is the Platte, which rises among the mountains of the great Rocky or Snowy Range in about longitude 112°. It winds through the Great American Desert to its union with the Missouri. Its sources are on the Spanish frontier not far distant from those of the Rio del Norte, which traverses the kingdom of New Mexico and empties into the Gulf of Florida. It is six hundred yards wide at its mouth, and is not more than six feet in depth, and from its rapidity and the great volume of sand it carries down, it is not navigable for boats larger than Indian canoes."

On the 22d of July the explorers camped on the east shore of the river ten miles above the mouth of the Platte to hold an interview with the Indians. The commanders had determined to cultivate the friendship of all Indian tribes they should meet on their journey through an unknown country and far beyond the reach of aid in any danger they might encounter. The regions they were to explore were known to be peopled with some of the most powerful and warlike Indian nations of America. It was realized that the success and safety of the little company of but forty-five must depend upon the establishment of friendly relations with the natives.

President Jefferson fully realized the perils likely to be

encountered by a small band of men cut off entirely for
months, or possibly years, from all communication with
their countrymen, in an unknown and unexplored region,
remote from civilization. But it was of great importance
to examine and learn something of the capabilities and
natural resources of this recently acquired region. The
prudence, skill and courage displayed by Lewis and Clark
in leading their party through this journey in safety, confirmed the excellent judgment of the President in his selection of the commanders of the successful expedition.

The first encountered were the Ottoe and Pawnee Indians on the Papillion and Mosquito, streams emptying
into the Missouri. The party at once established friendly
relations with them in a conference not far from where
Omaha stands. On the 29th they came to a region occupied by the Ayauway (Iowa) Indians before they moved
to the Des Moines Valley.

On the First of August they camped on a high wooded
bluff some distance back from the river, at an elevation
of more than seventy feet above the plains. From here
they obtained a fine view of the surrounding country, the
great prairies stretching in every direction as far as the
eye could reach; the winding valley of the river fringed
with woods in various places. On the 3d of August a
friendly council was held with six Indian chiefs, accompanied by many members of their tribes. Captain Lewis
explained to them that the Americans had now become the
rulers of this great valley and that they wanted to live at
peace with all of the Indians who occupied it. The tribes
at this council were the Ottoes and Missouris and they
asked that the Great Father would protect them from the
Omahas, with whom they were at war. After a friendly
conference presents were distributed among them and the
council closed. Lewis and Clark gave this camp the name
of '' Council Bluffs.''

A week later the explorers camped near the mouth of a
river named by the French '' Petite Riviere de Sioux ''

(the Little Sioux River). Most of the tributaries of the Missouri had been visited by French adventurers and trappers from 1705 up to the close of French dominion in the Mississippi Valley. They had given them names and to some extent explored them in their search for furs and game. Lewis and Clark were told by the Indians that the Little Sioux took its rise not far from the west branch of the Des Moines River; that within ninety miles of that river it passes through a lake sixty miles in circumference, divided into two parts, the banks of which approach very close to each other. '' It varies in width, contains several islands, and is the ' Lake of the Great Spirit.' ''

On the 10th the party passed a high bluff near the river where they were told by the Indians that the Omaha chief, Black Bird, was buried. He had died of smallpox four years before. Over the grave a mound twelve feet in diameter and six feet high had been piled up on an elevation three hundred feet above the river. Near this bluff was formerly a village of the Omahas, where were now buried nearly one thousand members of the tribe who had perished from smallpox the year their chief died. They had buried the dead and then burned their village consisting of three hundred wigwams.

Lewis and Clark now estimated that they had traveled by the river more than a thousand miles. On the 18th of August they landed on the west bank of the river opposite a point at the southwest corner of what is now Woodbury County, Iowa, and held a council with a band of Ottoe and Missouri Indians. The next day a young soldier of their party, Sergeant Charles Floyd, was prostrated with a sudden and very severe attack of bilious colic. The next morning presents were distributed among the Indians, who then mounted their ponies and departed westward over the prairie. The explorers embarked in their boats soon after and ascended the river thirteen miles, going into camp on the east shore. Here Sergeant Floyd died. His body was conveyed some distance to a high bluff overlooking the river, where he was buried with military honors. A cedar post, planted at the head of the grave, bore this inscription:

CHARLES FLOYD

Died August 20th, 1804.

He is the first white man known to have been buried on Iowa soil.

A river which the explorers passed emptying into the Missouri from the east, about a mile north of their camp, was named Floyd in memory of the young soldier whose grave was made in that lonely region. More than half a century later Sioux City was laid out near the spot where Floyd was buried.

For more than fifty years the annual floods of the great river encroached upon the bluff, wearing away its shore, until in 1857 the current had undermined the point upon which the grave was made, leaving the bones of the soldier exposed to view. Some of the residents of Sioux City assembled upon " Floyd's Bluff " and, with appropriate ceremonies, reburied the remains of Sergeant Floyd farther back from the shore. They found the red cedar-head board which had been planted by Captain Lewis fifty-three years before, thus identifying the grave.*

Remarkable windings of the river were frequently observed by the explorers. At a place at which they took meridian observations, they found themselves so near a point they had passed the day before, that a man was sent to step across the narrow neck which separated the two stations. He stepped nine hundred and thirty-four yards,

---

*On the 30th of May, 1901, a monument which had recently been erected to the memory of Charles Floyd, was dedicated   The monument was 100 feet in height and cost about $20,000. Congress and the Iowa Legislature made appropriations for the work, and Sioux City and private individuals also contributed. By invitation Hon John A. Kasson came from Washington to deliver the address. It was a valuable contribution to the history of the acquisition of Louisiana. There was exhibited a manuscript journal kept by Sergeant Floyd up to the time of his death, which was found in 1893, among the historical collections of Dr. Lyman Draper of Wisconsin.

while the distance by river was more than eighteen miles. No large bodies of timber were mentioned as occurring along the river valley, until the explorers reached the mouth of the Great Sioux River. Few Indians were found, and large flocks of prairie chickens, geese, ducks and sandhill cranes were frequently seen.

At the mouth of the Great Sioux River they were assured by the interpreter, M. Durion, that the river was navigable for a distance of more than two hundred miles, where the great falls would be found. He also described a creek which emptied into it just below the falls, which he said passed through a bluff of red rock, out of which the Indians made their pipes. These pipe stone lands were by agreement among the Indians, far and near, declared to be neutral grounds, where hostile tribes often met peaceably upon the banks of Pipestone Creek to secure their calumets of peace.

The further progress of the expedition cannot be given here in detail, as the history of its great explorations fills volumes. It need only be stated that it was conducted with courage and judgment and was eminently successful in procuring a vast fund of information as to the character of our newly acquired possessions. The explorers ascended the Missouri River to its source in the Rocky Mountains and crossed the divide to the head waters of the Columbia, which empties into the Pacific Ocean in Oregon. They proceeded down this river, making friends of all Indian tribes they met, often procuring supplies of them.

On the 16th day of November, 1805, they pitched their tents on the shores of the Pacific Ocean at Haley's Bay. Selecting a grove of lofty pines below the mouth of the Columbia River, the party erected comfortable cabins and went into winter quarters for the second winter since leaving St. Louis. Game was plenty and large numbers of Indians visited them, exchanging provisions for goods, and thus they passed a comfortable winter in the remote wilderness thousands of miles from the nearest white settlement.

On the 23d of March, 1806, they began their long journey homeward. Before leaving the winter camp, Captains Lewis and Clark took the precaution to post up in a secure place a brief statement, giving notice to whoever might visit that remote shore, that this party (giving their names) had explored the interior of the North American Continent by way of the Missouri and Columbia rivers, giving the date of the arrival on the Pacific coast and the time of the departure homeward. If any disaster should overtake them on the perilous return journey, here would be evidence of the success of the expedition and the results of their explorations would not be entirely lost to the world.

It is a remarkable fact that this brief notice was discovered by some Indians, taken by them and delivered to a Captain Hill, who was coasting near the Columbia River, carried by him to Canton, China, and sent from there to the United States, reaching Washington in January, 1807, nearly a year after the safe return of the explorers.

This was one of the most important expeditions ever sent out by our Government. It gave our country the first authentic information of its vast western possessions from the mouth of the Missouri along the eastern shores of Kansas and Nebraska, the western shore of Iowa, the interior of Dakota, Montana, Wyoming, Idaho and Oregon. It gave the first knowledge to civilization of numerous Indian tribes and nations, the lofty mountains of the Snowy Range, several of the greatest rivers and valleys of the west, the fir and pine forests, natural scenery not surpassed in grandeur by any other portion of the globe.

LIEUTENANT ZEBULON M PIKE
Explored Eastern Iowa in 1805

CHAPTER XI

THE year after the departure of Lewis and Clark the Government fitted out another expedition to explore the upper Mississippi and its valley. Zebulon M. Pike, a brilliant young officer, was placed in command.[*] On the 9th of August, 1805, the expedition, consisting of twenty soldiers, embarked in a keel boat seventy feet in length from St. Louis, under command of Lieutenant Pike. They carried provisions for a journey of four months and expected to explore the Mississippi to its head waters. By the 20th of August they had ascended the river two hundred and thirty-two miles above the mouth of the "Riviere des Moines," as Pike writes it. He describes it as coming in from the northwest at a point where the Mississippi is three-quarters of a mile wide. He says:

"We here arrived at the foot of the Rapids des Moines, which are immediately above the confluence of the river of that name with the Mississippi. Although no soul on board had ever passed them before we commenced ascending without delay. Our boat being large and moderately loaded, we found great difficulty. The rapids are eleven miles long, with successive shoals extending from shore to shore across the bed of the river. The channel, which is a bad one, is on the eastern side at the first two falls. It then passes under the edge of the third, crosses to the west side and ascends that side all the way to the Sac village. We had passed the first and most difficult shoal when we were met by William Ewing, an agent of the United States residing at the Sac village to instruct the Indians in agriculture. A French interpreter and fifteen men of the Sac nation came with Mr. Ewing in their canoes (with a United States flag) to assist me over the rapids. Taking a part of my load and putting two pilots in my barge, we soon reached Ewing's house at the village."

---

[*] Lieutenant Pike became a distinguished American officer in the War of 1812. In leading an army against the British at York (Toronto), in Canada, April 27, 1813, he was mortally wounded and died soon after the capture of the fort and city.

The next morning the chief men of the Sac village assembled and Lieutenant Pike explained to them the object of his expedition. The country here is described as hilly on both sides of the rapids, the soil fertile. On Thursday, August 22d, a number of islands were passed; the river was wide and full of sandbars. After ascending twenty-eight miles, Lieutenant Pike thus describes the country on the western shore:

" The channel of the river passes under a hill which rises up perpendicularly to a height of about sixty feet. On the summit is a level platform of about four hundred yards. In the rear is a small prairie of about eight or ten acres suitable for gardens. This would be a very good place for a garrison. Directly under the rocks is a limestone spring, which would supply a regiment of men with water. The landing is bold and safe, and a road could easily be made up the hill for teams. Black and white oak timber are here found in abundance. The hill continues for two miles, and gives rise to five springs in that distance. The view from this hill across the river east is very beautiful, showing broad prairies as far as the eye can reach, occasionally interrupted by groves of trees.* We remained here nine hours and saw traces of Indians. We learned that the largest Sac village was about two and a half miles eastward on the prairie, and that this point was about half way between St. Louis and Prairie du Chien."

On the 25th, the explorers landed on a prairie from which Lieutenant Pike writes: " There is a beautiful view for at least forty miles down the river, bearing S. E." The next day they passed the mouth of the Iowa River and camped at night on Grant's Prairie. Pike thus describes the river and vicinity:

" The Iowa River bears from the Mississippi S. W., and is one hundred and fifty yards wide at its mouth. In ascending the Iowa thirty-six miles you come to a fork. The right branch is called the Red Cedar from the great quantity of that wood found on its banks. It is navigable for bateaux nearly three hundred miles. It then branches into three forks called the 'Turkey Foot.' Ten miles up the Iowa from its mouth is a village of the Iowa Indians. From the Iowa to Rock River we generally found beautiful prairies on the west side, and in some places very rich

---

* From the general description, distance from the rapids, and other circumstances, it is believed that the spot here described is what was known in early days as the " Flint Hills," where the city of Burlington now stands.

land covered with black walnut and hickory timber. A short distance above the mouth of Rock River we came to the great rapids of the Mississippi, which extend up the river a distance of eighteen miles.* These shoals are a continuous chain of rocks, reaching in some places from shore to shore. They afford much more water than the Des Moines rapids, but the current is swifter and more difficult to ascend."

On Saturday, August 31st, Lieutenant Pike writes:

" We saw an encampment of Fox Indians on the west shore of the river, on a beautiful eminence, which appeared to be an old town. It is about ninety miles above Rock Island by the river."

At 12 o'clock the next day the explorers arrived at the " Mines of Spain." Lieutenant Pike writes:

" We were saluted with a field piece by Monsieur Dubuque, the proprietor. There were no horses to take us to the mines, which were six miles west of the river, and it was impossible for me to make an inspection of them from the river. I therefore proposed ten queries, which Dubuque answered. The substance of his answers was, that the mineral lands were supposed to extend twenty-seven leagues in length and from one to three leagues in width. The ore yielded about 75 per cent. and from 20,000 to 40,000 pounds were annually formed into pig lead. From the first Reynard (Fox) village to the lead mines the Mississippi became narrower, but the navigation became less difficult. The shores consist in general of prairie, which, when not immediately bordering the river, can be seen through the skirts of forest that in some places line the banks. The timber is generally maple, birch and oak, and the soil very excellent."†

On the 2d day of September the explorers reached Turkey River. The country is described as follows:

" From the lead mines to Turkey River, the Mississippi continues about the same width; the banks, soil and productions are entirely similar. Between the Iowa and Turkey rivers we found coming in from the west the Wabisapenkum (Wapsipinicon) river; it runs parallel with the Red Cedar, and has scarcely any wood on its banks. We next came to the

---

*The city of Davenport was afterward built on the west shore of the river at the foot of these rapids. The cities of Rock Island and Moline occupy the east shore, with a National Armory on Rock Island, which here divides the river. These, with the wooded bluffs rising from either side, form one of the most beautiful and picturesque landscapes to be found in the west.

†While here Lieutenant Pike met the Sac and Fox chief, Black Hawk, who had just returned from leading a war party against the Sauteurs.

Great Macottite (Maquoketa), and a little higher up the little river of the same name. The two streams approach each other, but present nothing remarkable excepting some lead mines, which are said to exist upon their banks. The Turkey River empties in on the west, bearing from the Mississippi about S. W., and is about one hundred yards wide at its mouth. Half a league up this river, on its right bank, is the third village of the Reynards, where they raise sufficient corn to supply all of the permanent and transient inhabitants of Prairie des Chiens."

Lieutenant Pike in writing of the Indians of this region says:

" It is surprising what a dread the Indians in this quarter have of the Americans. I have often seen them go around islands to avoid meeting my boat. The traders have impressed upon the minds of the savages the idea that we are vindictive, ferocious and very warlike people. They seem to fear us."

On the 4th of September, the explorers had reached Prairie du Chien, and from there Lieutenant Pike took a small boat to the mouth of the Ouisconsin (Wisconsin) River. He landed on the west shore of the Mississippi River nearly opposite the mouth of the Wisconsin and ascended a high hill. Here he found a level plateau commanding a fine view of the surrounding country. He held a council with the Puant (Winnebago) Indians. One object of the expedition was to meet and confer with as many of the tribes of the upper Mississippi Valley as he could reach in order to establish friendly relations with them. It was hoped that the way might thus be opened for treaties with them, which would enable the whites to establish settlements in this newly acquired territory. In this he was quite successful, for he was an officer of excellent judgment and in every way well qualified for the important mission intrusted to him.

Before leaving this point, Lieutenant Pike selected a site for a military post three miles from the mouth of the Wisconsin, on a hill called " Petit Gris." He writes:

" The Ouisconsin River is the grand source of communication between the great lakes and the valley of the Mississippi, and is the route by which all the traders convey their goods to the Mississippi River and the regions tributary to it as far down as St. Louis."

He describes the settlements and villages along the valley of the Mississippi at this time, September, 1805, as follows:

" The village of Prairie des Chiens was laid out in 1783 by M. Giard, Mr. Antoya and Mr. Dubuque. It consists of eighteen dwelling houses, on two streets. Sixteen were on Front Street, and two on First Street. There is a marsh or pond in the rear of the village, and behind the marsh are eight more houses. Some of the houses are framed, but most of them are built of small logs let in mortices, made in uprights joined close, daubed with mud on the outside and white-washed within. There are eight houses scattered in the country within a distance of five miles. On the west side of the Mississippi there are three houses on a small stream called Giard River,* making in all thirty-seven houses which contain on an average ten persons each, making a population of three hundred and seventy. During the fall and spring, when the traders gather in, there are at least six hundred people here. Most of the men have Indian wives, and more than half of the young people under twenty years of age are half-breeds."

On the 9th of September the explorers reached the mouth of the Upper Iowa or Oneota River, which is near the northern limits of the present State of Iowa. Lieutenant Pike extended his journey up the Mississippi, stopping wherever Indian camps or villages were found, to confer with the inhabitants and assure them of the friendship of his government. On the 22d of September, he reached the mouth of St. Peter River, near which he found a large Sioux village. Here he met Le Petit Corbeau, head chief of the Sioux nation and several other chiefs with whom he negotiated an important treaty by which the United States secured a grant of one hundred thousand acres of land in that vicinity. Proceeding up the river two hundred and thirty-three miles farther, he landed at the mouth of Pipe Creek and erected a fort in which to leave a part of his men and stores, while with a smaller party he extended his journey farther north. The

---

* These houses were where North McGregor has since been built.

river was now liable to freeze and Lieutenant Pike remained in camp until December 10th, building sleds and light canoes with which to pursue his explorations northward.

By the 8th of January, 1806, Pike with a corporal of his command reached a trading post on Lake Sable, in latitude 47°, kept by a Mr. Grant, for the Northwest Fur Company. This English company had extended its trade into this region in 1766, and from a small beginning in this section had built up gradually an immense concern. Its operations now extended from Hudson's Bay to the great lakes, up the St. Lawrence River, to the source of the Red River of the North, all of its tributaries west to the Rocky Mountains, including the territory since formed into the States of Iowa, Wisconsin, Minnesota, the Dakotas and Montana. From here Pike, with a small party, proceeded to the head waters of the Mississippi, which point he reached on the first day of February, 1806, arriving at Lake La Sang Sue at half-past two p.m. It was a proud moment for the young commander when he stood upon the shores of the lake from which the mighty Mississippi River takes its rise.

On the 12th of the month Lieutenant Pike, in company with the agent at the post, Mr. McGillis, ascended another fork of the Mississippi to its source in Red Cedar Lake, about thirty miles northeast of Leech Lake. They were now within six miles of the source of the Hudson Bay waters. On the 18th of February the lieutenant began his journey southward, accompanied by several Sauteur warriors.

He had been successful in establishing peaceful relations with all Indian tribes he had met, some of whom were the most fierce and warlike savages of the west. By the 7th of April, the ice having disappeared from the rivers, he started on his homeward journey, arriving at St. Louis on the 30th of April, after an absence of nearly nine months.

Previous to the explorations made by Lewis, Clark and Pike very little was known of the regions of the central west, drained by the two greatest rivers of North America. The reports of these explorers, who had only examined the country along the great water courses, awakened a deep interest among thoughtful Americans in the country recently acquired by Jefferson, known as Louisiana. The only people who had penetrated this unknown wilderness of woods and prairie were French missionaries who sought to convert the savages to Christianity; and the hunters and trappers who cultivated the friendship of the Indians in the interest of their traffic. Neither of these classes made homes, cultivated the soil, or left marks of civilization in their track. Hardly a trace of their wanderings for more than a hundred years within the limits of Iowa, Minnesota and Nebraska were found by the first actual settlers who came to the country to make permanent homes. No record even of the discoveries of the missionaries, hunters and trappers survived.

Thus a hundred and fifteen years passed from the time Marquette and Joliet discovered Iowa, before Julien Dubuque and his companions made the first white settlement within its limits. It was forty-four years later that the Indian title to any portion of its soil was relinquished. For the first half century after the new American Republic was established, it was the prevailing opinion that there was little country west of the Mississippi River valuable for agricultural purposes, and that portion of our possessions could be best utilized as permanent homes for the various Indian tribes which were being dispossessed of their lands east of the Mississippi. It was believed that having there an almost unlimited range, they could subsist largely upon game and fish, in the regions bordering upon an unexplored country marked upon the maps as the "Great American Desert."

As late as 1819, the *St. Louis Enquirer*, Thomas H. Benton, editor, said:

"After you get forty or fifty miles west of the Mississippi the arid plains set in. The country is uninhabitable except upon the borders of the rivers and creeks. The Grand Prairie, a plain without wood or water, which extends to the northwest farther than hunters or travelers have ever yet gone, comes down to within a few miles of St. Charles * and so completely occupies the fork of the Mississippi and Missouri rivers that the woodland for three hundred miles of each forms a skirt from five to twenty miles wide, and above that distance the prairie actually reaches the rivers in many places."

When it is seen that a statesman and editor so intelligent and eminent as Thomas H. Benton, as late as 1819, regarded the northwestern prairies covering a large portion of Missouri, Iowa, Minnesota, Kansas, Nebraska and the Dakotas as uninhabitable except along the borders of the rivers and creeks, it is not strange that the early pioneers, hunters and trappers entertained a similar opinion. For many years settlements were confined exclusively to the borders of streams where timber grew and to the forest regions. The first farms were hewn out of the forests; but as the fields were gradually extended out onto the prairies and they were found to be productive, yielding immense crops, the fertility of the prairies had to be recognized and a new value placed upon them.

But as the woods covered but an insignificant fraction of the surface of the prairie regions, it was generally believed many years later, that the prairies remote from woods could never become thickly settled or valuable for farms. Fuel and fencing, it was supposed, could never be supplied to make farms on the great prairies habitable. So for generations after the prairie regions were known, the hardy pioneers toiled in the dense forests of Ohio, Kentucky, Indiana and Michigan, hewing out farms among the sturdy trees which covered a large portion of the country. No more slavish toil can be found than that which the first settlers in these states patiently wrought to subdue the forests and remove the obstructing stumps from the rich soil. The natural meadows, unobstructed by

* A town on the Missouri River about twenty-five miles from St. Louis.

trees, waited long for the breaking plow of the pioneer; and were left as rich pastures for elk and buffalo and to feed the annual fires which swept over them unchecked, lighting the horizon with a lurid glow in the awful grandeur of their desolating march.

In 1806 the loyal American citizens of the Mississippi Valley were excited by rumors of a secret conspiracy said to be organizing under the leadership of the late Vice-President of the United States, Aaron Burr, to separate that region from the Union. It was reported that the scheme was to capture the adjacent Spanish provinces of Mexico and, uniting with them, found a western empire.

On the 5th of November the United States District-Attorney for Kentucky made formal charges in the United States Court against Aaron Burr, and followed with a brief statement explaining the nature of the alleged conspiracy. Henry Clay appeared as counsel for Aaron Burr and defeated the attempt to have him held for trial. Burr had caused to be built at Marietta, Ohio, ten large bateaux and had collected a great amount of provisions and stores for a voyage. He had secured the coöperation of many prominent men in various parts of the valley, and after the failure to indict him, took active steps to carry out his plans. General James Wilkinson,* who was Governor of Louisiana Territory, was approached and there was evidence that he had for several months possessed some knowledge of the enterprise. Captain Tyler, with a force of men and boats, accompanied by Harman Blennerhassett, a wealthy Irish gentleman occupying an island near Marietta, finally began the descent of the Ohio River. Below Louisville they were joined by Burr. The authorities now became thoroughly aroused over the gravity of the situation.

President Jefferson issued a proclamation warning all citizens against aiding the conspiracy and directing the

*General Wilkinson was a distinguished officer in the Continental Army in the War of the Revolution and the Indian War of 1794-6. In the latter year he became General-in-Chief of the army. He was appointed Governor of the new Louisiana Purchase in 1805.

arrest of all concerned in the unlawful enterprise. Burr
and his party were arrested near Natchez, his boats and
military supplies were seized and he was taken before the
Supreme Court and released on bail. The grand jury refused to indict him and Burr, failing to secure a discharge escaped. In attempting to make his way by night
to Pensacola to find shelter on a British vessel in that
harbor, he was captured and taken to Richmond, Virginia. He was there indicted, tried for high treason and
acquitted.

With the arrest of Burr the whole scheme failed, although there is little doubt that several influential men
were implicated. The mass of the people, however, were
loyal to the Union and gave no encouragement to Burr's
visionary scheme. Emigration now spread westward
along the rivers and many of the more courageous and far-
seeing home-seekers pushed out upon the treeless plains
of the Mississippi Valley.

The first newspaper published west of the river was
issued at St. Louis in July, 1808, called the *Louisiana
Gazette*. Its proprietor was Joseph Charless and, as there
was no print paper to be found in Louisiana at that time,
the first numbers of the new journal were printed on cap
writing paper. When the Territory of Missouri was organized the name of the paper was changed to the *Missouri
Gazette*, and in later years became the *Missouri Republican*,
afterward the *St. Louis Republic*. During this year the
southern portion of Louisiana was organized into the
District of Arkansas.

In 1805 General James Wilkinson was in command of
the Military Department of the West, with headquarters
at St. Louis. When he sent Lieutenant Zebulon M. Pike
on an expedition to the upper Mississippi River, he gave
him instructions to select a site for a military post some-
where between St. Louis and Prairie du Chien and procure the consent of the Indians for the building of a fort.
In Lieutenant Pike's report he says:

"I have chosen a site on a hill forty miles above the river De Moyen rapids, on the west side of the river. The channel of the river runs on that shore; the hill is about sixty feet perpendicular, nearly level on top."

In September, 1808, Lieutenant Alpha Kingsley was sent with a company of the First United States Infantry up the river to make a plat of the ground and begin the erection of the fort. During the fall and winter barracks and store houses were built and work pushed on the block houses and fort. In April of the next year it was garrisoned and named in honor of the new President, Fort Madison. It does not appear that the Indians had consented to the erection of this fort on the west side of the Mississippi, which was a direct violation of the treaty negotiated with the five Sac and Fox chiefs in 1804. By the eleventh article of that treaty the United States was entitled to build a fort in the vicinity of the mouth of the Wisconsin River; but the sixth article of the treaty provided that if any citizen of the United States, or any other white person, should form a settlement upon lands belonging to the Indians, such intruders should at once be removed. Notwithstanding this article, Fort Madison was built on lands belonging to the Sac and Fox Indians, without their permission, in clear violation of the treaty. It is not strange that the Indians complained of such an act of bad faith and hostility and under the lead of Black Hawk made an attempt to capture and destroy the fort.

Lieutenant Kingsley's force at the time he built the fort, and up to August, 1809, when he was relieved by Captain Horatio Stark, consisted of seventy men. In September, 1812, the fort was under the command of Lieutenant Thomas Hamilton, who had about fifty men. On the 5th of that month a band of about two hundred Winnebago warriors made an attack upon the fort. Among these Indians was Black Hawk, then a young man. A lively fight ensued, lasting until the 8th, when the Indians withdrew after having burned several buildings in the vicinity.

In 1813 the fort was again attacked by Indians, who

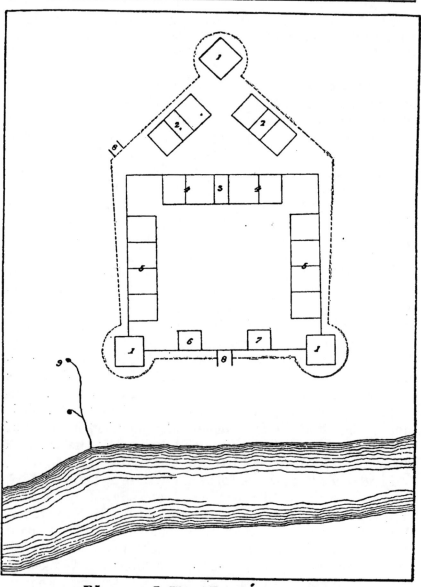

Plan of Ft. Madison, 1808.

1 Block Houses.	4 Officers Quarters.	7 Surgeons Office
2 Factory	5 Barracks	8 Gates
3 Passage-way	6 Guard-house	9 Spring

OLD FORT MADISON
Built in 1808

were defeated but several soldiers were killed. In August of that year a large force of Indians laid siege to the fort entirely surrounding it. The garrison, under Hamilton, made a brave defense until the provisions were exhausted and they were reduced to the verge of starvation. During the night of September 3d, Hamilton ordered a trench to be dug from the block house to the river where the boats were lying. There was no prospect of reinforcements being sent to their relief. Starvation, massacre or escape were the alternatives confronting them. They chose to attempt the latter. The night was dark and cloudy with a fierce wind roaring in the forest surrounding the fort. The little garrison, crawling on hands and knees along the bottom of the trench in perfect silence, at midnight entered the boats without alarming the watchful savages. The last man to enter the trench applied the torch to the fort. A moment later the boats pushed out into the rapid current of the Mississippi, and before the Indians were awakened by the roaring flames of the burning buildings, the fugitives were beyond the reach of rifle shot. They reached St. Louis in safety and the fort was never rebuilt. But the name clung to the spot where the ruins of the fort were long visible and later generations built a city on the historic site, giving it the name of Fort Madison.

In 1815 the Government sent Colonel R. C. Nichols with the Eighth United States Infantry to build a fort on Rock Island. His command, in keel boats, ascended the Mississippi to the mouth of the Des Moines River, where the channel was obstructed by ice and the party was compelled to land and spend the winter in that vicinity. Early in the spring of 1816, General T. A. Smith arrived and took command of the expedition, which reached Rock Island on the 10th of May. The day following his arrival General Smith sent messengers to all of the Indian villages in the vicinity inviting the chiefs to meet him in council, but none of them came. The Indians understood the significance of a fort and garrison and regarded it as un-

friendly but made no resistance. The island had long
been a favorite resort for the Indians, where they camped
among its beautiful groves and paddled their canoes along
the rocky shores. It was one of the most beautiful places
in the Mississippi Valley and they were reluctant to see
it occupied by a military force of the whites.

General Smith at once began the erection of a fortress
on a rocky elevation at the lower end of the island. When
completed the interior of the fort was four hundred feet
square. The lower half of the walls was of stone and the
upper half was constructed of heavy timber. At the northwest, southwest and southeast block houses were built
which were provided with cannon. On one side of the
square barracks were erected of hewn timber with roofs
sloping inward to protect them from the fire of the Indians and also that they might not furnish a safe lodging
place for the enemy in case of attack. The northwest corner of the fort stood about two hundred feet from the
bridge which now connects the island with the Iowa shore.
The west end of the island was at that time covered with a
dense forest of oak, black walnut and elm.

Colonel George Davenport, who came to Rock Island
with the first troops, was the contractor's agent who furnished the supplies for the army. He made his permanent home on the island, where he was murdered on the
4th of July, 1845. Fort Armstrong was completed in 1817,
and continued to be occupied by troops under various
commanders until May 4, 1836, when it was evacuated.
The last commander was Lieutenant-Colonel William
Davenport, of the First United States Infantry.

After the evacuation of the fort, attempts were made
by various parties to preëmpt and enter land on the island and to secure possession and title. Congress, by special acts, permitted George Davenport and David B. Sears
to enter the tracts of land upon which they had made valuable improvements, but held the island as a Government
reservation. Long litigation followed, but in the end the

OLD FORT ARMSTRONG, ON ROCK ISLAND
Built in 1816

Government purchased a number of the claims, others were abandoned and, in 1862, the Attorney-General held that the island was a military reservation. In 1863 extensive barracks were erected by the War Department for the safe keeping of thirteen thousand Confederate prisoners.

By act of Congress of July 11, 1862, an appropriation of $100,000 for the construction of an arsenal on Rock Island was made. There have been additional appropriations from time to time for the enlargement of the works first contemplated. The total amount appropriated up to 1871 was $3,220,000.

CHAPTER XII

IN 1809 the population north of the Ohio River and west of the Wabash had reached about ten thousand, located largely along the valleys of these rivers and the Mississippi. The western portion of the Territory of Indiana was detached and organized into Illinois Territory, embracing the great prairie region west of the Wabash, north of the Ohio and east of the Mississippi River. It extended north to the British possessions. Ninian Edwards was appointed Governor and the capital established at Kaskaskia.

Two years later great alarm was felt by the people in the Mississippi Valley over a succession of earthquake shocks which prevailed at intervals for several months. The point where the severest shocks were experienced was in the vicinity of New Madrid, in the southeast corner of what is now the State of Missouri. The convulsions were so great that immense sections of land sunk, the channel of the river was changed, lakes and swamps disappeared and low lands were elevated into hills. The waters of the Mississippi near New Madrid were rolled with a mighty force up stream for nearly ten miles, causing destruction of life and property. It was during the continuance of these convulsions that the first steamboat that ever navigated a western river was making its way cautiously down the Ohio and Mississippi rivers. The name of the steamer was the " Orleans," of four hundred tons, commanded by Captain Nicholas I. Roosevelt. It was built at Pittsburg, from whence it departed on the 6th of December, 1812, for New Orleans, and, reaching that place in safety, inaugurated steamboat transportation, which opened a new field of commerce on western waters. Heretofore the products of the West had found a route to the world's markets in the slowly floating flatboats, or bateaux, propelled by poles, oars or the current of the rivers. All of the goods and implements to supply this region were transported from distant cities by the same expensive and toilsome methods. The introduction of steam navigation on the rivers was the dawning of an era of incalculable prosperity for the West.

On the 4th of June, 1812, the Territory of Orleans was admitted into the Union as a State, under the name of Louisiana. William Clark, one of the commanders of Lewis and Clark's exploring expedition of 1804, was appointed Governor. The name Missouri was given to the remaining portion of the Territory of Louisiana.

During the War of 1812 the Mississippi Valley suffered but little. Colonel Nichols, the commander of a British fleet in 1814, attempted to revive the scheme for separating that region from the Union. He issued a proclamation in the name of the King of Great Britain to the citizens of Louisiana, calling upon the French, Spaniards, Englishmen, Indians and native Louisianians to rally to his standard and emancipate themselves from a usurping, weak and faithless Government. He declared that he had come with a fine train of artillery, experienced British officers and a large body of Indian warriors supported by a British and Spanish fleet. His avowed object was to put an end to the usurpations of the United States and restore the country to its lawful owners. To the Indians he offered a bounty of *ten dollars for every scalp* taken from the enemy. His address was distributed throughout the valley in the hope that the people of English, Spanish and French birth might be persuaded to conspire against the Government of the United States and aid Great Britain in her attempt to recover possession of the Mississippi Valley. A grim response to this appeal was given a few months later, when the loyal pioneers flocked to New Orleans with their rifles and met the British invaders on the field of battle. More than three thousand of Wellington's veterans fell before the unerring aim of the sturdy, loyal backwoodsmen under General Jackson.

Thus the third attempt to separate the Mississippi Valley from the eastern States, demonstrated the unswerving fidelity of the pioneers of the West to the new republic of which they were a most important factor, geographically, commercially and politically. No ambitious, plausible schemes of unscrupulous adventurers, or glowing visions of an independent nation, could win their favor or shake their loyalty to the American Union. They wisely preferred to form a part of a mighty nation, rather than become a weak member of petty confederacies.

At the beginning of the War of 1812 the entire white population of the northwest, embracing the territories of Indiana, Illinois and Michigan, was estimated at about forty thousand. During the war, British emissaries and officers had succeeded by aid of presents and promises in securing the friendly services and military assistance of many powerful tribes of Indians. The savages were encouraged to rob and massacre settlers on the frontier, so that for several years emigration to the Mississippi Vallay practically ceased.

In July, 1814, General William H. Harrison and Lewis Cass, commissioners on part of the United States, negotiated treaties with the Wyandots, Delawares, Senecas, Shawnees and other tribes by which they became allies of the United States during the war with Great Britain. After the close of the war treaties were made with nearly all of the tribes of hostile Indians. About the middle of July, 1815, a large number of Indian chiefs, representing most of the tribes of the northwest, assembled at Portage des Sioux, on the right bank of the Mississippi, a few miles below the mouth of the Missouri, to negotiate treaties with the United States. The Government was represented by Governor William Clark, of Missouri, who was Superintendent of Indian Affairs west of the Mississippi; Governor Ninian Edwards, of Illinois; and Auguste Chouteau, of St. Louis. General Henry Dodge was present with a strong military force to guard against treachery and to protect the commissioners. Treaties were concluded with the Pottawattamies, Piankeshaws, Sioux, Mahas, Kickapoos, Sacs and Foxes, Osages, Iowas and Zanzans. Several other treaties were made with various western tribes during the year 1816 and general peace was established throughout the West.

From this time forward thousands of settlers sought homes in the western Territories. Indiana had by this time acquired a population which entitled it to admission into the Union and was made a State on the 19th of April, 1816; Jonathan Jennings became its first Governor. On the 3d of December, 1818, Illinois also became a State. Michigan Territory had not, up to this time, attracted much immigration. The few settlers about Detroit and along the Raisin River had suffered greatly from the British and their savage Indian allies and many had abandoned their homes. The tide of immigration kept farther south, seeking homes in the rich lands of Indiana, Illinois and Missouri up to 1820. Iowa had not yet been named but was embraced in the great indefinite Northwest Territory and was occupied by Indians, as well as the traders, miners and trappers who had permission of the natives to come among them.

The first steamboat that ascended the Mississippi to the limits of Iowa, reached St. Louis on the 2d day of August, 1817. It was most appropriately named *General Pike*, in honor of the young commander of the first American expedition ever sent to explore the upper Mississippi Valley. It was commanded by Captain Jacob Reed.

In 1818 Missouri Territory made application for admission to the Union. When the bill was introduced in Congress for her admission, Mr. Talmadge, of New York, offered the following proviso:

" Provided that the further introduction of slavery or involuntary servitude be prohibited, except in punishment for crime where the party shall have been duly convicted; and that all children born within said State after the admission thereof, shall be free at the age of twenty years."

After a brief discussion the proviso was adopted in the House of Representatives by a vote of seventy-nine ayes to sixty-seven nays. This was the beginning of the great conflict between freedom and slavery in the new States and Territories, which forty-three years later brought on the armed attempt of the slave-holding States to overthrow the National Government and establish a slave-holding Confederacy.

After a lengthy and bitter contest over slavery in Missouri, a compromise was effected, largely through the influence of Henry Clay, who was Speaker of the House. This settlement became famous under the name of the "Missouri Compromise." The Senate favored the admission of Missouri as a slave State, while the House insisted upon the exclusion of slavery. The remarkable influence and eloquence of Henry Clay finally persuaded a majority of the members of the House to admit Missouri as a slave State, upon the condition that slavery should forever be excluded from that portion of the Louisiana Purchase lying north of latitude 36 degrees, 30 minutes, excepting Missouri.

This compromise was a guarantee by Congress that all States lying north of that line should in the future be admitted free, while slavery might be extended in Territories and States south of the compromise line, as far as the limits of the original Louisiana Purchase. During the controversy over the admission of Missouri, the District of Arkansas was detached and organized into the Territory of Arkansas. In defining the northern boundary of Missouri, the following language was employed.

"From the point aforesaid north along said meridian line to the intersection of the parallel of latitude which passes through the rapids of the River Des Moines, making the said line to correspond with the Indian boundary line; thence east from the point of intersection last aforesaid along said parallel of latitude to the middle of the channel of the main fork of said River Des Moines, to the mouth of the same, where it empties into the Mississippi River, thence due east to the middle of the main channel of the Mississippi River."

A serious conflict arose some years later between the states of Missouri and Iowa over the true meaning of the phrase " Rapids of the River Des Moines." Missouri contended that " it referred to certain ripples in the River Des Moines," which would carry the line some twenty-five or thirty miles farther north. Iowa held that the rapids in the Mississippi River, called by the early French explorers " *La Rapids de la Riviere Des Moines*," was the point meant. Lieutenant Pike in his journal of explorations of 1805 called the rapids beginning just above the mouth of the Des Moines River, in the Mississippi River, " The Des Moines Rapids."

In May, 1819, the first steamboat undertook to ascend the ever-shifting channel of the Missouri River. The Independence," with Captain Nelson in command, steamed up the rapid current of the " Great Muddy " for a long distance. It had been seriously doubted by experienced river navigators whether it was practicable to run steamers among the shifting sands and channels of that river.

In June of the same year Major S. H. Long was sent with a party to explore the Missouri, Platte and Yellowstone rivers and valleys to the Rocky Mountains. The trip to Council Bluffs was made on board the steamer "Western Engineer." Great difficulties were encountered in ascending the uncertain channel. The water was high, the current exceedingly rapid, while great masses of flood wood and the shifting sands formed bars obstructing the passage. Major Long found settlements at different points along the Missouri Valley and numerous rude forts and stockades which had been erected by the settlers during the late war with England, to protect themselves from Indian attacks. Several tribes of Indians in this remote region had been instigated by British emissaries during the war to attack these isolated settlements. Some fine farms were found which had been under cultivation for five to ten years, from which the explorers obtained poul-

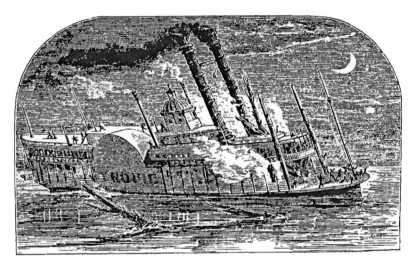

A MISSOURI RIVER STEAMER SNAGGED

try, eggs, vegetables and fruit. These pioneer farmers had immense cribs filled with corn, fine orchards of apple and peach trees, large double log houses and corn mills run by horse-power.

The advent of a steamboat created great excitement and was looked upon with wonder and amazement by the backwoodsmen, as it plowed its way up the mighty current of the Missouri at flood height. The only method of navigation ever witnessed by the pioneers was by canoes or flatboats, propelled by oars or poles. These farmers had no market for their products, no stores to furnish goods or groceries. Their nearest trading place was St. Louis, to which, at long intervals, journeys were made to exchange furs and skins of wild animals for such few goods as their simple life required. Major Long mentions a new disease which he found in some localities, coming from the use of milk, which at some seasons of the year communicates a distressing and sometimes fatal malady to those using it. He proceeds to describe the *milk sickness* which for many years afflicted the early settlers in some sections of Indiana, Illinois and Missouri.

On the 16th of September Major Long reached the mouth of the Platte. Trading boats from St. Louis were here found, which were to remain during the winter to collect furs and buffalo hides from the Ottoe and Missouri Indians.

No settlement had yet been found on the Iowa side of the Missouri. At the mouth of the Mosquito River, Major Long mentions the finding of the ruins of an old Ioway Indian village. A short distance above Fort Lisa was reached, which was a trading station of the Missouri Fur Company. On the 19th of September Major Long selected a place for winter quarters about five miles below Council Bluffs. This was the Council Bluffs named by Lewis and Clark in 1804, and it will be remembered was on the west side of the river and must have been about ten or fifteen miles above the city of Omaha. Major Long describes it as

a remarkable bank, rising abruptly from the brink of the
river to an elevation of about one hundred and fifty feet.
It had two important military advantages—security and
complete command of the river. It was three miles above
the mouth of the Boyer River coming in from the Iowa
side. The camp was made on a narrow beach covered with
woods reaching to the river, back of which rose a bluff
near two hundred feet high. The slope from the bluff
to the camp was gradual and easy of ascent. Here an
abundance of stone, wood and water was found, and
shelter from the bleak north and west winds. A council
was held here with the Ottoe Indians, bands of the Ioways,
the Missouris and Pawnees.

The principal Ioway chief at this council was Wang-ew-
aha, or Hard Heart, who had been engaged in over fifty
battles, in seven of which he had commanded. He was regarded as the bravest and most intelligent of all of the
Ioways. Beaver seem to have been plenty in the vicinity
of the camp, as sixty were caught by an Ioway chief on the
Boyer, and ten Omaha Indians brought in more than two
hundred taken on the Elk Horn. Game in the vicinity
consisted of bison, elk, deer, antelope, wolves, wild turkey,
otter, beaver and rabbits.

After making preparations for the winter encampment,
Major Long left Lieutenant Graham in command and,
descending the Missouri in a canoe, went to Washington.
Returning in the spring he left St. Louis on the 4th of
May, 1820, with a small party to make an overland journey to his camp at Council Bluffs, traveling by the com-
pass on as direct a line as practicable. From the mouth
of the Chariton to Grand River, the party passed through
a few settlements but the remainder of the trip was
through an unexplored region. They soon emerged from
the forests upon a prairie. Major Long writes:

"Upon leaving the forest there was an ascent of several miles to the
level of a great woodless plain. These vast plains, in which the eye finds
no object to rest upon, are first seen with surprise and pleasure, but their

great uniformity at length becomes tiresome. The grass was now about a foot high, and as the wind swept over the great plain, it appeared as though we were riding on the unquiet billows of the ocean. The surface is uniformly of that description not inaptly called rolling, and bears a comparison to the waves of an agitated sea. The distant shores and promontories of woodland, with here and there an insular grove, rendered the illusion more complete. Nothing is more difficult than to estimate by the eye the distance of an object seen on these plains. Soon after leaving our camp we thought we discovered several bison feeding at a distance of half a mile. Two of our party dismounted, creeping through the grass with great care for some distance, found them to be a wild turkey with a brood of half grown young. We often found hoofs, horns and bones of the bison and elk near former camping places of the Indians; also great numbers of tent poles and scaffolds."

On the 24th a camp was made on the banks of a beautiful river, and during the night a terrible storm came hurling the forest trees, uprooted and shivered, around them. Their terrified horses broke loose and ran wildly over the plains. The next day the party ascending a high range of hills, looked over a broad valley and saw the Missouri winding its way far off below. They had crossed the southwest corner of Iowa from some point on Grand River, probably passing through portions of Taylor, Page, Montgomery and Mills counties, striking the Missouri near the mouth of the Platte River. They were probably the first white men who ever traversed the beautiful rolling prairies of that region.

It had now been sixteen years since the western borders of Iowa had been partially explored by Lewis and Clark, and through their reports made known to the country; but so far as is known no permanent settlers had erected cabins in that region, or broken the prairie sod for farms. French and half-breed traders made their trips up and down the Missouri and its tributaries in pursuit of their vocation for many years after this before we find any attempts to open farms or lay out towns.

CHAPTER XIII

AFTER the death of Dubuque, the first white man known to have made a home in the limits of Iowa was Chevalier Marais, a scion of the French nobility and an adherent of Louis XVI. When the French Revolution swept over his country and the lives of the nobility were in danger, Marais fled to America and for twenty-two years was a wanderer of the west. In 1812 he married the daughter of the head chief of the Ioway Indians, established a trading post at the mouth of Buck Creek in the present limits of Clayton County, and lived there several years carrying on trade with the Indians and fur dealers.

An agent of the American Fur Company, Colonel J. W. Johnson, had in 1808 established a trading post at the Flint Hills, near where Burlington stands. His first shipment of merchandise was received on the 23d of August of the same year, from Bellefountain factory and was valued at $14,715.99. These goods were exchanged with the Indians for furs and skins. On the 28th of March, 1809, Colonel Johnson reports having procured the following:

710 lbs. of beaver skins valued	$1,420.00
1,353 muskrat skins at 25 cts	338.25
3,585 raccoon skins at 25 cts	896.25
28,021 lbs. of deer skins	7,256.45
Bear and otter skins	426.00
Beeswax and tallow	141.00
	$10,477.95

In 1812 the trading house was destroyed by fire and Colonel Johnson reports the loss of building and furs at $5,500. In 1820 Le Moliere, another French trader, had established a trading post six miles above the mouth of the Des Moines on the Iowa side.

In 1820 Dr. Samuel C. Muir, a surgeon in the United States army, was with a command stationed at Fort Edwards (now Warsaw, Illinois). He crossed the river and built a cabin where Keokuk now stands. He had married a beautiful and intelligent Indian girl of the Sac nation and their home was on a little Iowa farm where the cabin stood. Some years later an order was issued by the War Department requiring officers of the army at the frontier posts to abandon their Indian wives. Dr. Muir, who was a native of Scotland and a graduate of Edinburgh University, refused to desert his wife and resigned his commission. He lived happily with his wife in their modest and beautiful home on the banks of the Mississippi until 1832, when he was stricken with cholera and died suddenly, leaving his Indian widow and five children destitute, as his property became involved in litigation which consumed most of it.

In 1821 Isaac R. Campbell explored the southern portion of the territory embraced in Iowa and afterward settled near the foot of the Des Moines Rapids in Lee County, where he opened a farm and kept a public house. In writing his recollections of southern Iowa at that time, he says:

" The only indications of a white settlement at the time of my first visit at the Rapids was a cabin built by Dr. Samuel C. Muir on the site of the present city of Keokuk. The next cabin built by a white man in that vicinity was about six miles above, where a French trader, Le Moliere, had established a post. Another Frenchman, M. Blondin, had a cabin a mile farther up the river. At the head of the Rapids the Indian chief, Wapello, with a band of his tribe, had a village. This was near where Louis Honore Tesson, a French trader, had established a post and secured a grant of lands in 1799. The ruins of his buildings and his old orchard were here found."

Peter A. Sarpy, a French trader, had, as early as 1824, been engaged in the Indian traffic at a place called Traders'

FIRST IOWA SCHOOL HOUSE
Built in Lee County

Point on the east shore of the Missouri, near the south
line of Pottawattamie County. In the same year Mr.
Hart, a French trader, explored the western rivers and
valleys of Iowa along the Missouri and built a trading
post within the present limits of the city of Council Bluffs.
Quite a settlement of traders, hunters and trappers gathered in the vicinity. Francis Guittar, a French trader,
built a cabin there in 1827, and carried on trade with Indians and white hunters and trappers.

In 1828 Moses Stillwell with his family came to Puch-e-
chu-tuck (a name given by the Indians to the point at the
mouth of the Des Moines, where Dr. Muir had his home).
In the spring of 1829 Dr. Isaac Galland with his family
settled on the west shore of the Mississippi opposite the
upper chain of rocks in the lower rapids, where Nashville now is. It was called by the Indians Ah-wip-e-tuck.
Dr. Galland labored long and hard to build a city here,
but he was unsuccessful; the city went to Puch-e-chu-tuck
and became Keokuk. However, the establishment of the
first school,* and the birth of the first white child† within
the limits of the State made this place notable.

In his book descriptive of early Iowa, Dr. Galland says:

" As we passed up the river we saw the ruins of old Fort Madison about
ten miles above the rapids, near a sand bluff rising perpendicular from the
water's edge. On the second day after our keel boat reached Shoe-o-con or
Flint Hills. An Indian village of the Foxes stood at the mouth of the
Flint Creek; its chief was Ti-me-a. In 1825 I took a trip with an ox
team and an Indian guide up the river. We passed Wapello's village and
crossed the Des Moines River on a raft. We ascended the high lands above
Grave Yard Bluff (now Buena Vista). We followed the divide, passing a
lone tree standing on the bluff, which was a landmark for the Indians. In
the fall of 1825 I settled at Quash-qua-me village, where my father-in-law,
Captain James White, had purchased the old trading house and a tract of
land adjacent, which was an old Spanish grant made to Monsieur Julian,
on which he lived in 1805. Captain White made his first trip to this point
on the steamer Mandau, which was the first that came to the foot of the
Rapids."

* Established in 1830. Taught by Berryman Jennings.
† Eleanor Galland, a daughter of Dr. Galland, born 1830

In 1830 a trading post was established on the Iowa
River in the present limits of Johnson County. John
Gilbert was the agent in charge and was probably the first
white man to make a home in that part of the State. The
post was near Poweshiek's Indian village. Goods were
brought up the river in keel boats to be used in exchange
with the Indians for furs and skins. The following year
Colonel George Davenport explored the Cedar River in
a canoe to a point above the mouth of Rock Creek, where
he established a trading post and carried on a profitable
traffic with the Indians up to 1835.

In 1831 Mr. Campbell settled at Puch-e-chu-tuck. The
earliest settlers at this place after Dr. Muir and Moses
Stillwell, were Amos and Valencourt Vanausdol, John
Connelly, John Forsyth, James Thorn, John Tolman,
John Gaines and William Price, most of whom had Indian wives. Here the American Fur Company had erected on the river bank a row of hewn log buildings for the
use of their agent in his traffic with the Indians and for
the collection of skins and furs. The place was called
" Farmers' Trading Post."

In September, 1834, a meeting of half-breed Indians
was held at this place to prepare a petition to Congress
requesting the passage of an act to authorize them to sell
their lands in the tract known as the " Half-breed Reservation." There were nine families living in that vicinity
and, after the adjournment of the meeting above mentioned, the citizens held a council at John Gaines' saloon,
to consider the prospect of building a city at this place.
After some consultation, John Gaines proposed, and it
was agreed, that the future city should be named for the
Sac chief, Keokuk.

In August, 1835, Major Gordon with an escort of troops
crossed into the Black Hawk Purchase, traversing the region lying between the Mississippi and the upper Des
Moines rivers. He described the country as surpassing

in beauty and fertility almost any known region of the great West.

During the time occupied by the various explorations of the east and west borders of our future State, the territory had passed nominally under the jurisdiction of various organized territories. After Missouri was admitted into the Union as a State on the 4th of March, 1821, after the adoption of the famous "Missouri Compromise," all that portion of Missouri Territory north of the northern boundary was left without civil government until 1834. Although no portion of the territory west of the Mississippi River, north of Missouri, had yet been acquired of the various Indian tribes and nations occupying it, and white men could only enter the territory by permission of the Indians, still attempts were made from year to year to settle in that section.

In June, 1829, James L. Langworthy, a native of Vermont, purchased an interest in the Galena lead mines and attempted to procure an interest in Dubuque's old "Mines of Spain." Securing Indian guides he explored the country between the Turkey and Maquoketa rivers to find the lead mines formerly worked. He made friends with the Indians and gained their permission to work some of the mines. The next year with his brother, Lucius H. Langworthy and a company of miners, he began work. A village of the Sac and Fox Indians which stood at the mouth of Catfish Creek had been depopulated by an attack of Sioux Indians, who killed nearly all of its inhabitants. There were about seventy empty houses standing here when the miners from the Galena region crossed to take possession of the abandoned "Mines of Spain." Some of the reckless miners thought to intimidate the Indians by burning these cabins and thus prevent their return to the mines. In June, 1830, the miners on the west side of the river determined to organize a local government. They held a meeting and elected a legislature consisting of James L. Langworthy, H. F. Lauder,

James McPheters, Samuel Scales and E. M. Wren and instructed them to report a code of laws. This pioneer law-making body gathered around an old cottonwood log for a table and proceeded to business. Mr. Langworthy was chosen clerk and kept the records. The following is a copy of the code adopted:

" Having been chosen to draft laws by which we as miners will be governed, and having duly considered the subject, we do unanimously agree that we will be governed by the regulations on the east side of the Mississippi River, with the following exceptions:

" Article I. That each and every man shall hold two hundred yards square of ground by working said ground one day in six.

" Article II. We further agree that there shall be chosen by a majority of the miners present a person who shall hold this article, and who shall grant letters of arbitration, on application having been made, and said letters of arbitration shall be obligatory on the parties so applying."

The regulations referred to on the east side of the river were the laws established by the superintendent of the United States lead mines at Fever River (Galena). Under their code the settlers elected Dr. Jarote thir first Governor and it is known that their laws were obeyed and the acts of their legislature as rigidly enforced as have been the more formal acts of later years.

Settlers began to pass over to the new colony in large numbers, but as the invasion of the Indians' country was in direct violation of treaty compacts, the United States Government was called upon to expel the intruders. Under orders from the War Department, Colonel Zachary Taylor, commanding the military post at Prairie du Chien, sent Lieutenant Abercrombie with a company of soldiers to drive the invaders back to the east side of the Mississippi. A detachment was left at the mines to protect the Indians in possession of their property.

At the Flint Hills Samuel S. White and others had entered the Indian lands, erected cabins and staked off claims, but they also were driven out and their cabins destroyed.

FORT CRAWFORD AT PRAIRIE DU CHIEN

The treaty, by which the " Black Hawk Purchase " was acquired, was ratified on the 13th of February, 1833, and on the 1st of June following the Indians gave possession, removing to their reservations. The new territory thus opened to settlement had not yet been named Iowa, but was known as the " Black Hawk Purchase."

On the 1st of June, 1832, there were probably not more than fifty white people living within the limits of the future State; but for many years the fame of the beautiful valleys, groves and rivers, amid the fertile prairies covered with nutritious grass and brilliant with wild flowers, had reached the distant East. But it was reserved from settlement and in sole possession of Indians, their ideal hunting ground. Thousands of people were waiting impatiently for the removal of the red men from such a fair land. When the time came for the Indians to go farther west, the white top emigrant wagons thickly lined the paths leading into the land of promise. The home-seekers were crowding the ferries and exploring the creeks, rivers, groves and prairies for the best springs, timber and farm locations. Minerals, town sites and water power were sought for.

When the troops were withdrawn from the " Mines of Spain " in June, 1833, the Langworthy brothers crossed the river again and resumed work at the mines. Settlers flocked in, a frontier village began to grow up and a school was opened. All obstructions to settlement having now been removed, before the close of the year there was a population of about five hundred in the vicinity of the mines. A pioneer among the early inhabitants of this first Iowa village gives the following description of the place in that year:

" The valley resounded to the woodman's ax; the sturdy oaks fell before them on every side. The branches were used for fuel, and of the trunks were constructed rude log cabins without doors or windows. Three openings served for the entrance of light and the settlers, and the egress of the smoke. The winter of that year shut us in from all communication with the outside world, with a short supply of provisions, and not a woman in the entire settlement. There was plenty of whisky, and the demon intemperance stalked everywhere during the long winter evenings and short bleak days. The cholera claimed many victims, and the sick lay down and died with no gentle hand to nurse them, no medical aid to relieve, and no kindred or friends to mourn their untimely fate. We had no mails, no government, and were subject to no restraint of law or society. Drinking and gambling were universal amusements, and criminals were only amenable to the penalties inflicted by Judge Lynch, from whose summary decrees there was no appeal.

"In the spring of 1834 a transient steamer came up from St. Louis bringing provisions, groceries, goods and newspapers. A few women also came to join their husbands, and from that time on we began to exhibit some elements of civilization."

It is related by Eliphalet Price that the first American flag raised by a citizen of Iowa was made by a slave woman and run up in Dubuque by Nicholas Carroll immediately after 12 o'clock on the 4th of July, 1834. The same authority says that the first church in Iowa was built in Dubuque in the fall of 1834. Mr. Johnson, a devout Methodist, raised the money by general subscription among the citizens and the church was used by various denominations for several years. The first Catholic Church erected in Iowa was a stone edifice built in Dubuque in 1835-6, through the efforts of a French priest, Mazzuchelli.*

Next to Dubuque, Fort Madison was one of the earliest places in the limits of Iowa occupied by the whites. In 1832 Zachariah Hawkins, Berryman Jennings and several other young men, crossed the river and made claims in the vicinity of the old fort. Their claims were purchased the next year by Nathaniel and John H. Knapp, who proceeded in 1835 to plat a town.

In October, 1832, before Iowa was open to white settlers, a little colony crossed the Mississippi River at the head of Big Island, landing about two miles below the Flint Hills. They explored the country in that vicinity

---

*Eliphalet Price, in "Annals of Iowa," October, 1865.

WATERS' LEAD FURNACE, NEAR DUBUQUE
Erected in 1834, the Second in America

and selected claims for future farms. They built cabins
and fences, and in February, 1833, moved their families,
stock and farm implements to their claims. They had
begun to break up the land for crops, when the commander at Fort Armstrong sent a detachment of troops to
drive them off. Their cabins and fences were burned
by the soldiers and they retreated to the Illinois side,
but prepared to return as soon as the Indians were
removed.

Morton M. McCarver and Simpson S. White with their
families crossed and made claims within the limits of the
city of Burlington in 1833 and established a ferry across
the river to carry emigrants with their teams and goods.
They were the first settlers in Burlington. In the fall
William R. Ross brought a stock of goods and opened the
first store in the place. In November, 1833, the original
town was laid out and platted by Benjamin Tucker and
William R. Ross.*

In this same year of 1832 settlement was made near the
mouth of the Skunk River. This region was seen to be
especially fertile with convenient supplies of wood and
water. Among those who staked out claims in this vicinity were Joseph Edwards, Jeremiah Buford, William
Lee, Young L. Hughes, Joseph York, Jeremiah Cutbirth
and John Moore. Their claims were in the vicinity of the
town of Augusta as now located and in what is now Lee
and Des Moines counties. They cut logs and built cabins
and fenced and broke up land for farms. But the Indians
had not yet parted with possession of their lands, com-
plaint was made to the authorities and a company of soldiers came upon the settlers one day and drove them from
their claims to the east side of the Mississippi. They
were determined to hold their new homes and, after the
troops were sent away, the squatters again crossed to the
west side, took possession of their claims and thus became

---

*John Gray, a friend of the proprietors and a Vermonter, suggested the name, and it
was decided to call the new town Burlington for the city of that name in Vermont.

among the earliest settlers in Iowa. John Whittaker with
his family joined them early the following spring.

The first settler to cross the Mississippi River and open
a farm in the vicinity of old Fort Armstrong was Captain Benjamin W. Clark, a native of Virginia. He had
emigrated to western Illinois before the Black Hawk War
and, in 1833, when the lands west of the Mississippi were
opened to settlement, he took a claim. He soon discovered coal, which he mined; he planted an orchard and
established a ferry across the river, the only one between
Burlington and Dubuque. In 1835 he built a large public
house and the next year laid out the town of Buffalo, and
built a saw mill near the mouth of Duck Creek. His son,
David H. Clark, was the first white child born in the Black
Hawk Purchase in the country lying between Burlington
and Dubuque, April 21, 1834.

For several years Buffalo did a large amount of business and had the prospect of becoming an important city
in the future. But two rivals soon sprang up in Rockingham and Davenport, the latter destined to become the
large city of this region. Rockingham was laid out in
1836 by A. H. Davenport, Colonel John Sullivan and H.
W. Higgins. It was several miles up the river from Buffalo, opposite the mouth of Rock River.

The original claim upon which Davenport was laid out
was made in 1833 by R. H. Spencer and A. McCloud.
Soon after Antoine Le Claire purchased it for one hundred dollars. In 1835 it became the property of a company of eight persons who proceeded to lay out a town
named in honor of Colonel George Davenport. A long
and bitter contest arose between Rockingham and Davenport as to which should be the county-seat. It was finally
decided in favor of the latter. This proved a death blow
to Rockingham, which eventually disappeared from the
map.

CHAPTER XIV

BY order of the War Department, May 19, 1834, Lieutenant-Colonel S. W. Kearny was directed to proceed with three companies of the First United States Dragoons to establish a post near the mouth of the Des Moines River. He took Company B, Captain E. V. Sumner; Company H, Captain Nathan Boone and Company I, Captain J. B. Browne; with 107 men. On the 26th of September they reached their destination, making their camp where Montrose now stands. They immediately began the erection of log buildings and the post was named Fort Des Moines by order of the Secretary of War.

Colonel Kearny was ordered in March, 1835, to proceed up the Des Moines River to the Raccoon Fork and select a site for a military post in that vicinity. He started on the 6th of June with 150 men of Company B, commanded by Lieutenant H. S. Turner; Company H, Captain Nathan Boone, and Company I, Lieutenant Albert M. Lea. They were well mounted and followed a dividing ridge between the Skunk and Des Moines rivers. Their line of march led through that section of Iowa now embraced in the counties of Lee, Henry, Jefferson, Keokuk, Mahaska, Jasper and Polk. They camped at the mouth of the Raccoon River and spent some time exploring the country. A party was sent out, under Captain Boone, which for two weeks rode over the beautiful prairies in a northwesterly direction, finally coming into the Des Moines Valley in the vicinity of Boone County. Ascending the valley, on the 22d of June, they came to a river emptying into the Des Moines from a northeasterly direction. It was named Boone, for the commander of the party. From here they kept a northeasterly course along the divide between the Boone and Iowa rivers. The party spent nearly two months exploring the country, passing through Hamilton, Wright, Hancock, Cerro Gordo, Worth and other counties of northern Iowa. They had seen few Indians until the 30th of June. When in camp near the headwaters of the east fork of the Des Moines, they were suddenly attacked by a large party of Sioux warriors. Being in the heart of the Sioux country, that fierce tribe determined to resist a march through their possessions. Captain Boone made a successful defense until darkness put an end to the battle. Knowing that his little company was far beyond the reach of reënforcements, he ordered a retreat and, during the night, placed many miles between his command and the enemy.

By the 8th of August the expedition had returned to the Raccoon fork of the Des Moines River, where Colonel Kearny had established a camp and spent some time exploring the country north and west. They visited a portion of the Raccoon Valley, followed down the Des Moines to a village of Sac and Fox Indians, under the chief, Appanoose, located where Ottumwa now stands. Here they found a population of about three hundred and fifty Indians, with fine cornfields under cultivation.

One of the officers of the command was Lieutenant Albert M. Lea, who was a civil engineer and an accomplished draughtsman. He made a map of the region explored and to that added such information as he could collect from other sources. He prepared and had published a map of the "Iowa District." To accompany this map he published a little book with the following title:

"NOTES ON WISCONSIN TERRITORY.

The Iowa District,
or
BLACK HAWK PURCHASE.

By
Lieut. Albert M. Lea,

With Accurate Map of the District.

Philadelphia, 1836."

This was the first book ever published descriptive of Iowa or the Iowa District, as it appears to have been called, for this trip was made before the Territory of Wisconsin was organized and the entire region was a part of Michigan Territory. The following extracts are taken from Lieutenant Lea's book:

"The Iowa District lies between 40° 20' and 43° 30' north latitude, and 18° 10' and 15° 15' west from Washington. It is bounded by the Neutral Grounds between the Sauk and Sioux Indians on the north; by the lands of the Sauks and Foxes on the west; by Missouri on the south, and the Mississippi on the east. It is one hundred and ninety miles in length, fifty miles wide near each end, and forty miles wide near the middle opposite Rock Island. It is equivalent to a parallelogram one hundred and eighty by fifty miles, or nine thousand square miles, or 5,760,000 acres, including Keokuk's Reserve of 400 square miles. The District is sometimes called the ' Scott Purchase,' but more frequently the ' Black Hawk Purchase.'

" From the extent and beauty of the Iowa River, which runs centrally through it and gives character to most of it, the name of that river being both euphonious and appropriate, has been given to the District itself. The general appearance of the country is one of great beauty. It may be represented as one grand rolling prairie, along one side of which flows the mightiest river of the world, and through which numerous navigable streams pursue their devious ways toward the ocean. In every part of the District beautiful rivers and creeks are found, whose transparent waters are perpetually renewed by springs from which they flow. Many of the streams are connected with lakes, and nearly all are skirted by woods, often several miles in width, affording shelter from heat or cold to the wild animals of the prairies. The character of the population settling in this beautiful country is such as is rarely found in our new territories. With very few exceptions there is not a more orderly, industrious, energetic population west of the Alleghenies than is found in this Iowa District. For intelligence they are not surpassed as a body by any equal number of citizens of any country of the world.

" This District being north of Missouri is forever free from the institution of slavery, by compact made upon the admission of that State into the Union. What would not Missouri now have been if she had never admitted slavery within her borders? The Mississippi River is, and must continue to be, the main avenue of trade for this country; but there is a reasonable prospect of having a more direct and speedy communication with the markets of the East. New York is now pushing her railroad from the Hudson to Lake Erie; it will then connect with one that is projected around the southern shore of that lake to cross Ohio, Indiana and

Illinois, touching the foot of Lake Michigan in its route to the Mississippi River. This will place the center of the Iowa District within sixty hours of the city of New York. It is only a question of time when the business of this region will support such a road.

"Some of the most beautiful country of the world is lying immediately west of this District. The Indians are now moving over to the Des Moines, finding the country along the Waubisipinicon, Chicaqua (the Skunk) and the Iowa no longer stocked with game, they are ready to sell. The pressure of settlers along the border has already created a demand for its purchase. The western boundary will soon be extended, and it is hazarding little to say that this district will have a population that will entitle it to admission among the States of the Union by the time the census of 1840 shall have been completed. Taking this District all in all, for convenience of navigation, water, fuel and timber, richness of soil, beauty of landscape and climate, it surpasses any portion of the United States with which I am acquainted."

On the map accompanying this little book Lieutenant Lea has shown the territory now embraced in Iowa as it was then, 1835. Very much of it at that time had never been seen by white men. The southern boundary of the " Neutral Grounds " began at the Mississippi River nearly opposite Prairie du Chien and ran southwesterly to the Des Moines River near the south line of Webster County and the strip was about forty miles in width. The Iowa River above the junction of the Red Cedar was called Bison, and the Cedar was laid down as the Iowa. The Skunk was then the Chicaqua. The following lakes were shown on the map: Boyer Lake, Hahawa Lake, Clear Lake and Crane Lake. The town of Iowa on the Mississippi River, near the mouth of Pine River, was regarded at this time by Lieutenant Lea as the most promising city of the district, and likely to become the Capital of the future State of Iowa. He writes:

"Should the seat of government of the future State be located on the Mississippi River it will probably be fixed at Iowa, owing to its central position and commercial advantages. But if located in the interior it must be near the Iowa River, and then the town of Iowa will be the nearest port on the Mississippi to the capital of the State. There are some of the most beautiful sites for private residences on the river banks between Iowa and Rock Island that can be found anywhere."

This place was situated about ten miles up the river from Muscatine, at the mouth of Pine Creek. In 1834 Benjamin Nye and a Mr. Farnam had established a trading post at that point, on " Grindstone Bluff," where for several years a large trade was carried on with the Indians. But the prospective Capital of Iowa is now a farm.

The first record to be found in which the name *IOWA* is applied to the section of country which became the State of Iowa, is Lieutenant Albert M. Lea's report and book of 1835-6 descriptive of the " Black Hawk Purchase," as he saw it while accompanying the exploring expedition. He writes of it as the " Iowa District," as the Iowa River was the principal water course running through it. The name seemed at once to meet with favor among its inhabitants, for we find, soon after, that a writer in the *Dubuque Visitor*, alludes to that part of Wisconsin Territory as the future State of Iowa. In the following year when a convention assembled at Burlington to memorialize Congress on the subject of preëmptions, the disputed boundary, and for a division of the territory, that portion of Wisconsin lying west of the Mississippi was called the " Iowa District."

The name of the *Dubuque Visitor* was soon after changed to the *Iowa News*. In the summer of 1837 James Clark, of Burlington, gave his paper the name of the *Iowa Territorial Gazette*. William L. Toole, who was a delegate to the Burlington Convention in 1837, says that it was there decided to give the new Territory the name Iowa, after other names had been proposed and discussed. The name, however, was not used in the memorial asking for the organization of the new Territory, but was applied to it in the one on the subject of preëmptions. But by common consent before the act passed organizing the new Territory, the name *Iowa* given by Lieutenant Lea was accepted and to him must be accorded the honor of giving our State its beautiful name.

So far as can be ascertained the first time the name *Iowa*

is found in any public records was in 1829. At a session of the Legislature of the Territory of Michigan held in Detroit that year an act was passed and approved on the 9th of October by which all of the territory lying south of the Wisconsin River, west of Lake Michigan, east of the Mississippi River and north of Illinois, was formed into a new county, called *Iowa*, and the county-seat was located at Mineral Point.

A petition was sent in by the citizens of Mineral Point to Dr. William Brown, a member of the Council from Wayne County, praying for the establishment of a new county. He presented it on the 14th of September and it was referred to the Committee on Territorial Affairs. Henry R. Schoolcraft, the distinguished author of Indian books, who was a member of the Council, reported a bill to organize the county of Iowa, which became a law. It cannot now be ascertained who drafted this bill, but it lies between Dr. Brown and Mr. Schoolcraft. One of them undoubtedly suggested the name *Iowa*; but what the name signified, or from whence it was derived, will probably always remain an unsettled problem.

George Catlin, who became a famous Indian painter and historian, spent several months in Iowa during his tours among the Indians. He made a trip up the Des Moines Valley about this time and thus describes it:

"The whole country that we passed over was like a garden, wanting only cultivation, being mostly prairie. Keokuk's village is beautifully situated on a large prairie on the bank of the Des Moines River. Dubuque is a small town of about two hundred inhabitants, all built within two years. It is located in the midst of the richest country on the continent. The soil is very productive, and beneath the surface are the great lead mines, the most valuable in the country. I left Rock Island about eleven o'clock, and at half-past three I ran my canoe on the pebbly beach of Mas-co-tine Island. This beautiful island is so called from a band of Indians of that name, who once dwelt upon it, is twenty-five or thirty miles in length, without a habitation on it, or in sight, and throughout its whole extent is one great lonely prairie. It has high banks fronting on the river, and extending back as far as I could see, covered with a high and luxuriant growth of grass. The river at this place is nearly a mile wide. I spent two days strolling

PRAIRIE CHICKENS

over the island, shooting prairie hens and wild fowl for my meals. I found hundreds of graves of the red men on the island. Sleep on in peace, ye brave fellows, until the white man comes and with sacrilegious plowshare turns up your bones from their quiet and beautiful resting place! I returned to Camp Des Moines, musing over the loveliness and solitude of this beautiful prairie land of the West. Who can contemplate without amazement this mighty river eternally rolling its surging, boiling waters ever onward through the great prairie land for more than four thousand miles! I have contemplated the never ending transit of steamers plowing along its mighty current in the future, carrying the commerce of a mighty civilization which shall spring up like magic along its banks and tributaries.

"The steady march of our growing population to this vast garden spot will surely come in surging columns and spread farms, houses, orchards, towns and cities over all these remote wild prairies. Half a century hence the sun is sure to shine upon countless villages, silvered spires and domes, denoting the march of intellect, and wealth's refinements, in this beautiful and far off solitude of the West, and we may perhaps hear the tinkling of the bells from our graves."

These descriptions of the country from 1832 to 1835 when Iowa was beginning to attract the attention of eastern people present a vivid picture of the beautiful prairies, rivers, valleys and groves before its soil was broken for cultivation and before its Indian population had removed from their favorite hunting grounds.

The first settlers upon the public lands found it necessary to establish rules and regulations for taking and holding claims. As the lands had not been surveyed, and were not yet in the market, there were no laws for the protection of settlers in holding their claims. It became necessary therefore for the pioneers to organize associations and establish such regulations as were required to protect their homes in the absence of law. The claim laws, while not legally enacted, were founded upon the theory that a majority of the people had a right to protect their property by agreeing to such regulations as they deemed necessary to accomplish that object.

They proceeded to adopt certain rules and organized a Court of Claims. The important features of the claim clubs were as follows: the officers were usually a president, vice-president, a recorder of claims, seven judges or adjusters of the boundaries of claims, one of whom was an officer authorized to administer oaths, and two marshals. A record was kept of the acts of all meetings, descriptions of all claims, and all transfers of claims. It was the duty of the judges to decide all controversies relating to claims, settle all boundaries and make a return in writing of all acts and decisions. The marshals were required to serve all processes, enforce all decisions of the claim courts and call upon members of the club to aid in the enforcement of its laws and decisions. No person was permitted to take more than 480 acres of land, and he was required to make improvements on his claim within six months to the value of $50, and $50 worth of improvements each six months thereafter.

The decisions of this court were final, and as satisfactory as those made in modern times after expensive and tedious litigation carried through the various established courts of law. The expense of adjusting disputed claims was very small, as parties and their witnesses appeared before the courts without legal process; no lawyers were employed, sheriffs were dispensed with and justice has never since been so cheaply and equitably administered as in these early days under the claim laws. Disputes were few and easily adjusted and the decisions generally promptly acquiesced in.

Where claims had been staked out before government bounds were established, a record of such claims was kept in the various settlements. When the land sales were made, each settler was by common consent entitled to secure his claim without competition. Every bona fide settler was thus protected in his rights. Where claims did not correspond with the surveyed lines the adjustments were made by the claim committees or courts. A distinguished citizen who was one of the pioneers of that period said in later years:

" The law never did and never will protect the people in all their rights so fully as the early settlers protected themselves by these claim organizations."

Many of the early traders and trappers who made homes near the mouth of the Des Moines River married Indian wives, and their children usually adopted the habits of their Indian mothers as they grew up. When the treaty of August 4, 1824, was made by William Clark with the Sac and Fox Indians, the following stipulation was made:

" The small tract of land lying between the Mississippi and Des Moines rivers is intended for the use of the half-breeds belonging to the Sac and Fox nation; they holding it by the same title and in same manner that other Indian titles are held."

This reservation embraced about 113,000 acres of choice lands, lying in the southeast corner of Iowa, in the county of Lee. On the 13th of June, 1834, Congress passed an act authorizing the half-breeds to individually preëmpt, acquire title to and sell these lands. A company was organized under a special act of the Territorial Legislature for the purpose of buying and selling the half-breed lands. This tract had been divided into one hundred and one pieces, and the company had purchased forty-one of these tracts of land. The treaty making the reservation was very indefinite in its terms, failing to designate the number of persons or the names of those entitled to the lands. It was therefore impossible to determine who were the rightful owners, and those who purchased had no means of knowing whether the parties selling could convey good titles.

In order to settle the question of titles, an act was passed by the Wisconsin Territorial Legislature on the 16th of January, 1838, requiring all persons claiming title to file their respective claims with the clerk of the District Court of Lee County, within one year, showing the nature of their claims to title. Edward Johnston, Thomas S. Wilson and David Brigham were appointed a commission to

take testimony as to titles claimed and report to the court.
The lands not disposed of by the half-breeds were to be
sold and the money paid to such half-breeds as could establish a claim to them.

Before any sale of lands took place the Legislature repealed the act under which the commission was proceeding
with its work. The repealing act authorized the commissioners to bring suit against the owners of the lands for
their compensation for services. Suits were accordingly
brought, judgments rendered in favor of the commissioners and 119,000 acres of land were sold by the sheriff for
$5,773.32 to Hugh T. Reid to satisfy these judgments. The
sheriff executed a deed to Reid for the lands thus sold.

The Legislature had enacted a law providing that ten-
ants in common on any lands of which they were in possession might bring suits for a partition thereof. Under
this law suits were brought in the District Court of Lee
County by a large number of the claimants, and their
grantees, for partition of the half-breed lands among the
respective owners. Judgment was rendered for the plain-
tiffs and it was ordered that a partition of the lands be
made. A commission appointed divided the lands into one
hundred and one shares, which division was confirmed by
the court. The lands had been purchased of the half-
breeds mostly by non-resident speculators, and but few
of them were in actual possession. A large number of
settlers had entered upon the lands without title and were
occupying them when this partition was made by order
of court.

The Legislature of 1839 passed an act for the benefit of
these settlers. The act provided that any person who under color of title had settled upon the half-breed lands and
made improvements, before being dispossessed, should be
paid full value for such improvements. The Legislature
of 1840 passed a supplemental act, authorizing any settler
on the half-breed tract who had an interest in, or title to
land, to select not more than a section and hold such land

until the title was finally settled. A receipt for taxes paid
on the land should be held as sufficient evidence of title to
enable him to hold said land. At the next session an act
was passed to enable the settlers to have a lien upon the
land for improvements made. At the session of 1848 an
act was passed permitting the defendant in an action for
ejectment to raise a question of fraud in procuring title
by plaintiff, whatever the nature of the title claimed might
be, and the allegation of fraud should be investigated by
the judge. It was further provided that no writ of possession could be issued until payment for improvements
had been deposited with the clerk of the court.

The Legislature in all of its acts inclined to protect the
actual settlers upon the lands against the claims of speculators who were seeking to get possession of them. But
the Supreme Court decided that the act of 1840 could not
be interposed against a title confirmed by the judgment
of partition; that the act of 1840 became inoperative as
soon as the title to the lands was settled by law. The
Supreme Court also decided that nothing in the act of
1845 could be held valid which would impair vested rights.
The court also decided that judgment could not be enforced against the plaintiff for value of improvements in
excess of rents and profits for use of the land. Litigation
over the titles to these lands continued for many years,
sometimes favoring one class of claimants and again favoring the adverse interest.

In 1845 a decision was made in the case of Reid vs. Webster (a settler) in the Territorial Supreme Court, Charles
Mason, Joseph Williams and Thomas S. Wilson, judges,
which confirmed the title of Reid to the entire half-breed
tract of 119,000 acres for which he had paid less than
$6,000. But a judgment so manifestly unjust was not per-
mitted to stand. When the territory became a state, the
Supreme Court was reorganized, John F. Kinney and
George Greene having succeeded Mason and Wilson. The
court thus constituted, in another case brought by Reid

to dispossess another settler, Wright, decided Reid's title to be invalid. The case was taken to the United States Supreme Court where the decision was confirmed, setting aside Reid's title.

Judge Mason soon after purchased the New York Company's interest in the lands, and settled with the occupants upon fair terms, putting an end to the long years of litigation and uncertainty over the title to this valuable tract.

CHAPTER XV

I N June, 1834, Congress passed an act providing that

"all that part of the territory of the United States bounded on the east by the Mississippi River, on the south by the State of Missouri, and a line drawn due west from the northwest corner of said State to the Missouri River on the southwest, and west by the Missouri River and the White Earth River falling into the same; and on the north by the northern boundary of the United States, shall be attached to Michigan Territory."

It will be seen that this territory embraced the State of Iowa, a large portion of the Dakotas and Minnesota. For the purpose of temporary government all of this territory was attached to and made a part of Michigan.

At an extra session of the Sixth Legislative Assembly of Michigan held in September, 1834, the Iowa District was divided into two counties by running a line due west from the lower end of Rock Island. The territory north of this line was named Dubuque County, and all south of it was Des Moines County. A court was organized in each county, the terms of which were to be held at Dubuque and Burlington. The first court was held in a log house in Burlington in April, 1835. The first judges were appointed by the Governor of Michigan for the new counties and were Isaac Loeffler, of Des Moines County, and John King,* of Dubuque.

On the first Monday of October, 1835, George W. Jones, who lived at Sinsinawa Mound, in the present limits of Wisconsin, was elected a delegate to represent Michigan Territory in Congress. He secured the passage of a bill creating the new Territory of Wisconsin, which also embraced Iowa and a part of Minnesota and Dakota. General

---

*This Judge John King was the founder and publisher of the *Dubuque Visitor*, the first newspaper established in the limits of Iowa.

Henry Dodge, an officer of the regular army, was appointed Governor; John S. Homer, Secretary; Charles Dunn, Chief Justice; David Irwin and William C. Frazier, Associate Justices. Dubuque and Des Moines counties made up the judicial district over which David Irwin presided.

Governor Dodge ordered a census to be taken of the new Territory in September, 1836, and it was found that the two counties in the Black Hawk Purchase, Dubuque and Des Moines, had a population of 10,531, which entitled them to six members of the Council and thirteen members of the House of Representatives in the Territorial Legislature. At the election held on the first Monday in October of that year, Des Moines County elected to the Council, Jeremiah Smith, Joseph B. Teas and Arthur B. Ingham. In the House of Representatives were Isaac Leffler, Thomas Blair, John Box, George W. Teas, David R. Chance, Warren L. Jenkins and John Reynolds. The county of Dubuque sent to the Council, Thomas McCraney, John Foley and Thomas McKnight; to the House of Representatives, Loring Wheeler, Hardin Nowlin, Hosea T. Camp, Peter H. Engle and Patrick Quigley.

The first session of this Territorial Legislature convened on the 25th of October, 1836, at Belmont, which had been designated by the Governor as the temporary Capital of the newly organized Territory. Peter H. Engle, of Dubuque, was elected Speaker of the House, and Henry T. Baird, of Brown County, was chosen President of the Council.

An act was passed by this Legislature authorizing the establishment at Dubuque of the "Miners' Bank." The charter required that the bank should have a capital stock of $200,000 dollars, to be divided into shares of one hundred dollars each. Ezekiel Lockwood, Francis Gehon, John Kirk, William Myers, L. W. Langworthy, Robert D. Sherman, William W. Carrill, Simeon Clark and E. M. Bissell were named in the charter as the first directors,

MINERS' BANK BILLS
First Bank Established on Iowa Soil

who were to hold their positions until a new board should be chosen by the stockholders. One-tenth of the amount of each share was required to be paid in at the time of subscribing and the balance at such times as required by the directors. This was the first bank established in the limits of Iowa.

An act was passed organizing out of the territory embraced in Des Moines County, the counties of Lee, Van Buren, Henry, Louisa, Musquetine and Cook.*

By an act of this session, the permanent Capital of the new Territory was located at Madison. An act was passed incorporating the Belmont and Dubuque Railroad Company and authorizing it to construct a single or double track from Belmont to the most eligible point on the Mississippi River, " The road to be operated by the power and force of steam or animals, or any mechanical or other power." The company was prohibited from holding or speculating in any lands in the Territory other than those upon which the road should run—or that might be necessary to operate the same. It was further provided that the company should not charge to exceed six cents per mile for carrying passengers, nor more than fifteen cents per ton per mile for transporting any species of property. As this was the first act authorizing the construction of a railroad in Iowa, its provisions may be of interest as a matter of history, although the road was not built.

The site of Belmont, which was the first Capital of Wisconsin Territory when Iowa was included within its limits, was in the southwestern part of what is now the State of Wisconsin. The location of the little prairie village of that day is thus described by one who was there during the first session of the Territorial Legislature:

" The hill overlooking Des Moines cannot compare with the mounds between which the old capital stood, and the plain was at a greater height above the sea than any part of Iowa except portions of the northwest corner. The gem of the three Platte mounds was a perfect cone two hundred

---

*This county afterwards became Scott.

feet high, around which a race track one mile in length had been constructed, the exact circumference of the base of the mound. The beauty of the view from the summit of either of these mounds can never be forgotten."

Belmont contained but a few houses and was poorly prepared for the accommodation of the members of the Legislature. The sessions were held in a story-and-a-half frame building, designed for a store. Major J. Smith, who was a member from Des Moines County, proposed to erect a suitable building to accommodate the Legislature, if it would remove the capital to Burlington. His offer was accepted and on the 3d of December, 1836, an act was passed locating the seat of government at Burlington until March 4, 1839, unless public buildings were sooner completed at Madison. Belmont with its beautiful location was distanced in the rivalry of new towns and, failing to secure a railroad, gradually disappeared; a fine farm only marks the site of the first Capital.

John King, of Dubuque, published the first Iowa newspaper. He came from Ohio to the "Dubuque Lead Mines" in 1834. He was satisfied that the little village was destined to become an important city. In 1836 he determined to establish a newspaper, and returning to Ohio, purchased at Cincinnati a Smith hand-press with type and material sufficient to issue a small weekly paper. He also brought from Chillicothe a young man by the name of William Cary Jones, to take charge of the mechanical department of the office. The foreman and chief typesetter was Andrew Keesecker, who came from Galena. He set the type for the first number of the *Du Buque Visitor*, which was issued on May 11, 1836, and dated "Du Buque Lead Mines, Wisconsin Territory." As a matter of fact, Dubuque was then in Michigan Territory, which at that time comprised Michigan, Wisconsin, Iowa and Minnesota.

An act had been passed by Congress for the creation of the Territory of Wisconsin, which would take effect on the 4th of July. Judge King thought it allowable there-

BUILDING AT BELMONT, WISCONSIN
Where Iowa was First Represented in a Legislature in 1836

fore to anticipate what would soon be accomplished and give the location in Wisconsin Territory. In that remote frontier village beyond the reach of regular mails, it was found to be very difficult to issue a weekly newspaper and much more difficult to secure financial support. Consequently the paper experienced frequent changes of proprietors and names. In 1838 it became the *Iowa News;* in 1841 the *Miners' Express;* in 1855 the *Express & Herald;* and finally the *Dubuque Daily Herald.*

In 1842 the old hand-press was sold and moved to Grant County, Wisconsin, where it was used to print the *Herald.* In 1849 James M. Goodhue purchased the press and shipped it by steamboat to St. Paul, landing there April 18. Ten days later he issued the first number of the *Minnesota Pioneer,* the first newspaper established in that Territory. After service in various frontier towns in 1867 this press was purchased by Siminton Brothers, who used it to print the *Sauk Centre Herald.*

This pioneer press, which did service for twenty-six years in western frontier towns, was one of the important agents of civilization, and deserves a place in the history of the times. On this primitive machine were printed the first newspapers on the banks of the upper Mississippi, the first in western Wisconsin, in Iowa, and Minnesota. It was thus intimately associated with the early settlement and development of three States and Territories of the Northwest.

The first act regulating the sale of spirituous liquors in Iowa was passed at the session of 1836. It provided that the county supervisors might authorize any person to keep a *grocery* under such restrictions as a majority might deem expedient, with permission to sell spirituous liquors, provided he should pay into the county treasury nine dollars a month for one year. Any person selling such liquors without a license was liable to a fine of ten dollars for each offense. An act was also passed for the establishment of a territorial wagon road from Farmington, on the

Des Moines River, via Moffett's mill, Burlington, Wapello and Dubuque, to a point opposite Prairie du Chien.

It was during this year, 1836, that Dr. Isaac Galland established the second newspaper in the limits of Iowa, at Montrose, and called it the *Western Adventurer.* Two years later he moved to Fort Madison, and the paper was purchased by James G. Edwards, who converted it into an organ of the Whig Party, changing the name to the *Fort Madison Patriot.* The first number of the *Patriot* published a bill which had been introduced into Congress by the territorial delegate, George W. Jones, for a division of the Territory of Wisconsin, and the creation of a new Territory west of the Mississippi River to be named Iowa. The editor of the *Patriot,* in an article on the subject, writes:

" If a division of the Territory is effected, we propose that Iowans take the cognomen of ' Hawkeyes ' : our etymology can thus be more definitely traced than that of the ' Wolverines,' ' Suckers ' and ' Hoosiers,' and we can rescue from oblivion a memento at least of the old chief."

The suggestion met with general favor and the people of Iowa from that day became known as " Hawkeyes."

The second session of the Wisconsin Legislature assembled at Burlington (in Iowa) on the first Monday in November, 1837. Previous to its meeting, a call had been issued for a convention of delegates from the west side of the Mississippi River to assemble at Burlington on the 6th of November, for the following purposes:

First—To memorialize Congress to pass an act granting the right of preëmption to actual settlers on government lands.

Second—To memorialize Congress on the subject of an attempt by the State of Missouri to extend her northern boundary so as to embrace territory claimed as a part of Wisconsin.

Third—To memorialize Congress for the organization

of a separate territorial government in that part of Wisconsin lying west of the Mississippi River.

The convention assembled at the appointed time, and consisted of the following delegates, chosen by the counties represented:

Dubuque County—P. H. Engle, J. T. Fales, G. W. Harris, W. A. Warren, W. B. Watts, A. F. Russell, W. H. Patton, J. W. Parker, J. D. Bell and J. H. Rose. It will be remembered that Dubuque County at this time embraced all of the country north of the latitude of the south end of Rock Island, while the original county of Des Moines had been divided into Lee, Louisa, Van Buren, Henry, Muscatine and Des Moines counties. These counties sent the following delegates:

Des Moines County—David Rorer, Robert Ralston and Cyrus S. Jacobs; Van Buren County, Van Caldwell, J. G. Kenner and James Hall; Henry County, W. H. Wallace, J. D. Payne and J. L. Myers; Muscatine County, J. R. Struthers, M. Couch, Eli Reynolds, S. C. Hastings, James Davis, S. Jenner, A. Smith and E. K. Fay; Louisa County, J. M. Clark, William L. Toole and J. J. Rinearson; Lee County, Henry Eno, John Claypool and Hawkins Taylor.

The officers selected by the convention were: president, Cyrus S. Jacobs; vice-presidents, J. M. Clark and Wm. H. Wallace; secretaries, J. W. Parker and J. R. Struthers.

The following committees were appointed: to draft a memorial on the right of preëmptions, Engle, Kenner, Payne, Struthers, Patton, Rorer and Smith; to draft a memorial on the subject of the disputed boundary, Eno, Claypool, Kenner, Ralston, Davis, Watts and Toole; to prepare a memorial for a separate territorial organization, Rorer, Hastings, Caldwell, Myers, Claypool, Rinearson and Harris.

The session of the convention continued three days and on the last day the committees made reports, all of which were unanimously adopted. The report on preëmptions called attention to the facts that

"Twenty-five thousand people have settled on lands in Wisconsin Territory west of the Mississippi River, in what is called the 'Iowa District,' improved farms, erected buildings, built towns, laid out cities and made valuable improvements, but have not yet been able to secure any kind of title to their homes and farms. Congress is urged to enact a law authorizing all *bona fide* settlers to pre-empt for each actual occupant for land who has shown his good faith by making improvements the right to enter a half section of land before it shall be offered at public sale."

The report on settlement of the disputed boundary with Missouri, asked Congress to appoint commissioners to run the line between Missouri and Wisconsin and to adopt such measures as might be necessary to settle and establish said boundary line.

The memorial praying for a division of the Territory of Wisconsin was as follows:

"*To the Honorable Senate and House of Representatives of the United States in Congress Assembled:*

"The memorial of a general convention of delegates from the respective counties in the Territory of Wisconsin, west of the Mississippi River, convened at the Capitol at Burlington in said Territory, November 6, 1837, respectfully represents:

"That the citizens of that part of the Territory west of the Mississippi River, taking into consideration their remote and isolated position, and the vast extent of country included within the limits of the present Territory, and the impracticability of the same being governed as an entire whole, by the best administration of our municipal affairs, in such manner as to fully secure individual rights, and the rights of property, as well as to maintain domestic tranquillity and the good order of society, have by their respective representatives, convened in general convention as aforesaid, for availing themselves of the right of petition as free citizens, by representing their situation and wishes to your honorable body, and asking for the organization of a separate territorial government over that part of the Territory west of the Mississippi River.

"Without in the least designing to question the official conduct of those in whose hands the fate of our infant Territory has been confided, and in whose patriotism and wisdom we have the utmost confidence, your memorialists cannot refrain from the expression of their belief, that taking into consideration the geographical extent of her country, in connection with the probable population of western Wisconsin, perhaps no Territory of the United States has been so much neglected by the parent government, so illy protected in the political and individual rights of her citizens.

" Western Wisconsin came into possession of our government in June, 1833. Settlements were made and crops grown during the same season; and at that early day was the impulse given to the mighty throng of immigration that has subsequently filled our lovely and desirable country with people of intelligence, wealth and enterprise. In a little over four years, what has been the condition of western Wisconsin? Literally and practically a large portion of the time without a government. With a population of thousands she has remained ungoverned, and has been left by the parent government to take care of herself without the privilege on the one hand to provide a government of her own, and without any existing authority on the other to govern her. From June, 1833, to June, 1834, there was not even the shadow of government or law in all western Wisconsin.

" In June, 1834, Congress attached her to the then existing Territory of Michigan, of which Territory she nominally continued a part until July, 1836, a period of a little more than two years. During this time the whole country west, sufficient of itself for a respectable State, was included in two counties, Dubuque and Des Moines. In each of these two counties there were holden during this time of two years two terms of a county court of inferior jurisdiction, as the only sources of judicial relief, up to the passage of the Act of Congress creating the Territory of Wisconsin. That act took effect the 3rd of July, 1836, and the first judicial relief afforded under that act, was at the April term following, 1837, a period of nine months after its passage; subsequently to which time there had been a court holden in one solitary county of western Wisconsin only. This your memorialists are aware has recently been owing to the unfortunate indisposition of the esteemed judge of our district; but they are also aware of the fact that had western Wisconsin existed under a separate organization, we should have found relief in the service of other members of the judiciary, who are at present in consequence of the great extent of our Territory and the small number of judges dispersed at too great a distance, and too constantly engaged in the discharge of the duties of their own district, to be able to afford relief to other portions of the Territory. Thus with a population now of not less than twenty-five thousand, and of near half that number at the organization of the Territory, it will appear that we have existed as a portion of an organized Territory for sixteen months with but one term of court.

" Your memorialists look upon these evils as growing exclusively out of the immense extent of country included within the present boundaries of the Territory, and express their belief that nothing would so effectually remedy the evil as the organization of western Wisconsin into a separate territorial government. To this your memorialists consider themselves entitled by right, and the same obligation that rests upon their present government to protect them in the enjoyment of their rights until such time as they shall be permitted to provide protection for themselves; as well as from the uniform practice and policy of the government in relation to other Territories.

"The Territory of Indiana, including the present States of Indiana, Illinois and Michigan, and also much of the eastern portion of the Territory of Wisconsin, was placed under one separate territorial government in the year 1800, at a time when the population amounted to only five thousand six hundred and forty, or thereabouts. The territory of Arkansas was erected into a distinct Territory in 1820 with a population of about fourteen thousand. The Territory of Illinois was established in 1809, being formed by dividing the Indiana Territory. The exact population of Illinois Territory at the time of her separation from Indiana is not known to your memorialists, but her population in 1812 amounted to but eleven thousand five hundred whites, and a few blacks, in all less than twelve thousand inhabitants. The Territory of Michigan was formed in 1805 by again dividing the Indiana Territory, of which until then she composed a part. The population of Michigan in 1810, five years after her organization, was only four thousand seven hundred and sixty; and in 1820, fifteen years after the Territory was established, it was only about nine thousand. Michigan thus existed as a separate Territory for fifteen years with a population less than half as great as that of western Wisconsin now. Each of the above named Territories, now grown into populous and prosperous States, were organized into separate Territories with much less population than that of western Wisconsin, at a time too when the nation was burdened with a debt of many millions.

"Your memorialists therefore pray for the organization of a separate territorial government over that part of Wisconsin Territory lying west of the Mississippi River."

This was the first organized effort of the citizens of what was then called western Wisconsin to secure the establishment of a separate government and territory. The memorial was sent to General George W. Jones, the delegate in Congress from Wisconsin, who at once began to work for the establishment of Iowa Territory, although he lived on the east side of the Mississippi River and would remain a citizen of Wisconsin.

The assembling of the Wisconsin Legislature at Burlington at this time, was the first meeting of a legislative body within the limits of the future State of Iowa. As the members of the Council were elected for four years, and of the House for two years, this was the second session of the First Territorial Legislative Assembly, which had first convened at Belmont.

Early in the session an act was passed dividing Dubuque County and organizing from its territory the counties of Clayton, Jackson, Clinton, Scott, Johnson, Linn, Benton, Jones and Delaware. The counties of Dubuque, Delaware, Jackson, Jones, Linn, Clinton, Cedar and Scott, as constituted at this session, embraced the same areas of territory and boundaries as now. Clayton County as then organized included a portion of Allamakee and only a part of the present county of Clayton. The county-seat, Prairie La Porte, was afterward named Guttenberg.

Fayette County as first established extended westward to the limits of the Territory and north to the British Possessions, embracing in its vast area most of what afterward made twenty-eight counties of northern Iowa, and all of Minnesota west of the Mississippi River (excepting a small tract in the southeast corner) and all of the Dakotas east of the Missouri and White Earth River. It covered an area of nearly 140,000 square miles, being nearly three times the size of the State of Iowa. Buchanan extended west to the Missouri River, embracing territory which has since been divided into ten Iowa counties. Benton embraced all of the territory in that range west of Linn County, to the western boundary of the State, including in its limits nine future counties. Keokuk embraced all of that range west of Johnson County to the Missouri River, taking in territory afterward contained in nine counties, but embracing only the northern tier of townhips in Keokuk County as now bounded.

Johnson County as organized at this time included in its limits three of the northern townships in the present county of Washington. The Legislature at this session provided a board of commissioners, consisting of three electors in each county to transact its ordinary business. It abolished all laws authorizing imprisonment for debt, also authorized a census to be taken of the inhabitants of the Territory. Later in the session an act was passed defining the boundaries of the counties of Lee, Van Buren, Des Moines, Henry, Louisa, Muscatine and Slaughter and locating their county-seats. All of these counties had been established at the first session of the Legislature, excepting Slaughter, but as the government survey of the public lands had not been completed at the time, the act designated the boundaries to correspond with the recent survey. A resolution was passed at this session providing for an investigation of the Miners' Bank of Dubuque, the report to be made at an extra session to be held in June following. At the extra session held at Burlington, beginning June 11, 1838, an act was passed providing that all territory lying west of Van Buren County and east of the Missouri River, not embraced in any other county, should be attached to Van Buren.

In the fall of 1837 the United States negotiated another treaty with the Sac, Fox and Sioux Indians by which 1,250,000 acres of land lying west of, adjoining the Black Hawk Purchase of 1832, was ceded to the Government and opened to settlement. This tract consisted of a strip of land about twenty-five miles in width, lying immediately west of the Black Hawk Purchase. The Sacs and Foxes also ceded to the United States all of their interest in the country south of the boundary line established between them and the Sioux, August 19, 1825, and between the Mississippi and Missouri rivers. This was rather an indefinite claim to lands on the Missouri slope. The lands opened to settlement west of the Mississippi were now attracting a large immigration and the people of that portion of Wisconsin Territory were working earnestly for a division and establishment of a new Territory on the west side of the river.

CHAPTER XVI

The first census of Wisconsin Territory, taken in August, 1836, showed the population on the west side of the Mississippi to be as follows:

Dubuque County	4,274
Des Moines County	6,257
Total	10,531

In May, 1838, a second census was taken in the sixteen counties organized from the territory of the two original counties, with the following result:

Lee	2,839
Slaughter	283
Clayton	274
Henry	3,058
Scott	1,252
Clinton	445
Muscatine	1,247
Des Moines	4,605
Van Buren	3,174
Cedar	557
Johnson	237
Dubuque	2,381
Linn	205
Jones	241
Jackson	881
Louisa	1,180
Total population	22,859

In June, 1838, the bill pending before Congress entitled, " An Act to divide the Territory of Wisconsin and to establish the territorial government of Iowa," became a law, having been approved by the President on the 12th inst. It provided that

" From and after the 3d day of July next all of that part of the present
Territory of Wisconsin which lies west of the Mississippi River, and west
of a line drawn due north from the head waters of said river to the territorial line, shall be constituted a separate territorial government by the
name of Iowa."

It will be seen that the Territory thus established included all of Iowa, most of Minnesota and a portion of Dakota.
The act provided for the appointment by the President of
a Governor to hold office three years, unless sooner removed by the President, who should also be commander-
in-chief of the militia and superintendent of Indian affairs. He should approve all laws enacted by the Legislative Assembly before they took effect. The Secretary of
the Territory was appointed for four years, and in case of
death or removal, or necessary absence of the Governor
from the Territory, the Secretary was authorized and required to perform all duties of the Governor during such
vacancy.

The Legislative Assembly consisted of a Council and
House of Representatives; the Council composed of thirteen members, and the House of twenty-six. Members of
the Council were chosen for two years, and of the House
for one year. The election was to be called by the Governor after a census of the Territory had been taken; the Assembly to meet at such time and place as the Governor
might designate. The courts consisted of supreme, district and probate judges, and justices of the peace, appointed by the Governor. The Supreme Court was composed of a Chief Justice and two associate judges with
terms of four years. The Territory was divided into three
judicial districts, court to be held in each district by one
of the judges at such times as may be fixed by law. The
Chief Justice and associate judges, Attorney and Marshal of the Territory to be appointed by the President for
four years, a delegate in Congress to be elected by the
voters of the Territory for a term of two years.

The Governor was further empowered to grant pardons,

ROBERT LUCAS
First Governor of Iowa Territory, 1838-1841

appoint all minor judicial officers, sheriffs and militia officers. He was authorized to divide the Territory into judicial districts and select the place for meeting of the first Legislative Assembly.

President Van Buren first selected Brigadier-General Henry Atkinson for Governor of Iowa Territory, because of his intimate acquaintance with Indian affairs in the Mississippi Valley. But General Atkinson preferred to retain his position as commander of the western division of the army and declined the office.

The President then made the following appointments for officers of the new Territory; Robert Lucas, Governor; William B. Conway, Secretary; Francis Gehon, Marshal; Cyrus S. Jacobs, United States Attorney; Charles Mason, Chief Justice; Joseph Williams and Thomas S. Wilson, Associate Judges; A. C. Dodge, Register; and J. P. Van Antwerp, Receiver of the United States Land Office at Burlingtou; B. R. Peterkin, Register, and Thomas McKnight, Receiver of the Land Office at Dubuque. Cyrus S. Jacobs, who had been elected to the Territorial Legislature, was killed in a political affray soon after his appointment as United States Attorney and the vacancy filled by the appointment of Isaac Van Allen, of New York. Mr. Van Allen died soon after his appointment and was succeeded by Charles Weston.

Governor Lucas received his commission on the 17th of July, 1838, and, on the 25th departed for the distant Territory by way of the Ohio River. Stopping at Cincinnati to purchase a library, for the Territory for which Congress had appropriated $5,000, he made the acquaintance of a young college graduate, Theodore S. Parvin. The Governor was favorably impressed with the young man and tendered him the position of private secretary which Mr. Parvin accepted. They reached Burlington on the 13th of August, the Governor having selected that city for the capital of the new Territory.

When he arrived he was surprised to learn that William

B. Conway, the Secretary, when notified of his appointment at his home in Pittsburg, had hurried to the Territory and assumed the duties of Governor, issued a proclamation for an election, signing the document "Acting Governor." Governor Lucas quietly ignored the presumptuous act of the Secretary and at once entered upon the discharge of his duties.

The first official act of the Governor was to issue a proclamation, dated August 13, 1838, dividing the Territory into eight representative districts and apportioning the members of the Council and House among the nineteen counties then organized. The Legislature elected met at the old Zion Church in Burlington on the 12th day of November, 1838. Jesse B. Browne, of Lee County, was chosen President of the Council and William H. Wallace, of Henry County, Speaker of the House. The Democrats had a large majority in each branch of the Legislature but partisan considerations were ignored in the election of presiding officers, both being members of the Whig Party. The members were largely young men, fourteen of the twenty-six in the House were under thirty-five years of age and ten of the fourteen members of the Council were under forty. Among the youthful members of this First Territorial Legislature of Iowa were several of marked ability, who attained high positions in the State and Nation. James W. Grimes, who was the youngest member of the House, being but twenty-two years of age, became Governor of the State and later a distinguished United States Senator. Stephen Hempstead, a member of the Council, who was but twenty-six years of age, became the second Governor of the State in 1850. S. C. Hastings, a member of the House, twenty-four years old, was afterward elected to Congress and in 1846 was Chief Justice of the State Supreme Court.

Governor Lucas in his message recommended a careful revision of the judicial system from which should be excluded all technical and ambiguous rules of practice, that

OLD ZION CHURCH
In which the Legislative Assembly Met from 1838 to 1841

their proceedings might tend toward prompt adjustment of cases in controversy by the simplest and most direct methods; the enactment of a general road system; laws to supress gambling and intemperance; the organization of the militia; the selection of commissioners to locate the seat of government; a system of common schools; the laying out of the surveyed portion of the Territory into counties of uniform size as nearly as practicable; the prohibition of the subdivision or change of county boundaries and the location of county-seats by impartial commissioners.

He strongly urged the appointment of commissioners to prepare a code of civil and criminal laws and practice, to be reported at the next session of the Legislature. The Governor expressed a determination to appoint no man to a public office who was intemperate or a gambler.

The Legislature had a most important work to perform in providing an entire system of laws for the government of the new Territory; and it must be conceded, in view of the absence of legislative experience on the part of most of its members, the work was remarkably well done. Its acts fill a book of nearly five hundred pages, embracing a system of civil and criminal practice, probate courts, organization of the militia, revenue laws, location of the capital and penitentiary, provision for a board of county commissioners and establishment of a common school system. The only discreditable act was one prohibiting free negroes from settling in the Territory, unless able to give a bond of $500 as security for good behavior, and prohibiting such negroes from becoming a charge upon the county. This act provided that any negro who should settle in the Territory without giving such a bond should be arrested and forcibly hired out to the highest bidder for cash, to serve six months. Any citizen who sheltered or employed a colored man who had failed to give a bond was subject to a fine of one hundred dollars. Any slave holder was authorized to come into the Territory to procure the arrest

and surrender to him, by an Iowa officer, of any slave who
had escaped from bondage and sought freedom on Iowa
soil. The House journal shows no opposition to this infamous law, but in the Council, James M. Clark, Robert
Ralston and Jonathan W. Parker voted against it. The
name of Slaughter County was changed to Washington
and Jefferson County was established and named for the
author of the Declaration of Independence.

During the session an unpleasant contest arose between
the Legislature and the Governor over the exercise of the
veto power. The organic act provided that '' The Governor shall approve all laws passed by the Legislative Assembly before they shall take effect.'' Under this provision it would seem that the power of absolute veto was
conferred upon the Governor and that no act could become a law without his approval. The two branches of
the Legislature had by joint resolution directed the Secretary to pay certain of its officers and employees.

The Secretary doubting the legality of such payment
without the authority of a law having the approval of the
Governor, submitted the resolution to Governor Lucas and
asked his opinion as to whether the resolution would be
legal authority for payment of public money. The Gov-
eruor replied that, in his opinion, it would not; holding
that a law must first be enacted by the Legislature and
approved by the Governor before the Secretary could
legally pay for the services of the legislative officers.

The Secretary submitted the Governor's opinion to the
Legislature. A committee was appointed to consider the
communication, which reported that in the opinion of the
members of the Legislature, the Secretary had a legal
right to pay the expenses of the Legislature when directed
so to do by the resolution of that body, upon a certificate
of the presiding officers of each House. On motion of
Hawkins Taylor, the House declared by resolution that
'' the Secretary of the Territory is the only disbursing officer known to the organic law, and that a certificate

signed by the Speaker and Clerk is a sufficient voucher upon which to pay for services rendered by any employee of the House.''

Upon the passage of a similar resolution by the Council the Secretary decided to make payment as directed by the Legislature, without the approval of the Governor. Many of the acts of the Legislature were vetoed by the Governor and these disagreements between the Legislature and the Executive were apparently fomented by the Secretary, as would appear from his official acts. A joint resolution was passed requesting the Governor to immediately notify the Assembly upon his approval of a bill. The Governor declined to do so, stating that upon his approval of bills or joint resolutions they were as required by law immediately deposited with the Secretary of the Territory.

The Governor returned the joint resolution without his approval. The House then passed a resolution calling upon the Secretary for the information desired. James W. Grimes, one of the representatives from Des Moines County, from a special committee appointed to consider the Governor's vetoes, made a lengthy report of which the following is a summary:

" Several bills of importance have been vetoed by the Governor, some approved in part, and to some he has attached exceptions and explanations. We do not consider that the Governor has treated the Assembly with dignity or fairness due to it or himself as executive. We deny the power of the Governor to unconditionally veto bills. We claim that the act organizing the Territory makes it the imperative duty of the Governor to approve all bills passed by the Legislative Assembly. We believe that Congress never intended that the veto power should be exercised by the Governor. We believe the principle claimed by the Governor is dangerous and pernicious, and as representatives of a free people we cannot acquiesce in it."

The report was signed by James W. Grimes, C. Swan, Laurel Summers and Hawkins Taylor and was adopted by a vote of sixteen yeas to six nays. Upon receipt of a report of the Secretary showing the action of the Governor upon bills and joint resolutions passed by the Assembly, Mr. Bankson offered a resolution declaring that

"Robert Lucas is unfit to be the ruler of a free people and that a committee be appointed to report a memorial setting forth our reasons to the President and praying for his immediate removal from office."

The resolution was adopted by the close vote of twelve ayes to ten nays. Bankson, Hall, Summers, Taylor and Nowlin were the committee appointed to prepare the memorial. A lengthy memorial was reported reciting the grievances complained of, and requesting the removal of the Governor from office. It was adopted by a vote of sixteen for and eight against it. The minority requested permission of the House to enter a protest against the removal of the Governor, that their protest be entered upon the journal and a copy be forwarded to the President. The House, by a vote of sixteen to eight, refused to permit the minority to be heard. The memorial for the removal of the Governor was signed by the presiding officers of the two Houses and forwarded to the President.

A protest was also sent to the President against removal, signed by eight members of the House. In reply to the charges made against the Governor, the minority said in conclusion:

"Believing the Governor is acceptable as Executive to a large majority of the people of the Territory, and believing him to be an honest and pure man, and in all respects well qualified for the high station he now holds, we desire his continuance in office."

The President inclosed the memorial for his removal to Governor Lucas requesting an explanation. The Governor with candor and dignity explained the unfortunate controversy and forwarded it to the President, accompanied with a strong petition from the people for his retention in office. That was the last heard of the affair.

A controversy had arisen between the people of the Territory of Iowa and the State of Missouri over the boundary line between them. By the act of Congress of March 6, 1820, defining the boundaries of Missouri, the northern line was described as follows:

"The parallel of latitude which passes through the rapids of the River Des Moines, thence east along said parallel of latitude to the middle of the channel of the main fork of the said River Des Moines; thence down along the middle of the main channel of said River Des Moines to the mouth of the same, where it empties into the Mississippi."

A line had been run in 1816 by J. C. Sullivan and marked by mounds and stakes to establish the northern boundary of the Territory of Missouri. It began one hundred miles north of where the Kansas River empties into the Missouri, thence east along that parallel of latitude to the Mississippi River. The "Rapids Des Moines" were thus first designated by Lieutenant Pike in his report of the exploration of the upper Mississippi in 1805. As he passed up that river by the mouth of the Des Moines River, he writes:

"On Tuesday, the 20th of August, we arrived at the foot of the Rapids Des Moines, which are immediately above the confluence of the river of that name with the Mississippi. The Rapids are eleven miles long with successive ledges and shoals extending from shore to shore across the bed of the river."

These rapids in the Mississippi River were thus called by Lieutenant Pike "Rapids des Moines" and from that time to the present have been known as the Des Moines Rapids. But many have supposed that the "Des Moines Rapids" were in the Des Moines River, not only at the time of the controversy over the boundary line, but up to the present day, hence the misapprehension which led to the long and bitter controversy. There is no doubt that Missouri officials so understood, as this was the chief point upon which their claim was based in attempting to

establish their northern boundary nearly thirty miles
north of the mouth of the Des Moines River. Lieutenant
Pike, however, in his map of 1805, locates the " Rapids
des Moines " in the Mississippi River, above the mouth
of the Des Moines.

In 1837 the State of Missouri appointed commissioners to run the northern boundary line and mark it. In
a search for rapids in the Des Moines River they
found ripples near Keosauqua, which they assumed
to be the " Rapids of the Des Moines " named in the
act of Congress defining the boundary in 1820. But
these ripples had never been called the " Rapids of the
Des Moines," until so designated by these Missouri commissioners. The conflict first arose over the disputed
territory when Clark County, Missouri, enrolled the citizens within its limits, and placed their names on its tax
list. When the Missouri tax officer undertook to collect
the taxes for Clark County, the settlers who lived in the
territory in dispute refused to pay. The collector levied
upon their property, was arrested on a warrant issued by
a magistrate in Van Buren County, and delivered into
custody at Muscatine.

Governor Boggs of Missouri sent General Allen with a
thousand armed men to aid the officers of Clark County in
collecting the tax. Governor Lucas promptly ordered
General J. B. Browne to call out the militia and march to
the defense of the Van Buren County officials; 1,200
men responded to the call. Before proceeding to hostilities, General Browne selected A. C. Dodge, of Burlington; General Churchman, of Dubuque; and Dr. Clark, of
Fort Madison, to act as commissioners to negotiate a
peaceable settlement. In the meantime the sheriff of
Clark County had been directed to postpone the collection
of taxes and a delegation had been sent to Governor Lucas
to propose an amicable adjustment of the controversy.

General Allen had withdrawn his army and awaited the
result of negotiations. The Iowa militia was disbanded.

Colonel McDaniels and Dr. Wayland, the Missouri commissioners, went to Burlington and conferred with the Governor and Legislature then in session, and it was agreed that hostilities should be postponed and the matter in dispute be referred to Congress for settlement.

On the 18th of June, 1838, Congress passed an act authorizing the President to cause the southern boundary of Iowa to be ascertained and marked. Lieutenant Albert M. Lea was appointed commissioner for the United States and Dr. James Davis was appointed by Governor Lucas for Iowa. No appointment was made by the Governor of Missouri. The two commissioners made an examination of the various lines claimed, and Lieutenant Lea made a report to the commissioner of the General Land Office in January, 1839. The controversy was not finally settled until December, 1848, when the United States Supreme Court decided that the line run by Sullivan was the true northern boundary of Missouri. This decision gave Iowa all the territory claimed by her public officials.

H. B. Hendershott, of Iowa, and W. G. Minor, of Missouri, were appointed commissioners to resurvey and mark the boundary line. This they proceeded to do, erecting iron pillars ten miles apart along our southern boundary. By decree of the United States Supreme Court the line surveyed and marked was made the permanent boundary between Iowa and Missouri, thus settling the long pending controversy.

The commissioners chosen by the Legislature to locate the capital of the Territory were Chauncey Swan of Dubuque, John Ronalds of Louisa and Robert Ralston of Des Moines County. They were required by law to meet at the town of Napoleon, in Johnson County, on the first Monday of May, 1839, and to locate the seat of government at the most suitable point in that county. The location was made on the east bank of the Iowa River, about two miles northwest of Napoleon, where 640 acres of land were procured. By the terms of the act providing for the location of the Capital it was named " Iowa City." A portion of the land was cleared of brush and timber and laid out into lots.

The Governor was required to order a sale of lots at the newly chosen Capital, under the supervision of the commissioners, the proceeds thereof to be paid into the treasury of the Territory. The selection had been made on the 4th of May and designated by a stake driven into the ground bearing the following inscription:

" Seat of Government
City of Iowa."

A sale of lots was widely advertised for August 18, 1839. A few log houses had been built before the sale took place. The first sale lasted three days and was then postponed until October. Two hundred and six lots were disposed of at these sales for $28,854.75, which amount was estimated to be about one-fourth of the value of the entire plat.

When the city was laid out one rude log cabin stood on the site of the future Capital of Iowa. Matthew Tenrick with his family occupied it. The commissioners and surveyors boarded at this cabin while engaged in platting the city. The first substantial log house was erected by Mr. Tenrick during the summer at the corner of Iowa Avenue and Dubuque Street. It was constructed of hewn logs and was two stories in height. The first frame building was put up the same summer by Wesley Jones, south of the University Square, in which the first store was opened. Walter Butler came with his family, and before winter erected and opened a hotel on the corner of Clinton and Washington Streets. Young men began to arrive at the new backwoods Capital and open offices for future business. The first lawyer was William L. Gilbert; the first doctor was Henry Murray; the first minister Rev. Mr. Ferree, of the Methodist Episcopal Church; the first post-

master was Samuel H. McCrory; and the first blacksmith
Henry Usher.

There were no roads leading into the town, and in order
to guide travelers to the new Capital from the Mississippi
River, the enterprising first settlers employed Lyman Dillon to run a furrow across the prairie and through the
groves to guide strangers to the new seat of government.

Dillon started from Iowa City with his huge breaking
plough, drawn by five yoke of oxen, a two-horse emigrant wagon carrying provisions, cooking utensils and
bedding for the journey. All day the patient ox-team
drew the plough, turning over the tough prairie sod, mile
after mile, to mark the way for travelers. At noon and
night the oxen were turned out to graze on the rich prairie
grass, while the men cooked their food and slept in the
wagon. For nearly one hundred miles the longest furrow
on record marked the way and soon a well-beaten road
was made beside it by the white-top wagons of the coming
settlers.

During the autumn of 1839 Governor Lucas, accompanied by two daughters, with General Fletcher, of Muscatine, as guide, all traveling on horseback, visited the
new Capital. They met a most cordial reception. The
hospitality of the most commodious house in the village,
the only one having an attic, was tendered the distinguished guests. The way to their sleeping room was
up a rude ladder through a small opening in the upper
floor. Before his return the Governor purchased a claim'
near the city which in after years became his home.

No mail line had yet been established between the new
Capital and the outside world; letters and papers were
brought from Muscatine for the citizens by any one who
happened there on business. There was no flouring mill
nearer than Muscatine, corn meal, ground in coffee mills,
took the place of wheat flour with many. The food was
plain, the houses rudely constructed and cold, this first
winter in the history of Iowa City; but her pioneer in-

habitants cheerfully endured all the privations of frontier life and looked hopefully to the future for realization of their visions of coming good fortune.

These first settlers in and about the new Capital are described, by one who was among them, as

"Mostly young men without families, who have left the paternal roof in the older States in search of homes on the frontier, there to work out their own way in life's battles and toils. The young pioneer is not encumbered with extra baggage; with a gun and knife, a bake-pan, tin cup, some corn meal and bacon, all packed on his back, he explores the country on foot. He selects his claim, builds a rude log cabin, cooks his coarse food, and freely shares his scanty supply with any traveler who comes along. When absent, his cabin door is left unfastened, and some cooked food left in sight for any weary, hungry pioneer who may chance to come in to rest. When several settlers have taken claims in one vicinity, the first act towards civil government is to meet at one of the cabins and form a ' claim association' for mutual protection of their new homes. They select officers, record the names of the members, as well as the number of each member's claim. They pledge themselves to stand by each other in holding possession of their respective homes until they can be purchased from the United States. In the absence of laws protecting their claims from mercenary speculators, they organized and enacted homestead and pre-emption laws long in advance of the legislation which was subsequently founded upon the recognition of the justice of this principle thus first established by the necessities of the early pioneers."

One of the most important and notable of the early decisions of the Territorial Supreme Court was the case of Ralph, a colored man, who had been a slave in Missouri, belonging to a man by the name of Montgomery. His master had made a written contract with Ralph to sell him his freedom for $550 and to permit him to go to the Dubuque lead mines to earn the money. Ralph worked industriously for several years, but was not able to save enough to pay Montgomery the price of his freedom. Two Virginians at Dubuque who knew of the agreement, volunteered to deliver Ralph to his former owner in Missouri for $100.

Montgomery accepted the offer. Ralph was seized at

CHARLES MASON
First Chief Justice of the Supreme Court of Iowa

the mines while at work, hand-cuffed and taken to Belle-vue to be sent by a steamer to Missouri. Alexander But-terworth, a farmer working in his field, saw the kidnap-ping and hastened to the office of Thomas S. Wilson, one of the Judges of the Supreme Court and demanded a writ of habeas corpus, which Judge Wilson promptly issued and served, by which Ralph was returned to Dubuque. The case was one of so much importance that at the re-quest of Judge Wilson it was transferred to the Supreme Court for trial.

The court consisted of three judges, Charles Mason, Chief Justice, with Thomas S. Wilson and Joseph Wil-liams, associates. After a full hearing it was unanimously decided that Montgomery's contract with Ralph, whereby he was permitted to become a citizen of a free territory, liberated him, as slavery did not and could not exist in Iowa. Judge Mason, in delivering the opinion, said:

" Where a slave with his master's consent becomes a resident of a free State or Territory he could not be regarded thereafter as a fugitive slave, nor could the master under such circumstances exercise any rights of ownership over him. When the master applies to our tribunals for the purpose of controlling as property that which our laws have declared shall not be property, it is incumbent upon them to refuse their co-operation."

When it is remembered that the three judges (all Demo-crats), thus early enunciated the doctrine of humanity and equity, that slavery was local and freedom a natural right, the liberty loving people of Iowa will forever honor these pioneer judges who, in their sturdy manhood and love of justice, immortalized their names in an opinion in direct conflict with the infamous later decision of the National tribunal in the case of Dred Scott.

CHAPTER XVII

THE conflict which had arisen between Governor Lucas and the first Territorial Legislature over the exercise of the veto power had induced Congress to amend the act providing for the territorial government. It was determined that when a bill was not approved by the Governor he should return it with his objections to the house in which it originated. If both branches then passed it by a vote of two-thirds of the members it should become a law without approval by the Governor. The electors of the Territory were authorized to elect sheriffs, probate judges, justices of the peace and county surveyors. The term of the delegate in Congress was extended to the 11th day of October, 1840. The term of his successor was made to expire on the 4th of March thereafter and from that date the term of the delegate ran for two years, the same as members of Congress from the States.

At the election held on the first Monday of August, 1839, members of the House of Representatives of the Legislature were elected, the members of the Council holding over. The session convened at Burlington on the 4th of November, and was organized by the election of Stephen Hempstead, President of the Council, and Edward Johnston, Speaker of the House. Governor Lucas sent in his message on the 5th instant. In relation to the condition of the Territory he says:

"It has advanced since its organization in improvement, population and wealth beyond a parallel of all former history. With a genial climate, soil unsurpassed for fertility, abounding with pure water, navigable rivers, and inexhaustible mineral resources, it already has a population estimated at 50,000, which will probably be doubled by the time the United States census of 1840 shall be taken."

He recommended the Legislature to request Congress
to pass an act providing for the admission of Iowa as a
state at an early day. He advised the passage of an act
providing for calling a convention to form a state constitution. He recommended an act providing for the election by the people of all territorial and county officers not
prohibited by the organic act. He urged the Legislature
to memorialize Congress to make a grant of public lands
for the support of schools equal in amount to the grant
made to Wisconsin.

Soon after the Legislature assembled, William B. Conway, Secretary of the Territory, died, leaving a vacancy,
and there was no provision of law authorizing any person
to discharge the duties of the office until the vacancy was
filled. As the Secretary was the custodian of the funds
for payment of expenses of the Legislature, that body by
joint resolution appointed Charles Weston fiscal agent until the vacancy should be filled. James Clarke editor of
the *Territorial Gazette*, at Burlington, was soon after appointed by the President to fill the vacancy. In November, 1845, he was appointed Governor of the Territory,
holding the office until Iowa became a state. The Legislature created the offices of Auditor and Treasurer.
Thornton Bayless was appointed Treasurer, and Jesse
Williams Auditor. An act was passed requiring the Capitol commissioners to adopt a plan for a building to be
erected at a cost not exceeding $51,000. Chauncey Swan
was selected to superintend the work. The corner-stone
was laid with impressive ceremonies on the 4th of July,
1840, Governor Lucas making the principal address.

There were four candidates in the field for Delegate in
Congress for the new Territory at the first election, held
in September, 1838, viz.: William W. Chapman and David
Rorer, of Des Moines County; P. H. Engle, of Dubuque
County; and B. F. Wallace, of Henry County. Wallace
was a Whig, the others were Democrats, but politics had
little influence in the election; local and personal con-

siderations largely determined the result. Chapman was declared elected, having received more votes than his highest competitor. Mr. Chapman made an excellent representative for the new Territory. In the contest between Missouri and Iowa over the boundary line, Mr. Chapman contended successfully with two distinguished United States Senators from Missouri, Benton and Linn, for the true line, which was finally established as claimed by Iowa. Mr. Chapman originated the bill which became a law, granting Iowa 500,000 acres of the public lands within its limits for the support of public schools. At the August election in 1839 Francis Gehon* was chosen Delegate to Congress.

The last session of the Legislature had passed an act changing the time for holding the general election to the first Monday in October, and authorizing an extra session of the Legislature to be held, beginning the second Monday in July. At the extra session the apportionment was made for representative districts; an act passed for organization of the militia; and a proposition was submitted to the people at the next election to call a convention to adopt a constitution for admission into the Union.

A period of general depression in business prevailed throughout the country during the last part of Van Buren's term as President, and Whig politicians charged the " hard times " to the financial policy pursued by the Democratic administration. Seeing a favorable condition for the overthrow of their adversaries, the Whig politicians called the first political National Convention ever held and proceeded to nominate General William H. Harrison for President.

The Democrats also held a convention and nominated Martin Van Buren for reëlection. Although there were no well defined issues on national affairs involved in the contest, the campaign was one of intense enthusiasm on

---

* A change in the law fixing the time of the beginning of the term, Mr. Gehon was legislated out of the office to which he had been elected.

part of the Whigs. Their rallying cry was " hard cider " and " log cabins," and with songs, public meetings, and rallies throughout the country, General Harrison was borne into the Presidential chair on a wave of popular enthusiasm. Party feeling ran high and extended into the new Territory of Iowa, although its citizens had no voice in the election. The two parties in Iowa now organized and made strictly partisan nominations and the enthusiasm of the national contest spread over the Territory in the pending election.

The first call for a Democratic convention in Iowa, was written by Edward Johnston, in January, 1840, and is as follows:

"The undersigned, members of the Democratic party of the Territory of Iowa, conceiving it highly necessary that immediate steps should be taken to effect an organization of the party, hereby pledge themselves to use all honorable means in the several counties where they reside to bring about that result, and they further agree to use their exertions to have Democratic delegates sent from their respective counties to a Territorial convention to be held in the ensuing summer for the purpose of nominating a candidate to Congress.

"Edward Johnston, Shepherd Leffler, Laurel Summers, Jos. T. Fales, G. S. Bailey, John B. Lash, Jacob L. Meyers, Daniel Brewer, W. G. Coop, S. C. Hastings, J. M. Robertson, Jacob Minder, H. Van Antwerp, Thomas Cox, J. W. Parker.

"January, A. D. 1840."

A Democratic convention was accordingly held, and General A. C. Dodge was nominated for Delegate in Congress. The Whigs held a convention and placed in nomination Alfred Rich. General Dodge was reëlected by a majority of five hundred fifteen.

A proposition had been submitted to the people of the Territory at this election to call a convention for the framing of a constitution, preparatory to the admission of Iowa as a state. It was defeated by a vote of 937 for the convention, to 2,907 against it.

The census of the Territory taken in 1840 showed a population of 43,112, of which 172 were negroes. The

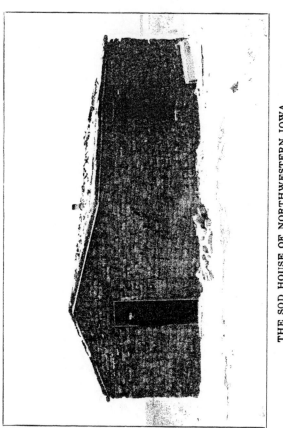

THE SOD HOUSE OF NORTHWESTERN IOWA
As Built by the Early Homestead Settlers.

Legislature having created the offices of Auditor and Treasurer, on the 14th of January, 1840, Morgan Reno was appointed Treasurer, and Jesse Williams, Auditor.

By the Federal Census of 1840 it was shown that Iowa had produced 1,406,241 bushels of corn, 154,693, bushels of wheat, 216,385 bushels of oats, 6,212 bushels of buckwheat, 3,792 bushels of rye, 728 bushels of barley, and 234,063 bushels of potatoes. Corn was the principal grain crop for many years and was largely used for bread by the pioneers. Prairie grass furnished pasture for stock and all of the hay required for more than twenty years.

During these pioneer days most of the houses were built of logs and covered with staves held in place by other logs, the floor being made of puncheon or hewn logs, and all done without the aid of a carpenter. Grain was stored in rail pens covered with straw, and stables were built of logs or slabs, with roofs of prairie hay or straw held in place by poles.

Where settlers ventured out on the prairies remote from timber, sod took the place of logs in the construction of cabins and stables. Barns for the shelter of hay, grain, live-stock or farm implements were very few in number for twenty years after the first settlements began in Iowa. Springs and creeks furnished water for house use and stock for many years before wells were dug. Fuel and rails for fencing were procured in the numerous groves and belts of timber which bordered many of the larger streams. Game and fish were plenty and took the place of beef and mutton; and clothing for the family was for the most part home-made linsey-woolsey, colored with dye made from butternut and hickory bark. Skins of animals tanned at home furnished the materials for moccasins, boots, shoes and rude harness.

The Third Territorial Legislature assembled at Burlington on the 2d of November, 1840. Mr. Bainbridge was chosen President of the Council: Thomas Cox was elected Speaker of the House. In his message, Gov-

ernor Lucas gives a report of his action in relation to the
boundary controversy with Missouri; recommends the
organization of rifle companies to protect settlers from
the Indians; urges the Legislature to provide a plan for
raising revenue to meet expenses not provided for by the
General Government.

The Legislature created the office of Superintendent of
Public Instruction; changed the time of meeting of the
Legislature to the first Monday of December; provided
for a Superintendent of Public Buildings and an agent
to conduct the sale of lots in Iowa City. It provided a
law for raising revenue, and authorized a loan of $20,000
to aid in the completion of the Capitol building, to be repaid from proceeds of lots in Iowa City. Chauncey Swan
was appointed Superintendent of Public Buildings with
an annual salary of $1,000, and Jesse Williams was ap-
pointed Territorial Agent at a salary of $700 per year.

The election of General Harrison, the Whig candidate
for President, was speedily followed by a removal of Democratic Federal officers and the filling of their places with
Whigs. Governor Lucas was superseded on the 13th of
May, 1841, by the appointment of Hon. John Chambers,
of Kentucky, a warm personal and political friend of
President Harrison. He was appointed Governor of the
Iowa Territory on the 25th of March. Governor Lucas
retired after nearly three years' service and settled near
Iowa City, where he spent the remainder of his life. In
looking back over his administration, after the animosi-
ties of his stormy term have passed away, the verdict will
be that he gave to the new Territory wise, able and faithful service. He brought to the office large experience in
public affairs, sterling integrity and firm convictions of
duty. Tenacious in his opinions, dignified in bearing,
strong in purpose, he became involved in numerous sharp
controversies and conflicts with the first Legislature over
the exercise of the veto power, but he acted strictly within
the letter of the law. In his firm and prompt resistance

JOHN CHAMBERS
Governor of Iowa Territory, 1841 to 1845

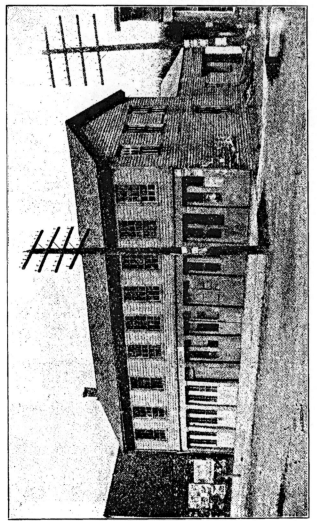

BUILDING AT IOWA CITY, FIRST USED FOR A STATE HOUSE IN 1841

to the claim of Missouri to a strip of Iowa Territory, Governor Lucas was sustained by the final decision of the United States Supreme Court. He was largely instrumental in procuring the enactment of a liberal public school system, at that early day one of the most advanced in operation in the West.

Governor John Chambers had been a prominent member of the Kentucky Legislature for many years, had served three terms in Congress and was for three terms Attorney-General of his State. Upon his appointment Governor Chambers selected for his Private Secretary J. O. Phister, of Maysville, Kentucky. O. W. H. Stull was appointed by the President, Secretary of the Territory. It is related of Mr. Stull while Secretary of the Territory, that wanting a servant, he purchased a negro boy of a Mr. Clancy for two hundred fifty dollars. After Mr. Stull was removed from office by President Tyler, it is stated that the boy was taken to Maryland and held as a slave.* Secretary Stull left no records to show the official business transacted in that office during his term.

On the 20th of June, 1841, a steamer, the "Ripple," ascended the Iowa River to Iowa City and was welcomed by a great assemblage of people who hoped this was the beginning of regular navigation of the Iowa. On the 22d of June, Governor Chambers made his first visit to the new Capital and was cordially received by the citizens. He was at this time past middle age, and is described as a plain, unostentatious man, cordial in manner, who made a favorable impression on the pioneer population.

The last Legislature had, by joint resolution, decided that the next session should be held at Iowa City, provided the citizens would furnish a suitable building in which its sessions could be held. Walter Butler, a public-spirited man, erected a building at his own expense for the use of the Legislature, upon a pledge of the citizens that they would aid in reimbursing him for the expendi-

---

* History of Johnson County, page 463.

ture. They failed to redeem the pledge and their enterprising neighbor was financially ruined by the outlay.

The first grist mill in that part of the Territory was erected during this season on Clear Creek by David and Joshua Switzer, taking the place of the hand mills, coffee mills and other pioneer methods of converting corn and wheat into meal and flour. The *Iowa Standard*, a weekly Whig paper, was started at the Capital by William Crum on the 10th of June, 1841. A Democratic paper, the *Iowa Capital Reporter*, was also established on the 4th of December of that year.

The Fourth Legislative Assembly convened at Iowa City on the 6th of December, 1841. J. W. Parker, of Scott County, was elected President of the Council and Warner Lewis, of Dubuque, was elected Speaker of the House.

Governor Chambers again recommended the submission of a proposition to the voters for a convention to frame a constitution preparatory to admission as a state. The Legislature passed an act providing that, if at the next election a majority of the votes cast were "for a constitution," then there should be another election held on the first Tuesday in October for the election of eighty-two delegates, who should meet at the Capital on the first Monday in November for the purpose of framing a constitution. The constitution thus framed was required to be published in all of the newspapers in the Territory and submitted to a vote of the people at the next election. The first proposition was defeated at the election; a majority of the voters after consideration were opposed to assuming the duties and burdens of a state government. Every county in the Territory gave a majority against a convention.

Governor Chambers, who was Superintendent of Indian Affairs, in September, 1842, negotiated a treaty with the Sac and Fox Indians by the terms of which they ceded to the United States all of their remaining lands in Iowa, to

FORT SANFORD
Established in 1842

the Missouri River and agreed to remove to their Kansas reservation at the expiration of three years. Long before this treaty was ratified by Congress adventurous settlers crowded into the newly purchased Territory to secure the choice claims.

Governor Chambers called upon the War Department for troops to expel these intruders. Captain John Beach was sent with a detachment of the First Dragoons to perform that duty. He removed the squatters to the south side of the Des Moines River. In September, 1842, Captain James Allen, with Company K, was sent by way of Iowa City to establish a post on the Des Moines River to guard the Indian reservation from intruders. He marched his command to the Sac and Fox Agency, occupied a building belonging to the American Fur Company and named the post Fort Sanford, in recognition of the courtesy of Mr. J. Sanford, the agent of that company. The post was located on the left bank of the Des Moines River about sixty-five miles west of Fort Madison, four miles west of the Sac and Fox Agency and twenty-five miles north of the Missouri line. The nearest post-office was Fairfield, twenty-one miles distant. Fort Sanford was abandoned on the 17th of May, 1843 and Captain Allen proceeded with his command to the mouth of the Raccoon River. The settlers, in spite of the military guard, rushed in along the entire line by hundreds, to secure town sites, water powers and timber claims. The treaty was ratified by Congress and the title thus acquired to a vast tract of fertile land, estimated at 10,000,000 of acres.

The year 1842 brought to the people of Iowa severe financial depression, which had begun in the east two or three years earlier. The banks of the country had generally suspended specie payment and many had failed. The Miners' Bank of Dubuque was the only one in Iowa. It had been badly managed and was soon compelled to suspend. Money was scarce throughout the Territory, and exchange of products was the only method of carrying on business.

The Legislature assembled at Iowa City on the 5th of December, 1842, and organized by the election of John D. Elbert, of Van Buren County, President of the Council; and James M. Morgan, of Des Moines County, Speaker of the House. John M. Coleman, Territorial Agent, reported sales of lots at Iowa City, amounting to $22,871 since he had come into office. W. B. Snyder, Superintendent of Public Buildings, reported a portion of the new Capitol inclosed and in condition to accommodate the Legislature. He estimated that $34,143 would complete it. It is a singular fact that the only act of a general nature passed at this session was the appropriation bill, providing for compensation of members and officers of the Legislature.

The winter of 1842-3 was one of the severest known since the first settlements were made in Iowa. Snow began to fall early in November and continued at frequent intervals throughout the entire winter, the first snow remaining on the ground until April. The cold was intense, with fierce winds and before spring, in many parts of the country snow reached a depth of from three to four feet. The settlers were poorly prepared for such a winter, their cabins were cold and little shelter had been provided for live stock. Great suffering ensued. Provisions became nearly exhausted; cattle perished by the thousands; deer, prairie chickens and quail were nearly annihilated. Half-starved wolves prowled about the settlements, seizing pigs, sheep and poultry wherever they could be found. The failure of banks had left the people without money; business of every kind was prostrated and the collection of debts became almost impossible. The only market for farm produce was the limited demand from immigrants moving into the Territory. Good cows could be purchased for ten dollars each; pork for one dollar per hundred, wheat twenty cents a bushel, corn and oats for ten cents. Money commanded from twenty-five to forty per cent. interest and the currency in circulation was of doubtful value.

Under this condition of affairs the Sixth Legislative Assembly met at Iowa City on the 4th of December, 1843. Thomas Cox was elected President of the Council and James Carlton was chosen Speaker of the House. Governor Chambers in his message strongly urged the Legislature to again take steps to organize a state government. In order to afford some relief, the Legislature enacted a valuation law, the provisions of which protected property of a debtor from being sold on execution for less than two-thirds of its appraised value. The Legislature also provided for a revision of the laws, which work was done by O. W. Stull and Samuel J. Burr. The work of Mr. Stull was but partially completed when he was removed from office by President Tyler. Mr. Burr was appointed to succeed him as Secretary of the Territory and, after a long delay, completed the revision. An act was again passed submitting to the people a proposition to frame a constitution for a state government. Acts were also passed providing for a census to be taken in May and for an extra session to be held in June; also for the organization of the counties of Keokuk, Wapello and Davis.

The census of the Territory taken in 1844 shows the population by counties as follows:

Cedar	2,217	Kishkekosh	386
Clayton	1,200	Lee	9,830
Clinton	1,201	Linn	2,643
Davis	2,622	Louisa	3,238
Delaware	300	Muscatine	2,882
Des Moines	9,109	Scott	2,750
Dubuque	4,049	Van Buren	9,019
Henry	6,017	Wapello	2,814
Jackson	2,000	Washington	3,120
Jefferson	5,694		
Johnson	2,949	Total	75,150
Jones	1,112		

The counties of Kishkekosh and Appanoose were created. The county of Madison was established in the Half-breed Tract, embracing a portion of Lee, with the county-seat at Nashville. An attempt was made to repeal the charter of the Miners' Bank, the only one in the Territory because it had suspended specie payment and been badly managed. The Territory had borrowed $5,500 of the bank which it was unable to pay, and, under these circumstances, a majority of the members refused to force the bank out of existence.

At the election held in April for a convention to frame a state constitution, the vote stood 6,719 for a convention, to 3,974 against, being a majority of 2,745 for the convention. Governor Chambers issued a proclamation for the election of seventy-three delegates for this purpose at the August election. Party nominations were made and the Democrats elected a large majority of the delegates.

Among the men of note chosen to frame a constitution were: Ex-Governor Lucas, Shepherd Leffler, J. C. Hall, James Grant, Stephen Hempstead and Francis Gehon, Democrats; Ralph P. Lowe, Elijah Sells, Ebenezer Cook and Stephen B. Shelledy, Whigs. The Whigs generally favored the establishment of a banking system, while a large majority of the Democrats were opposed to banks, either State or National, and to the issue of paper currency. The convention assembled at Iowa City on the 17th of October, 1844, and organized by the election of Shepherd Leffler, of Des Moines County, President; and George S. Hampton, of Johnson County, Secretary. It remained in session until the First of November, framing a constitution and fixing the boundaries of the proposed State to include a large portion of southern Minnesota. The boundaries as fixed by this convention were as follows: the south line between Iowa and Missouri as it is now; the west line the middle of the channel of the Missouri River, north to the mouth of the Big Sioux, thence in a direct line in a northeasterly direction to the middle of the channel of the St. Peter River (Minnesota), where the Watonwan (Blue Earth River) enters the same, thence down the middle of that river to the middle of the channel of the Mississippi and thence down the middle of that river to the place of beginning. These boundaries would have included all of the present State of Iowa except the county of Lyon and a part of Sioux and Osceola, about half of Plymouth and a small fraction of the corners of O'Brien and Dickinson. It would have taken from southeast Minnesota about seventeen counties.

The proposed Constitution provided for biennial sessions of the Legislature; the biennial election of State officers consisting of a Governor, Secretary of State, Auditor, Treasurer and Superintendent of Public Instruction; a Supreme Court to consist of three judges to be chosen by the Legislature; district judges to be elected by the voters of the respective districts; all judges to hold office for four years. Banks were prohibited, and the State debt was limited to $100,000. The limit of all corporations was fixed at twenty years, the private property of stockholders was made liable for corporate debts and the Legislature empowered to repeal all acts of incorporation. Private property could not be taken for the use of corporations without the consent of the owner, a provision which would have enabled any land owner to prevent the building of a railroad over his premises. The Constitution thus framed was forwarded to A. C. Dodge, Delegate in Congress, who was working to secure the admission of Iowa.

The growing conflict between the North and South over the extension of slavery in new States was renewed with bitterness when application was made for the admission of Iowa. After a lengthy contest in each house, a bill finally passed for the admission of Iowa as a free State and Florida as a slave State, on the 3d of March, 1845.

The act of Congress approved June 12, 1838, creating the Territory of Iowa, appropriated $20,000 to be used in the construction of public buildings at the seat of government. A subsequent act appropriated one section of public land to be used for the location of the Capitol. This section was laid out in blocks and lots which were offered for sale by act of the Legislative Assembly, the proceeds used in the construction of the State House. Iowa City was built up on this section, twelve acres of which were reserved for the Capitol Square.

The plan for the Capitol was made by Rev. Samuel Mazzuchelli, and John F. Rague was the first architect. The corner-stone was laid July 4, 1840, and an address made by Governor Lucas. The stone for the building was taken from quarries on the banks of the Cedar and Iowa rivers.

The building was erected on a foundation six feet thick and six feet below the surface of the ground. The walls of the basement were four feet thick, and the upper stories three and two feet in thickness. The size of the building is one hundred and twenty feet long by sixty feet wide. The roof was surmounted by a cupola. On the first floor were rooms for the Governor, Secretary of State, Auditor, Treasurer, Supreme Court and Library. The second story was divided into two rooms for the General Assembly, each fifty-four by forty-three feet in size; the Senate Chamber in the north wing and the House of Representatives in the south. More than fifteen years were consumed in the construction of the building, which was completed in the fall of 1855. In 1842 four rooms on the first floor and the Representatives' Hall were partially completed so that the Legislative Assembly and State officers occupied the building. The cost of the structure when completed was about $123,000. Four Territorial, six State Legislatures and three Constitutional Conventions were held in this Capitol. Upon the removal of the Capital of the State to Des Moines in 1857 the State House at Iowa City was granted to the State University and has been remodeled and since occupied by that institution.

OLD STATE CAPITOL AT IOWA CITY
Since Used by the State University

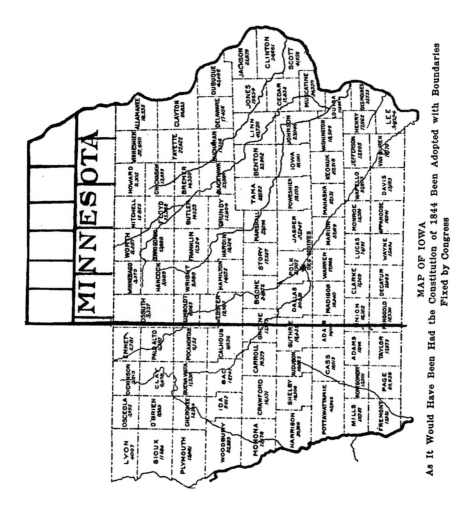

MAP OF IOWA

As It Would Have Been Had the Constitution of 1844 Been Adopted with Boundaries
Fixed by Congress

THE boundary of Iowa as fixed by Congress would have taken eleven counties from southeastern Minnesota, extending the northern boundary of Iowa about forty-two miles farther north than now. But the western boundary was on the line of the west side of Kossuth County and thence south, dividing the counties of Calhoun, Greene, Guthrie and Adair, following the west line of Union and Ringgold to Missouri. This would have cut off from Iowa as now formed, thirty-one counties of the Missouri slope and the Des Moines valley. It would have brought the western boundary of the State within about forty miles of Des Moines. The State would have been about one hundred and eighty miles wide from east to west, and about two hundred and fifty miles long from north to south. This would have brought the geographical center near Cedar Falls and probably made that town or Waterloo the permanent Capital.

Hon. A. C. Dodge, the Iowa Delegate in Congress, opposed the change in boundaries with all the ability and influence he could command, but when it was finally approved by Congress and the President, he acquiesced, believing that no more acceptable boundaries could be obtained. He issued an address to his constituents advising them to accept the boundaries fixed by Congress and ratify the new Constitution. In that address he said:

" A majority of the Committee on Territories was composed of members from the slave-holding portion of the Union. The Delegate from Florida, supported by the members from the South, brought forward a proposition for a division of that State, although its whole territory was three thousand square miles less than that embraced within the constitutional boundaries of Iowa. The object of this move being to increase the number of slave

states, and the weight of slave representatives in Congress. It met with
warm opposition from the non-slave-holding states, and as a counter movement they came forward with a similar proposition in regard to Iowa.
After being fully, freely and even angrily discussed at various meetings of
the committee, the proposition to divide Florida was carried, and that to
divide Iowa was rejected by *a strictly sectional vote*. When the bill came
into the House, where the relative strength of the sectional parties was
reversed, the action of the committee was overruled by a large majority.
The clause for the division of Florida was stricken out, and the boundaries
of Iowa, in opposition to my earnest protest, were subjected to considerable
curtailment.

" This was effected by votes of members from north, east and west, irre-
spective of party divisions. The amendment to reduce was proposed by
Mr. Duncan (Democrat) from Ohio, and supported by Mr. Vinton (Whig),
who in a lucid and cogent manner represented the injury which the creation of large states would inflict upon the western country. He forcibly
exhibited the great wrong done to the West in times past by Congress in
dividing its territory in overgrown states, thereby enabling the Atlantic
portion of the Union to retain supremacy in the United States Senate.
He showed that it was the true interest of the people of the valley of the
Mississippi that new states should be of reasonable size, and he appealed
to western members to check that legislation which had heretofore de-
prived the western country of its due representation in the Senate.   I
advert to the remarks of Mr. Vinton, because their irresistible force was
admitted by all except the delegations from the South. The House had a
few days previous to this discussion passed a law for the annexation of
Texas, by which five new states may be added to the Union. This furnished an additional reason why my protest was disregarded, inasmuch
as our fellow citizens from the non-slave holding states were desirous by
moderate division of remaining free territory of the Union to give to the
free states a counterbalancing influence."

Mr. Dodge was again nominated for Delegate in Congress by the Democratic Convention which met at Iowa
City on the 11th of June, 1845.   The Whigs nominated
Ralph P. Lowe on the 13th of June.   The last Legislature,
in anticipation of the admission of Iowa as a State, had
during the winter of 1844-5, postponed the session of the
Legislature until May, 1845.   But the Constitution with
the boundaries of the proposed State as fixed by Congress,
met with determined opposition from the people.   The
natural western boundary was the Missouri River, and

THEODORE S. PARVIN

many of the most sagacious and patriotic citizens were unwilling to permit the Missouri slope, embracing one-third of the most fertile portion of the Territory, to be forever severed from the State. They preferred to postpone the time when it should take its place in the Union, feeling confident that by rejecting the obnoxious boundaries now, they could in the near future secure to Iowa its natural and more desirable area.

On the other hand, there was a powerful and influential party urging the adoption of the Constitution with boundaries fixed by Congress which would secure the immediate admission of Iowa. It was urged that such action would at once by the election of Senators and Representatives in Congress and with the various Federal officers apportioned to it, greatly promote its influence in national affairs. The Governor and all State officials would be chosen by the people, all of which would enlarge the rights and privileges of its citizens and lead to greater prosperity. The Democratic party had elected a majority of the delegates who framed the Constitution, and it was regarded as a product of that party. A decided majority of the voters of the Territory were Democrats, and expected to be able to fill all of the important offices in the new State with men of their own political faith. Consequently the Democrats as a party, worked for the adoption of the Constitution. The Whigs were opposed to several of its important provisions and resisted its adoption. At this juncture, Enoch W. Eastman, Theodore S. Parvin and Frederick D. Mills, all young men and Democrats, realizing the irreparable mistake this dismemberment of Iowa would be, organized an opposition to the acceptance of the Constitution with the proposed boundary and at once took the field to work for its rejection. They enlisted the coöperation of two more influential Democrats, Shepherd Leffler and James W. Woods and made a thorough canvas of the Territory, holding public meetings in which they eloquently set forth the fatal mistake it would be to accept the proposed dismemberment of the fair proportions of Iowa. The contest was fierce and bitter but patriotism and good judgment prevailed.

The Constitution was rejected by a majority of 996, thus securing the preservation of Iowa, embracing the entire western slope to the Missouri River. It was a critical period in Iowa history, and the people of the State will never cease to honor the three young men who, by their courage and wisdom, preserved for all time its symmetrical proportions.

A new Legislature was chosen at this election, which convened at Iowa City on the 5th of May, 1845. It was organized by the election of S. C. Hastings, of Muscatine, President of the Council; James M. Morgan, of Burlington was elected Speaker of the House.

The Democrats had a large majority in each branch of the Legislature and the leaders of that party were exceedingly anxious for the admission of Iowa as a State. They secured the passage of an act providing that the rejected Constitution should again be submitted to a vote of the people at the August election with the boundaries as fixed by the Constitutional Convention. It was expressly provided in the act for submission that, if the Constitution should be adopted, it should not be held to be an acceptance of the boundaries designated by Congress and the admission of the State should not be completed until the conditions that might be imposed by Congress should be ratified by a vote of the people; and that the election of State officers should be postponed until the State was finally admitted. The proposition was strongly opposed by the Whig members of the Legislature, but was carried by a strict party vote.

The Whigs prepared a protest, embracing their objections to the bill, which was entered upon the journal of the House and subsequently published in the Whig papers of the Territory. When the bill was submitted to Governor Chambers he promptly vetoed it, but it was approved

ENOCH W. EASTMAN

JAMES CLARKE
Last Governor of Iowa Territory
1845-6

by a two-thirds vote of each branch of the Legislature, and became a law.

Among the important acts of this session was the repeal of the charter of the Miners' Bank of Dubuque; abolition of the office of Territorial Agent, conferring his duties upon the Treasurer; incorporation of a University at Iowa City; a change of the name of Louisville to Ottumwa; the organization of Iowa and Marion counties.

The following joint resolution was passed:

" Resolved by the Council and House of Representatives, that our Delegate in Congress be instructed to insist unconditionally on the convention boundaries, and in no case accept anything short of the St. Peter on the north, and the Missouri on the west, as the northern and western boundaries of the State of Iowa."

Mr. Dodge in his canvass for reëlection as Delegate, led his party in advocating the adoption of the rejected Constitution of 1844. The result of the election was 7,235 votes for the Constitution, and 7,656 against it. Thus it was again rejected by a majority of 421. General Dodge was reëlected over Ralph P. Lowe, Whig, by a majority of 831. Dodge had influence enough with President Tyler to prevent the removal of the Democratic Judges of the Territory—Mason, Wilson and Williams—but Governor Chambers, who was a Whig, was removed by President Polk in November, 1845, and James Clarke, a Democrat. was appointed his successor. Mr. Clarke had been Secretary of the Territory from 1839 to 1841, and was a member of the Constitutional Convention of 1844. Jesse Williams was made Secretary of the Territory to succeed Samuel J. Burr, and Robert M. Secrest succeeded William L. Gilbert as Auditor.

The Eighth and last Territorial Legislature assembled at Iowa City on the 1st of December, 1845, and elected Stephen Hempstead President of the Council and George W. McCleary was chosen Speaker of the House.

Governor Clarke in his message deplored the rejection

of the Constitution and urged the speedy admission of
Iowa as a State, calling attention to its great increase of
population until settlements now extended nearly to the
Missouri River. He urged the Legislature to ask Congress
for a grant of public lands for the improvement of the
navigation of the Des Moines River.

Among the acts of the Legislature was one conferring
upon married women the right of ownership and control
of real estate, and providing that they should not be
liable for the debts of their husbands. An act was passed
authorizing the levy of a tax for the support of public
schools. The Legislature provided for another constitutional convention, consisting of thirty-two members, to
be chosen at the April election to meet at Iowa City the
first Monday in May, 1846, to frame a constitution. This
constitution, when framed, to be submitted to a vote of the
people for adoption. The name of Kishkekosh County
was changed to Monroe, in honor of the fifth President.

In 1841 J. B. Newhall, of Massachusetts, visited the
Territory of Iowa, traveling extensively over the prairies,
along the rivers and among the new towns. He wrote a
series of articles for an eastern journal under the title,
"Sketches of Iowa." He also lectured in the eastern
States and England upon the natural advantages and resources of "Western America." Through these lectures
and his sketches, published in book form, the public received much valuable information in relation to Iowa and
the Mississippi Valley. He visited the far West as early
as 1836, finally made Iowa his home and in 1845 became
the Secretary of Governor James Clarke.

In 1846 he wrote and published a book called, "Glimpse
of Iowa," which gives much valuable information relating to the new State in the first year of her statehood. Mr.
Newhall writes that

"In the year 1836-7 the great thoroughfares leading through Indiana
and Illinois were literally lined with the long blue wagons of the emigrants
bound for the 'Black Hawk Purchase.' Following the wagons were cattle,

EMIGRANTS COMING TO IOWA FROM 1833 TO 1854

hogs, men and dogs, and frequently women and children forming the rear of the van—often ten, twenty or thirty wagons in company, all going into the new region west of the Mississippi River. These people had with them all of their possessions and very little money. They depended upon their own labor, ingenuity and resources to create homes in the wild uninhabited region into which they were going. Their wants were few, for generations they had descended from the self-reliant pioneers who had subdued the forests and populated the Eastern States of the Union. The ax and rifle were their chief implements and dependence, and every man and boy was an expert in the use of both. The men built their own houses and constructed nearly all of their farm implements, while the women of the household, in addition to the ordinary work, spun the yarn, wove the cloth and made all the clothing for the family. Such people could make homes beyond the reach of mills, stores, mails, churches or schools, and regard it no hardship."

In the little book published in 1846 by Mr. Newhall are found many items of interest, showing the condition of Iowa when it became a State. He enumerates the principal towns as Fort Madison, Keokuk, West Point, Montrose and Franklin. In a directory of each of the chief towns are found names of men who became prominent in its history and development. In Fort Madison at this early day can be found in the list of lawyers: Edward Johnston, Hugh T. Reid, John F. Kinney, B. S. Roberts, Philip Velie and D. F. Miller. C. H. Perry kept a hotel. There were six churches and one weekly newspaper, the *Lee County Democrat*, published by R. W. Albright, with T. S. Epsy, editor. Thomas A. Walker was postmaster. In Bloomington (now Muscatine) were R. P. Lowe, W. G. Woodward, Jacob Butler, J. S. Richman and S. C. Hastings, lawyers; D. C. Cloud was a carpenter and a magistrate; T. S. Parvin also magistrate and lawyer. There were five churches, and one select school taught by Miss Sherer. William E. Leffingwell was a boat builder. The *Bloomington Herald*, a weekly paper, edited by M. T. Emerson, was the only paper published in the little city. Dr. James Weed had an extensive nursery of 100,000 fruit trees near the city. Joseph Williams, judge of the Supreme Court, lived there.

In Davenport among the merchants were Hiram Price,
J. L. Davenport and A. C. Fulton. The lawyers named
were James Grant, Ebenezer Cook, James Thorington
and G. C. R. Mitchell. The *Davenport Gazette*, edited by
Alfred Sanders, was published every Thursday. There
were seven churches and three private schools. James
Thorington was one of the teachers. The postmaster was
John Forrest. The "Directory of Keosauqua," enumerates among its lawyers: J. B. Howell, J. C. Knapp,
G. G. Wright and A. C. Hall. Edward Manning was a
merchant. The *Des Moines Valley Whig* was published
weekly by J. B. Howell, and the *Iowa Democrat*, another
weekly, was published by J. and J. M. Shepherd. But
two churches are named.

At Mount Pleasant, Alvin Saunders was a merchant;
William Thompson, John F. Morton and W. H. Wallace
were among the lawyers. John S. Bartruff was the postmaster and Samuel S. Howe was principal of a female
seminary. There were five churches, and a collegiate institute, with Rev. A. J. Huestis as president. Fairfield
had among its lawyers, C. W. Slagle, Caleb Baldwin and
Charles Negus. The postmaster was E. S. Gage. There
were two private schools and three churches. At Keokuk
there was a weekly paper, *The Iowa Argus*, owned by Wm.
Pattee. The postmaster was Adam Hine. There were
six lawyers, four physicians, three churches and three
hotels. Fifty buildings had been erected during the year
past. Forty thousand bushels of wheat had been shipped
by river during the fall.

Iowa City had seven general stores, seven churches and
twelve lawyers. Among the latter were Curtis Bates, Wm.
Penn Clark and Geo. S. Hampton. The city had the State
University, Iowa City College and a female academy. The
two weekly papers were the *Iowa Capital Reporter*, edited
by A. H. Palmer, and the *Iowa City Standard*, by Foster &
Morris. C. Trowbridge was the postmaster.

Burlington had two newspapers published weekly—

The Iowa Territorial Gazette, a Democratic journal, published by Thurston & Tizzard; the *Burlington Hawkeye,* owned by Edwards & Broadwell, a Whig paper. Among the merchants were W. F. Coolbaugh, J. G. Lauman, J. G. Foote and Silas A. Hudson. There were five hotels and five churches; a historical society, of which David Rorer was president, and a public library. Among the lawyers were James W. Grimes, J. C. Hall, L. D. Stockton and E. W. Eastman. The mayor was J. L. Corse, and the postmaster, Levi Hager. Dubuque had at this time eighteen mercantile establishments, and among the merchants were Thomas H. Benton, Jr. There were six hotels and five churches and one printing office. The only paper was the *Miners' Express,* of which George Greene was editor and publisher. A. P. Wood was just about to establish another. There were five flouring mills in the city and vicinity and one steam saw mill. There were six private schools. Six smelting establishments were turning out 4,000,000 pounds of lead annually. John King was postmaster, J. K. O'Farrall mayor of the city.

The following are some of the prices prevailing at this time: "horses, from $50 to $60; oxen, from $40 to $60 a pair; farm wagon, $75; plows from $8 to $20; sugar, 10 cents; coffee, 10 cents; tea, 75 cents to $1 per pound; flour, $4 a barrel; unbleached cotton sheeting, 18 cents, and calico from 10 to 20 cents per yard. Good board was furnished at $1.50 or $2 per week. The wages of common labor were from 75 cents to $1 per day. Government land sold at $1.25 per acre, and an ordinary log house cost from $50 to $75." There were no canals, railroads or telegraph; few stage lines. and no daily mails, or daily papers. The weekly mail was carried on horseback. There were no banks and very little money in circulation. There were few buyers of farm products who paid cash. Exchange was the common method of dealing.

Such, in brief, is a view of Iowa as it was in 1846, when the State government was organized with a population of

96,088. The total number of votes polled at the first election for Governor was 15,005. There were few church buildings, and, outside the chief towns, the school houses were built of logs, as were nearly all of the farm houses, a large majority of the residences and many of the business and public buildings in the towns. There were no labor saving farm implements, and the scanty household furniture was largely of home manufacture. Salaries of public officials were small—the Governor received but $1,000; the Secretary of State, $500; the Treasurer, $400; and the State Librarian, $150 per annum.

The annexation of Texas brought on a war with Mexico in the spring of 1846. Iowa was still a Territory but was taking the steps necessary to become a State. The President was authorized by Congress to call into the field, arm and equip fifty thousand volunteers. He issued his proclamation and Iowa was requested to furnish a regiment. On the 1st of June, 1846, Governor Clarke, from the Executive office at Burlington, issued a call for a regiment of volunteers. There was great enthusiasm, mass meetings were held in many of the towns and enlistment began at once. By the 26th of June twelve companies had been enlisted, consisting of two companies in each of the counties of Lee, Van Buren and Des Moines and one in each of the counties of Dubuque, Muscatine, Johnson, Louisa, Washington and Linn.

Governor Clarke offered the command of the Iowa regiment to ex-Governor John Chambers, but because of ill-health he was not able to take the field, and, with reluctance, declined. In the meantime Captain Edwin Guthrie, of Fort Madison, and Frederick D. Mills, of Burlington, had raised an independent company of one hundred men, which was accepted and became ''Company K'' of the Fifteenth United States Infantry. The company had enlisted for one year, entered the service in July, 1847, and, in General Scott's army of invasion, marched to the City of Mexico after fighting several battles in which this Iowa company took part. Mills was commissioned Major of the Fifteenth Regiment and was a most gallant officer. He was slain on the 20th of August after the Battle of Cherubusco, while leading a detachment in pursuit of a portion of the Mexican army, near the walls of the City of Mexico. Isaac M. Griffith, a sergeant in the Iowa company, lost an arm at Cherubusco. In June, 1848, Captain Guthrie was mortally wounded while gallantly leading his company in battle.

In June, 1846, soon after the war began, Captain James Allen, of the First Dragoons, was sent by the War Department to Iowa to confer with the Mormon leaders at Mount Pisgah and Kanesville for the purpose of procuring volunteers for the army. Brigham Young, then at the head of the Mormons, urged his people to raise a battalion for the war. In a short time five hundred men were enlisted and organized into what was known as the "Mormon Battalion," which joined the army of General Stephen W. Kearny, then gathering at Forth Leavenworth. This army marched over the plains by way of Salt Lake to California. The Mormon Battalion remained with the army of General Kearny, doing good service in California until the term of enlistment expired. The first were mustered out at Los Angeles in July, 1847 and the remainder at San Diego in March, 1848. The loss of the battalion during the term of service was nine men.

The twelve companies which had been raised in Iowa under the President's first call for fifty thousand were never organized into an Iowa regiment. The men were anxious to go to the seat of war, but so many regiments had been accepted from the various States that the Secretary of War, on the 25th of November, 1846, notified Governor Clarke that the Iowa regiment would not be needed. An Iowa officer who greatly distinguished himself in the war, was Benjamin S. Roberts, of Fort Madison. He went into the army as a lieutenant of mounted riflemen at the beginning of the war, was in General

Scott's army and participated in all of its battles. He led
the advance into the Mexican capital and pulled down
their flag with his own hands. He was promoted to lieutenant-colonel in the regular army. In 1849 the Iowa
Legislature voted him a sword in honor of his brilliant
services.

The Mexican War furnished names for several Iowa
counties and towns. The Legislature of 1850 created
new counties of the remaining portion of the State. The
battle-fields and heroes of the late war were fresh in the
minds of the people and their memory was perpetuated
in many of the counties named. Buena Vista, Cerro
Gordo and Palo Alto were the names of battle-fields used;
and Taylor, Ringgold, Mills, Yell, Worth, Butler, Hardin
and Guthrie were the names of officers who had distinguished themselves in the Mexican War. Numerous townships and towns commemorated other heroes of the war.

CHAPTER XIX

A T the April election of 1846 thirty-two delegates were chosen to frame a State constitution. The convention met at Iowa City on the 4th of May and was organized by the election of Enos Lowe, President, and William Thompson, Secretary. The work was completed on the 19th day of the same month. The boundaries of the State were fixed as they now exist and many of the provisions of the Constitution were almost an exact copy of the one lately rejected by the people. The most important changes were those prohibiting the establishment of banks and the issue of paper money, and dispensing with a Lieutenant-Governor. At an election held on the 3d of August this Constitution was adopted by the people by a vote of 9,492 for, to 9,036 against it. The absolute prohibition of banks aroused a strong opposition which came near defeating the Constitution.

The boundaries proposed were generally acceptable, though the conflict with Missouri was not settled until several years later. It must be conceded that this first Constitution was, in the main, wisely framed and well adapted to the conditions of the people of the new State. The country had suffered severely from bank failures, depreciated and worthless bank bills, until public confidence in banks and paper currency was nearly destroyed. The only bank chartered by the Territory had failed and the people of Iowa determined to protect themselves from further disaster in that direction by absolute prohibition. The majority could not then foresee that such a policy would result in flooding Iowa with currency of doubtful value from the banks of distant States, over which our State exercised no control.

In September Governor Clarke issued a proclamation for the election of State officers and members of the Legislature. The Democratic State Convention was held at Iowa City on the 24th of September, at which Ansel Briggs was nominated for Governor; Elisha Cutler, Secretary of State; J. T. Fales, Auditor; and Morgan Reno, Treasurer. Shepherd Leffler, of Des Moines County, and S. C. Hastings, of Muscatine, were nominated for Representatives in Congress, for since no apportionment had yet been made of Congressional Districts, the Representatives were to be elected by the State at large. The platform adopted by this first Democratic State Convention embraced the following declarations:

1. Endorsed the administration of James K. Polk.
2. Approved the independent Treasury bill and settlement of the Oregon boundary.
3. Endorsed the repeal of the tariff of 1842 and approved tariff for revenue only.
4. Pronounced unalterable opposition to all banking institutions of whatever name, nature or description.
5. Favored unlimited suffrage to free men without property qualification or religious tests; opposed the grant of exclusive privileges to corporations.
6. Declared in favor of less legislation, few laws, strict obedience, short sessions, light taxes and no State debt.

The first Whig State Convention met at Iowa City on the 25th of September and placed in nomination the following candidates:

For Governor, Thomas McKnight; Secretary of State, James H. Cowles; Auditor, Easten Morris; Treasurer, Egbert T. Smith; Representatives in Congress, Joseph H. Hedrick, of Wapello, and G. C. R. Mitchell, of Scott County.

The platform adopted declared in favor of,

1. A sound money currency.
2. A tariff for revenue and protection to American labor.
3. Restraint of the Executive from exercise of the veto.
4. Distribution of proceeds of the sale of public lands among the States.

5. One term only for the President.

6. Improvement of rivers and harbors by the general Government.

7. Condemned the administration of James K. Polk.

8. Condemned the State constitution recently adopted, with pledge to labor for its speedy amendment.

The Legislature to be chosen was expected to elect two United States Senators and three judges of the State Supreme Court. The election resulted in the success of the Democratic candidates. S. C. Hastings and Shepherd Leffler, Democrats, were elected to Congress.

On the 15th of December, A. C. Dodge, Delegate from Iowa, presented to the House of Representatives the Constitution of the State of Iowa.

It was referred to the Committee on Territories and on the 17th Stephen A. Douglas, of Illinois, from that committee, reported a bill for the admission of Iowa into the Union. On the 21st the bill passed the House and was sent to the Senate. On the 24th it was taken up in the Senate, having been approved by the judiciary committee. After an attempt to amend it had failed, the bill passed the Senate. On the 28th of December, 1846, the President signed the bill and Iowa became a State. On the 29th Shepherd Leffler and Serranus C. Hastings, who were in Washington, took the oath of office and their seats as the first Representatives in Congress from the State of Iowa. Congress granted to the new State for the support of public schools the sixteenth section of each township, amounting in the aggregate to 1,013,614 acres.

On the 5th of June, 1846, a treaty had been concluded with the Pottawattamie Indians, who occupied a large tract of country in the western portion of the State, by which they relinquished their lands in Iowa to the United States. By the terms of the treaty the Indians were not required to remove from their lands until two years had elapsed. But a series of events transpired in neighboring States which hastened the occupation of their lands before the time fixed.

The first attempt to found a colony of the followers of the Mormon Prophet, Joseph Smith, was made at Kirkland, Ohio, where Sidney Rigdon lived. Rigdon had been an eloquent minister of the Christian (Campbellite) church in Kirkland and had met Joseph Smith soon after he claimed to have found the plates on which a revelation was inscribed, and from which the Mormon Bible was produced. Rigdon assisted Smith in procuring the printing of the Bible and on the 6th of April, 1830, they organized the "Church of Latter Day Saints." Converts were made by the eloquent preacher, Rigdon, who acted as a missionary and on the First of January, 1831, they had secured more than one thousand members and believers in the new religion. Smith claimed to have a second revelation commanding him to found a colony of the saints in the far West and build a temple in the New Jerusalem. A location was chosen in the vicinity of Independence, Missouri, where a large tract of land was secured, houses built, farms opened and the foundation laid for the temple. The Mormons from Kirkland and converts from all quarters gathered at the New Jerusalem until several hundred were assembled. But the citizens of western Missouri were intensely hostile to the new sect and finally a large mob gathered, attacked the Mormon colony, destroying their printing office and other buildings and flogging some of their members. Governor Boggs finally called out nearly five thousand of the State militia, under General J. B. Clark, with instructions " to exterminate the Mormons, or drive them beyond the borders of the State." This militia general at once proceeded to execute the orders. A large number of the leaders were arrested, their families driven from their homes at the point of the bayonet and the entire colony hurriedly sent destitute out upon the bleak prairie late in November, without even tents to protect them from the driving storms. The rivers and creeks were unbridged and filled with floating ice; the snow was deep, impeding their progress, many were killed, others desperately wounded, families separated, women and children sick and dying for want of food, shelter and proper care. The oxen, which were their only teams, died of starvation. Disease and death daily claimed victims.

Mothers carried their starving children, themselves perishing with hunger and fatigue. The dead were thrust into rude bark coffins and sunk in the rivers. At last 1,200 emaciated people in all stages of disease and starvation reached the banks of the Mississippi River, where the strongest crossed. The people of Iowa and Illinois treated them kindly, furnished food and such shelter as was available. Their leaders had been captured, such as were not killed, and paraded from one jail to another, tormented in a manner that stamps their enemies as more cruel and barbarous than Indians. At Howe's Mills twenty prisoners were confined in a log building, the door fastened and the mob, joining the State militia, fired upon the helpless prisoners through the crevices between the logs until all were killed or desperately wounded. One little boy, nine years of age, who had escaped the massacre at the log shop by hiding under a forge, was dragged out and murdered in cold blood, while the savage white men cheered and danced around the dying boy and the nineteen other victims.

These whites were the ancestors of the "Border Ruffians," who, a quarter of a century later, invaded the Territory of Kansas and slaughtered her citizens in a war waged to spread human slavery; and in the Civil War, under the lead of Quantrell, murdered more than a hundred defenseless citizens of Lawrence in the presence of their families. The State authorities finally grew sick of the atrocities perpetrated by the militia that they were unable to control and permitted the escape of the survivors of the Mormon leaders, who finally reached the refugees who were finding shelter in Iowa and Illinois.

It was in the fall of 1838 that the Mormons were ex-

pelled from Missouri and some of them settled in Lee
County, Iowa, but the larger number crossed the Mississippi and erected temporary shelter for the winter. Dr.
Isaac Galland, a Mormon elder, was the owner of a large
tract of land on both sides of the river and sold it to the
refugees on liberal terms. In February, 1839, Dr. Galland
wrote to Governor Robert Lucas, of Iowa, inquiring
whether their people would be permitted to purchase land
and settle in the Territory of Iowa. The Governor replied that he knew of no authority that could deprive them
of that right; that as citizens of the United States they
were entitled to the same rights and legal protection as
other citizens.

Thus encouraged a few Mormon families expelled from
Missouri settled in the southeast corner of the Territory
in 1839 and 1840. Bishop Knight bought for his church
a part of the town sites of Keokuk, Nashville and Montrose, in Lee County, and larger tracts of the vicinity. In
1840 there were over one hundred Mormon families living
in that county. Across the river from Montrose was the
little town of Commerce, started by New York speculators; this the Mormons purchased, changing its name to
Nauvoo. Joseph Smith, their Prophet, came from imprisonment in Missouri and pronounced Nauvoo the seat of
the church. It soon grew into a large city, as the Mormons gathered from all of their former settlements and
the foundation of a large temple was laid. Great numbers of converts came from England and joined the Nauvoo colony.

A revelation in July, 1843, permitting a plurality of
wives, raised a storm of indignation in the surrounding
settlements, and it was charged that the Mormons har-
bored criminals. Joseph Smith was arrested in June,
1844, together with other leaders. The arrests had been
made by a company of soldiers on order of Governor
Ford, of Illinois. The Mormon leaders were lodged in
jail at Carthage and charged with riot. On the 27th a

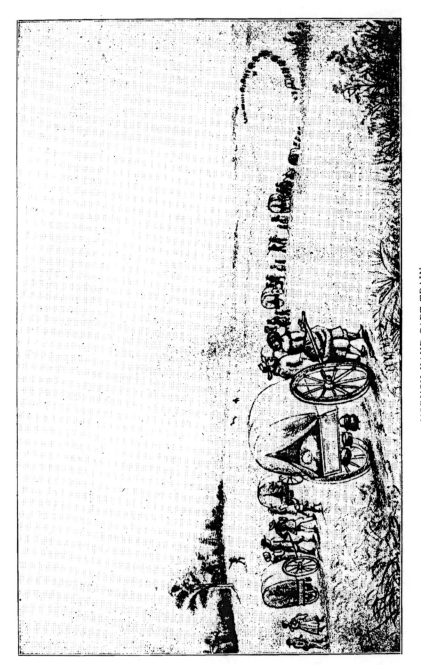

MORMON HAND-CART TRAIN
Passing Over the Iowa Prairies in 1846-7

mob numbering about two hundred men, disguised as Indians, attacked the guards at the jail, overpowered them, broke down the door, killing Joseph Smith and his brother Hiram, and severely wounding several others. From time to time conflicts arose between the citizens and the Mormons, some of whom had purchased claims and settled on the half-breed lands in Iowa. Although the Mormons had built a city of nearly 20,000 at Nauvoo and erected a temple for public worship and had become the owners of valuable farms in the vicinity, their lives and property were so continuously in jeopardy, that they finally determined to abandon all and seek safety by emigration. Their religion and peculiar social practices were so obnoxious to their neighbors, that they realized the necessity of colonizing their people in distant, unsettled regions, if they would secure religious freedom.

In the fall of 1845 they began to dispose of their property and prepared to emigrate westward into Iowa. Brigham Young, who had succeeded Joseph Smith, led the main body across the river, beginning the journey in February, 1846. A large number, including many sick, aged and poor, had to be left behind until a new home could be provided. The transfer of 16,000 into Iowa was finally completed. The line of 3,000 wagons, 30,000 head of cattle, horses and mules, large flocks of sheep and the thousands of men, women and children made up such a vast caravan as had never before been seen in America.

Heavy cold rains fell and the rich black soil was converted into deep mud. Some days but two or three miles' progress could be made before the weaker gave out, and a camp had to be made on the water-soaked ground where death came often to end the suffering of the sick. The burials were pathetic. In place of a coffin the body was inclosed in bark stripped from green logs and buried in a shallow trench and the grave was marked by a post.

On the 27th of April, 1846, the first party stopped in what is now Decatur County and built rude log houses for shelter, while breaking up the prairie to raise crops upon which to subsist when they should resume their march. This settlement they named Garden Grove and here several hundred made a temporary home for such as were worn down by suffering. When the high bluffs of Grand River were reached, in what is now Union County, on the 17th day of June, seven hundred of the Mormons determined to stop and raise crops to supply provisions for themselves and those who were to follow them. They selected a ridge on the east side of Grand River, covered with a beautiful grove of oak and elm and gently sloping into the broad valley. Here they built log cabins and dug caves on each side of the long street on the summit of the ridge.

A mill was built by their mechanics; native bowlders were dressed into mill stones and the machinery run by horse power. They erected a tabernacle in the grove and provided a cemetery in which their numerous dead were buried. A great spring on the east slope of the ridge furnished an abundance of pure water for the entire population of "Mount Pisgah," the name they gave to this rude city in the wilderness. During the two and a half years the Mormons occupied this place, thousands of their brethren found it a most welcome stopping place on their journey to Kanesville and westward. The remnant left at Nauvoo was persecuted beyond endurance by the people who had flocked into the city after the main body of the Mormons had left, and on the 17th of September they were driven out. Crossing the river under the lead of Heber C. Kimball, wagons and hand carts were procured and in October they started West.

Poorly equipped for such a journey over the unsettled prairies, the women and children suffered greatly from insufficient clothing and food. Traveling by day over the trackless prairie, fording unbridged and swollen streams, amid floating ice and fierce snow storms, camping nights on the snow-covered ground, protected only by tents, their sufferings were fearful. Sickness from exposure prevailed to an alarming extent, and death by the wayside ended the misery of hundreds.

.Their trail could be followed for years by the graves that marked the pathway of their journey through Van Buren, Davis, Appanoose, Decatur and Union counties. No such scenes have ever been witnessed in Iowa as marked the winter march of the Mormon refugees over its unsettled prairies. When Mount Pisgah was reached they found rest and shelter and kind hands to minister to their wants. More than four hundred men, women and children who died from the effects of exposure and hardships of the exodus of 1846-7 were buried in the Mormon cemetery at this place.

In 1888 the Mormon authorities at Salt Lake caused a monument to be erected here to the memory of the dead, who for the most part sleep in unmarked graves in this inclosure. On the monument are inscribed the names of William Huntington, the First Presiding Elder of Mount Pisgah and sixty-seven others. C. A. White, a pioneer settler here, has long had charge of this Mormon cemetery, which is often visited by high officials of the Latter Day Saints and surviving friends of those who perished during the exodus of 1846-7. A number of the Mormon families remained at Garden Grove, Mount Pisgah, Lost Grove, Sargent's Grove and Indiantown. Others made claims, built cabins and opened farms along the line of march. But the main body pushed on to the Missouri River, where a village was built in the southwest corner of Mills County. The greater number, however, went northward and located on Indian Creek and built a town near where Council Bluffs now stands, which they named Kanesville.

In the persecution which the Mormons endured in the early years of their residence in the western States and Territories, Iowa never joined. Our people and State officials have respected the right of American citizens to

hold such religious opinions as they chose and to enjoy the
protection of our laws. Bigotry has never obtained
among our citizens. Claiming the utmost freedom of religious opinion for themselves, they have always conceded to others the same constitutional right. The kind
treatment of the Mormons by Governor Lucas is in
marked contrast with that of the officials and citizens of
Missouri and Illinois.

In 1847 Brigham Young led an expedition over the
plains to Salt Lake, where he selected a location for the
future home of the Mormons. In June 1848 the second
expedition, consisting of six hundred and twenty-three
wagons and nearly two thousand persons, joined the colony at Salt Lake. Those who remained spread over the
country now embraced in Mills and Pottawattamie counties, making their headquarters at Kanesville. Elder
Orson Hyde was their leader. Under his direction a large
tabernacle of logs was erected for their religious meetings and another for school purposes. The farmers
among them settled along the creeks and in the groves, and
opened farms to supply provisions for the colony. During the year 1849 cholera of a deadly type was brought
into their settlements and prevailed for nearly two years.
The people, who were almost destitute of experienced
physicians and suitable medicines, were living in poor
cabins and in every way little prepared to encounter this
terrible pestilence. Hundreds died without medical attendance. The bluffs were thickly dotted with new-made
graves. Each year large parties of Mormons left the
Iowa settlement to join the Salt Lake colony.

In 1852 an imperative order was issued for all to emigrate to Utah, and, disposing of their houses and farms,
and under the lead of Elder Orson Hyde, they crossed the
great plains. Some, however, who were opposed to po-
lygamy, remained in Iowa and reorganized the '' Church
of the Latter Day Saints,'' and finally established headquarters at Lamoni, in Decatur County, under the lead of

Joseph Smith, Jr., son of the founder of the Mormon Church.

When Iowa became a State, the era of railroad building had not begun. Inland transportation was largely by canals, lakes and rivers. In the absence of these, stage coaches carried passengers and freight was transported by wagons. Navigable rivers were the natural highways and a liberal policy was pursued by the general government in removing obstructions and otherwise improving these arteries of inland navigation. The people of Iowa believed that by a system of dams and locks the Des Moines, Iowa and Cedar rivers could be made navigable for many miles during a large portion of the year. With the two rivers of the continent navigable to the ocean making the east and west boundaries of the State, Iowa products could reach the markets of the world by continuous water navigation. The improvement of the largest inland river flowing into the Mississippi, it was believed, would extend navigation far into the interior of the new State. Congress had been persuaded in August, 1846, to make a grant of lands for the improvement of the navigation of the Des Moines River. The grant conveyed for this purpose every alternate section of public land on each side and within the limits of five miles from the river. This grant was to become the property of the State as soon as it was admitted and to be devoted to the improvement of the river from its mouth to the Raccoon Fork.

The lands thus granted, and accepted by the State upon the conditions imposed by Congress, were to be selected by agents to be appointed by the Governor, and could only be disposed of as work of improvement of the river progressed. Jesse Williams, J. H. Bonney and Robert Cock were the commissioners appointed to select the lands. The population of Iowa at this time was 102,388.

The first Legislature convened at Iowa City on the 30th of November, 1846. The Senate consisted of nine-

teen members, and elected Thomas Baker (Democrat), of
Polk County, President. The House consisted of forty
members, and elected Jesse B. Browne (Whig), of Lee
County, Speaker. The Democrats had a majority in the
Senate and the Whigs a majority in the House. But local
issues had, in Lee County, overshadowed party considera-
tions to such an extent that it was doubtful whether the
Democrats would be able to command a majority on joint
ballot for their candidates for Supreme Judges and United
States Senators.

On the 3d day of December, 1846, Ansel Briggs was
inaugurated the first Governor of Iowa and delivered
a brief address to the General Assembly, making no recommendations. The Democrats held an early caucus and
made the following nominations: for United States
Senators, Thomas S. Wilson, of Dubuque; and Augustus
C. Dodge, of Burlington; for Judges of the Supreme
Court, S. C. Hastings, John F. Kinney and George
Greene. It required thirty votes on joint ballot to elect.
The Democrats had eleven members of the Senate, the
Whigs eight. In the House the Whigs had twenty members and the Democrats seventeen, with three Independents. Huner, of the Senate, and Conlee and Clifton of the
House, all from Lee County, had been elected on the ''Settlers '' ticket, and King of Mahaska had been elected as
an Independent. These four votes were uncertain. Clifton, Conlee and Huner were Democrats but would not
support the Democratic candidates for Senators. Jonathan McCarthy, of Lee County was the only Whig these
men would support and as the Whigs had no hope of
success without their votes, they reluctantly agreed to
support McCarthy as one of their candidates. Huner was
personally hostile to A. C. Dodge and refused to vote for
him. On the 18th day of September the joint convention
was held. The House was packed with people from over
the State. Amidst suppressed but intense excitement the
roll call began. Every eye turned upon the doubtful mem-

ANSEL BRIGGS
First Governor of the State, 1846-1850.

bers as their names were called. Clifton, Conlee and Huner all voted for McCarthy, but to the surprise of all, a stanch Whig, Fullenwider, cast his vote for Mitchell, thus defeating McCarthy's election. The vote stood, McCarthy twenty-nine, Wilson twenty-eight, and Mitchell one. It required thirty votes to elect. As Huner, Conlee and Clifton would under no circumstances vote for the regular Democratic candidates, their election was impossible. As Fullenwider would not vote for McCarthy, and the three Lee County Independents would support no other Whig, it became evident that the Senators could not be elected. With the aid of Conlee and Clifton the Democrats adjourned the joint convention to January 5, 1847. The next day, December 19, the Legislature also adjourned until the same date. Before the time fixed for reassembling Mr. Conlee died.

Senator Huner now determined to become a candidate. He divulged his plan to Clifton. The votes of these two members added to the entire Democratic strength would elect. As Huner and Clifton were Democrats, they believed the Democrats might accept Huner as one of the Senators, rather than fail to elect Senators and Supreme Judges. But when the scheme was proposed the Democrats declined to accept Huner in place of A. C. Dodge. They proposed, however, to drop Dodge (to whom Huner was hostile) and elect in his place Verplank Van Antwerp. But Huner refused to help them elect any one unless he could be one of the Senators. Rather than submit to such a disreputable bargain the Democrats determined to prevent the reassembling of a joint convention and allow the State to remain unrepresented until the meeting of the next General Assembly. Having a clear majority in the Senate, they were able to defeat all efforts of the Whigs of that body to again meet the House in joint convention and the Legislature adjourned without electing Senators or Judges.

The salaries of State officers were fixed as follows:

Governor, $1,000; Auditor, $600; Secretary of State,
$500; Treasurer, $400; Judges of the Supreme Court
and District Courts, $1,000 each. For the purpose of de-
fraying the expenses of the State government an act was
passed authorizing the issue and sale of bonds to the
amount of $55,000, bearing interest at ten per cent. and
payable in ten years. Acts of general interest were passed
as follows: to complete the change from Territorial to
State government; to provide for election of United
States Senators; to authorize general incorporations; to
establish the new counties of Ringgold, Taylor, Page and
Fremont; to provide a system of common schools, a general revenue law, for the election of a Superintendent of
Public Instruction and the management of the school fund;
to accept the grant of lands to improve the navigation of
the Des Moines River; to create a Board of Public Works
to carry on improvement. John Brown, Joseph D. Hoag
and John Taylor were appointed commissioners to locate
the permanent seat of government for the State near the
geographical center, to lay off one section in lots, reserve
a square of five acres for a Capitol building, sell two lots
in each block, the proceeds to be held for the erection of
a State House. An act was passed to provide for the
navigation of the Skunk River and to remove obstructions
below the forks in Keokuk County. Joint resolutions were
passed asking for a grant of lands to improve the navigation of the Iowa and Cedar rivers and also to aid in the
construction of a military road from Keokuk, via the
Raccoon Forks of the Des Moines River to the Missouri
River opposite the mouth of the Platte, to be a part of a
national highway to Oregon Territory.

The State was divided into two Congressional districts.
The first consisted of the counties of Lee, Van Buren, Jef-
ferson, Wapello, Davis, Appanoose, Henry, Mahaska,
Monroe, Marion, Jasper, Polk, Keokuk and all territory
south of a line running from the northwest corner of
Polk to the Missouri River. The remainder of the State

constituted the Second District. The State was divided
into four judicial districts, in each of which a judge was
to be elected for a term of five years. An act was passed
providing for a State University at Iowa City. The two
townships of land granted by Congress were donated to
the University. After accomplishing a vast amount of
work in the establishment of a complete system of State
government, the Legislature closed its session on the 25th
of February.

CHAPTER XX

A T the April election in 1847 the several counties voted on a proposition to grant license for the sale of intoxicating liquors. All but two counties refused to license the traffic. Four district judges were chosen at this election. Charles Mason, who was Chief Justice of the Territorial Supreme Court, had been nominated by the Democrats for Superintendent of Public Instruction. James Harlan was nominated by the Whigs. Mr. Harlan, who was a recent graduate of an eastern college, and a young man of fine ability, entered upon the campaign with great energy, speaking in most of the populous counties. He made a favorable impression and greatly to the surprise of his competitor was elected, receiving 8,038 votes, to 7,625 for Mason.

When it was found that Harlan was elected the Secretary of State, Elisha Cutler, a stanch Democrat, declared that the law under which the election was held had not taken effect prior to the election and refused to issue a certificate of election but finally gave Mr. Harlan a certified statement of the votes cast which showed a majority of 413 over Judge Mason. Mr. Harlan presented this statement to Governor Briggs and also handed him the official bond required by law. The Governor approved the bond but refused to issue his commission on the ground that he had no authority. A writ of *quo warranto* was served on Mr. Harlan, requiring him to show by what authority he undertook to discharge the duties of the office. But the trial was delayed until after the meeting of the Legislature and Mr. Harlan proceeded to discharge the duties of the office.

At the August election for a Board of Public Works, in

1847, the Democratic candidates were: for President, H. W. Sample; Secretary, Charles Corkery; Treasurer, Paul Bratton. The Whigs nominated for President, George Wilson; Secretary, Madison Dagger; Treasurer, Pierce B. Fagan. The vote stood as follows:

Sample, Democrat................................. 10,297
Wilson, Whig...................................... 9,204
                                                   ———
Sample's Majority................................ 1,093

The average Democratic majority was about 1,000. The Democrats of the First Congressional District nominated William Thompson of Henry County for Representative in Congress and the Whigs nominated Jesse B. Browne, of Lee County. In the Second District the Democrats nominated Shepherd Leffler, of Des Moines County and the Whigs nominated G. C. R. Mitchell, of Scott County. Charles Mason, Chief Justice of the Supreme Court having resigned in June, 1847, the Governor appointed Joseph Williams to fill the vacancy. John F. Kinney was appointed Supreme Judge on the 12th of June and George Greene was appointed Supreme Judge in place of Thomas S. Wilson, resigned.

Governor Briggs called an extra session of the Legislature to meet on the 3d of January, 1848. In his message he gives the following as the reason for which the Legislature was convened:

First—To provide remedies for the confusion arising from defects in the school laws by which officers elected in April were declared by the Supreme Court not legally chosen. Second—The election of Supreme Judges and United States Senators. Third—The election of a commission to revise and codify the laws of the State.

The controlling influence, however, which brought the extra session came from the leaders of the Democratic party. At the August election Josiah Kent, a straight Democrat, had been elected to fill the vacancy caused by the death of Reuben Conlee, representative from Lee

County. Clifton, of the same county, under great pressure from his Democratic friends, had given them reason to believe that he would now vote for the Democratic candidates for United States Senators and Supreme Judges. With these votes the Democrats felt confident of being able to elect these important officers. But when the session convened the Whigs learned that John N. Kinsman, a Democrat from Polk County, had removed from that district and at once the charge was preferred against him and a committee was appointed to investigate the case. The charge was found to be true and so reported to the House. By a strict party vote the seat was declared vacant. This gave the Whigs a majority of one in the House and enabled them to defeat every attempt of the Democrats to meet the Senate in joint convention for the purpose of electing United States Senators and Supreme Judges. Thus the chief purpose for which the extra session had been called was defeated.

The first reports of the State officers, made at the close of 1847 show the financial condition of the new State at that time. The report of the Auditor gives the total value of the taxable property at $11,277,139, on which a tax of two mills should give a revenue of $22,554.27. But only $15,788, or about sixty per cent. of the amount had been collected. The Treasurer's report shows the entire revenue received from all sources for the year ending November 1, 1847, to be $50,782.36. There had been paid out on warrants for that period $59,184.36. The report of the Superintendent of Public Instruction gives the number of children of school age 20,928, of which only 2,439 were in the public schools, the small proportion in attendance being due largely to a failure of the districts to provide school-houses. There were at this time thirty-one organized and twenty unorganized counties in the State.

The Legislature having failed to elect Supreme Judges, and as the terms of those appointed by the Governor were held to have expired upon the meeting of the General As-

sembly, after its adjournment, he reappointed Joseph
Williams, John F. Kinney and George Greene. An act
was passed at the extra session for the appointment of a
commission to prepare a complete code of laws for the
new State. The commissioners selected for the work were
Charles Mason of Burlington, William G. Woodward of
Muscatine and Stephen Hempstead of Dubuque. Their
work when completed embraced a careful compilation of
all laws then in force and a code of civil and criminal
practice which was known as the "Code of 1851." The
principal provisions of their work remained in force until
the adoption of the Constitution of 1857 required a revision.

The commissioners chosen at the regular session of 1847
to locate the permanent Capital of the State, selected a
location remote from any town, river, grove or settlement, possessing no natural advantages for a city or State
Capital. It was in Jasper County, which at that time had
a population of but five hundred and sixty persons. The
site chosen was the west half of sections three and ten, and
all of sections four, five, eight and nine in Congressional
township, seventy-eight north, in range twenty, west of
the 5th principal meridian. It was five miles west of the
Skunk River and about two miles southeast of the present
town of Prairie City. The commissioners laid out a tract
two miles north and south, by two and a half miles east
and west in size and named it "Monroe City." They advertised a sale of lots to begin October 28, 1847 and continue from day to day. The sale opened with a large attendance and continued until the 3d of November. Four
hundred and twenty-five lots were sold for an aggregate
sum of $6,189.72, or a little more than $14 a lot; $1,797.40
only was paid in cash, notes being given for the balance,
payable in two, four and six years. Two of the commissioners showed their confidence in the new city by purchasing fifty-two lots. Some of the favorite lots sold at
from one hundred to three hundred dollars each. The

commissioners secured for themselves large interests in lands near the new Capital, and their work bade fair to bring them ample remuneration for their services.

The policy of granting public lands to aid works of internal improvement had been adopted by Congress as early as 1802, when a grant was made (long before the building of the first railroads), to aid in the construction of a turnpike wagon road in the interior of the State of Ohio to the Ohio River. Other grants for similar purposes followed and in May, 1824, a grant of lands was made to aid in the construction of a canal in Indiana. Grants were made to Ohio and Illinois for similar purposes and one for the improvement of the navigation of the Tennessee River. The first railroad built in the United States, upon which a steam engine was used, was constructed in 1829, but it was not until 1832 that much progress was made in railroad building. In 1835 there were but ninety-five miles of railroad in the United States. Up to 1841 no railroad had been built in Ohio, Indiana, Michigan or Illinois. Transportation was by river, lake, canal and wagons. In 1848 there were but twenty-two miles of railroad in Illinois, eighty-six miles in Indiana and none in Wisconsin or Missouri.

In 1833 Congress made the first grant of public lands to aid in the construction of a railroad by authorizing the State of Illinois to use the land heretofore granted to aid in the construction of canals.

As early as 1837 the people of Iowa had, through the efforts of John Plumb (a citizen of the State) become interested in a project for building a great trunk line of railroad to connect the Atlantic States with the Pacific Coast, to be aided by a grant of public lands along the route. Such a line would be likely to pass through Iowa and open up its inland prairies to settlement. Asa Whitney, of New York, had projected a line of railroad across the great plains and Rocky Mountains to the Pacific Coast and had written able articles showing the feasibility of

such a line. The proposed route passed through Iowa and
the citizens of our State felt a deep interest in the project
and some of the far-seeing men believed that the benefits
of this commercial highway might be secured to Iowa by
prompt action in obtaining a valuable land grant for a
railroad to the Missouri River.

In 1838 George W. Jones, Delegate in Congress for Wisconsin, secured an appropriation of $10,000, which was
expended in making a survey from Lake Michigan through
southern Wisconsin for a railroad from the great lakes to
the Mississippi River. In 1839 a memorial was prepared
and circulated by Samuel R. Curtis, then living in Ohio,
asking for a grant of lands to aid in building a railroad
to the Pacific Ocean. It was presented by John Quincy
Adams. The Legislature, in 1844, memorialized Congress
to make a grant of public lands to the State to aid in the
construction of a railroad from Dubuque to Keokuk; the
grant to consist of alternate sections, extending five miles
in width on each side of the road, or its equivalent in adjacent government lands. During the following winter a
convention was held at Iowa City, representing various
sections of the State, for the purpose of procuring grants
of public land to aid in building other lines of railroad
east and west. One of the proposed lines was to run from
Davenport west to Iowa City, Monroe City, Raccoon
Fork of the Des Moines River, to a point on the Missouri
River near Council Bluffs. The first grant of public lands
in Iowa for transportation lines was that made in 1846
to aid in the improvement of the navigation of the Des
Moines River.

The Legislature of Iowa, by joint resolution, approved
January 9, 1847, accepted the grant. A Board of Public
Works chosen at the next election met and organized on
the 22d of September, 1847 and proceeded with the improvement. Agents appointed by the Governor selected
the unsold alternate sections designated by odd numbers,
for a width of five miles on each side of the river from

mouth to source. The selections were approved by the Secretary of the Treasury. A question having arisen as to the extent of the grant, the Board of Public Works was instructed by Richard M. Young, Commissioner of the General Land Office, February 23, 1848, that the grant embraced the alternate (odd numbered) sections within five miles of the river, throughout the whole extent of that stream within the limits of Iowa.* The public had reason to believe that this decision of the Land Department of the United States settled the limits of the grant. But it proved to be but the beginning of one of the most complicated, vexatious and expensive controversies that has ever arisen over a grant of public lands, as will be seen as its history progresses.

The Constitution of 1846 provided that a census of the State should be taken within one year after its adoption, and each two years thereafter for eight years. The census of 1847 gave the population 116,454, making an increase during the year past of 14,066. There were at this time thirty-two organized counties in the State. The report of the Auditor, made November 30, 1847, shows the total amount of State tax collected that year to be but $5,782.36. A loan was made by the issue and sale of bonds to the amount of $55,000. The assessed value of the property of the State for 1847 was $11,277,139.

The Whig State Convention assembled at Iowa City on the 11th of May, 1848, and placed in nomination the following candidates: Secretary of State, J. M. Coleman; Auditor, M. Morley; Treasurer, Robert Holmes. The resolutions adopted condemned the administration of James K. Polk for making war upon Mexico; declared in favor of the application of the principle of the " Wilmot Proviso."†

---

* Letter of Commissioner, in Report of State Land Office, 1865, page 30.

† In 1846 the House of Representatives was discussing the acquisition of territory from Mexico when David Wilmot, a Democrat from Pennsylvania, offered the following amendment to the bill: " Provided that slavery shall be forever prohibited in all territory acquired from Mexico." This "Wilmot Proviso" although defeated at the time eventually divided and defeated the Democrats.

The Democratic Convention was held at Iowa City on the 1st of June and nominated the following ticket: Secretary of State, Josiah H. Bonney; Auditor, Joseph T. Fales; Treasurer, Morgan Reno. The resolutions indorsed the national administration and State government of Iowa, and eulogized the army engaged in the War with Mexico.

For Presidential electors the Whigs nominated Fitz Henry Warren, Wm. H. Wallace, Jesse Bowen and Stephen B. Shelledy. The Democrats nominated A. C. Dodge, Joseph Williams, Lincoln Clark and J. J. Selman. For Congress the Whigs nominated, in the First District, Daniel F. Miller; the Democrats nominated William Thompson. In the Second District, the Whigs nominated Timothy Davis, the Antislavery Party, James Dawson, and the Democrats, Shepherd Leffler. The campaign in Iowa was a vigorous one and the Democrats carried the State as usual, electing both members of Congress. The vote for Secretary of State was as follows:

Bonney, Democrat	12,367
Coleman, Whig	11,155
Wm. Miller, Ind	523
Democratic plurality	1,212

The vote for President at the November election was as follows:

Cass, Democrat	12,093
Taylor, Whig	11,144
Van Buren, Free Soil	1,126

By throwing out the vote of Pottawattamie County the plurality of Cass over Taylor was declared to be 1,434, and his majority over Taylor and Van Buren, 308. The vote of Pottawattamie County was for Taylor 527, for Cass 42.

The State had been regarded as very close between the Democrats and Whigs and as the Mormon vote was generally cast nearly solid which ever way the leaders advised, it might possibly in this election determine the contest in favor of the party securing it. Fitz Henry Warren, chief manager of the Whig campaign, conferred with the Mormon leaders at Kanesville, where some six hundred voters were then living and succeeded in securing that vote for his party. Had the Mormon vote been counted in the returns, Daniel F. Miller, Whig, of the First District, would have been elected to Congress. The Democrats objected to the canvass of the vote of Pottawattamie County, when it became known that the Mormons living there had voted the Whig ticket. The ground for rejecting the vote was as follows. The county had not yet been organized, but the preliminary steps had been taken. Wm. S. Townsend, a Democrat, had been appointed by the judge of that district, sheriff, for the purpose of completing the organization, and had ordered an election on the first Monday in April. But Townsend having learned that the Mormon vote was likely to be given to the Whig party, refused to serve, and the county organization was not completed. The Mormons seeing that they were likely to lose their votes, petitioned the county commissioner of Monroe (the nearest organized county on the east) to organize a township embracing enough territory to include the Mormon settlement and thus enable them to take part in the elections. The petition was granted, and they voted at the August election. When the poll books of the Mormon township were returned to the county-seat of Monroe, the clerk refused to receive or recognize them. It was known, however, that the vote of that township stood thirty votes for Thompson and 493 for Miller. Had the vote of that township been counted, Miller would have been elected. The messenger who brought the poll books to Albia, laid them on the clerk's desk, while an exciting controversy was going on between A. C. Hall, who represented the

Democrats, and J. B. Howell, who appeared for the Whigs. During the discussion the poll books disappeared. It afterward appeared that Israel Kester found the books on the floor and put them in Hall's valise. Hall did not discover them until he reached home. Miller contested the election of Thompson before Congress and made a search for the lost poll books, but they were not found. Congress declared the seat vacant.

The Democrats elected a majority of the members of the Second General Assembly, which met at Iowa City on the 4th of December, 1848, and organized by the election of John J. Selman, President of the Senate. In the House, Smiley H. Bonham was chosen Speaker. George W. Jones appeared as a candidate for United States Senator against Judge T. S. Wilson, who was the nominee of the Democratic party two years before, when they were unable to elect. A bitter contest ensued between the two Dubuque candidates. Jones secured the caucus nomination by one majority.

There was no opposition to A. C. Dodge in his own party and he received a unanimous nomination in the caucus which nominated Joseph Williams for Chief Justice, and John F. Kinney and George Greene for Associate Judges of the Supreme Court. The Whigs nominated Ralph P. Lowe and William H. Wallace for United States Senators, and Stephen Whicher, James B. Howell and Timothy Davis for Supreme Judges. At the joint convention held on the 7th of December, the Democratic candidates were elected, as that party had a majority of nineteen on joint ballot. The Democrats now had control of every branch of the State government and there was great rejoicing in the party over the sweeping victories.

The Auditor's report for 1848 gave the total value of the taxable property of the State at $14,449,920, from which a revenue of $36,129 had been derived on a tax of 2½ mills on the dollar. The State debt, exclusive of the bonded indebtedness, was reported at $22,651.62. The

GEORGE W JONES
United States Senator, 1848 to 1859

value of the improved farms of the State was $8,031,698; manufactories, $237,655. There were 27,180 horses valued at $992,946; 72,840 head of cattle, valued at $723,326; 114,623 sheep, worth $131,338; 170,445 swine, worth $215,-361. Cattle and horses over two years old and sheep and swine over six months old, only were enumerated in this statement. The number of acres of improved land was 2,316,704. The total value of personal property subject to tax was $110,417, exclusive of money, notes, mortgages and bonds.

There was at this time gold and silver coin and bank notes to the amount of only $183,426 reported, while notes, mortgages, bonds and other securities were found to the value of $106,357. The number of watches in the State is given as 3,112, valued at an average of about $11.50 each. As the population at this time was 154,573, the poverty of the people can be realized when it is seen that the money in circulation was but one dollar and eleven cents per capita.

The report of the Board of Public Works on the progress made toward the improvement of the navigation of the Des Moines River showed facts of interest. The receipts from the sale of lands embraced in the grant up to November 30, 1848, amounted to $50,151.65. Each head of a family was allowed to take 320 acres of land at $1.25 per acre. Samuel R. Curtis, who had been appointed chief engineer, had made a survey of the river from its mouth for a distance of ninety-three miles to Ottumwa. The survey showed that, owing to the low banks near the mouth of the river, it would be necessary to construct a canal for a distance of ten miles. The plan proposed was that, above this canal, dams should be erected to raise the water in the shoals and rapids to sufficient depth to enable steamers of medium size, by a system of locks, to navigate the river up to the Raccoon Fork. A contract had been let for the construction of the canal, and the building of three dams and four locks to be completed by

March 1, 1851. Contracts were also made for nine additional dams and locks. The estimated cost of the first
three dams, four locks and work in the river between
them, was $201,633. It was estimated that thirteen locks
and dams would be required to render the river navigable
to Ottumwa, the cost of which was estimated at $477,357.

General Curtis was of the opinion that when the system was completed to the Raccoon Fork, freight could be
carried from St. Louis via Keokuk and the Des Moines
River, and thence by wagon to Council Bluffs, at a saving
of nine-two cents per hundred pounds over the cost by
steamer up the Missouri River. He further says:

> "It is mathematically certain (except in times of high water in the
> Missouri) that the trade of Council Bluffs will incline to follow down this
> improvement. We enter the great valley of the Nebraska and all branches
> of the Missouri and offer to the commerce of these valleys the cheapest and
> most expeditious route for their products. A country of a thousand miles
> extent, capable of furnishing vast agricultural and mineral products, may
> by wise and discreet energy in the prosecution of this work, become tribu-
> tary to the improvements now in progress on the Des Moines River."

Such were the expectations entertained by the people of
Iowa at this time, of the importance and feasibility of the
Des Moines River improvements inaugurated. General
Curtis was probably the ablest civil engineer in the West.
He had been engaged in a somewhat similar work on the
Muskingum River, was familiar with the general system
of internal improvements of the country and his opinion
of this enterprise had great influence with Iowa people.
He even expressed the belief, in his enthusiastic report,
that the making the Des Moines River navigable to the
Raccoon Fork could be accomplished at less than half the
cost per mile of a good railroad, and he adds:

> "Most of the heavy agricultural and mineral products will float down
> the channels of our rivers when railroads have intersected them with a
> thousand lines."

The Board of Public Works estimated that the land grant would amount to nearly 1,000,000 acres and that with the annual tolls derived from the completed portion of the work, the grant would pay the expense of improvements above the Raccoon Fork. The Legislature omitted no act deemed necessary to secure to actual settlers on the lands embraced in this grant, undisturbed possession and good titles to their homes.

CHAPTER XXI

THE act providing for the relocation of the Capital of the State was repealed at the session of the Legislature of 1848, the plat of Monroe City was vacated and the State Treasurer was directed to refund with six per cent. interest, all money paid for lots in that short-lived Capital city. The commissioners, who had purchased a large number of lots in the city, were excluded from the benefits of the refunding section of the act. The Legislature instructed our Senators and Representatives in Congress to use their influence to secure a grant of lands or money, for the improvement of the navigation of the Maquoketa, Skunk, Wapsipinicon and Iowa rivers. A joint resolution was passed extending thanks of the people of Iowa to Captain Benjamin S. Roberts for his gallant conduct in the Mexican War and a finely wrought sword was ordered presented to him by the Governor. Congress was urged to grant a liberal pension to Isaac W. Griffith, a soldier from Iowa, who lost his right arm in the Mexican War at the Battle of Cherubusco.

The report of the Superintendent of Public Instruction for 1848 shows the number of children of school age to be 41,446, of which but 7,077 were in the public schools. The number of teachers employed was one hundred and twenty-four, of which one hundred and one were men, and twenty-three women. The average salary of the men was sixteen dollars per month, of the women but nine dollars. There were six hundred and seventy-three organized school districts. The State Library at this time contained 1,660 volumes, one-third of which were law books. The expense of maintaining the Library for the year past was $109.31.

The first homestead law, providing for the exemption of the home of the head of a family from sale for debt, was enacted by the Second General Assembly. The author of the bill was Lemuel B. Patterson, a young man then living at Iowa City, who had served two terms as Librarian of the Territory. At that time, when nearly all of the young men of the new State were poor and struggling to secure homes, the common rate of interest exacted by professional money lenders was forty per cent. Hundreds of men had given mortgages on their homes at this ruinous rate of interest, had found themselves unable to meet their obligations and had seen their families left homeless. Mr. Patterson was deeply impressed with the destitution and misfortunes of so many industrious families and determined to secure legislation for the protection of the home. He drafted a bill embracing the principle of the homestead exemption laws now so generally prevailing and secured its enactment into law against strong opposition. This law has been amended and improved from time to time but the important features devised by its author in 1849, remain as the settled policy of our State.

When the new Senators from Iowa took their seats in Congress, General A. C. Dodge drew the short term which expired March 4, 1849. The Legislature being in session, reëlected him for a full term of six years. The Whig votes were given to Francis Springer. Upon the accession of General Zachary Taylor as President, he appointed Fitz Henry Warren, of Iowa, First Assistant Postmaster General, much to the gratification of the Whigs of the State, of which he was one of the ablest leaders.

The Democratic State Convention met at Iowa City on the 29th of June, 1849, and nominated for President of the Board of Public Works, W. M. Patterson; Secretary, Jesse Williams; Treasurer, George Gillaspy. The resolutions denounced the removal of Democrats from Federal offices. A low tariff was favored, and gold and silver as the money of the country; the Wilmot Proviso was con-

AUGUSTUS C. DODGE
United States Senator, 1848 to 1855

demned but the exclusion of slavery from California and
New Mexico was favored. The Whig State Convention assembled at Iowa City June 30th and nominated Thomas J.
McKean for President of the Board of Public Works;
Wm. M. Allison for Secretary; and Henry G. Stewart for
Treasurer. The resolutions indorsed the administration
of President Taylor, favored the exclusion of slavery from
the free territories, condemned the acts of the Democratic
party in the late Legislature and favored a revision of
the Constitution of the State.

The election was warmly contested but resulted in the
choice of the Democratic candidates by a plurality of
about seven hundred. The vote for President of Board
of Public Works was as follows:

Patterson, Democrat............................. 11,672
McKean, Whig................................... 10,960
John H. Dayton, Free Soil....................... 564
Patterson's plurality, 712; majority, 148.

At the opening of the session of the Thirty-first Congress in December, 1849, Daniel F. Miller appeared and
contested the seat of William Thompson, who had been
admitted on a certificate of election given by the board
of canvassers after they had rejected the vote of Kanesville. The House of Representatives was nearly evenly
divided between the two parties, being classified Democrats one hundred and sixteen, Whigs one hundred and
eleven, with three Independents. The contest over the
election of Speaker had continued from the 12th to the
24th of December, when Howell Cobb, Democrat, was
chosen by a plurality of one vote. Under the circumstances a deep interest was taken in the contest of Thompson's election. The committee on elections consisted of
six Democrats and four Whigs. After a lengthy investigation a majority report, signed by the six Democrats,
was presented, declaring Thompson entitled to the
seat. The four Whig members made a minority report

which found that the votes of Kanesville were legally cast
and should have been counted. The debate which followed was not closed until the 29th of June, 1850, when
the House, by a vote of one hundred and two to ninety-
four, decided that Thompson had not been legally elected.
The House further declared, by a vote of one hundred and
nine to eighty-four, that a vacancy existed in the First
Iowa District, and directed the Speaker to so inform the
Governor of that State. A special election was called to
fill the vacancy at which Miller was chosen by a plurality
of two hundred and fifty-seven.

In February, 1848, an event occurred in California
which largely affected the settlement of Iowa for several
years. A laborer employed by Colonel Sutter (a Swiss
immigrant, who had built a mill on the Sacramento River),
while digging a race for the mill, discovered gold dust in
the excavation. It was soon found that gold in large
quantities existed in the alluvial deposits of many of the
streams of the Territory which had recently been acquired
from Mexico. The discoveries soon became known to the
public, causing great excitement. The contagion reached
the Mississippi Valley, as glowing accounts came of rich
deposits and sudden fortunes made by the gold diggers.
Then began an exodus from Iowa and other western
States. The tide of immigration which had been flowing
into the prairie States was suddenly diverted toward the
newly discovered gold-fields of California.

Early in 1849 thousands of citizens of Iowa, allured by
the prospect of acquiring sudden wealth, formed companies in various localities for the purpose of making the
journey over the plains. Wagons were fitted up with
camp equipments, provisions, tools and arms for defense
against the Indians. They were generally drawn by oxen,
for cattle could subsist on grass along the route, while
horses would require grain to be transported the entire
distance. It was necessary for the emigrants to carry
with them enough supplies to last for the entire journey,

which took from four to six months. Large, strong wagons were made for these trips, as rough roads were encountered through the mountain regions. These wagons were also used as the night camps for defense against Indian attacks. Almost the entire journey was through an unsettled country, portions of which was in regions infested by roving bands of hostile Indians. The wagons were covered with canvas and drawn by from three to six pair of oxen. At night the encampment was made secure by forming a corral with the wagons, while the oxen were left to graze on the plains. Progress was slow, as the cattle could only travel from fifteen to twenty-five miles a day. During the years 1849, '50, '51, '52, long lines of California teams traversed the main roads leading westward through Iowa, from the Mississippi to the Missouri. They furnished a good home market to Iowa farmers for their surplus hay and corn, early in the spring before the grass had grown to supply feed for the slowly moving teams. Thousands of gold seekers from Illinois, Indiana, Michigan and Wisconsin made their journey thus over the Iowa prairies in those years. It is doubtful, on the whole, whether as much wealth was brought back by the thousands of Iowa men who swelled the army of gold seekers as was expended by them in outfits, subsistence, loss of time and the various unavoidable expenses attending the venture.

Whether Iowa gained or lost in population from the great hegira is not easy to determine. Thousands of Iowa men remained in California, but other thousands from eastern States, who traversed its fertile prairies on their journey in search of gold, remembered the beautiful country they had passed through and, after a few years, returned to make it their home.

The gold discoveries and consequent emigration to California revived with vigor the controversy over the extension of slavery in the territories. The new population of California was largely composed of industrious, self-reliant men, who were inured to toil and abhorred slavery. President Taylor, who was anxious to avoid the reopening of a bitter contest upon which the Whig party was hopelessly divided, sought to forestall the danger by sending a trusted agent to the Pacific Coast, immediately after his inauguration, to urge the early application of the citizens of California for its admission into the Union as a free State, before the slavery propagators would gain a formidable foothold on its soil.

A convention was called, a constitution framed prohibiting slavery. But the " irrepressible conflict " could not be prevented. It was in vain that compromises were agreed to, they only postponed the day when it must be settled by physical force. The compromise measures finally agreed to by the Thirty-first Congress were: the admission of California as a free State, settlement of the Texas boundary, organization of Utah and New Mexico as Territories without prohibiting slavery within their limits, the enactment of a rigid law for the arrest and return to their masters of all slaves escaping from bondage and the abolition of the slave trade in the District of Columbia.

General Dodge of Iowa took an active part in the discussion of these measures, he and Senator Jones voting for the fugitive slave law and against the exclusion of slavery from the territories. General Dodge, in a speech, rejoiced that Iowa had never indorsed the " Wilmot Proviso," which sought to exclude slavery from the territories.

There can be no doubt that Senators Dodge and Jones truly represented a majority of the people of Iowa at this time, as it was almost the only northern State which had refused to instruct its members of Congress to support the " Wilmot Proviso." President Taylor died on the 9th of July, 1850, in the midst of the bitter controversy and was succeeded by Millard Fillmore, who was an earnest supporter of the compromise measures.

On the 15th day of May, 1850, the Whigs held their State convention at Iowa City. The resolutions declare the Whig party of Iowa to be in favor of free men, free territory, free States and a revision of the Constitution of the State. The candidates nominated were John L. Thompson for Governor; Isaac Cook for Secretary of State; Wm. H. Seevers for Auditor; Evan Jay for Treasurer; and Joseph Nosler for Treasurer of the Board of Public Works. The Democratic Convention assembled at Iowa City on the 12th of June. The resolutions condemned the administration of President Taylor and approved of the compromise measures of Congress. The following nominations were made: Stephen Hempstead for Governor; G. W. McCleary for Secretary of State; Israel Kester for Treasurer; Wm. Pattee for Auditor; George Gillaspy for Treasurer of Public Works.

The election resulted in the success of the Democrats by an average plurality of 2,000.

The vote for Governor was as follows:

Hempstead, Democrat	13,486
Thompson, Whig	11,403
Wm. Penn Clark, Free Soil	575
Hempstead's plurality	2,083
Hempstead's majority	1,058

The election of members of Congress for the full term resulted in the choice of Bernhart Henn in the First District, and Lincoln Clark in the Second, both Democrats.

The Third General Assembly met at Iowa City on the 2d of December, and was organized by the election of the following officers: President of the Senate, Enos Lowe; Speaker of the House, George Temple.

Governor Briggs, in his retiring message to the General Assembly, congratulated the people of the State upon the final settlement, by the Supreme Court of the United States, of the controversy long pending with Missouri over our southern boundary. The award was in favor of the line claimed by Iowa.

The financial condition of the State was reported as follows: the amount of money on hand and received for the two years ending November 4, 1850, $90,444.33; amount paid out for the same period, $90,442.94; balance in the treasury, $1.39. The estimated revenue for the next year, $56,538.33, exclusive of the delinquent taxes of former years. On the 4th of December the votes for Governor were canvassed by the General Assembly in joint convention, and Stephen Hempstead was declared elected for the term of four years and delivered his inaugural address.

During the session the following new counties were established:

Union, Adams, Adair, Cass, Montgomery, Mills, Bremer, Butler, Grundy, Hardin, Franklin, Wright, Risley, Yell, Greene, Guthrie, Audubon, Carroll, Fox, Sac, Crawford, Shelby, Harrison, Monona, Ida, Wahkaw, Humboldt, Pocahontas, Buena Vista, Cherokee, Plymouth, Floyd, Cerro Gordo, Hancock, Kossuth, Palo Alto, Clay, O'Brien, Sioux, Howard, Mitchell, Worth, Winnebago, Bancroft, Emmet, Dickinson, Osceola and Buncombe.

The act providing for a Board of Public Works was repealed and provisions made for a Commissioner and Register to carry on the improvement of the Des Moines River. Wm. G. Haun of Clinton County, introduced a bill in the House to prohibit free negroes and mulattoes from settling in the State. It met with strong opposition, but finally passed the House by a vote of twenty yeas to fifteen nays. In the Senate the vote stood nine yeas to seven nays. The Governor approved it and it became a law.

The commissioners appointed to revise and codify the laws of the State had completed their work and reported to the Legislature for approval. Upon consideration some amendments were made, after which it was adopted and ordered printed. The law was to take effect July 1, 1851. There were printed with the code the following documents: The Declaration of Independence, Articles of Confederation, Ordinance of 1787, Constitution of the

STEPHEN HEMPSTEAD
Governor of Iowa, 1850 to 1854

United States, Acts Establishing the Territories of Michigan, Wisconsin and Iowa, Constitution of Iowa, Acts of Congress Relating to the Admission of Iowa into the Union, Acts of Congress Relating to Naturalization of Foreigners and other State papers of minor importance —the whole making a volume of six hundred and eighty-five pages, known as the " Code of 1851."

In the House Journal for 1850-1 was published several documents of historic interest, among which were the following: Decree of the United States Supreme Court settling the boundary controversy between Missouri and Iowa, report of the commissioners who surveyed and established the line with the full field notes, showing the establishment of mile-posts and monuments and a description of the character of the land on each side of the entire route, the streams, surface of the country, varieties of timber, etc. The entire length of the line as established was two hundred and eleven miles and thirty-two chains. There was also published a complete list of the teachers of the public schools of the State for the year 1850, showing the name, age and birthplace of each teacher and the county in which each school was taught. This is probably the only published record ever made of Iowa teachers in pioneer times. In looking over this roll of teachers we find the names of many who became prominent as lawmakers, judges, editors and educators.

The season of 1851 will long be remembered for the vast amount of rain which fell during the spring and summer. The floods began early in May and continued into July. Rain fell in torrents until the sloughs and ravines were filled with water which flowed into the swollen creeks and rivers, carrying fences and bridges away. The roads became almost impassable, the cultivated fields were quagmires, the river bottoms were inundated miles in width.

In a large portion of the State farmers were unable to put in crops, and where they had been planted the floods destroyed them. The low lands became vast lakes, while

mud and water seemed to take possession of the farms,
flat lands and valleys. The Mississippi River encroached
upon the towns and cities along its banks, flooding business houses and dwellings and driving people with their
movable property to the high lands. At Des Moines the
river at one time reached a height of twenty-two feet
above its ordinary stage. At Eddyville, Ottumwa, Iowaville and other towns, the people were driven from their
homes, while driftwood and sand lodged in their lots, filling wells and cellars with mud and water. The farms
along valleys and broad river bottoms suffered most.
Stock was drowned, houses, barns and premises flooded,
great ditches were cut through the fields, bridges and
fences carried away and general desolation prevailed.
When the rains ceased in July, hot dry weather came, bak-
ing the saturated soil, parching the vegetation which had
survived the floods, so that crops were almost a failure
throughout the State. Cholera broke out along the Des
Moines and Mississippi rivers and the ravages of that
plague added to the misery of the people. The fright-
ful disease struck down hundreds in apparent robust
health, often terminating in death within a few hours.
In some localities famine threatened to add to the horrors of floods and pestilence, as the crops were so nearly
destroyed that there was little food left for the people.
This was the darkest period in Iowa's history. The loss
of crops had impoverished thousands. The scourge of
cholera had alarmed them; famine threatened and many
sold their farms for half their value and left the State.
Those who remained soon found the best market they had
ever known for horses, oxen, cows and corn from the
crowds of emigrants who were crossing Iowa for the
California gold-fields.

Early in 1849 Colonel Mason, of the 6th United States
Infantry, was ordered to select a site for a military post
on the upper Des Moines River. The Sioux Indians in
that part of the State had been committing depredations

upon surveying parties and pioneers and it was for the protection of settlers from the Sioux that the post was to be established. Colonel Mason selected a site on the high table land of the east side of the Des Moines River, a short distance below the mouth of Lizzard Creek. The place selected was on the extreme western border of the " Neutral Grounds," between the Sioux, Sac and Fox Indian lands. Early in the spring of 1850 Major Samuel Woods, with a detachment of the Sixth United States Infantry, was sent to the new post, which had been named Fort Clark. Another fort on the frontier had been given the same name, by order of the Secretary of War, and the name of the Iowa post was changed to Fort Dodge, in honor of General Henry Dodge, the United States Senator from Wisconsin. The commissioned officers of Major Wood's command when stationed at Fort Dodge were Captain L. A. Olmstead, Lieutenants L. S. Corey and Stubbs and Surgeon Charles A. Keeney.

The command marched from Fort Buckner on the Iowa River on the last day of July. Because of the heavily-loaded wagon train it was necessary to bridge many streams and sloughs. Reaching the Des Moines River about the middle of August camp was made on the table land, where the business portion of Fort Dodge has since been built. The command proceeded at once to erect twelve substantial log buildings, which were completed and occupied by the 20th of November. During the three years the troops occupied Fort Dodge, the Government expended $80,000 in buildings and other improvements. The post was abandoned on the 3d of October, 1863, when the troops were ordered one hundred and fifty miles north in Minnesota to build a new fort on the north line of the new purchase made from the Sioux Indians.

CHAPTER XXII

AT the April election in 1851, Thomas H. Benton, Democrat, was chosen Superintendent of Public Instruction over Wm. G. Woodward, Whig, by a vote of 10,353 to 9,002.

The Fourth General Assembly convened at Iowa City on the 6th day of December, 1852, and was organized by the election of William E. Leffingwell, President of the Senate, and James Grant, Speaker of the House. Governor Hempstead's message, which was read in each House on the 7th, states the financial condition as follows: amount paid into the treasury for the two years ending October 31, 1852, $139,681.69, disbursements for the same period, $131,631.49, leaving a balance of $8,051.59. The funded debt of the State was $81,795.75.

Among the recommendations he urges the establishment of the office of Attorney-General and also a State Land Office, the erection of a monument to the memory of Major Mills, who fell in the Mexican War, the prohibition of the circulation of bank notes of less denomination than ten dollars, a general license law for the sale of intoxicating liquors, that the Legislature urge Congress to make a grant of public lands to aid in the construction of railroads in Iowa.

General Van Antwerp, Commissioner of the Des Moines River Improvement, in his report to the Governor, made November 30, 1852, stated that $300,000 had been expended in the work, and that by a recent decision of the Interior Department it was held that the grant of lands extended to the source of the river; a million of acres was now available for the completion of the work. He says:

"If these lands can be held in reserve until the improvements are completed and sold for their actual value, the proceeds will pay for the work twice over."

He adds:

"The Des Moines River improvement is the only public work Iowa has yet undertaken. Build as many railroads as we may the Des Moines River improvement once finished from its mouth to Fort Des Moines, will remain forever Iowa's greatest work, and will float to the "Father of Waters" the largest portion of the products of her entire valley, probably of the entire State, of which that valley is the great heart and center."

The Whig State Convention held at Iowa City on the 26th of February, 1852, nominated the following ticket: J. W. Jenkins for Secretary of State; Asbury Porter, Auditor; Hosea B. Horn, Treasurer. The resolutions favored a convention to revise the Constitution, indorsed the administration of President Fillmore and the compromise measures of 1850.

The Democrats held their convention at the Capital on the 28th of May and made the following nominations: for Secretary of State, George W. McCleary; Auditor, Wm. Pattee; Treasurer, M. L. Morris. The resolutions indorsed the compromise of 1850, opposed a national bank and a protective tariff. At the election, McCleary, Democrat, received 16,884 votes, and Jenkins, Whig, 15,027—McCleary's majority, 1,857.

At the Presidential election in November, the vote of Iowa was as follows: For Franklin Pierce, Democrat, 17,762; General Winfield Scott, Whig, 15,856; John P. Hale, Free Soil, 1,606—plurality for Pierce, 1,906. Pierce's majority, 300.

On the 21st of December the General Assembly in joint convention proceeded to the election of a United States Senator. James W. Grimes, on behalf of the Whigs, nominated George G. Wright; Freeman Alger, for the Democrats, placed in nomination George W. Jones. Upon the roll call Jones received fifty-nine votes and Wright thirty-one. George W. Jones was declared elected for the term of six years from March 4, 1853.

At this session of the Legislature strong efforts were made to secure land grants to aid in the construction of several lines of railroad in the State. James W. Grimes, who was an influential member of the House from Des Moines County, was one of the most active in these efforts. The project to aid a line of road from Dubuque to Keokuk failed, but a combination of the friends of east and west trunk lines across the State was finally effected, which procured the passage of memorials for aid to three roads. First, a railroad from Burlington to a point on the Missouri River at, or near, the mouth of the Platte River. Second, a road from Davenport via Muscatine to Kanesville on the Missouri. Third, a road from Dubuque to Fort Des Moines.

As early as 1828 Wm. C. Redfield suggested substantially the route upon which the Chicago, Rock Island and Pacific Railroad was located and built, as the most feasible line for such an enterprise. Twenty-two years later, in Iowa City, on the 14th of October, 1850, a company was organized to build a railroad on a portion of that route. James P. Carlton was chosen President, H. W. Lathrop, Secretary and Le Grand Byington, Treasurer of this company. Richard P. Morgan, of Kendall, Illinois, made the preliminary survey for the road between Davenport and Iowa City, in November and December of the same year, receiving therefor $400. The right of way was easily secured, but there was very little surplus capital in Iowa at that time that could be spared for railroad building.

From Chicago a railroad was being slowly constructed over the unsettled prairies then lying between that city and the Mississippi River. The people of Iowa were watching its progress with deep interest. In October, 1852, the Mississippi and Missouri Railroad Company was organized to build a railroad from Davenport to Council Bluffs. At the head of this new company were capitalists from the eastern States and Chicago, and such prominent citizens of Davenport as Hiram Price, John P. Cook, James Grant and Ebenezer Cook. As it became apparent that this company could command capital to build the road, negotiations were opened with its directors by the officers of the Iowa City and Davenport Railroad Company, by which its franchises were transferred to the Mississippi and Missouri Company, upon the condition that the road should be built through Iowa City.

Meanwhile the Chicago road was approaching Rock Island. The following announcement shows its progress at this time:

" On Monday, March 14, 1853, and until further notice, a passenger train on the Chicago and Rock Island Railroad will run daily (Sunday excepted), between Chicago and La Salle, leaving Chicago at 8 o'clock a. m., arriving at La Salle at 1.20 p. m., connecting with steamers at La Salle for St. Louis and intermediate places on the Illinois River, and with stages west for Davenport, Iowa, and northward to Dixon, Galena and Dubuque.   A. R. GILMORE, Superintendent."

The Legislature having created the office of Attorney-General, D. C. Cloud, Democrat, was elected over Samuel A. Rice, Whig, by a vote of 14,464 to 6,900. In 1854 the California immigration had subsided and the tide again turned into Iowa. The Chicago and Rock Island Railroad reached the Mississippi River opposite Davenport early in February, and on the 22d of that month thousands of citizens of Iowa and Illinois gathered at Rock Island to witness the arrival of the first train. At 5 p.m., the engine, Le Claire, profusely decorated with flags, came in sight and sounded its whistle. A mighty shout from the assembled people, roar of cannon and firing of rockets was the welcoming response. Two other trains loaded with visitors followed in rapid succession. Then came a great mass meeting, speeches of welcome, enthusiastic cheering and general rejoicing, which continued late into the night. All realized that it was the dawning of a new era of prosperity for Iowa. For the first time the State was in direct daily communication with the eastern world, and in the near future the railroad extension would build up inland cities, distribute coal, lumber and goods, stimulate immigration, carry farm products to eastern markets at all seasons of the year and greatly increase the value of farms and their products. The first line of railroad having now reached the Mississippi River on its way to the Pacific coast, the necessity for a bridge across the river became apparent.

On the 17th of January, 1853, the Legislature of Illinois had incorporated "The Railroad Bridge Company" to build a bridge across the Mississippi River at or near Rock Island. Powerful opposition on part of river cities and steamboat interests was now organized. The construction of a bridge across this great waterway was opposed on the ground that it would be an obstruction to navigation. But the courts decided in favor of the bridge and the work was begun in the fall of 1853 and completed in April, 1856.

The railroad was completed to Iowa City on the 1st of January, 1856, with a branch to Muscatine, which was opened in July.

The census of 1852 had shown a population of 229,929. In the beginning of 1854 it had increased to 324,401, a gain of 94,472. Capital in a much larger ratio was also coming in to develop industries, build up towns and cities and promote public enterprises. The slow progress of river improvements, the great cost of canals, the closing of water navigation for several months of each year by freezing and low water, had finally convinced all classes of people that the country must rely largely upon railroads for transportation. The prairie States were sparsely settled, their people had no surplus capital to invest in railroad building. There were millions of acres of government land unsalable for lack of home markets, or means of transporting crops to distant markets. If por-

tions of these lands could be used to aid in building railroads, it would greatly increase the value of all and hasten
by many years the construction of needed lines through
the State. Without some such valuable aid, it must be
many years before the immense prairies of Iowa could be
traversed by railroads and made available for rapid settlement and profitable cultivation. Congress had been
urged by the Legislature and by our Senators and Representatives to make grants of public lands to aid in the
building of railroads, but without success. Renewed efforts were now made by public meetings, newspapers and
our members of Congress.

On the 9th of January, 1854, the Democratic State Convention met at Iowa City and nominated the following
candidates for the several offices: Curtis Bates for Governor; Geo. W. McCleary for Secretary of State; Joseph L. Sharp for Auditor; M. L. Morris for Treasurer;
D. C. Cloud for Attorney-General. The resolutions indorsed the administration and policy of President Pierce
without reserve.

The Whig Convention assembled at the Capital on the
22d of February and placed in nomination the following
ticket: for Governor, James W. Grimes; Secretary of
State, Simeon Winters; Auditor, A. J. Stevens; Treasurer, A. McMakin; Attorney-General, J. W. Sinnett. The
resolutions condemned the repeal of the Missouri Compromise and the attempt of Congress to legislate slavery
into the free Territories, favored the establishment of
banks and a law prohibiting the sale and manufacture of intoxicating liquors. The Whig party at this
time was rapidly breaking up. Many of its members had united with the " Know-Nothings," a party
opposed to the naturalization of foreign emigrants. It
was divided into two hostile factions—the " Silver
Greys," who were willing to let slavery alone, and
the " Seward Whigs," who were opposed to slavery.
The Democratic party was also divided on the slavery

JAMES W. GRIMES
Governor of Iowa, 1854 to 1858

issue; the " Hunkers " favored slavery, and the " Free Soilers " were antislavery. There was also an " Antislavery " party, which in 1854 nominated a full ticket for State officers. James W. Grimes was known to be outspoken in opposition to the extension of slavery and he was willing to make a vigorous campaign if he could receive the support of all of the opponents of the extension of slavery. He therefore held a private conference with the antislavery leaders, and persuaded them to withdraw their ticket and support the Whig candidates. Mr. Grimes now entered upon the campaign with great vigor and with strong hopes of success. He attacked the National Democratic administration, denouncing in scathing language its persistent efforts to extend slavery into the new Territories. He became the champion of the opposition to slavery and won the support of a large portion of the Free Soil Democrats. It was the beginning of a union of all who opposed the extension of slavery and the forerunner of the coming Republican party. The campaign resulted in the election of James W. Grimes, by a vote of 23,325 to 21,202 for Curtis Bates, giving Grimes a majority of 2,123. The Whigs also elected A. J. Stevens, Auditor, while the Democrats elected G. W. McCleary, Secretary of State; M. L. Morris, Treasurer; and D. C. Cloud, Attorney-General. James D. Eads, Democrat, had been elected Superintendent of Public Instruction in April.

The Fifth General Assembly, which convened on the 4th day of December, at Iowa City, was organized by the election of Maturin L. Fisher President of the Senate, and Reuben Noble Speaker of the House. The Democrats had sixteen members of the Senate; the Whigs and Free Soil, fifteen. In the House they stood, Whig and Free Soil, forty; Democrats, thirty. The Democrats organized the Senate and the Whigs the House.

Governor Hempstead, in his retiring message, reported the financial condition of the State to be as follows:

amount paid into the treasury for the two years ending
November 1, 1854, $125,462.57, adding $8,602.88, the
amount in the treasury October 31, 1852, made a total of
$134,065.45. There had been paid out on Auditor's war-
rants $118,542.90, leaving a balance in the treasury of
$15,522.55. The funded debt of the State was $79,745.75.
He renewed his advice that no change should be made in
the Constitution to authorize the establishment of banks
in the State; and also again urged the enactment of a
general license law. He recommended the organization
of the militia and the appointment of a Commissioner of
Immigration and again urged the Legislature to memorialize Congress for a grant of public lands to aid in
building a railroad from the Mississippi to the Missouri
River. On the 9th of December, James W. Grimes was
sworn into office as Governor, and delivered his inaugural
address to the General Assembly in joint convention. He
recommended a general revision of the laws relating to
public schools, that they should be supported by taxation
instead of by rate bills. He urged the establishment of
charitable State institutions; that the University Fund
be appropriated to establish a scientific or polytechnic
school; and a revision of the Constitution. He made a
powerful argument against the extension of slavery in
the Territories, saying:

" It becomes the State of Iowa, the only free child of the Missouri Compromise, to let the world know that she values the blessings that compromise has secured to her, and that she will never consent to become a
party to the nationalization of slavery."

On the 13th of December the General Assembly met in
joint convention to elect a United States Senator and Supreme Judges. Two ballots were taken without an election, when the convention adjourned to the next day, at
which time the convention adjourned to the 21st without
taking a vote on the election of Senator. A. C. Dodge
and Edward Johnston had received the votes of most of

GEORGE G. WRIGHT
Chief Justice, Supreme Court, 1855 to 1864

the Democrats, while the Whig and Free Soil members divided their votes among seven candidates, the most prominent of which were Fitz Henry Warren, James B. Howell, Ebenezer Cook and James Harlan. On the 21st, three votes were taken for Senator. On the third ballot Harlan had forty-seven votes, and A. C. Dodge forty-three, Cook seven. On the fifth ballot Harlan received forty-five votes, Cook forty-four, scattering eight. The Democrats being in a minority had no chance to elect a member of their own party, and as Cook was a conservative Whig, and Harlan a Free Soil Whig, most of them on the fifth ballot-voted for Cook, hoping to elect him over Harlan. The convention now adjourned to January Fifth. On the seventh ballot Harlan received forty-seven votes, Cook twenty-nine, W. D. Browning nineteen.

The convention then decided to proceed to the election of Supreme Judges. On the vote for Chief Justice, George G. Wright, Whig, was elected over Edward Johnston, fifty-three to forty-five. Wm. G. Woodward, Whig, was then elected Associate Justice by fifty-one votes, the opposition being divided among eight candidates. After several ballots for another Associate Justice were taken without an election the convention adjourned to the next day when the Senate met and, by a strict party vote, adjourned to Monday to avoid meeting the House in joint convention at the time agreed upon, proposing to thus invalidate any election that might be made. When the time arrived to which the joint convention had adjourned, the Whig Senators entered the House and the Speaker announced the joint convention was then in session. Mr. Samuels raised the point that the convention was not properly convened. The Speaker overruled the point and ordered the roll called. Most of the Democratic members absented themselves or refused to answer to the call. Fifty-seven members answered, however, making a majority of the joint convention. The President being absent, W. W. Hamilton was elected to fill the position. The

convention then proceeded to elect an Associate Justice
of the Supreme Court, and Norman W. Isbell was chosen
by a vote of fifty-one to five. A vote was then taken for
United States Senator. James Harlan received fifty-two
votes to four scattering and was declared elected for six
years from March 4, 1855.

The most important act of the session was the passage
of a bill submitting to a vote of the people at the August
election a proposition for a convention to revise the Constitution of the State. Among other important acts were
the following: to provide for relocation of the Capital
of the State to within two miles of the Raccoon Fork of
the Des Moines River; to provide for a Geological Survey,
to be made by the geologist, to be appointed by the Governor and confirmed by the Senate; an act to establish
an asylum for the deaf and dumb; an act for the suppres-
sion of intemperance, known as the prohibitory liquor law;
an act adding to the county of Kossuth the territory of
Bancroft County and the north half of Humboldt, and an
act to establish a State Land Office.

The principal contests before this Legislature were the
election of a United States Senator; the revision of the
Constitution and prohibition of the liquor traffic. The
election of James W. Grimes, as Governor, was the first
victory of the Antislavery movement in Iowa. Up to
1854 the Territory and State had been controlled by the
Democrats, and its votes in Congress, with one exception,*
had uniformly been given against the Antislavery or
Free Soil movement, which was rapidly growing in the
Northern States. Grimes was an earnest and outspoken
opponent of the extension of slavery. A majority of the
Legislature of 1854 was opposed to the Democratic party
and sympathized with the growing Free Soil movement.

The election of James Harlan to the United States Senate over the combined strength of the Democrats and con-

---

* Daniel F. Miller, Whig, member of Congress in 1849-51. John P. Cook, member of the
33d Congress, was a conservative Whig, and not in sympathy with the Free Soil wing of
that party.

JAMES HARLAN
United States Senator, 1855 to 1873

servative Whigs was regarded as the most important victory of all for the Free Soil cause. Mr. Harlan was the most radical Antislavery candidate presented to the Legislature and, although the opposition had finally resorted to revolutionary methods to prevent his election, he had received the votes of a majority of all of the members of the General Assembly.

A strong movement had been organized in the State by the friends of temperance for the enactment of a law prohibiting the manufacture and sale of intoxicating liquor. The State Temperance Alliance had delegated to Hiram Price, D. S. True and John L. Davies the preparation of a bill to be presented to the Legislature, similar to the "Maine Liquor Law." The bill was drafted with great care and sent to Dr. Amos Witter, a Democratic Representative from Scott County, who, on the 13th of December, 1854, introduced it into the House. It met with most determined opposition at every stage of progress, but finally passed both houses and was approved by Governor Grimes. One of its provisions required the act to be submitted to a vote of the people at the following April election. The vote stood 25,555 for the law, to 22,645 against. Having thus been adopted by a majority of 2,910, it went into effect on the First of July following. The act prohibited the manufacture and sale of intoxicating liquors, excepting for mechanical or medical purposes. The penalties were fine and imprisonment. With some amendment and modifications this law remained upon the statute books for more than forty years.

The Democratic State Convention was held at Iowa City, January 24, 1855 and nominated the following candidates: Commissioner of River Improvement, O. D. Tisdale; Register, Wm. Dewey; Register State Land Office, S. H. Samuels. The Whig Convention, held at the same place on the following day, nominated the following ticket: Commissioner of River Improvement, Wm. McKay; Register, J. C. Lockwood; Register Land Office, An-son Hart. The Whig ticket was elected. The vote for Commissioner was for McKay, Whig, 24,743; Tisdale, Democrat, 20,006. McKay's majority, 4,737.

This was the last contest between the Democrats and Whigs in Iowa. Before the next election the Whig party was largely absorbed by the new Republican party. The Silver Grey Whigs had United with the Democrats, while the Free Soil Whigs and Antislavery Democrats had together become Republicans. The conflict in Kansas over slavery had been growing in bitterness. Thousands of people from Missouri and other slave States entered the Territory to aid in the attempt to make it a slave State. Immigration from the North poured in and the contest between the advocates of free and slave States became bitter, not only in Kansas but throughout the entire Union. In spite of the Compromise of 1850, the conflict between freedom and slavery was growing more intense year by year, and armed collisions were becoming frequent in Kansas.

During the years of conflict between the defenders of slavery in Congress and the rapidly growing Antislavery sentiment, which grew warm at the close of the Mexican War, our Senators, Jones and Dodge, voted against the "Wilmot Proviso" and later for the Fugitive Slave Law and the whole of the Compromise measures of 1850. In the debates, which extended through many years, no voice was raised in Congress from Iowa Senators or Representatives against the extension of slavery until 1855 when James Harlan and James Thorington took their seats. Elected by a union of the Free Soil Whigs and Abolitionists, they were the first Iowa Congressmen to oppose the growing aggression of the slave power. The sentiment of the people of Iowa on the absorbing topic was undergoing a change.

The Legislature of 1856 passed joint resolutions strongly opposing the extension of slavery. These resolutions were sent to the Iowa members of Congress. No more Democrats were elected to Congress from Iowa until after slavery had ceased to exist. The Democratic party in Iowa never opposed the extension of slavery and thousands of its former members left the ranks, uniting with the Free Soil movement which organized the Republican party. The National Whig party, in trying to remain neutral, was going to pieces, and the opponents of the extension of slavery were coming together in a new political organization, known as the Republican party.

Early in January, 1856, the following call appeared in many Iowa newspapers:

" *To the Citizens of Iowa*:

" Believing that a large majority of the people of Iowa are opposed to the introduction of slavery into territory now free, and that the Democratic party is striving to make slavery a national institution, contrary to the principles laid down in the Declaration of Independence and the Constitution as taught by the Fathers of the Republic, we call upon all such citizens to meet in convention at Iowa City on the 22d day of February, 1856, for the purpose of organizing a Republican party to make common cause with a similar party already formed in several other States of the Union.

Signed   MANY CITIZENS.

" January 3, 1856."

It has been ascertained in late years, that the call which brought this convention together was made in the following manner: Robert Lowry, Hiram Price and Alfred Sanders, of Scott County, united in a letter to Governor Grimes in December, 1855, urging him to prepare a call for a State convention to organize a Republican party in Iowa. The Governor conferred with Samuel McFarland, of Henry County, and a few others. The call was written and sent by them to the *Burlington Hawkeye* and *Mt. Pleasant Journal*, which papers published it, and from them it was widely copied throughout the State.

The convention which assembled under this call was large and enthusiastic, and proceeded to organize the Republican party of Iowa. The following resolutions of the platform adopted make a comprehensive statement of the chief purpose of the new party:

" The mission of the Republican party is to maintain the liberties of the people, the sovereignty of the States and the perpetuity of the Union. Under the Constitution and by right, freedom alone is national. If this plain Jeffersonian and early policy was carried out, the Federal Government would relieve itself of all responsibility for the existence of slavery, which Republicanism insists it should and intends it shall do. Regarding slavery in the States as a local institution, beyond our reach and above our authority, but recognizing it of vital concern to every citizen in its relation to the Nation, we will oppose its spread, and demand that all national territory shall be free."

An effort was made by Hiram Price and others to procure incorporated in the platform of the new party an indorsement of the prohibitory liquor law, but a majority decided that it was better to unite in the new organization all who were opposed to the extension of slavery, which could only be accomplished by omitting all minor issues, upon which wide difference of opinion would arise. The convention then elected delegates to a national convention which would convene to organize a national Republican party and nominate candidates for President and Vice-President. Candidates for Presidential electors were chosen and the following ticket nominated for State officers: Elijah Sells for Secretary of State; John Pattee, Auditor; M. L. Morris, Treasurer; Samuel A. Rice, Attorney-General. Among the prominent Democrats who left their old party and were active in organizing the Republican party were, Hiram Price, Samuel J. Kirkwood and Martin L. Morris.

ELIJAH SELLS
Member of Constitutional Convention of 1844

JAMES THORINGTON
First Republican Member of Congress, 1855 to 1857

CHAPTER XXIII

THE efforts through many years by the people of Iowa to secure from Congress a grant of public lands to aid in building railroads across the State from east to west, were finally successful. James Thorington, the Republican member from the Second District, had devoted his energies to the accomplishment of this work from the time he took his seat in the House and largely through his judicious and untiring efforts, an act was passed by the Twenty-fourth Congress making a liberal grant. The act was approved on the 15th of May, 1856, and on the 3d of June, Governor Grimes issued his proclamation calling an extra session of the General Assembly to meet July 2d to act upon the grant.

The act granted every alternate section of land six miles in width on each side of three lines of railroad to be constructed from Burlington, Davenport and Lyons, westward across the State, said grants subject to the disposal of the Legislature. The Legislature passed a bill accepting the grant and, with proper restrictions, conveying it to the Burlington and Missouri River Railroad Company, the Mississippi and Missouri Railroad Company and the Iowa Central Air Line Railroad Company. Acts were also passed at this extra session to provide for a commission to revise the school laws; to permit a band of Sac and Fox Indians to reside in the State; to authorize certain towns to issue bonds to aid railroads.

The Democratic State Convention met at Iowa City June 26th and nominated the following ticket: Secretary of State, George Snyder; Auditor, James Pollard; Treasurer, George Paul; Attorney-General, James Baker. The convention indorsed the national Democratic party,

its policy and candidates. At the August election the
vote on the State candidates stood as follows:

Elijah Sells, Secretary of State, Rep................ 40,388

George Snyder, Dem............................ 32,920

Majority for Sells................................ 7,468

The vote on a constitutional convention was, for a convention, 32,790, against a convention, 14,162; majority
for a convention, 18,628.

The Republicans elected Samuel R. Curtis to Congress
in the First District, and Timothy Davis in the Second
District. They also elected a majority of each branch of
the Sixth General Assembly and now had control of every
department of the State government. The vote of Iowa
for President was cast as follows: for John C. Fremont,
Republican, 45,196; James Buchanan, Democrat, 37,663;
Millard Fillmore, Whig, 9,669; plurality for Fremont,
7,784.

An election was held on the 4th of December, 1856, for
delegates to the Constitutional Convention, at which one
delegate was chosen from each Senatorial District and two
from the First and Fourth Districts. They assembled at
Iowa City on the 19th of January, 1857 and organized
by the election of Francis Springer, President and T. J.
Saunders, Secretary. The convention consisted of thirty-
six delegates, of which twenty-one were Republicans and
fifteen Democrats. The session lasted until the 5th of
March. The following are the most important changes
made in the Constitution:

1. No lease of agricultural lands was valid for more than twenty years.

2. Biennial sessions of the Legislature were begun on the second Monday in January after the election of members.

3. Time of the General Election was changed to the second Tuesday in
October.

4. The votes of a majority of the members elected in each branch of the
General Assembly were required to pass a bill.

FRANCIS SPRINGER
President of the Constitutional Convention of 1857

5 Local or special laws were not to be passed on certain subjects, and in no case where a general law could be made applicable.

6. No money was to be appropriated for local or private purposes, unless by a vote of two-thirds of the members of each branch of the General Assembly.

7. The number of Senators was limited to fifty, and the number of Representatives to one hundred.

8. The office of Lieutenant Governor was created.

9. The office of Supreme Judge was made elective.

10. The limit of State indebtedness was increased from $100,000 to $250,000. In case of insurrection, invasion or defense in time of war this limit might be exceeded.

11. Banks could be established under laws enacted by the Legislature, provided such laws were approved by a majority of voters at a general or special election.

12. A State Board of Education was created.

13. The Capital of the State was permanently fixed at Des Moines, and the State University was permanently located at Iowa City.

14. To submit to a vote of the people a proposition to strike the word "White" from the article on suffrage (the effect of which would be to permit negroes to vote if the proposition should be adopted).

The census of 1856 gave the population of the State 517,875, an increase in two years of 193,474, more than double the population of four years before. The past two years had been a period of great prosperity in Iowa. The crops had been good, prices satisfactory, railroads were now entering the State, settlements were spreading over the prairies at a rate unprecedented. Spring wheat was the principal crop, yielding often from twenty-five to thirty-five bushels per acre, of plump grain, selling at from $1.10 to $1.35 per bushel. Very often the crop on forty acres would pay for one hundred and sixty acres of the best prairie land. Two years before the first railroad had reached the Mississippi, opposite Iowa, and now two hundred and forty-six miles had been built within its limits.

The Sixth and last General Assembly, under the old Constitution, met at Iowa City on the first day of December, 1856. The Senate was organized by the election of W. W.

Hamilton, President.   Samuel McFarland was chosen
Speaker of the House.   Governor Grimes sent his message
to the two Houses on the third day of the month.   The
financial condition was stated as follows: amount in the
treasury, October 1st, 1854, $10,106.86; paid in from that
date to October 31st, 1856, $250,399.45.   Amount paid out,
$249,149.85, leaving a balance of $11,156.46.   The Governor recommended an investigation of the affairs of the
Des Moines Improvement Company which was not making satisfactory progress with the work.

The Senate of the United States having declared the
former election of James Harlan illegal, on the 17th of
January, 1857, the Legislature reëlected him for the un-
expired portion of the term, ending March 4, 1861.   Acts
were passed providing for the payment of State bonds, $57-
000, due January 1, 1857; creating the counties of Humboldt and Hamilton; transferring the school fund to the
State treasury; providing for the distribution of the five
per cent. fund; amending the prohibitory liquor law;
fixing the salaries of the Governor, Supreme and District
Judges and other officers; authorizing certain cities and
counties to issue bonds and subscribe for stock in building
railroads; authorizing the McGregor Railroad Company
to accept a land grant.

James D. Eads, of Lee County, was elected Superintendent of Public Instruction at the April election, 1854,
gave bonds which were approved and entered upon the
duties of the office.   It was discovered in 1856 that the
financial affairs of the office were in a state of confusion,
and the funds belonging to the State, in the custody of the
Superintendent, were being loaned on doubtful security.
The Sixth General Assembly passed an act concerning the
school funds in which the Governor was authorized to
appoint an agent to make a thorough investigation and
report the condition in which they were found.   Under
this authority Governor Grimes appointed Joseph M.
Beck, of Lee County.   He soon discovered a state of af-

fairs that demanded prompt action, and on the 3d of March the Governor suspended James D. Eads from office and appointed as his successor, Joseph C. Stone, of Johnson County. He was not able to take possession of the office, as Mr. Eads refused to acknowledge the right of the Governor to remove him and retained the books, papers and funds. At the April election the Democratic candidate, Maturin L. Fisher, was elected over the Republican candidate, L. A. Bugbee, and on the 9th of June following he entered upon the discharge of the duties of the office.

The Superintendent was the custodian of the school funds of the State, and it was his duty to apportion them among the several counties and make loans to individuals. In his report to the Governor, made in November, 1857, J. M. Beck says:

"I found in possession of the Auditor of State fifty-four notes which were received from James D. Eads, late Superintendent of Public Instruction, as notes taken for loans of the five per cent. school fund, amounting in the aggregate to $155,199.99. Thirty-eight of these notes were accompanied by mortgages as security thereon. Fourteen of these mortgages had not been recorded. One of the notes was given by James D. Eads himself for $20,000, secured by a mortgage on lots in Fort Madison upon which were mechanics' liens and another mortgage given by him to his sureties on his official bond. Forty-seven thousand three hundred and fifty dollars had been loaned to the members of the syndicate in Des Moines, which built the temporary State House. Their notes were secured by mortgages on lots and lands."

After a careful examination of such securities as could be found, the agent reported a deficit of $65,150.78. He says:

"I made examination of the books, papers and vouchers in the office of the Superintendent of Public Instruction. *I found that no books of account had been kept by Mr. Eads.* He appropriates to his own use in one case $20,000, calls it a loan to himself, hands over as vouchers therefor a note signed by himself, secured by a mortgage on property worth about half the amount. To recognize this note in any other light than evidence

of crime would be setting a premium upon the violation of law and giving
free license to the embezzlement of public funds. His reports do not agree
with each other; his vouchers do not agree with his reports, and in several
cases the books and statements of officers receiving money from him, con-
tradict both his vouchers and reports."

Long before the first white settlements in Iowa, the
beautiful group of lakes near the head waters of the little
Sioux and west fork of the Des Moines River had been
a favorite resort of the Dakota or Sioux Indians. As
early as 1680, Louis Hennepin in exploring the upper
Mississippi Valley, was captured and held a prisoner by
the Yanktons. In 1700, when Lesueur was exploring
the region about Blue Earth and Minnesota River, he
found one of the Sioux nations occupying all of that region, and these Indians gave the name of Minne-Waukon
to Spirit Lake, which signifies ''Spirit Water,'' or as in-
terpreted by Major Long, '' Mysterious Medicine.'' It
was with great reluctance that the Sioux Indians consented to surrender this favorite hunting and camping
ground to the whites, as they did by the treaty of 1851.

As early as 1848, when Mr. Marsh, a government sur-
veyor, was running the correction line near Fort Dodge,
the party encountered a band of Sioux Indians, under the
chief, Si-dom-i-na-do-tah, and were ordered to turn back
and leave the country. When they attempted to proceed,
the Indians destroyed their wagons, instruments and
other property, seized their horses and forced them to re-
cross the river and leave the country .

In 1849 some adventurers settled on the Des Moines
River, near the mouth of the Boone. The Indians soon
discovered them, destroyed their cabins and drove them
out of the country. These and other collisions led to the
establishment of Fort Dodge. Si-dom-i-na-do-tah, signifying '' Two Fingers,'' was the chief of a roving band of
Sisseton Sioux Indians, numbering about five hundred.
He had led them in several battles with the Pottawattamies
in northwestern Iowa. One was fought near Twin Lakes,

in Calhoun County. Their last battle was on the Lizzard, in the present limits of Webster County. Si-dom-i-na-do-tah was a brave and skillful commander and had concealed his warriors in the heavy woods and brush of a high bluff.

The Pottawattamies were led into ambush, where they encountered the terrible fire from the concealed Sioux. They fought bravely, but were defeated with great slaughter and the survivors who reached their own country were so few that their tribe made no more raids into the Sioux country.

SIDOMINADOTA

SIOUX CHIEF MURDERED BY HENRY LOTT AND SON

In 1847 a desperado, named Henry Lott, built a cabin, which became a rendezvous for horse thieves and outlaws, near the mouth of the Boone River. Horses were stolen from the settlements below and from the Indians, secreted on Lott's premises and from there taken to the eastern part of the State and sold. In 1848, Lott's marauders stole a number of ponies from the Sioux Indians, who were hunting along the river. Si-dom-i-na-do-tah and six of his party tracked the ponies to Lott's settlement, found them concealed in the woods, recovered them and the chief ordered Lott to leave the country within five days. This he refused to do and, at the expiration of the time, the Sioux chief ordered his men to burn the cabin and kill his cattle. Lott was now alarmed and fled down the river with a stepson, abandoning his wife and small children. Upon reaching the Pea settlement in Boone County, he spread the report that his family had been massacred by the Indians. The settlers at once organized a party to punish the Sioux. Che-meuse, or '' Johney Green,'' a Musquakie chief, was at Elk Rapids, sixteen miles below, with several hundred of his band. He furnished twenty-six warriors for the expedition, which was placed under his command and piloted by Lott. When they reached his claim the Sioux had gone, and the wife and children of Lott were there without food or shelter. A son twelve years old had attempted to follow Lott when he fled, but after wandering twenty miles alone had perished from cold. Lott remained on his claim, where his wife died during the year, as Lott reported, from exposure and abuse from the Indians. Lott swore vengeance upon the Sioux chief, but made no haste to execute it. In the fall of 1853, he and a son passed through Fort Dodge with an ox team and a wagon loaded with provisions, goods and three barrels of whisky. He went into what is now Humboldt County and built a cabin on the bank of the creek which has since been named Lott's Creek.

Here he opened trade with the Indians in goods and whisky. In the month of January, 1854, Lott learned that Si-dom-i-na-do-tah with his family was camped on another creek since named Bloody Run. Taking his son one day, Lott went to the camp of the Sioux chief. Finding that he was not recognized, Lott made professions of warm friendship for the Indians. He told the chief that there was a large herd of elk on the river bottom and induced him to set off to find them. Lott and his son started toward their own cabin, but as soon as the old chief was out of sight, they skulked back, hiding in the tall grass, and as the chief returned from the hunt they shot him dead as he rode by on his pony. They then stripped him and, disguising themselves as Indians, waited until night, when, returning to the Indian tepees, they gave the war cry and as the Indian women and children came out in alarm, butchered them one by one. The victims were the aged mother, wife and children of Si-dom-i-na-do-tah and two orphans living with them. One little girl hid in the grass and escaped, and one little boy, terribly wounded and left for dead, recovered. The murderers then plundered the camp of every article of value and left the mutilated bodies of their victims to be devoured by wolves. Returning to their own cabin, they burnt it, to throw suspicion on the Indians, loaded a wagon with plunder and fled down the river. Ink-pa-du-tah, a brother of the murdered chief, was encamped with another band of Sioux Indians a few miles from the scene of the massacre. A few days later he discovered the dead and mangled bodies of his mother, brother and his entire family.

A careful examination by Major Williams, of Fort Dodge, and Ink-pa-du-tah, led to the discovery of facts which left no doubt that Lott was the perpetrator of the murders. His heavily loaded team was tracked down the river on the ice to the mouth of the Boone. Lott stated that he had been driven from his claim by the Indians, and he here sold to the settlers the pony, gun, furs and other property belonging to his victims. Lott hurried on his flight down the river, leaving one of his children at T. S. White's, six miles below Fort Dodge, and his two little girls at Dr. Hull's in Boone County.

Major Williams, with several of the Indians, followed rapidly on the trail of Lott and his son, hoping to overtake and arrest them. But Lott having several days the start, left the Des Moines River, struck out westward upon the unsettled prairie, crossed the Missouri River north of Council Bluffs and disappeared on the great plains.

Several years after his flight, it was learned by a letter from his son to an acquaintance in Boone County, that after settling in California, Henry Lott met his fate at the hands of the " Vigilance Committee " for crime committed in the gold regions. Ink-pa-du-tah brooded sullenly over the cruel murder of his mother and brother, believing that some of the white settlers were parties to the massacre and had aided Lott and his son to escape. The Sioux were greatly incensed upon learning that the head of their murdered chief had been taken to Homer and nailed upon the outside of a house, and they threatened to be revenged upon the whites. These facts were all procured from Major Williams, who had been active in his efforts to bring the murderers to justice, and was familiar with the true history of the massacre. Ink-pa-du-tah never fully renewed his friendship with the whites after this slaughter of his relatives, but looked upon them as treacherous enemies. There can be no doubt that he determined to bide his time for retaliation, which resulted a few years later in the Spirit Lake massacre.

During 1855-6, adventurous pioneers had prospected the valley of the Little Sioux and made claims at various places near the river, built cabins and settled with their families at Correctionville, in Woodbury County, Pilot Rock, in Cherokee, Peterson and Gillett's Grove, in Clay County.

An Irish colony had settled near Medium Lake, on the west fork of the Des Moines River, in Palo Alto, and a Mr. Granger had built a cabin in Emmet County, near the north line of the State. A small colony had ventured farther up the river and made a settlement in Minnesota, called Springfield (now Jackson). Asa C. and Ambrose A. Call, brothers, had settled near the present town of Algona, on the east fork of the Des Moines River, in 1854.

The settlements at Okoboji and Spirit Lake, in Dickinson County had been made in 1856 and embraced about fifty persons. Most of the Indians had by this time removed from northwestern Iowa, but parties frequently returned to hunt and fish at their favorite resorts of former years. Ink-pa-du-tah, who often came with his band, had professed friendship for the whites in these isolated settlements, but those familiar with the Indian character were apprehensive that some day he would take revenge upon them for the massacre of his relatives by Lott.

The winter of 1856-7 was one of unusual severity. Frequent storms had swept over the prairies, covering them with a depth of snow that made travel very difficult. They continued late into March, filling the ravines with drifts so deep that communication between the scattered settlements was almost impossible for weeks and months. Provisions were for the most part consumed during the long blockade by the fierce blizzards. Ink-pa-du-tah had carefully noted the condition of the settlers and with the relentless cruelty of his race, laid his plans to visit an awful retribution upon the countrymen of Henry Lott. It mattered not to him that these settlers were wholly innocent of any part, knowledge, or sympathy with the murders; they were of the white race to which Lott belonged and their lives must atone for his crime.

During the summer of 1856, Ink-pa-du-tah, with a portion of his band, had visited most of these frontier settlements and carefully noted their helplessness in case of a sudden attack. In February, 1857, the Sioux chief selected about thirty of his warriors and, accompanied by their squaws, to allay suspicion on part of the settlers, started up the Little Sioux Valley. The chief sent detached parties to the settler's cabins to take their arms, ammunition, provisions and cattle, and leave them defenseless and destitute. The snow was deep, the cold intense, the settlers few and widely separated, beyond reach of aid, and were compelled to submit to every outrage the

Sioux chose to perpetrate. Resistance would have brought certain death.

As the Indians advanced their depredations began to assume a savage character. At Gillett's Grove ten armed warriors forced an entrance into a house occupied by two families, seized the women and girls and subjected them to horrible outrages. They destroyed the furniture and beds, killed the cattle and hogs and robbed the terrified families of every article they took fancy to. Near midnight the settlers fled through the deep snow wandering for thirty-six hours, thinly clad, until they reached the house of Abner Bell, the nearest neighbor, utterly exhausted and nearly frozen to death. The Indians went from cabin to cabin, perpetrating outrages too horrible to relate, carrying off some of the girls to their camps where they were held until the savages moved on. Up to this time, however, no one had been killed.

As soon as the Indians moved on toward the lakes, Abner Bell, Mr. Weaver and Mr. Wilcox made their way through the deep snow to Fort Dodge, seventy miles distant. Their story of the Indian outrages created great indignation and excitement, as all realized that the frontier settlements were in imminent danger. But several days elapsed, no one knew where the Indians had gone; the snow was so deep that there was no hope that they could be overtaken by the time an organized force could be fitted out to pursue them.

PILLSBURY POINT, WEST OKOBOJI LAKE
Near Where the Massacre Began in 1857

CHAPTER XXIV

THE pioneers who first erected a cabin in the beautiful groves that lie along the shores of Okoboji and Spirit Lakes, were Rowland Gardner and Harvey Luce, his son-in-law. They had recently emigrated from the State of New York. Crossing the prairies in their canvas-covered wagons drawn by oxen, they found no settlement west of Algona, but continued on over the prairie going northwest until the evening of July 16, 1856, when they camped on the wooded shore of West Okoboji. They were so enchanted with the beauty of the lakes, forest and prairie that they decided to here make their homes. They explored the country about them and found the clear blue waters of Okoboji fringed by alternate stretches of sandy beach, pebble shores, walls of bowlders and forests reaching down to the water's edge. Away in the distance were prairies, while eastward were other lakes and groves. Not a sign of human habitation or smoke of camp fire was to be seen in any direction from the highest point on the lake shore. They were the only inhabitants of the little paradise they had discovered, far away from the nearest settlement. Elk and deer were grazing on the prairies, water fowl were coming and going from lake to lake, great flocks of prairie chickens were seen, squirrels and song birds were heard on every side.

The emigrants selected a site for their cabin on the southeast shore of West Okoboji, near the rocky projection since known as Pillsbury Point. The families consisted of Rowland Gardner, his wife Frances, little Rowland, six years old, Abbie, fourteen, Eliza, sixteen, and Mary, the oldest daughter, wife of Harvey Luce, and their two little children, Albert, four years old, and Amanda, a year old. A short time after their arrival a party of four young men from Red Wing, Minnesota, camped on the straits separating the two Okoboji lakes. They were Dr. I. H. Herriott, Bertell Snyder, William and Carl Granger. They were the first white men to paddle a canoe on these lakes. Fascinated by the loveliness of the country each took a claim, and together they built a cabin on a peninsula, now known as Smith's Point. The next settlers were from Delaware County, Iowa; James H. Mattocks, his wife Mary, and four children, Alice, Agnes, Jacob and Jackson. They built a cabin opposite Granger's on the slope extending down toward the straits from the south side. Robert Mathieson and a son lived with them. Both of these cabins overlooked East and West Okoboji Lakes. Some weeks later Joel Howe, his wife Millie, with six children (Lydia, Jonathan, Sardis, Alfred, Jacob and Philetus), settled on the east shore of East Okoboji. A daughter, Lydia, had married Alvin Noble, and they had a son two years old, named John. This family, with Joseph M. Thatcher and his young wife, Elizabeth, with their infant daughter, Dora, occupied a cabin a mile north of Howe's, at the upper end of the grove. A trapper, Morris Markham, boarded with Noble and Thatcher. These people were all from Hampton, in Franklin County.

Six miles northeast, on the west shore of Spirit Lake, William Marble and his young wife, Margaret, recently married in Linn County, had taken a claim and built a cabin. These made a settlement among the lakes, separated by distances of from one-half to six miles, of six families, in which were living sixteen men, eight women and fourteen children. This little colony, coming to the lakes in the summer of 1856, had not been able to raise crops sufficient to furnish food for the winter. Early in February their supply of provisions was nearly exhausted. It was a long perilous journey to the nearest settlements where provisions could be procured. But with starva-

EAST OKOBOJI LAKE
At the Time of the Massacre

tion staring them in the face, Harvey Luce and Joseph M. Thatcher started for Waterloo with an ox team and sled for supplies. After a journey over trackless prairies, working their way through immense drifts, they reached Waterloo, loaded their sled, started on their return and reached a cabin ten miles below Emmetsburg, where their team gave out. Thatcher remained here several days to rest the oxen, but Luce, feeling anxious about his family, determined to go on. Here he found Jonathan Howe, Enoch Ryan and Robert Clark who joined him on his homeward journey. Jonathan was a son of Joel Howe; Clark and Ryan were young men, the former from Waterloo, and the latter from Hampton.

After a desperate struggle amid huge snow drifts and blinding storms, Luce and his three companions reached the Gardner cabin on the evening of March 6. On the second day after their arrival the weather had greatly moderated, and Mr. Gardner determined to go to Fort Dodge for provisions. As the family sat down to an early breakfast, the cabin door was opened and fourteen fierce-looking Sioux Indians walked in, led by Ink-pa-du-tah. The Indians at first professed friendship until they had eaten all of the food in the house, when they undertook to seize the guns and ammunition.* But Luce resisted them and a most unequal struggle began. At this moment Dr. Herriott and Carl Snyder entered. Seeing four determined men the savages withdrew. Mr. Gardner, believing that the entire settlement was in danger, urged the young men to notify all of the neighbors to assemble at the Gardner house, which was the largest and strongest, and there defend themselves, if the Indians should become hostile. The young men thought there was no danger and soon after went to their cabin.

The Indians prowled around until near noon when they approached the Mattocks cabin, driving Gardner's cattle

*Many of the facts relating to the massacre and captivities are taken from the History of the Spirit Lake Massacre written by Mrs. Abbie Gardner Sharp.

and shooting them on the way. Gardner, Luce and Clark
now realized the great peril and made a heroic effort to
warn their neighbors. Mr. Gardner remained to protect
his family, while Luce and Clark started about two o'clock
to give the alarm. Soon after, the rapid firing of guns
at the Mattocks house and the screaming of the terrified
women warned the Gardner family that the terrible work
had begun. Mr. Gardner now barricaded the door and
prepared to defend his family to the last, but his wife,
who still had hope that the Indians would spare them for
the many acts of kindness in times past, begged of her
husband not to fire upon them. The Indians now forced
their way into the house and shot Mr. Gardner, killing
him instantly. They then turned upon the women and
children and beat their brains out with clubs; the only
one spared was Abbie, the daughter, fourteen years of
age. The terrified child begged of the savages to kill her,
too, as she could not endure the thought of the terrible
tortures and outrages inflicted on helpless prisoners. But
heedless of her entreaties, they dragged her away, while
the moans of her dying mother, sister and brother, crazed
her with anguish and horror. At the Mattocks house a
brave resistance was made. When the attack began Dr.
Herriott and Carl Snyder seized their guns and hastened
to the assistance of their neighbors. But outnumbered
five to one as they were by the Sioux warriors, there was
no hope of successful resistance. The five men fought
here with a bravery unsurpassed to save the women and
children, and as they fell one by one, with rifles grasped
in their hands, the terror of those remaining, for whom
their lives had been given, was appalling.

When Abbie was dragged to this scene of slaughter the
mangled bodies of the five men, two women and children
were lying about the burning cabin, while the shrieks of
other children roasting in the flames, made a succession
of horrors too hideous to be described. No witness survived to tell the fearful story of the heroic fight and

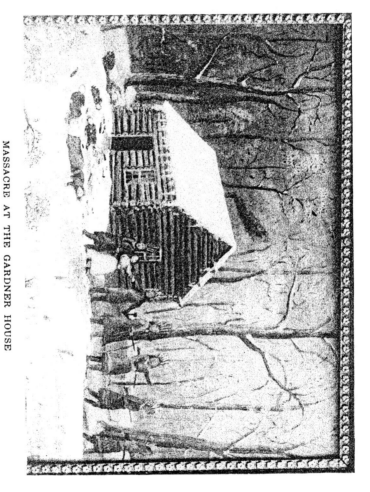

MASSACRE AT THE GARDNER HOUSE
From an Old Painting)

DR ISAAC H HERRIOTT
Killed in Defending the Mattocks Family

WILLIAM BURKHOLDER
Perished on the Relief Expedition

bloody massacre here, but eleven mutilated bodies were left to mark the spot. A careful examination of the vicinity later, by the party who buried the dead, throws some light upon the struggle.

Dr. Herriott and Carl Snyder doubtless heard from their cabin the shrieks of the women and children, when the attack began at the Mattocks house. Then came the reports of firearms as Mr. Mattocks, Mathieson and the young man seized their rifles and fought desperately with the savages. Dr. Herriott and young Snyder might have escaped now by flight but, heroic men as they were, no such attempt was made. With rifle in hand they hurried to the rescue, regardless of overwhelming numbers. At the first fire Dr. Herriott brought down one of the Sioux warriors; then rushing into the thickest of the fight, the two brave men shattered their empty guns over the heads of the savages in a vain effort to save the terror-stricken women and children. How many Indians were killed or wounded in the unequal conflict can never be known. Abbie Gardner believes that none were killed and but one was wounded. But Major Wm. Williams, the veteran commander of the relief expedition that buried the dead, is of a different opinion.* In his report to Governor Grimes, made on the 12th of April, immediately after the return of the burial party to Fort Dodge, he writes:

"The number of Indians killed or wounded must be from fifteen to twenty. From the number seen to fall, and judging from the bloody clothes and clots of blood left in their encampments, the struggle at the lakes must have been severe, particularly at the house of Esquire Mattocks. Eleven bodies were found at this house, together with several broken guns. They appear to have fought hand to hand."

* When it is remembered that Abbie was but fourteen years old at the time of the massacre, and was almost paralyzed with the horrors surrounding her, and that her book was written twenty-eight years after her captivity, it is not strange that such a discrepancy between her estimate of the Indian losses and that of Major Williams should be found. The Major's report was written about a month after the massacre. It is not likely that the wily Sioux would let their captive know the extent of their losses, but Williams had an intimate knowledge of the customs of the Sioux Indians and their cunning concealment of their losses in battle.

Luce and Clark, who started from the Gardner house to
warn the settlers, went toward Mr. Howe's. They were
overtaken near the outlet on the south shore of East Okoboji, by the stealthy savages, shot down and scalped. This
closed the first day's horrid work, the 8th day of March,
1857. That night the Sioux warriors celebrated the butchery of twenty men, women and children in the true Indian
fashion, with blackened faces, keeping time in their war
dance to the beating of drums, circling over the blood-
stained snow with unearthly yells among the mutilated
bodies of their victims, until exhausted by their horrid
orgies. Crouched in an Indian tepee, Abbie Gardner, the
only survivor of the first day's massacre, prostrated by
grief and terror and the awful deeds she had been compelled to witness, endured such anguish as seldom falls
to the lot of a human being.

While this awful butchery was going on, the neighbors
on the east side of the lakes had no warning of their impending danger. Luce and Clark were lying dead on the
south shore. Mr. Howe had started early in the morning
of the 9th, wading through the deep snow drifts toward
the Gardner cabin to borrow flour. He was met by the
Indians who were going to his house to continue their
work. They shot him, then severed his head from the body
and hurried on to his cabin. Mrs. Howe, her son Jonathan, his sister Sardis and three young brothers, all unsuspicious of danger, were in the house. Suddenly the
door was burst open, a wild rush of yelling Indians with
gleaming tomahawks and scalping knives filled the house,
and a few moments later, amid screams of terror and
groans of anguish, the dead and dying bodies of the entire
family were lying in the blood-stained snow. Going on
to the Thatcher cabin, the Indians found Mr. Noble, his
wife and child, Mrs. Thatcher and her child and Mr. Ryan.
Seeing two stalwart young men at home, the cowardly
savages professed friendship as they entered the house.
When Noble and Ryan were thus deceived, the Indians

SIOUX INDIAN SCALP DANCE
After the First Day's Massacre at the Okoboji Lakes

suddenly turned their guns upon them and fired, killing both men before they could seïze their rifles. They then caught the two children from their mother's arms and swinging them by their feet against a tree near the door, crushed their brains out. They plundered the house, killed the cattle and hogs, then dragging Mrs. Noble and Mrs. Thatcher with them, started for their camp. With a refinement of cruelty peculiar to their race, they took Mrs. Noble back to the Howe cabin, where with unspeakable horror she saw the mangled bodies of her mother, sister and four brothers. Jacob, her thirteen year old brother, was still alive, and while the Indians were killing the cattle, she tried to get him into a bed in the house, hoping he might be saved, but the savages discovered him and beat his brains out, while his sister stood by powerless to protect him.

The Indians remained about the lakes until the 13th, while William Marble and his young wife in their cabin on the shores of Spirit Lake knew nothing of the terrible fate that had overtaken every family of their neighbors. They were several miles from any other house and, as the snow was very deep, Mr. Marble had not ventured away from home and had heard nothing to alarm him. On that morning, soon after breakfast, as Mrs. Marble relates, looking out of the cabin window, a band of painted and armed Indians was seen approaching. They came into the house and professed friendship. One of them wanted to exhange his rifle for a very fine one belonging to Mr. Marble, who, fearing to offend them, agreed to the trade. They then proposed shooting at a mark. Mr. Marble fired first and stepped forward to examine the target, when the treacherous savages shot him in his back. Mrs. Marble, who had been anxiously watching them from the window, in fear for her husband's safety, sprang out with piercing screams as he fell, and threw her arms around her murdered husband, in the agony of dispair. He was dead, and she was alone, in the hands of his brutal mur-

derers. They flung her aside and searched the body of
their victim, taking from it a belt containing $1,000 in
gold. This was the little fortune the young couple had
brought with them to improve and stock the beautiful farm
they had selected on the banks of the lake. The Indians
then plundered the house, took Mrs. Marble's gold watch
and placed her upon a pony. In one brief hour the young
wife had lost husband and home, and was a captive, reserved for a fate worse than death.

The Indians returned with their plunder to the main
body, and here Mrs. Marble found the other three captive
women and from them learned the terrible fate that had
overtaken the entire settlement. They realized now that
none were left to attempt their rescue, and torturing visions of the slaughter of fathers, mothers, sisters, brothers,
husbands and children were stamped on their memory in
a hideous intensity that paralyzed them. They prayed
for death to end it all and save them from a fate too awful
to be contemplated. The captive women were soon separated, each being taken to a different lodge, where their
hair was braided and their faces painted, after the manner
of the Sioux squaws. They were held as slaves and suffered treatment as brutal as has ever befallen helpless
women in the hands of savages. Before leaving Marble's
Grove, the Indians pealed the bark from a large tree, and
on the white surface pictured in signs the record of their
horrid deeds. This ghastly record was visible for several
years, and was seen by many of the early settlers.

Thus did Ink-pa-du-tah bide his time, and after the
lapse of more than three years, wreak a terrible vengeance
upon innocent white families, for the massacre of his nearest relatives by Henry Lott and his son. Not a person was
left in the entire colony at the lakes to carry the news of
the great tragedy to the nearest settlement. But it so
happened that the discovery was made on the day on which
the Howe, Noble and Thatcher families were slaughtered.

Morris Markham, who lived at Noble's, had started for

the Des Moines River on the 7th, in search of some cattle
that had strayed away. Returning on the evening of the
9th, cold, hungry and exhausted, he reached the Gardner
cabin near midnight. It was very dark and cold, and
Markham was surprised to find the doors open and the
house deserted. Upon examination he came upon the
bodies of the family. some lying on the floor and others
about the yard. Horror stricken by these evidences of a
terrible tragedy, he cautiously went on through the dark
forest toward the Mattocks house. When near it, he discovered the Indian camps, and at once realized that the
fierce Sioux had appeared in his absence, at the isolated
settlement and murdered his friends and neighbors. He
saw the smouldering ruins of the Mattocks cabin and the
mutilated bodies of other settlers lying about. Almost
overcome with the horrors confronting him he turned
back toward the Howe settlement, hoping it had escaped
the massacre. But upon reaching Howe's cabin he again
came upon the ghastly bodies of women and children.
Almost paralyzed by the horrid sights, he turned toward
his own home, hoping against hope that it might have
escaped. But there before him lay the mangled forms of
Noble, Ryan and the children. Markham had walked more
than thirty miles since morning, through deep snow without rest or food. He was now completely exhausted and
his feet were frozen. He managed to start a fire in a
ravine, not far away, and here, without shelter or food,
he spent the remainder of the night, not daring to lie down,
lest he too might be murdered by the Indians. Before
daylight he started for the nearest settlement, Springfield,
Minnesota, eighteen miles distant. He reached that place
completely exhausted and spread the news of the fate of
the Okoboji colony.

- Fortunate it was that Markham's strength had held out
to warn them of the danger, or they too would have shared
the fate of their neighbors. After a hurried consultation
the people decided to gather all the families at the houses

of Messrs. Thomas and Wheeler for mutual protection. Two messengers were sent to Fort Ridgely for aid. For seventeen days the settlers at Springfield were kept in suspense, hourly expecting an attack from the Indians. There were sixteen men, women and children at the Thomas house when the attack began. Most unexpectedly to the Indians, they found the people prepared to give them a warm reception.

The cowardly savages dressed one of their number in citizen's clothes, and he approached the Thomas house in a friendly manner, calling the people out upon a cunning pretext. The remainder of the band was concealed behind trees in the forest surrounding the cabin. They opened fire upon the settlers who had been decoyed outside. The volley mortally wounded William Thomas, a little boy eight years old, and severely wounded Mr. Thomas, David Carver and Miss Drusella Swanger. There were but three men now left in the house unhurt—Morris Markham, Jareb Palmer and John Bradshaw. Hastily barricading the doors, the three men, assisted by Mrs. Thomas and Louisa Church, Eliza Gardner* and Miss Swanger, prepared for a vigorous defense.

All of the wounded had now succeeded in reaching the house, except little Willie Thomas, who had fallen outside, and was overlooked in the excitement until after the doors were barricaded. It was then too late to rescue him without endangering the lives of all. His father was severely wounded and his mother begged piteously to be permitted to open the door and bring him in; but the others felt it would be certain death to all and he was left to his fate. The Indians gradually crept nearer the house while keeping up a constant fire on the besieged settlers. They, however, kept in shelter of the log stable and large trees. Eliza Gardner and Miss Swanger cast

---

* Eliza was a daughter of Rowland Gardner, who with his family had been among the first victims of the massacre of the lakes She was visiting Mrs. Church and thus escaped the slaughter of the family. Mr Markham had brought the terrible news to her a few days before the attack at Springfield. She did not know that her sister Abbie was alive and a captive.

bullets and loaded guns, while Mrs. Church took the place
of one of the wounded men at a port-hole and fought as
bravely as the men. Watching a tree behind which an
Indian was firing upon the cabin, Mrs. Church gave him
a load of buckshot as he was aiming his rifle at the house.
He fell back howling into the snow. So the fight went on
until sunset, the well directed shots from the cabin pre-
venting an assault by the Indians. At dark they joined
others of the band who were butchering isolated settlers.

William and George Wood, who kept a store and were
on friendly terms with the Indians, were confident that
they would not be molested and refused to unite with their
neighbors in preparing for defense, as they discredited
Markham's report of the massacre at the lakes. A party
of Sioux, upon their arrival, went to Wood's store and
purchased a keg of powder and a quantity of lead, which
was used in the siege of the Thomas house and in the
slaughter of the Stewart family. The Wood brothers
suffered a terrible penalty for their folly, as some days
later the treacherous Sioux returned to the store, shot the
proprietors with some of the ammunition recklessly sold
to them, plundered the store and, piling brush over the
mutilated bodies of the victims, set it on fire. Johnny
Stewart, a little eight-year-old son of Joshua Stewart, had
escaped into the woods when the family was massacred by
the Indians. After dark he made his way to the Thomas
house and was taken in. Soon after a Mr. Sheigley also
arrived. There were now seventeen persons in the house,
three of whom were badly wounded and in need of medical
aid.

A consultation was held, and it was determined to attempt to escape in the night, before the Indians could assemble to renew the attack and probably set fire to the
house. Whether they should stay or go, there was but
little hope of escape from the doom that had overtaken
their neighbors. They believed themselves to be the only
survivors of the colony. No assistance could be expected,

and they determined to try to reach the nearest settlement.
There was great fear that the Indians were concealed near
by in the woods. Some one must venture to make a careful examination of the surroundings. It was a perilous
undertaking and all hesitated. A young man stepped forward and volunteered to risk his life in behalf of the
others.

It was the brave Morris Markham who had discovered
the massacre at the lakes and had already saved the lives
of all present by warning them of the impending danger.
Carefully examining his rifle by the dim fire-light, he told
his companions that if he discovered Indians, he would
warn them by firing, if possible, even if he was stricken
down in the dark by the lurking savages, and they should
immediately barricade the door and defend themselves
without waiting for him. He stepped out into the darkness with his rifle cocked and noiselessly disappeared.
His comrades waited with intense anxiety. Markham
crept silently through the snow from tree to tree, listening for the first movement of a stealthy foe. He cautiously made a wide circuit around the house and stable, expecting any moment to hear the crack of a rifle or the
sudden rush of armed savages. Half an hour passed and
the suspense of his companions in the house, intently listening, seemed unendurable. Not a sound reached them,
and a terrible fear came to them that he had been toma-
hawked by the stealthy Sioux before he could give the
alarm.

At last they heard approaching footsteps and hastily
barricaded the door. Another moment of intense waiting
and peering through the port-holes with loaded guns, then
they heard the well-known voice of Markham. He informed them that the Indians had disappeared and he had
found a yoke of oxen which had escaped the general
slaughter. He had hitched them to a sled and all hands
hastened to bring out the small children, the wounded,
blankets and provisions, and they started on their dan-

gerous journey, sorrowfully leaving the dead body of little Willie Thomas where he fell. The brave women tramped through the deep snow, following the well-armed men and the heavily loaded sled. The only coward among the settlers at Springfield was a Dr. Strong. In October he went from Fort Dodge to Mr. Gardner's at the lakes. When he afterward settled at Springfield, his wife persuaded Eliza Gardner to go with them and spend the winter and thus she escaped the fate of the other members of her father's family. When the news of the massacre reached Springfield, Dr. Strong took his wife and child and Eliza to the Thomas house for safety. On the morning before the attack Dr. Strong had been called to Mr. Wheeler's to attend two men who had lost their legs by freezing. While there, he heard the guns all through the day at the Thomas house, where the fight was going on and where his wife and child were. He was so terrified that he did not venture out of the Wheeler cabin until dark. When the firing had ceased and he had seen the Indians retreating, he made no effort to learn the fate of his family. The next morning he persuaded Mrs. Smith to go over and learn the fate of the settlers at the Thomas cabin. When she returned with the report that it was deserted, and that a boy was lying dead in the yard, Dr. Strong left the three women, their two children and his two crippled patients and fled without an effort to learn the fate of his wife and child.

There was now but one able-bodied man left at the Wheeler house, J. B. Skinner. The others were Mrs. Skinner, Mrs. Wm. Nelson and her child, Mrs. Smith and her crippled husband, whose leg had recently been amputated, Mr. Sheigley's little boy and Mr. Henderson, who had lost both legs. To remain now until the Indians returned seemed to be certain death for all, with but one man able to defend them. They had no team and no way to carry the wounded men. Hard as it was they had to abandon Henderson and Smith and start through the deep

snow, expecting to be pursued by the Indians upon discovery that they had left the house. In their haste and
terror, Mr. Sheigley's little boy was also left behind. On
the second day they fortunately fell in with Markham's
party, and Mr. Sheigley learning that his little boy had
been abandoned in the flight, started back alone to rescue
him. Late in the afternoon the fugitives came in sight of
a grove on the Des Moines River, where George Granger
lived. In the distance they saw a man running toward
the grove, and in his terrified flight he pulled off his
boots and threw them away, to increase his speed. He
was recognized as Dr. Strong, making his way alone down
the river after having abandoned his wife and child two
days before.

This fleeing coward kept on his flight alone down the
river to the Irish colony in Palo Alto County where he
was found by Major William's Relief Expedition on its
way to the lakes. Dr. Strong was not man enough to join
them and return to learn the fate of his family whom he
had abandoned. His wife and child survived the sufferings of that dreadful winter march, and were with the
party rescued, but she refused to return to the husband
who had so heartlessly deserted her in that time of deadly
peril.

The party remained two nights at the Granger cabin,
waiting the return of Mr. Sheigley, who was unable to
find his boy.* The next day the entire party went on
toward Fort Dodge, with a scanty supply of food and
clothing and the wounded suffering greatly for medical assistance. At night all slept in the snow without shelter,
their shoes and clothing wet with melting snows and the
water of icy streams. Miss Swanger, with a painful bullet wound in her shoulder, gave up her place on the sled
to the children and marched on foot through the snow.
The sufferings of the entire party were enough to ex-
haust the strongest men, as they dragged themselves

---

*The boy was afterwards found safe with a neighbor who had escaped the massacre.

through the deep drifts and plunged into icy waters that filled the ravine and sloughs.

Monday, the 30th of March, they had been out three days, and it was doubtful whether the wounded, or women and children, could survive another night, so deplorable was their condition. Toward noon they sighted in the distance a party approaching, which they had no doubt were the pursuing Indians. It was felt by all that escape was impossible. But Morris Markham, John Bradshaw and Jareb Palmer were not men to abandon the helpless or tamely surrender. A hurried consultation was held and it was determined to divide the guns among the men who were not disabled. John Bradshaw volunteered to advance upon the Indians with six loaded guns and pick them off one by one at long range as they approached. Markham, Palmer and the other men remained with the women, children and wounded to defend them to the last. Brave John Bradshaw advanced alone, placed his loaded guns in easy reach, cocked his rifle and sternly watched the approach of the enemy. Every eye of the fugitives was fixed upon him as they awaited the hopeless conflict. Suddenly a loud shout and signals from the advancing party proclaimed them friends. It was the advance guard of Major William's Relief Expedition coming to their aid. In order to protect themselves from the fierce north wind, they had drawn shawls and blankets about their heads, thus resembling Indians in their wrappings. Language cannot describe the emotions of the suffering fugitives, as the sudden transition from hopeless terror to the joy of rescue came over them. As they came nearer, S. J. Church, who was one of the party, recognized among the fugitives his wife and children, whom he had feared were victims of the massacre. Another of the party, J. M. Thatcher, now learned from Markham of the butchery of his child and the probable worse fate of his young wife taken into captivity. Everything in their power was now done by the relief party for the comfort of the sufferers.

Dr. Bissell dressed the wounds of the injured and all rested in safety for the first time since their flight began. An escort was sent the next day, which conveyed them safely to the Irish colony. Mrs. Smith turned back with the soldiers who were going to the lakes to find and rescue her crippled husband, who had been abandoned when the party fled from the Wheeler house. She found her husband and Henderson, who had also been left, and both were rescued.

CAPT. J. F. DUNCOMBE

CAPT. C B RICHARDS
Officers of he Rel ef Expedi on of 1857

MAJ. WILLIAM WILLIAMS

CHAPTER XXV

THE news of the massacre at the lakes was carried to Fort Dodge by O. C. Howe, R. U. Wheelock and B. F. Parmenter, of Jasper County, who had taken claims the fall before at Spirit Lake. They started for the lakes early in March, and reached the Thatcher cabin at midnight on the 15th. No one could be aroused to let them in, but upon opening the door they came upon the lifeless bodies of Noble and Ryan. Horror-stricken by the sight, they next approached the house of Mr. Howe and there found the mutilated bodies of seven women and children. They now realized that the Indians had probably exterminated the entire settlement, and hastened back to Fort Dodge, reaching there on the 22d.

The terrible news aroused the people in every direction. Prompt steps were taken to send a relief expedition at once to the lakes. Major William Williams issued a call for volunteers, and in three days one hundred men were enlisted. They were organized into three companies—Company " A," of Fort Dodge, C. B. Richards, captain; Company " C " of Fort Dodge, and vicinity, John F. Duncombe, captain; Company " D " of Webster City, J. C. Johnson, captain. So intense was the excitement and desire to overtake and punish the savages, that the little army started out in haste, poorly equipped for a long winter march over unsettled prairies. The winter, which had been the severest on record, was still unbroken.

The snow storms had continued for months, filling sloughs and ravines in many places to a depth of from six to fifteen feet. But few tents could be procured and the blankets, clothing and provisions that were hastily collected were insufficient for such an expedition. Major Williams, the commander, was a vigorous man but he was

sixty-two years of age. He had been commissioned by
Governor Grimes two years before to act upon his own
judgment in any trouble with the Indians. News of the
outrages perpetrated along the Little Sioux some time before had reached Fort Dodge and the people were not
wholly unprepared for tidings of further depredations.
Howe, Parmenter and Wheelock joined the expedition at
Fort Dodge; J. M. Thatcher, at the Irish colony, Morris
Markham, John Bradshaw and Jareb Palmer turned back
with it, after conducting the Springfield refugees to safety.
A hard crust on the snow rendered the march slow and
difficult, as it was not sufficiently hard to bear the weight
of a man. At the close of the second day the party camped
at Dakota, in Humboldt County, but eighteen miles from
Fort Dodge. From this place onward the obstructions,
hardships and sufferings increased. In many places the
ravines they had to cross were filled with snow in depth
of from ten to twenty feet, in which the teams were helpless. Long ropes had to be fastened to the floundering
horses and they were pulled through by the men one at a
time. The loaded wagons were drawn through in a similar
manner. Sometimes it required the entire brigade to haul
one loaded wagon through the immense drifts. Often the
men were compelled to wade two abreast in long lines,
up to their waists in snow, to break a road for the teams
and wagons.

On the third night the expedition was obliged to camp
on the unsheltered prairie in the deep snow, without fuel,
with a bleak northwest wind sweeping down upon the exhausted men. They made a supper of crackers and raw
pork, chained the oxen to the wagons, which were arranged close together to break the wind, while the men
crowded together on their beds of snow, to keep from
freezing. The next day was a renewal of the hardships
until night, when they were able to reach the shelter of
McKnight's Grove, where they found plenty of fuel to
cook their food and cabins in which to sleep.

On the morning of the 28th, after roll call, Major Williams made a brief address to his men, alluding to the hardships encountered and complaints of some of the faint-hearted. He told them plainly that greater sufferings were ahead of them and if any lacked the courage or endurance to encounter them, now was the time to say so and return to their homes. Nine men turned their steps homeward, leaving the command with weakened ranks to face the dangers ahead. No record has been kept of the names of these deserters.

On the 29th, the little army reached the Irish colony, near where Emmetsburg now stands and exchanged some of their worn out teams for fresh animals. They were also reënforced by several young men, bringing the number of the command up to one hundred and twenty-five. Dr. Strong, who had deserted his wife and child, was found here, but could not be persuaded to join the Relief Expedition. Major Williams knew that another day's march might bring them within reach of the Indians, and so sent a company of nine picked men in advance as scouts. They were C. C. Carpenter, Frank R. Mason, J. M. Thatcher, W. L. Church, Wm. K. Laughlin, A. N. Hathaway, Wm. Defore and A. H. Johnson, under command of Lieutenant J. N. Maxwell. They carried corn bread to last three days. This was the 30th of March, and traveling northward about twelve miles, by noon, upon reaching an elevation, one of the company shouted "Indians!" Far away could be seen a party twice as large as their own, slowly advancing. Lieutenant Maxwell quickly formed his men in line for the attack, and followed a high ridge to keep in sight of the enemy, as the approaching party was seen to be preparing for battle. Coming nearer, Mr. Church, who was in advance, suddenly dropped his gun, sprang forward, exclaiming, "My God! there's my wife and babies!"

Governor Carpenter, years after, thus described the scene which followed:

"They had surrounded the ox-sled in an attitude of defense, as they had supposéd us to be Indians, and had resolved, if overpowered, never to fall into the hands of the savages alive. On discovering that we were friends, such a heartrending scene I never before witnessed, as the relatives and friends of the refugees had supposed they were dead. In the party were Mrs. W. L. Church and her children; her sister, Drusella Swanger, shot through the shoulder; Mr. Thomas, who had lost an arm; Mr. Carver, also severely wounded in the fight at Springfield; Mrs. Dr. Strong and child, who had been deserted by her craven husband. In the haste of their flight they had taken but few provisions and scanty clothing. The women had worn out their shoes; their dresses were worn into fringe about the ankles; the children were crying with hunger and cold; the wounded were in a deplorable condition for want of surgical aid. Their food was entirely exhausted; they had no means of making fire: their blankets and clothing were wet and frozen; and in their exhausted condition it is hardly possible that many of them could have survived another night's exposure from the fearful storm then coming on. The refugees were so overcome by the sudden transition from deadly peril and impending death that seemed to confront them, changed in an instant to relief in their desperate extremity, that they sank down in the snow, crying and laughing alternately, as their deliverers gathered around them. If nothing more had been accomplished by the Relief Expedition, every member felt that the salvation of eighteen perishing refugees, from almost certain death by exposure and starvation, had richly repaid them for all the hardships encountered."

On the 31st the expedition pushed northward, finding frequent indications of Indians, until it reached the Granger house, on the west fork of the Des Moines River, near the Minnesota line. Here Major Williams learned that a company of soldiers from Fort Ridgely was at Springfield for the protection of settlers, and that the Indians had moved on westward. Learning that those murdered at the lakes were unburied, Major Williams called for volunteers to go to the lakes and bury the mutilated bodies. Captain J. C. Johnson, Lieutenant J. N. Maxwell, and Privates W. E. Burkholder, Henry Carse, W. N. Ford, J. H. Dailey, O. C. Howe, Geo. P. Smith, O. C. Spencer, S. Van Cleve, C. Stebbins, R. U. Wheelock, R. A. Smith, B. F. Parmenter, Jesse Addington, R. McCormack, J. M. Thatcher, W. R. Wilson, James Murray, A. E. Burtch, W. K. Laughlin, E. D. Kellogg and John Dalley promptly stepped forward and volunteered to go on the perilous mission. On the morning of the 2d of April, the command separated, the main body under Major Williams turned back to the Irish colony, while Captain Johnson's party started for the lakes. They reached East Okoboji about two o'clock, guided by Thatcher to his own cabin. A horrible sight confronted him. His home was in ruins, and lying in the yard were the dead bodies of his friends, Noble and Ryan, as they had fallen three weeks before, when surprised and shot down by the treacherous Sioux. Inside of the cabin nothing was left but the ghastly forms of the two little children who had been snatched from the arms of their terrified mothers, Mrs. Thatcher and Mrs. Noble. The fate of the two young mothers who were dragged off by the Indians was then unknown. From cabin to cabin, all through the settlement the company went, burying the dead, until all were laid beneath the snow-covered ground.

Not a living person of the entire colony was found. Mr. Marble's body had been buried by the soldiers from Fort Ridgely. The body of young Dr. Herriott was found near Mattocks' cabin, with his right hand still grasping his broken rifle, the barrel empty, where he had fallen in a hand-to-hand struggle with the Indians, bravely defending his neighbors. The bodies of Luce and Clark were not found until some weeks later, near the outlet of the lake. Their sad mission ended, the burial party started on the 4th of April on their homeward march, their provisions entirely consumed.

The weather was warm and the melting snow filled the sloughs with water, in many places waist deep, through which the men had to wade, wetting their clothing to the shoulders. About four o'clock the wind, which had been in the south, suddenly changed to the northwest and in half an hour a howling blizzard was sweeping down upon them. Their clothes were soon frozen stiff. Some of the party had taken their boots off to wade the sloughs, and

others had cut holes in them to let the water out. Many
had their boots frozen before they could put them on and
were compelled to walk on through the snow and freezing
water in their stockings, which were soon worn out.

As night came on the piercing winds nearly chilled them
to death. They dare not lie down in the snow for it was
only by violent exercise that they were able to keep warmth
and life in their stiffening limbs and bodies. They separated into two companies, one led by Captain Johnson, the
other by Lieutenant Maxwell. They dare not go on in the
blinding storm and darkness, fearing to lose their way,
so all that long fearful night, they tramped back and forth
in a desperate effort to save themselves from freezing.
Often the weaker ones would fall down benumbed in the
drifting snow and the stronger comrades would lift them
up and force them to keep moving.

In the morning, says Lieutenant Maxwell:

" I saw Johnson and Burkholder some distance from us, going in a
southerly direction, while we were traveling east. They were following
the directions of an old trapper, and we soon lost sight of them. Henry
Carse became unconscious during the day, and sank in the snow, blood
running from his mouth. We carried him to the river, where a fire was
started by saturating a damp wad with powder and shooting it into the
weeds. Carse was now helpless, and when we cut the rags from his feet,
the frozen skin and flesh came off with them."

As soon as the fire was well started, Maxwell and Laughlin, who were the strongest of the party, determined to
cross the river and go to the Irish colony for help. They
reached the settlement and sent assistance to their comrades, who were brought in badly frozen but alive. Major
Williams gives the following account of the sad fate of
Captain J. C. Johnson and Wm. E. Burkholder:

" G. P. Smith was the last one who saw them. He fell in with them
after they separated from their comrades and traveled with them for some
time. They were very much exhausted from wading ponds and sloughs;
their clothes frozen and covered with ice. Their feet were badly frozen,

and unable to walk farther, they finally sank down in the snow, and Smith helped them to pull off their frozen boots. They tore up a part of their blankets and wrapped them around their freezing feet, which were very painful. Smith urged them to get up and make another effort to reach the Des Moines River timber, which was in sight, but they were so chilled and exhausted by the bleak wind, frozen feet and icy clothing that they were unable to rise, and said they could go no farther. After vainly trying for a long time to get them to make another effort to reach the timber, Smith at last realized that to save his own life he must leave them. After going some distance he looked back and saw them still on their knees in the snow, apparently unable to arise. It is not likely they ever left the spot where Smith left them, but finally, overcome with cold, they sank down and perished side by side."

Eleven years after two skeletons were found near where they were last seen and identified by the guns and powder flasks lying by them as the remains of Johnson and Burkholder.*

The main body of the expedition which had gone back to the Irish colony experienced no trouble until near night of the second day's march. Having a very small supply of provisions they were put upon short allowance. The water in the river was now very high and the melting snow was filling the creeks and sloughs. When the command reached Cylinder Creek, late in the afternoon of April 4th, it had overflowed its banks and had spread out over the valley a mile in width and twelve feet deep, with a strong current in the channel. All efforts to find a place where it could be crossed failed. The wind had now suddenly changed to the northwest and it was rapidly growing cold. Captains Richards and Duncombe saw serious work and danger before them and sent Major Williams and Mr. Dawson (both of whom were old men) back to the settlement, while they sought for a way to get the men across the flooded stream. An effort was made to convert the

---

* Capt. J. C. Johnson had recently come to Webster City from Pennsylvania, a young man who was universally esteemed. His courage, patient endurance and considerate care for his men on that long fearful march, had endeared him to every member of his company

Wm. E. Burkholder had recently been elected Treasurer of Webster County and was a young man of great promise. He had cheerfully shared all the hardships of this winter campaign, volunteering to go on to the lakes to bury the dead. He was a brother of Governor Carpenter's wife.

wagon box into a raft on which to cross and with a long rope establish a ferry. But the raft was swamped as its four occupants reached the opposite shore and the rope was lost. A messenger was sent to the nearest house for help and material for a raft. Captain Richards says:

" The wind was now blowing a terrific gale and the cold was intense, so that our wet clothing was frozen stiff upon us as we traveled up and down the banks of the swollen current in a vain search for a better place for the men to cross. When help and material for a raft came, so strong and cold was the wind, and so swift the current, filled with floating ice, that all of our efforts to build a raft failed. It was now dark and still growing colder, and the roar of the blinding storm so great that we could no longer hold communication with our companions on the other side. We were benumbed with cold, utterly exhausted, and three miles from the nearest cabin. We were powerless to aid our comrades, and could only try to save ourselves. It was a terrible walk in the face of the terrific blizzard, our clothes frozen, our feet freezing, and our strength gone. After wandering in the blinding storm until nine o'clock, we fortunately found the cabin. Here we passed a night that will never be obliterated from my memory. We gathered about the fire vainly trying to dry our frozen clothing. We had no blankets, and the piercing wind was driving through every crevice of the cabin, and we walked the floor in the most intense anxiety over the fate of our companions, left on the banks of the creek, exposed to the fury of the blizzard, without shelter, food or fire. All through the night we kept looking out on the wild storm in hopes it would cease, but the cold ever grew more intense, and the wind howled more fiercely, and no one slept. We knew that Carpenter, Stratton, Stevens and Wright were men endowed with courage equal to any emergency, and we trusted they would find some way to keep the men from perishing; still a harrowing fear would come over us that we should in the morning find them frozen to death. Terrible visions of their fate tortured us through the long hours of the night, and with the first dawn of light Duncombe, Smith, Mason and I were wading through the drifts toward Cylinder Creek. The mercury was now 28 degrees below zero, and the blizzard at its wildest fury. Mason gave out and sunk down in the drifts. I got him back to the cabin and soon overtook the others. Strong ice was formed on the creek from the shore, and we hurried over it to the main channel where the current was so swift that it was too weak to bear us up. We could go no farther, could not see across for the drifting snow, and could hear no sound on the other side in answer to our loud shouts. Our faces and hands were now freezing, and we had to return to the cabin and wait until the ice should be strong enough to support us. Toward night we made another vain effort to cross, and had to return to the cabin, oppressed with the conviction that not one of our companions could survive until morning. But soon after dark three of the men came to the cabin and reported the command safe."

Governor Carpenter tells how they managed to save themselves.

" We took the covers from the wagons and some tent canvas and stretched them over the wheels and made a rude shelter. We then put all of the blankets together on the snow and crowded in, lying down close together in our wet and frozen clothing, where we remained from Saturday evening until Monday morning, with nothing to eat until we reached the Shippey cabin Monday noon. We had waited until the ice was frozen over Cylinder Creek hard enough to bear up our loaded wagons and teams. I have since marched with armies from Cairo to Atlanta and up to Richmond, sometimes traveling continuously for three or four days and nights with only a brief halt occasionally to give the exhausted soldiers a chance to boil a cup of coffee. Under burning suns, through rain, sleet and snow, we endured great suffering; but never in all the weary years could our suffering be compared with that of the two terrible days and nights we endured on the banks of Cylinder Creek."

Lieutenant Mason says:

" How we survived those fearful nights I do not know, when the mercury sunk to 34 degrees below zero the last night. The poor boys were slowly freezing, and many of them were insane; I think all of us were more or less insane the last night. The tongues of many of the men were hanging out, and the blood was running from the mouth or nose as we got up the last morning."

The command now broke up into small parties and spread out over a wide range of country. In no other way could they find food in the scanty supply the few settlers had who lived along the river. The sufferings of some of the small parties reached the last degree of endurance as they traveled on homeward. But for the help of the settlers many must have perished. All at last reached their homes, however, except Johnson and Burkholder, though many were severely frozen.

Captain Duncombe, in writing of this relief expedition thirty years afterward, says:

"For severe hardships, continuous toil, constant exposure, bodily and mental suffering, I do not believe it has ever been surpassed by men who have risked their lives to rescue their fellow men from peril and death."

CHAPTER XXVI

WHILE the events recorded in the previous chapters were transpiring, four young women, who had been dragged from their homes by the merciless savages, were cowering in the Indian camp. Soon after their repulse at the Thomas cabin the Indians loaded their ponies, squaws and captives with plunder and started westward. Mrs. Thatcher was ill of a fever and scarcely able to walk, but the savages had no mercy. She was compelled to carry a heavy load and wade through snow and ice cold water, sometimes up to her waist. At night she was forced to cut and carry wood and assist in all the camp drudgery until she often sunk fainting in the snow. When she at last could go no longer, she was lashed to the back of a pony and carried along. She bore her sufferings with great patience in the knowledge that her husband, to whom she was devotedly attached, had escaped the massacre and would do all in his power for her rescue.

On the third day the Indians discovered that they were pursued by a company of soldiers. The warriors prepared for battle, while the squaws hastily tore down the tents and hid among the willows. One Indian was left with the captive women with orders to *kill them when the attack began.* An Indian sentinel in a tree watched the soldiers and signaled their movements to the warriors.

After an hour and a half of intense excitement on the part of the Indians and captives it was known that the soldiers had turned back and abandoned the pursuit. The pursuing party was a detachment of twenty-four men, under Lieutenant Murray, which had been sent by Cap-

tain Barnard E. Bee,* from Springfield, in pursuit of the
Indians. Captain Bee had arrived from Fort Ridgely
and secured two half-breed guides for Lieutenant Murray.
They reached the grove at 3 p.m. in which the Indians had
camped the night before. Lieutenant Murray, upon examination of the camp, believed he was close upon the Indians, but the treacherous guides assured him the camp
was three days old and that further pursuit was hopeless.
Thus deceived, Murray turned back, when actually in
sight of the sentinel of the Indians who was watching his
movements. The Indians were in ambush in superior
force and the result of an attack would have been doubtful, as they were well armed. It was better that no attempt was made since the four captives would have been
massacred at once. The Indians were thoroughly alarmed
and fled for two days and nights without stopping. The
captives suffered greatly in this hurried retreat, wading
through deep snow and swollen streams, cold, hungry and
worn out, and it is a wonder they survived. Before they
reached the Big Sioux River, the horses taken from the
massacred settlers had died from starvation, their bodies
were cut up for food and the loads they had carried were
transferred to the backs of the squaws and the four white
women.

Six weeks of terrible suffering and horrors unspeakable
had been endured by the four young women when they
reached the Big Sioux River. As they were preparing to
cross an Indian came up to Mrs. Thatcher, who was carrying a heavy load, took the pack from her shoulders and
ordered her to go onto the driftwood bridge. She realized
at once that some harm was intended. She turned to her
companions and bade them " good-by," saying, " If any
of you escape, tell my dear husband that I wanted to live
for his sake." The savage drove her along before him
and when about half across seized Mrs. Thatcher and

---

* Capt. Bee was an officer of the regular army, a native of South Carolina and when
that State seceded in 1861, left the United States service and was made a Brigadier-
General. He was killed at the first battle of Bull Run.

KILLING OF MRS THATCHER
(From an Old Painting.)

hurled her into the river. With wonderful strength and courage she swam in the icy current until she reached and clung to a fallen tree on the shore. Some of the savages beat her off with clubs and with their tent poles pushed her back into the swift current. Again the brave woman swam for the opposite shore, when the merciless wretches beat her back into the rapids. As she was carried along by the current, the savages ran along the shore throwing clubs and stones at the exhausted and drowning woman, until one of the warriors raised his rifle and shot her as she clung to a ledge of driftwood. The annals of Indian cruelty nowhere record a more cowardly crime. She was but nineteen years of age, a lovely girl in the bloom of youth, who had come with her husband to make a home on the beautiful wooded shore of Okoboji. Mrs. Noble and Mrs. Thatcher had been intimate friends in their girlhood days. They had married cousins and together had moved to the distant frontier with bright anticipations of long, happy lives in each other's society. Now, as Mrs. Noble closed her eyes to shut out the horror of the dying struggles of her dearest friend, and thought of her murdered husband, child, father, mother, brothers and sister, she felt that death alone could relieve her hopeless anguish. That night she begged Abbie and Mrs. Marble to go with her and end their sufferings beneath the dark waters of the river, where her last dear friend had perished. From that day Mrs. Noble seemed weary of life and anxious to end the horrors that every night brought to the captives.

When news of the massacre of the settlers at the lakes and the capture of four women reached the Indian Agency on Yellow Medicine River, the agent, Charles E. Flandreau, with S. R. Riggs and Dr. Thos. Williamson, missionaries, began to devise plans for the rescue of the captives. Two friendly Indians had visited the Sioux camp, had there seen the three captive women and at once opened negotiations for their purchase. They finally suc-

ceeded in purchasing Mrs. Marble. On the morning of
May 6th, she learned that she had been sold by Ink-pa-du-
tah to two strange Indians. She bade her companions a
sorrowful good-by. Mrs. Marble assured them that if she
should reach a white settlement she would do all in her
power for their rescue. Mrs. Marble was taken to the
Agency at Yellow Medicine where, after several weeks, she
was ransomed by Mr. Riggs and Dr. Williamson, who paid
the Indians $1,000 for her release, which sum had been
raised by Major Flandreau. Mrs. Marble at once did
everything in her power to effect the rescue of her two
surviving companions. Major Flandreau was also untiring in their behalf.

The Minnesota Legislature promptly appropriated $10,-
000 to be used by the Governor for the rescue of the captives. Large rewards were offered to friendly Indians
and volunteers came forward at once. Major Flandreau
procured an outfit and, on the 23d of May, a party started
with orders to purchase the captive women at any price.
Four companies of soldiers were to be marched at once
from Fort Ridgely, as near Ink-pa-du-tah's camp as was
prudent, to fall upon the Sioux as soon as the captives
were secured and exterminate the perpetrators of the massacre, if possible. But as the troops were ready to start,
orders came for them to join General Johnston's Utah
expedition and Ink-pa-du-tah's band thus escaped punishment. While these events were transpiring, the two captive women were being taken farther into the wilds of Dakota and were hopeless of rescue.

One evening after the two women had gone to their tent,
Roaring Cloud, a son of the chief, came in and ordered
Mrs. Noble to come with him to his tepee. She indignant-
ly refused to go. He seized her and attempted to drag her
off. She resisted with all of her strength, determined then
and there to end her wretched life, rather than again submit to the horrors from which there was no other escape.
She alone of the helpless captives had often resisted the

ABBIE GARDNER SHARP

brutal savages, until her strength was exhausted and she was overpowered. Since the cruel murder of her friend, Mrs. Thatcher, she had felt life a burden. This night she nerved herself to welcome death. Wild with rage at her unyielding resistance, the young savage dragged her out of the tent, seized a club in his mad fury, beat her head again and again, leaving her mangled form by the door. For half an hour her dying moans reached the ears of the terrified girl, Abbie, who was cowering in a corner, now alone in the hands of the savages.

The next morning the Indians cut off the two dark heavy braids of hair from the head of the murdered woman, fastened them to a stick, and followed Abbie, switching her face with them, thus adding to her agony. Hurrying on day after day they reached the James River, where Ashton now stands. Here was an Indian village of about two thousand Sioux and Abbie abandoned all hope of rescue. But powerful friends were at work, spurred on by the urgent entreaties of Mrs. Marble. Major Flandreau had procured Indian goods of great value to tempt them and selected three of the most trusty of the race to proceed with all possible haste to overtake Ink-pa-du-tah's band. John Other Day led the party and, on the 30th of May, reached the vicinity of the Sioux encampment, secreting the team and wagon. Entering the village he and his men soon learned that there was but one white woman remaining. After three days' negotiations they succeeded in purchasing Miss Gardner. They took her to St. Paul, delivered her to Governor Medary and received $1,200 for their faithful services in rescuing the last of the surviving captives. The two women who were rescued never recovered from the brutal treatment they endured from the Indians while in captivity. While their lives were spared, their suffering, bodily and mentally, could only end with death. Abbie never saw Mrs. Marble after her release from captivity but found Mr. Thatcher and conveyed to him the last message of his young wife and the

full particulars of her sad fate. At Hampton she found
her sister, Eliza, who made her escape from the Springfield massacre. In 1885 Abbie Gardner Sharp wrote and
published a full history of the massacre and her captivity,
from which many of the facts here given were procured.

In all the narratives of Indian wars and barbarities
that, for more than two hundred years, have marked the
advance of civilization across the American continent,
there are no pages in the bloody record more thrilling or
pathetic than those recording the horrors which exterminated the first colony planted on the shores of Okoboji
and Spirit Lakes. Of all the horrors endured by white
women in Indian captivity, none have surpassed those of
Elizabeth Thatcher, Lydia Noble, Abbie Gardner and
Margaret A. Marble.

A son of Si-dom-i-na-do-tah (who was murdered with
his family by Henry Lott, the desperado) saved the lives
of one family. John B. Skinner, who had settled at the
lakes, often befriended this boy, Josh, who was badly
wounded at the time his father and family were massacred
by Lott and his son. The boy recovered and at times
found a home at Skinner's. When his uncle, Ink-pa-du-
tah, planned his raid for a terrible vengeance on the whites,
Josh learned that the blow was to fall on the innocent, isolated colony at the lakes. He warned Skinner of danger,
and so impressed it upon him, that Mr. Skinner moved
back to Liberty and escaped the fate which befell his
neighbors. Whether Mr. Skinner warned any others of
the danger is not known. Josh also warned Mr. Carter,
of Emmet County, of the impending massacre, and spent
a part of the winter in Kossuth County. He was seen and
recognized by Mrs. J. B. Thomas as one of the leaders in
the attack upon their house at Springfield. He was undoubtedly engaged in the massacre at the lakes.

In 1862 Josh was one of the most active in the terrible
Minnesota massacres, leading a band at Lake Shetek,
which exterminated nearly the entire settlement. Thus

can be traced back to Henry Lott's fearful crime, the primary cause leading to the bloody retribution visited upon the innocent, as the attack was led by surviving relatives of Si-dom-i-na-do-tah. Forty-one innocent men, women and children were the direct victims, while the suffering of the captives, relatives and members of the Relief Expedition make up a record of horror and misery seldom surpassed.

It can never be known how many of the Indians were killed but the soldiers and friendly Indians, under Major Flandreau and Lieutenant Murray, killed Roaring Cloud, the murderer of Mrs. Noble and three other members of Ink-pa-du-tah's band. It is probable that several were killed by Dr. Herriott, Snyder and Mattocks and two or three in the battle at the Thomas house. Ink-pa-du-tah's party was among the most ferocious of the butchers in the Minnesota massacres of 1862 and it is not unlikely that some of them were among the Indians who were killed, or the thirty who were hung at Mankato. Ink-pa-du-tah was last heard of among the Sioux who fled to the far West pursued by General Sibley's army in 1863.

On the 12th of April, 1857, Major Williams made a lengthy report to Governor Grimes of the Relief Expedition under his command from which the following extracts are made:

"Being called upon by the frontier settlers for aid in checking the horrible outrages committed upon the citizens living on the Little Sioux River at the Spirit Lake settlements, and in Emmet County, by the Sioux Indians, by authority you invested in me, I raised, organized and armed three companies of thirty men each, which were as we proceeded increased to thirty-seven men each. By forced marches through snowdrifts from fifteen to twenty feet deep, and swollen streams, we made our way up to the State line. Never was harder service rendered by any body of men than by the one hundred and ten volunteers under my command. We had to ford streams breast deep every few miles, and often to drag by band with ropes our wagons, horses and oxen through deep ravines drifted even full of snow. Wet all day to our waists, we had to lie out on the open prairie without tents, wrapped in blankets in the snow. Eighty miles out we met the survivors of the massacre at Springfield, nineteen men, women and children. We found them in a wretched condition, destitute of food, three of them wounded. They had fled in the night, thinly clad; several of the women without bonnets or shoes wading through snow and water waist deep carrying their crying children. They had eaten nothing for two days and could hardly have survived another night. We built fires in a small grove near by, supplied their wants, our surgeons dressed their wounds and sent a party to convey them to the Irish settlement, where a blockhouse was being erected for defense against the Indians.

" We pushed on, throwing out thirty scouts in advance to examine the groves and streams for signs of Indians, which were often found. At the State line we camped in a grove, where I detailed sixty men, armed with rifles and revolvers, to march all night in two divisions to surprise the Indians before daylight. Our guides reported Indians camped at the trading house of a half-breed named Gaboo. But we found they had fled at the approach of the fifty regulars from Fort Ridgely.

" Finding the troops from Fort Ridgely had not buried the dead, I detailed twenty-five men under Captain Johnson and Lieutenant Maxwell to march to the lakes and perform that sad duty. They found and buried thirty-one bodies, including the bones of those burned in the Mattocks house. Seven were killed at Springfield. I may sum up the total number of casualties to the settlers as follows: killed, 41; missing, 12; badly wounded, 3; prisoners, 4 women. At every place the Indians broke up and destroyed the furniture, burned houses and killed in all more than one hundred head of cattle. It seems to have been their purpose to exterminate the entire settlement in that region. Too much praise cannot be bestowed on the men under my command. Fourteen were badly frozen; Captain Johnson and William E. Burkholder perished in a terrible snow storm. Several men were deranged from their sufferings. We have a host of destitute and wounded persons thrown upon us to provide for, both from the Little Sioux River and the upper Des Moines, besides our own frozen and disabled men.

" We have driven all of the Indians out of the north part of the State, unless there may be some near the mouth of the Big Sioux."

In Governor Grimes' message to the Seventh General Assembly, on the 12th of January, 1858, is a statement of the massacre and the Relief Expedition under Major Williams' command, and he recommends that the State make an appropriation to compensate the men " who so gallantly and humanely periled their lives for others;" and for the expense of their outfit.

He further says:

"I submit to the General Assembly whether some public recognition of
the noble gallantry and untimely death of Captain Johnson and W. E.
Burkholder is not alike due to their memory and to the gratitude of the
State."

CHAPTER XXVII

IN early days, before Iowa Territory was organized, Bellevue, in Jackson County, became infested with men of disreputable character, who were guilty of many crimes and gave that locality a bad reputation.

In 1857 a party of immigrants landed in Bellevue, claiming to have come from Michigan. They had considerable property, consisting of good teams, wagons, household furniture and money. The land had not yet been surveyed and the only titles were claims held by the occupants. But as these were respected by all reputable persons and protected by rigid claim laws, towns were laid out on these claims, lots and blocks staked off and recorded, which were bought and sold with as much confidence in the claim titles as ever existed in later years after titles had been secured from Government sales and patents.

The leader of this Michigan colony was W. W. Brown, a man of intelligence and engaging manners. He built a hotel and was elected a magistrate. He was liberal and charitable, always ready to assist the unfortunate and soon became one of the leading citizens of the new town.

He employed a number of men in various enterprises and it was soon discovered that a large amount of counterfeit money was in circulation. Upon investigation it was in almost all cases traced to some employee of Mr. Brown. Citizens on both sides of the river began to lose horses, and it was discovered that some of them were found sheltered in the vicinity of Bellevue. Many horses were brought into the town by strangers and exchanged for other horses which were brought by other strangers, who claimed to have come from Wisconsin and northern Illinois.

It was ultimately discovered that Bellevue was the headquarters of a large gang of counterfeiters and horse
thieves who had confederates scattered through portions
of Wisconsin, northern Illinois and extending down the
Mississippi River into Missouri. The large body of timber in Jackson County, known as the "Big Woods," made
an almost secure place for secreting stolen property.
There were stations extending through Jones, Cedar,
Johnson, Mahaska, Scott, Louisa and Lee counties.
Brown's hotel was one of the stations and it was there
that a battle was fought in 1840 that went far for a time
to banish the boldest of the gang from Jackson County.
Among the desperadoes who belonged to the gang were
William Fox, Aaron and John Long, Richard Baxter,
Granville Young and Mr. Birch, all of whom were afterward concerned in the robbery and murder of Colonel
George Davenport. On the 8th of January, 1840, many
of the citizens of Bellevue were attending a ball given to
celebrate the anniversary of the Battle of New Orleans.
James Thompson got several members of the gang of desperadoes together and robbed the residence of J. C. Mitchell, and grossly abused a young lady who was the only
person in the house. She recognized Thompson in the
struggle and after a desperate resistance made her escape
to the ball-room and gave the alarm. Mitchell armed himself and started out to find Thompson. They met in the
street. Thompson fired first and missed. Mitchell sent a
bullet through his heart before he could fire again and the
desperado fell dead. Brown hastily gathered members of
his gang and they swore vengeance on Mitchell, whose
friends armed themselves and standing at the head of the
stairs awaited the attack. A number of shots were exchanged, when Brown's party retreated, and going to a
saloon nearby formed a plot to blow up Mitchell's house
and destroy him and his family. They broke into a store
and secured a tin can holding fifteen pounds of gun
powder. The can was placed in the cellar by William Fox,

HEADQUARTERS OF BROWN'S BANDITTI
Erected in 1837 near Bellevue in Jackson County

and in casting lots to determine who should apply the slow match it fell to Mr. Chichester. Fortunately a gap had been left in strewing the powder and thus the can was not reached by the fire, and a terrible tragedy was narrowly averted.

The citizens now became thoroughly aroused and began to organize for mutual protection and the arrest and conviction of the members of the gang. A consultation was held in Dubuque, at which there were present Sheriff W. A. Warren of Jackson County, James Crawford, the prosecuting attorney, and Judge Thomas S. Wilson. A warrant was issued, charging W. W. Brown, William Fox and Aaron Long and twenty others as confederates, with theft, robbery, passing counterfeit money and other crimes. As soon as it became known to Brown's gang that warrants were out for their arrest they armed themselves and swore that they would resist to the last extremity.

Captain Warren called to his assistance a posse of about forty determined men, and all, well armed, marched to Brown's hotel, where the gang had decided to give battle to the sheriff and his party. The squad moved in double file and as it arrived within thirty paces of the hotel Captain Warren gave the order "charge," and the men sprang forward, quickly surrounding the house. Brown was seen standing at the head of his men with a rifle raised to his shoulder. Warren demanded instant surrender, and as Brown's rifle was lowered it was discharged and his men opened fire generally, wounding several citizens, one fatally. The sheriff's men returned the fire and Brown fell dead. His gang fought desperately for fifteen minutes as the posse forced an entrance and drove them up the stairs where a hand to hand struggle with gun barrels, pitchforks and bowie knives continued. Finding it impossible to force a barricade on the stairs, Captain Warran gave the command to fire the house. Before the fire reached the second story the gang began to escape by jumping from a window to a shed in the rear.

Thirteen of them were captured as they leaped down and fled, while six escaped. The sheriff's party lost four men killed and seven wounded. Three of the gang were killed and several wounded.

Fox, Long and Chichester were among the prisoners and when the battle was ended and the wives and children of the slain citizens were weeping over the mangled remains of the husbands and fathers, a fierce cry arose, "hang them." Ropes were quickly thrown round their necks when they begged and pleaded in the most abject manner for their lives.

The venerable Colonel Cox mounted a box and urged the citizens to let the law take its course, pledging his word that the fate of the prisoners should be determined by a majority of the citizens when they had time to deliberate.

A strong guard was placed over the prisoners while the leading citizens retired to the residence of James L. Kirkpatrick to determine their fate. A long and heated discussion then ensued between the advocates of the execution of the desperadoes and the more merciful who favored whipping. Colonel Cox presided over the deliberations and it was finally determined to take a vote on the penalty and every man pledged himself to abide the decision of the majority. Two men were selected to conduct the ballot. They secured two boxes, one of which contained white and colored beans. Two more were chosen to pass the box around. Each person present was told to put one of the beans in the empty box; white meant hanging and colored meant whipping. The prisoners were present trembling and begging for mercy. The venerable chairman commanded order and a deathlike silence ensued. One by one the unique ballots were silently dropped into the box until all had voted. The result was handed to the chairman who commanded the prisoners to rise and hear the verdict. Colonel Cox then called upon all present who would pledge themselves to abide the pending decision to rise. Every man arose. There was three majority for whipping. It now developed upon the chairman to pass sentence upon each of the prisoners by deciding how many lashes he should receive. The chairman then proceeded to give the culprits their quota and warn them that they were to leave the State as soon as each sentence was executed and, he added, " if you ever return you will be promptly hanged." Executioners were appointed to lay on the lash and when the ordeal was ended the cowering, groaning wretches were placed in skiffs with three days' rations and sent down the river. Fox, the smoothest villain of the gang, used his tongue to such effect as to get off with the lightest punishment; and after several years of criminal career planned and helped to perpetrate the murder of Colonel Davenport.

The banditti were also numerous in Rock Island, Carroll and Ogle counties, in Illinois, and their haunts extended across the State into Indiana. In many localities their sympathizers were strong enough to control elections and choose justices of the peace, constables and sheriffs from members of the gang. In Ogle County, Illinois, they burned the court-house and jail, released criminals, destroyed court records and organized a reign of terror.

On the Fourth of July, 1854, Colonel George Davenport was at home alone on Rock Island. He was known to be wealthy and was supposed to keep large sums of money in his house. Five members of the banditti were chosen to rob his house. They were secreted on the island several days taking observations and on the morning of the Fourth saw the members of Colonel Davenport's family cross to Stephenson (now Rock Island) to attend the celebration. They hastened to force an entrance into the house and shot the colonel as he was seated in his chair, found the key to his safe, procured six hundred dollars, the family jewelry and fled into the heavy timber. For many weeks no trace of the murderers could be obtained, when

Edward Bonney, a fearless officer, determined to ferret
out the perpetrators of the crime. Disguising himself,
and knowing some members of the banditti, he passed himself off to their confederates as a member of the gang.
In that guise he soon learned that Fox, Birch, John Long
and Richard Baxter were the murderers. One by one he
ran them down, arresting one at a time until he had all of
them in jail. Aaron Long and Granville Young were arrested as accessories. Birch turned State's evidence, escaped from jail and was recaptured. Baxter was convicted and died in the penitentiary, while Granville Young,
John and Aaron Long were executed after making a confession. For a time the banditti sought other parts of the
country for their depredations.

During the next ten years fifteen murders were committed in Jackson and Clinton counties, and in all but
one case the murderers escaped punishment. Lawyers
found a way to secure the acquittal of their clients or they
escaped from jail and it seemed impossible to punish crime
through the courts.

A particularly atrocious murder was committed in
March, 1857, where a citizen, John Ingle, was murdered
by Alexander Gifford for parties who paid Gifford to do
the deed. He was arrested and lodged in jail at Andrew
to await his trial. The impression prevailed that his attorney would secure his acquittal and the citizens, exasperated by the continued escape of the guilty, secretly organized a "Vigilance Committee." One afternoon, about
three weeks after the murder, a hundred men marched
into Andrew, battered down the door of the jail with
sledges, took Gifford from his cell, placed a rope around
his neck, threw the other end over the limb of a tree, and
called upon the prisoner to confess. The trembling
wretch, hoping to receive lighter punishment by a full
confession, told the story of the crime. He said that he
had been hired by Henry Jarret and David McDonald to
put Ingle out of the way and had received $150 for doing

so. But the confession only sealed his doom. There could now be no doubt of his guilt, and strong men grasped the rope and quickly put an end to his career of crime. His confederates escaped, as no legal evidence could be secured to corroborate the confession of the murderer.

The citizens of Jackson and several adjacent counties now assembled in conference and effected an oath-bound organization for the purpose of ridding the State of the remaining members of the gang of desperadoes who were stealing horses, robbing houses and farms and circulating counterfeit money. In 1854 a cruel murder had been committed by a Mr. Barger, in Jackson County, whose wife had secured a divorce from him.

He went one dark night to the house where she was living with her children, and watching until she came to the door, shot her dead with his rifle. He was seen by a neighbor running from the scene of the murder, was arrested and tried three times, always convicted, but through the skill of William E. Leffingwell, the best lawyer in the county, secured rehearings and new trials on technicalities, finally got a change of venue to Clinton County, and was removed to the De Witt jail to await another trial. The respectable citizens became thoroughly exasperated at the continued thwarting of justice and determined to take the punishment into their own hands. On the 28th of May, 1857, more than three years after the murder, the "Vigilance Committee" to the number of fifty assembled at the jail, secured the keys, took the murderer back to Andrew and hanged him to the same tree upon which Gifford had been executed.

Soon after this affair the members of the "Vigilance Committee" sent a statement of their object and purpose to the Jackson *Sentinel* for publication, from which the following extracts are taken:

"We, the Vigilance Committee of Jackson County, are determined that the criminal laws of the State shall be enforced to the very letter. When our legal officers neglect their duty, we will spare no pains either of time, life or property to secure the punishment of all guilty of horse stealing, counterfeiting or murder; and we will be governed by the penal laws of the State so far as it is convenient.

" We further warn all officers that they must not commence proceedings of any kind against those who helped to hang Gifford or Barger, as we believe they should have been hung long before they were.

" We will avenge the unjust death of any member of the Committee at the cost of life or property.

" We will further punish with death any person joining this Committee whom we find has been or is concerned in horse stealing, counterfeiting, robbery or murder, and all spies will share the same fate."

It was ascertained that not less than seven hundred citizens of the counties of Jackson, Jones, Clinton, Scott, Cedar and Johnson were members of this organization. They were bound together by the most solemn oaths to stand by each other under all circumstances and permit no member to be arrested or subjected to punishment for any acts of the committee.

For fifteen years the law had seemed to be powerless to effectually protect peaceable people in person or property in this region and the most atrocious crimes generally went unpunished. The members of the gang of desperadoes usually lived in sparsely settled sections among the brush and timber lands bordering on the Maquoketa, Wapsipinicon, Cedar and Iowa rivers and their numerous tributaries. Every member knew where the log cabins of their confederates were located, and that they would be sheltered and the stolen property secreted until it could be disposed of at places distant from where it was taken. Thus banded together in the perpetration of crime, with witnesses always ready to prove an alibi, there was small chance of punishment.

Early in the " '50's " there was living on Camp Creek, in Polk County, a man by the name of J. W. Thomas, who was usually called by his neighbors " Comequick." He was the terror of the entire settlement. He took long trips to the eastern part of the State and often returned with plenty of money and good horses. He never was known to work and no one doubted that he was a member of the gang of desperadoes so numerous in the Mississippi Valley. He frequently changed his residence and no one dared to offend him as he was known to be a reckless and dangerous man. In 1852 he robbed an old man living on Camp Creek of $1,000 that was kept in his cabin. He was arrested by Lewis Todhunter and Dr. Sellers and lodged in jail. But some of his confederates were on the grand jury and prevented an indictment being found against him and he was released.

In September, 1856, a young man and his wife stopped at the Nine Mile House, near Oskaloosa, took dinner and inquired for a good piece of land. They said they had a thousand dollars with which to purchase a farm. Old Mr. Thomas ('' Comequick ''), who was present, said he lived near Des Moines and knew a farm that would suit them. The young man and his wife were traveling in an emigrant wagon and Thomas started off with them on horseback to take them to the farm. Nothing more was seen of them until about two weeks later when the bodies of the man and wife were found, hidden in shocks of corn near the Skunk River, in Poweshiek County. A brother of the murdered woman procured a description of ''Comequick,'' and, after a long search found him, with the stolen wagon and horses which he had sold. He was arrested and lodged in jail, but afterward released on bail through the efforts of M. M. Crocker, of Des Moines, whom he had secured as his attorney with the stolen money. When the time for trial came his attorney secured a continuance to the next term.

When the case was called up next term Crocker secured a change of venue. The principal witness was the brother of the murdered woman, who lived in Illinois, and had spent all the money he could raise in hunting the criminal and trying to bring him to justice. The murder was so atrocious that intense excitement prevailed in that region and more than 2,000 citizens had gathered at

Montezuma to hear the trial. When Judge Stone
granted a change of venue the rage of the people was intense. The brother of the murdered woman mounted a
log and said to the crowd of excited men:

" I was willing the man should have a fair trial. I have followed his
trail for weeks until I at last discovered one of the stolen horses; then
after a short time I found where he sold the wagon and other horse.
Finally I caught the man and brought him here and he was released on
bail. When the time for trial arrived 1 came here again to testify, and
the lawyer got the case continued. Now I have come again and they have
got a change of venue. I have spent every cent I have in the world and I
can't come again. Gentlemen, that villain up there—pointing to the court
room—butchered my sister and hid her in a corn shock, and his lawyer is
going to get him cleared next time because I have nothing left to pay my
expenses here again. Will you let that murderer get cleared when I cannot come to tell the horrid story to the jury? " He paused a moment, while
a mighty shout went up. " No; never! "

They made a wild rush for the court room, dragged the
struggling wretch to the nearest tree, put the rope around
his neck and raised his writhing body high in the air,
where it was left until cut down for the coroner's inquest.

During the years of 1855-56-57 many horses were stolen
from the farmers of Jackson, Jones, Clinton, Scott, Cedar
and Johnson counties. The settlers at that time possessed but little property, many being in debt for their
land, paying in most cases from twelve to twenty-five per
cent. interest on their indebtedness. Prices of farm products brought little and they were working hard and econ-
omizing in every possible way to support their families,
improve their farms and meet their obligations. Good
horses were worth from $200 to $300 a team and the loss
of a horse or team, at that time, meant deep distress, and
often left the farmer without means to cultivate his land
or save his crops. Many arrests were made, but the employment of the best lawyers and the testimony of other
members of the gang were almost sure to prevent conviction. This emboldened the thieves to continue their depredations, and finally many of the farmers determined to

join the " Vigilance Committees " and take the arrests, trials and punishment of the thieves into their own hands. The persons who resorted to such remedies became known as " Regulators " and eventually a large majority of the farmers in the section infested by the thieves became members of the organizations.

The little town of Big Rock was for some time the headquarters of the " Regulators." It was situated in the northwestern part of Scott County and close to the Clinton County line, about three miles from Clam Shell Ford, on the Wapsipinicon River. Here many of the meetings were held and plans formed for hunting down the thieves. No records were kept of the proceedings and no member of the organization has ever been known to divulge the names of the members, or make a full revelation of their transactions. Hence it is difficult to give a reliable history of the terrible punishment they inflicted upon sus- pected persons who fell into their hands.

Alonzo Page was a young married man, who lived near the east line of Cedar County, about two miles east of the present town of Lowden, in what was called " the barrens." His cabin was built of logs and was surrounded by scrub oak trees, near which was a small clearing cultivated by him. He was an intelligent, industrious young man, often working out among his neighbors in haying and harvest. He had in some way incurred the enmity of a Mr. Corry, living on Rock Creek and soon after the Regulators were organized, this man caused a report to be circulated that Page was connected with a gang of horse thieves. Acting upon this report in June, 1857, a party of Regulators rode to the Page cabin and notified him to leave the country. When informed of the charge against him, Page solemnly protested against the attempt to drive him from his home and declared that he was innocent of the charge. He was again warned to leave the country by a certain time or take the consequences. He consulted with some of his neighbors after the Regulators had gone and they advised him to remain and pay no attention to the threat.

One dark night some time after the expiration of the date fixed by the Regulators for him to leave, Mr. Page heard the tramp of horses near his cabin and the furious barking of his dog. He hastily barred the door, looking out of the window, saw strange men riding up near the house. Soon raps came on the door and a request for admission. He inquired who was there and what was wanted, but received no satisfaction. He could now see from the window that the house was surrounded by armed horsemen. Mrs. Page was very ill and greatly alarmed for her husband's safety. The pounding on the door continned with threats that it would be broken down unless opened. Mr. Page told the mob of his wife's condition and that no strangers could come into the house. He realized his danger, remembering the threats made on his life when warned to leave the country, and prepared to defend himself and protect his wife to the last. He loaded his double-barreled gun with buckshot and warned the Regulators to leave or take the consequences. After further parleying the door was broken down and Page stepped to the opening to fire upon the crowd. As soon as he stepped in sight a rifle ball pierced his body and he fell in the doorway mortally wounded. The Regulators then retreated leaving the dying man and his frantic wife. It was not believed that the Regulators engaged in this tragic affair intended to deliberately kill Mr. Page, and it was charged that the fatal shot was fired by his personal enemy, who instigated the raid on his house. The Regulators were led to believe that Page was connected with the horse thieves and expected to be able to drive him out of the country, but the young man, conscious of his own innocence, refused to be driven from his home and died in its defense.

The next victim was Peter Conklin, who had committed many crimes in Johnson County and was believed to be a prominent member of the gang of horse thieves. A band of Regulators was scouring the country near Yankee Run, in Cedar County, on the 27th of June, and came upon Conklin in the woods on horseback. He fled, was pursued, overtaken, shot down and instantly killed. There was little doubt that he was a desperado of a very dangerous character.

Charles Clute, a carpenter, living on a farm nine miles northeast of Tipton, fell under suspicion and suffered persecution, if not death, at the hands of the Regulators. He married the daughter of Mrs. J. D. Denson, a widow, and for several years attended to her business. They kept a hotel and carried on the farm. The widow finally married J. A. Warner and the two men worked harmoniously together at farming, building and hotel keeping. One day in the winter of 1856, a peddler, named Johnson, stopped at the Denson House, and becoming blockaded by a snow storm, remained several days. Some months later Johnson came to the Denson House with a good team, and left it to be sold by Mr. Clute. Johnson was arrested some time later for stealing horses in Wisconsin, taken to that State and lodged in the jail. As Mr. Clute had sold the horses for Johnson, he was charged by some of his neighbors with harboring horse thieves. He was arrested, but no evidence could be found against him and he was released. One night a gang of men called upon him, took him to the woods and gave him a terrible whipping. He was then released and returned home. Late in the summer Mr. Clute was again arrested, charged with assisting Johnson in disposing of stolen horses. But there was no evidence produced against him when the time for trial came and he was again discharged. After the organization of the Regulators, in 1857, a body of them seized Clute and Warner, who were building a house in Scott County, claiming to have a warrant for them. They were taken across the Wapsipinicon at Clam Shell Ford, and given a trial by the Regulators in the woods near the residence of

Bennett Warren, who was also a prisoner in their hands.
As in all previous arrests there was no evidence whatever
against them, but the Regulators decreed they must leave
the country. They were compelled to witness the hanging of old Mr. Warren; then taken back to Big Rock, kept
over night at Goddard's tavern and terrified into promising to leave the country. In a few days Clute disappeared
and was never seen or heard of even by his family. It
was afterward proved by Johnson that Clute was in no
way implicated with him in horse stealing, and there is
little doubt that he was entirely innocent of all charges
made against him. It was believed by his friends that he
never got out of Scott County, but was made way with by
the Regulators. On the other hand, many believed that
Mr. Clute had become convinced that his life was in continual danger from the Regulators, and that his only safety
was in going to some distant State.

In 1857 there was living in Clinton County, near the
Wapsipinicon River, about four miles northeast of Wheat-
land, a farmer named Bennett Warren. He was about
sixty years of age and an old settler in that section. He
kept a sort of public house, entertaining travelers. Persons strongly suspected of belonging to gangs of horse
thieves and counterfeiters often stopped at his house, and
it was believed by many that Mr. Warren was in some
way connected with these law breakers. The Regulators
had organized for the express purpose of breaking up
and bringing to swift punishment these bands of horse
thieves.

On the 24th of June, 1857, several hundred of the Regulators gathered at Big Rock in Scott County and marched
into Clinton County to Warren's house. They took him to
a grove near by to select a jury of twelve men from their
number, R. H. Randall, a well-known citizen of Clinton
County, presiding over the court thus constituted.
Charges were preferred against Mr. Warren of harboring horse thieves knowing them to be such; keeping and

secreting stolen horses knowing them to be such; passing counterfeit money knowing it to be such. Mr. Warren had no voice in the selection of a jury, was given no time or opportunity to prepare for defense and no chance to procure counsel to aid or advise him. Witnesses were called and sworn to convict, but none in his defense. It is not strange that after such a trial the jury found him to be guilty of all the charges. The chairman then called upon all who were in favor of punishing him to step to one side of the road. The vote was unanimous for punishment. Then came the vote on the nature of the punishment—shall the prisoner be whipped or "hung." The vote was taken in the same way as before.

The accounts disagree as to what followed. The History of Clinton County says:

"At first the majority was largely for the milder punishment. Those who favored the extreme measure said, 'What satisfaction will there be in whipping the old, gray-headed man? What good will come of it? We are here to make an example that will protect our property and deter others from these crimes.'"

As the argument progressed one by one and in knots of twos and threes, the people passed over the road so fateful to the doomed man who was a silent witness to these proceedings, until a clear majority stood for the death sentence. A rope was placed around Warren's neck and he was asked if he had anything to say. His only response was, "I am an old man and you can't cheat me out of many years." The rope was thrown over a limb, men seized it and amid silence the signal was given and Bennett Warren was ushered into eternity. The body was taken down and carried to the house and left with his agonized and terror-stricken wife and children.

R. H. Randall, of Spring Rock, one of the best known and most respectable citizens of Clinton County, gives the following items relating to the Warren tragedy:

"Many of the people of Scott, Cedar, Clinton, Jones and Jackson counties had become convinced 'that no horse thieves could be convicted in the courts, and from four to five hundred of the most respectable men of these counties assembled at the various meetings to devise measures to rid the country of these law breakers. I presided at most of these meetings, including the one at Warren's. When the jury found Warren guilty, the question arose, 'What shall be done with him?' Many motions were made and voted down, when someone moved that he be hung. When the vote on this motion was to be taken, I requested all who were in favor of hanging to walk over to the east side of the road, and all opposed to hanging should go to the west side. Only a few went on the west side. I was astonished and did not endorse the decision. I got upon a wagon and began to tell my reasons for opposing their vote as best I could for about ten minutes, and was making many changes of votes when a man came to me and said, 'Randall, if you don't stop that you will be shot inside of five minutes.' I replied, 'One murder is enough,' and ran out of sight. I am not ashamed of anything I did that day, so you may use my name."

Edward Soper was a young man living three miles southeast of Tipton, and Alonzo Gleason was staying at various places in that vicinity, having no regular occupation. In the spring of 1857 these two young men, in company with three other bad characters, stole a valuable horse belonging to Charles Pennygrot, who lived two miles from Lowden. With this horse and another they had stolen from near Solon, they started for Illinois to dispose of the property. By traveling nights and avoiding the public roads, they escaped without detection, crossing the Mississippi and going on to the Illinois River. Here they sold the horses and after some weeks returned to Cedar County to resume their stealing. But the citizens became aroused and caused their arrest by the sheriff. They were taken to the old court-house at Tipton on the 2d of July, confined in a room on the ground floor, guarded by twenty men selected by the sheriff, John Byerly. About midnight a large body of Regulators overpowered the guard, seized the prisoners and conveyed them to a grove on the farm of Martin Henry, south of Lowden. The Regulators came from all directions, generally armed, until more than two hundred had gathered. They organized a court, and selected a jury to try the prisoners, who stood surrounded by determined-looking men and trembling with fear. They remembered the terrible fate of Page and Warren and had little hope of escaping the same fearful punishment. After the evidence was presented the jury brought in the verdict—" Guilty! "

Then in the hope that their lives might be spared, the two men confessed their guilt, and told of the particulars of the theft of the last horses taken, and where they had been sold. But there was no mercy for them and the death sentence was sanctioned by a large majority. Very little time was given them, although Soper broke down and begged piteously for mercy. Gleason was firm and reckless to the last. Ropes were fastened around their necks, they were placed in a wagon beneath the white oak tree that was used for the gallows. A score of men caught the ropes and the wagon was drawn from under them, leaving two more victims of the Regulators.

The law abiding people now began to denounce these lynchings, the killing of men for stealing and in some cases without evidence of guilt. It was felt that no citizen was safe, when suspicion could be aroused by personal enemies and innocent men be executed to gratify malice. The lawless acts of the Regulators were denounced and efforts were made to stop the crimes of armed bands called Regulators. A determined effort was made by Judge Tuthill, of Cedar County, to secure the indictment and arrest of the known leaders but so threatening were the demonstrations that the witnesses and jurors were notified that such action would imperil their lives. Citizens who denounced the deeds of Regulators were threatened, and for several months there was a reign of terror prevailing in that section of the State. Those who approved of the lawless acts, together with the large number engaged in them, were a vast majority of the citizens and it soon became apparent that they would not tolerate the punishment of any who had participated in the lynchings.

The last victim was a farmer of Jones County, named
Hiram Roberts. He had long been suspected of being connected with the horse thieves, as he frequently made visits
in Cedar County among the bad characters. On the last
of October, 1857, Roberts went to James W. Hanlin's,
four miles northwest of Tipton. The Regulators, hearing of his visit, quietly notified a large number of the
members, who, at a time fixed by the leaders, gathered at
Hanlin's and captured Roberts. He was taken over the
line into Jones County and placed in a barn belonging to
George Saum. Here he was left in charge of several men
who had been engaged in his capture, while the others retired to some distance for consultation. After a short
time a young man from Cedar County, fearing that another tragedy was about to be enacted, refused to be a
party to the crime and went to the barn to get his horse to
ride home. Upon opening the door he was horrified to see
Roberts suspended by the neck from a beam overhead and
writhing in the agonies of death. It was soon learned that
the men left in charge of the prisoner, while waiting for
the result of the consultation, had tried, condemned, sentenced and executed the helpless victim. Six of the prominent actors in the tragedy were arrested and bound over
to appear at the next term of court at Anamosa. In the
meantime witnesses were got out of the way, friends of
the accused were on the grand jury and, as the prisoners
appeared at court, surrounded by several hundred armed
Regulators, no indictments were found and the perpetrators of the crime escaped punishment as had all of their
confederates. While public opinion was largely on the
side of the Regulators, there was a minority of the best
citizens who were firmly opposed to their defiance of law
and to the summary lynching of persons accused of crimes.
Their influence was making a strong impression in the
community against the lawless acts of the Regulators.

In view of the danger of severe punishment that might
be inflicted upon them, a number of Regulators under-

took to intimidate the most active advocates of legal trial for all charged with crime. Canada McCollough, a near neighbor of Alonzo Page (who was killed by the Regulators), one of the most highly esteemed citizens of Cedar County, was outspoken in his denunciation of that cruel deed and firmly believed that Page was innocent of any wrong doing. He was waited upon and warned that he must cease his denunciations of the Regulators or leave the country. McCollough was an old pioneer, skilled in the use of the rifle and fearless of personal danger. He owned a large farm and had no idea of abandoning his home and property or the right of free speech and determined to defend both with his life if need be.

One day after the time had expired in which he was warned to leave, he saw a large band of horsemen approaching his house. His rifles were loaded and ready for use. He stood in the doorway of his strong log house, rifle in hand, as the Regulators approached, led by William George, a well known farmer from Rock Creek. As the band came within easy rifle shot, McCollough drew a deadly bead on the leader and ordered him to halt. The party stopped and a lengthy conference ensued. McCollough assured them that he should defend his home with his life, that they knew he was a law abiding citizen, guilty of no crime, that he had a legal right to express his opinions and should do so; that they might murder him but he should kill one or two of them first, as they well knew he never missed a deer within gunshot and that he had friends who would surely avenge his death. They hesitated, parleyed with him and tried to get a promise that he would keep still in future. But he stood firm for his rights as an American citizen and would make no concessions. His fearlessness convinced the Regulators that he had armed friends in the house who would defend him to the last. They were aware that a large number of law-abiding citizens, whom they had sought to intimidate, had counseled together and had an understanding that they would aid each other in case violence was threatened. This band also knew that they would not be supported by the better class of those who had acted with them in driving good citizens from their homes; so after conference they decided to give McCollough further time and rode away. This was the last organized effort to intimidate good citizens.

While the terrible tragedies enacted by the Regulators must be condemned, the effect was to terrify lawbreakers in that part of the State so effectually as to banish the gangs of horse thieves and counterfeiters who had long defied the law and carried on their criminal traffic with impunity. While all efforts to secure the arrest, trial and punishment of persons engaged in lynching were unsuccessful, the Regulators realized the fact that their defiance of law would no longer be tolerated, and no further attempts were made by them to usurp the duties of courts and legal officers and we hear no more of their meetings.

THE OLD CAPITOL AT DES MOINES
Erected in 1857 ; Occupied Until 1886

CHAPTER XXVIII

IN 1857 it became apparent that the practical navigation of the Des Moines River by a system of dams and locks could not be accomplished. Edwin Manning, in a report to the General Assembly, made January 1, 1857, states that $475,000 had been expended in six years, that but two dams and locks had been completed, that the total amount expended on the work up to 1857 had been nearly $800,000 and but three dams completed. The Legislature, on the 29th of January, passed an act by which commissioners were authorized to ascertain and pay off all just claims against the improvement and contract with any company for the sale of all lands, tolls and water rents, who would give good security for the completion of the work, such contract to be valid when approved by the Governor.

A building having been erected by the citizens of Des Moines for a State House in the fall of 1856, the State officers moved the records and furniture from Iowa City and the Capital of the State was established at Des Moines in 1857.

There were three elections held in that year. The first was for minor State officers, held in April. The Democratic candidates were M. L. Fisher for Superintendent of Public Instruction; T. S. Parvin, Register of Land Office; G. S. Bailey, Commissioner of Des Moines River Improvement. The Republicans nominated L. A. Bugbee for Superintendent, W. H. Holmes for Register and Edwin Manning, Commissioner. The election was very close, resulting in the choice of Fisher, Democrat, by a majority of 505, in a total vote of 75,279; Parvin, Democrat, by a majority of 502; Manning, Republican, by a majority of 315.

In August the election on the adoption of the new Constitution resulted as follows: for the Constitution, 40,311; against the Constitution, 36,681; majority for, 3,630. The Republicans generally voted for, and the Democrats largely voted against the Constitution.

The Democrats held their State Convention at Iowa City on the 26th of August and nominated the following ticket: for Governor, Ben M. Samuels; for Lieutenant-Governor, Geo. Gillaspy. The resolutions indorsed the administration of James Buchanan, the recent decision of the United States Supreme Court in the Dred Scott case, denounced the new Constitution and negro suffrage, and approved the acts and votes of Senator Jones and Representative Hall in Congress.

The Republican Convention was held at Iowa City on the 19th of August and placed in nomination for Governor, Ralph P. Lowe and for Lieutenant-Governor, Oran Faville. The resolutions declared that under the Constitution of the United States freedom alone is national; condemned the repeal of the Missouri compromise, the Dred Scott decision and the attempt to force slavery into Kansas. They declared in favor of a banking system, indorsed the new Constitution and the administration of Governor Grimes.

The year 1857 closed with great financial depression throughout the country. Most of the banks suspended specie payment and redemption of their bills and a large number of them failed. There were no banks in Iowa permitted to issue bills and it was impossible to get good money in sufficient quantities to buy farm produce or carry on the ordinary business.

In the Territory of Nebraska on our western border there was no restriction to the establishment of banks. Some of our Iowa financiers conceived the plan of establishing banks in that sparsely settled Territory to supply Iowa with currency. Thomas H. Benton, a well-known citizen, made the first venture in March, 1855, by estab-

ORAN FAVILLE
First Lieutenant-Governor of Iowa.

SPECIMEN OF WILDCAT CURRENCY

lishing '' The Western Fire and Marine Insurance Company,'' which proceeded to issue bank bills and put them in circulation in Iowa. Soon after Cook and Sargent, of Davenport, established a bank at Florence, issued bills and proceeded to put them in circulation from their Iowa banking houses at Davenport, Iowa City and Des Moines. B. F. Allen of Des Moines, established the '' Bank of Nebraska,'' putting its bills in circulation from his Iowa banking house. Greene and Weare of Cedar Rapids, had the Bank of Fontanelle in Nebraska, where they manufactured paper money for their Iowa customers. This firm had numerous banking houses in various Iowa towns from which the Fontanelle bank bills were put in circulation. Iowa City, Bentonsport and several other cities issued scrip, beautifully engraved, on bank note paper in the usual denominations, form and style of bank bills, which were paid out as money. The Western Stage Company and Burrows and Prettyman, merchants and produce dealers of Davenport, manufactured handsomely engraved promises to pay which circulated as money in the region where the proprietors were known.

Thus for about two years the people of Iowa had no choice but to take this worthless paper in place of money. It would not pay taxes, buy eastern exchange or enter government land, and would only pay debts or buy groceries, because money had disappeared and could only be purchased at a large premium. For a few months after the manufacture of these substitutes for money began, business temporarily revived; but as no one had confidence in this currency, everyone sought to exchange it at once for something that had real value or pay debts with it. No one dared to hold it. When the Nebraska banks began to fail the distress was widespread and every branch of business was paralyzed. In the newer frontier settlements the effects of the depression brought greater hardships. R. A. Smith, of Dickinson County, says:

"Real estate became valueless. It was necessary to adopt a system of self-denial never before known in Iowa. It was with the utmost difficulty that the common necessaries of life could be obtained. Tea, coffee, salt, and all kinds of groceries were out of reach of nearly all. It was not uncommon for families to live for days on wild meat with only such breadstuffs as could be ground in a coffee mill. Musk-rat pelts were almost the only resource for raising money to pay taxes. The people had to cut up grain sacks for clothing, supplemented with deer skins for moccasins in place of shoes and stockings."

Thousands of citizens were unable to get money to pay taxes or to save their property from sale under the summary process of deeds of trust from which there was no redemption at that time. Thousands were reduced from prosperous farmers, merchants and mechanics to poverty and destitution. Such was the financial situation when the Seventh General Assembly met at Des Moines, the new Capital, on the 11th of January, 1858. This was the first session under the new Constitution and in many respects was the most important legislative body that ever convened in Iowa. For the first time the Senate was presided over by a Lieutenant-Governor, chosen by the electors of the State, Oran Faville. In the House, Stephen B. Shelledy was elected Speaker.

Governor Grimes, in his message, said:

"Your labors will exercise a potent influence upon the future character and prosperity of the State, long after the last of you shall cease to be interested in human affairs. All the general laws of the State will require some modifications to adapt them to the provisions of the new constitution."

He recommended a registry law to record all legal voters; a revision of the revenue laws; a restoration of township assessors; a sound banking system; the support of public schools by taxation, and the enactment into laws of the school system prepared by Horace Mann and Amos Dean and submitted to the last General Assembly.

The financial condition of the State was reported as follows:

RALPH P. LOWE
Governor of Iowa, 1858-1859

Amount in the Treasury October 3, 1856........ $ 11,254.91
Paid into the Treasury during the year........   231,234.42

Total $242,489.33
Amount paid out during the year............   228,806.23

Balance in the Treasury November 1, 1857.... $ 13,683.10
Due on the assessment of 1857...............   418,709.59

The defalcation of James D. Eads, late Superintendent
of Public Instruction of school funds, was reported to
amount to $46,403.81.

The Governor urged the Legislature to provide for the
payment of the volunteers, who marched under Major
Williams to protect the settlers of northwestern Iowa from
the Sioux Indians, in March, 1857. On the 14th of January, 1858, the General Assembly in joint convention proceeded to canvass the votes cast for Governor and Lieutenant-Governor and declared the following result:

Ralph P. Lowe .... 38,498 votes.
Ben M. Samuels 36,088
T. F. Henry   1,004

Ralph P. Lowe was declared elected.
For Lieutenant-Governor:

Oran Faville .... 37,633 votes.
George Gillaspy .... 35,310.
Eastin Morris   1,000

Oran Faville was declared elected and on the same day
the newly elected Governor and Lieutenant-Governor were
sworn into office, and Governor Lowe delivered his inaugural address to the General Assembly.

The most important acts of this session were the framing of laws providing for the organization of a State Bank,
with branches, and also a general banking law. These acts
were to be submitted to a vote of the electors of the State.

The banking laws enacted provided for two systems. The first was the incorporation of the State Bank of Iowa and provision for the organization of five or more branches, with capital of not less than $50,000 and not more than $300,000 each; all notes for circulation to be furnished by the State Bank, and good security required for their redemption in gold or silver. The number of branches of the State Bank was limited to thirty and ample security was provided for depositors. The branches were required to be mutually responsible for each other's liabilities on all notes circulated as money; each stockholder to be individually responsible to its creditors for all of its liabilities to an amount equal to the amount of shares held by him; and in case of insolvency the bill holders to have preference over other creditors; the suspension of specie payments never to be permitted or sanctioned. The act passed the Legislature in March, was submitted to a vote of the electors at a special election held on the fourth Monday of June, 1858. The vote stood for the law, 41,588; against the law, 3,697. It went into effect on the 29th of July, upon the issue of a proclamation by the Governor. The Commissioners named to carry into effect the provisions of the law, were C. H. Booth of Dubuque County; E. H. Harrison of Lee; Ezekiel Clark of Johnson; J. W. Dutton of Muscatine; W. J. Gatling of Polk; C. W. Slagle of Jefferson; Elihu Baker of Linn; W. S. Dart of Mahaska; L. W. Babbitt of Pottawattamie; and T. W. Edgington of Lucas, who organized and received applications for the establishment of branches. After a careful examination of securities offered by the applicants, branches were authorized at Muscatine, Iowa City, Des Moines, Dubuque, Oskaloosa, Mount Pleasant, Keokuk and Davenport. In accordance with law, the affairs of the State Bank of Iowa now passed under the control and supervision of a Board of Directors, consisting of one chosen from each branch. The first Board consisted of W. T. Smith of Oskaloosa; Samuel

BILL OF THE OLD STATE BANK OF IOWA

F. Miller, Keokuk; P. M. Casady, Des Moines; Samuel J:
Kirkwood, Iowa City; Chester Weed, Muscatine; R.
Bronson, Dubuque; Hiram Price, Davenport; with Hoyt
Sherman and Benjamin Lake Directors for the State. The
first officers of the Board were Chester Weed, President;
W. T. Smith, Vice-President; Elihu Baker, Secretary;
Samuel J. Kirkwood and Hiram Price, with the Vice-
President, formed the Executive Committee.

Among the important acts of this first Board of Directors was the adoption of a carefully considered series
of by-laws clearly defining the duties of the officers. The
President was required to make a personal examination
of the affairs of each branch and retain in his custody
the bonds of the bank officers. The Executive Committee
had general supervision of the branches; it was required
to hold monthly meetings and special sessions whenever
it became necessary. The high financial standing of this
Board of Directors was the best guaranty to the people of
the State that the new banking system would be conducted
with fidelity and at once inspired confidence in the sta-
bility of the State Bank of Iowa. This confidence was
never shaken during the existence of this admirable institution which met the most sanguine expectation of its
framers.

A general banking law was also enacted under which
any person or persons could establish a bank, but it was
so rigid in its requirements for the security of bill holders
and depositors, that bankers preferred to organize under
the act for the establishment of a State Bank and branches.
The State Banks were sound institutions, always paying
their depositors in full in specie and redeeming their
currency whenever presented. It is probable that no better or safer banking system was ever devised and it did
the banking business of the State to the entire satisfaction
of the people until superseded by the National Banks.

An act was passed providing for the establishment of
a State Agricultural College. The bill for this act was

introduced by R. A. Richardson into the House and referred to the committee of ways and means. That committee reported the bill back with a recommendation that
it be indefinitely postponed. The friends of the bill hastily
conferred together and decided to make a vigorous fight
for it and B. F. Gue, of Scott County, was selected to lead
in a speech advocating the establishment of such a college.
After a warm debate the bill was amended and ordered
engrossed, passed both Houses and became a law. An act
was passed providing for a loan of $200,000 and the issue
of State bonds. Provision was made for the erection of an
asylum for the blind at Vinton.

It having become evident that it was impracticable to
render the Des Moines River navigable with the proceeds
of the grant of land made for that purpose in 1846, the
Legislature passed an act diverting the grant to the Keokuk, Des Moines and Minnesota Railroad Company, for
the purpose of aiding the construction of a railroad up the
valley of the Des Moines River. Joint resolutions were
also passed providing for a final settlement with the Des
Moines Navigation Company by granting to said company
a portion of the old land grant.

An act was passed providing for a commission to revise and codify the general laws of the State, to conform
all laws to the new Constitution, prepare a code of civil
and criminal procedure, all to be published in one volume,
" which shall contain all the general laws in force in the
State." William Smyth, W. T. Barker and C. Ben Dar-
win were the commissioners chosen to do this work.

An entire new school system was enacted; its framing
was largely the work of Horace Mann and Amos Dean,
who had been employed by the State previous to the meeting of the former General Assembly, but which had not
been adopted. This system was a step in advance of former laws and its main features were long retained, resulting in the advance of modern methods in our public
schools.

Early in the session an effort was made to impeach Thomas W. Clagett, a judge of the First District and a special committee was appointed to take evidence and report. Petitions and remonstrances in large numbers were presented to the General Assembly from Lee County, for several weeks for and against impeachment and a large amount of testimony on the subject was taken by the committee. It became evident that Judge Clagett was arbitrary in his treatment of attorneys practicing before his court but there was no evidence impeaching his integrity, and the non-partisan committee finally reported· "That we find no cause of impeachment," and the House concurred in the report.

There was a bitter controversy existing between the residents of the old city of Des Moines and the people of East Des Moines over the location of the new Capitol and, early in the session, a memorial was presented to the General Assembly, charging fraud and corruption on part of the commissioners, stating that they did not act for the best interests of the State in making the location. A special committee was thereupon appointed by the House of Representatives for the purpose of taking evidence and making a thorough investigation of the charges made against the commissioners. The committee made a careful examination of the evidence obtainable in support of the charges and gave the commissioners opportunity to testify and bring witnesses to exonerate them from the allegations of fraud and corruption. The evidence, with all the papers and documents brought before the committee, was reported to the House just before the close of the session and ordered printed in pamphlet for distribution among the members and one copy sent to each newspaper in the State.

The report was signed by four of the five members of the committee and may be summarized briefly as follows:

"Your committee is of the opinion that the Commissioners did not act with a strict regard to the interest of the entire State in preferring the location on the east side of the river. Several of the witnesses refused to testify upon important points; but without this, sufficient evidence has been elicited to convince your committee that Mr. Pegram, one of the Commissioners, was influenced in making the location by personal and private considerations, and that he did receive a bribe or bonus in consideration of his vote for the location of the Capitol. With regard to Mr. Goodrell there appears nothing in the testimony implicating him in the frauds alleged in the second charge."

George W. McCrary, the fifth member of the committee, did not unite with the others, but states his position in a separate report, in which he says:

"I do not desire that the Commissioners should suffer on account of having acted contrary to what I might conceive to be for the best interest of the State. As one of the committee, bound to believe that the Commissioners acted in accordance with their oaths, until the contrary is proven, the undersigned feels bound to say that, with the exception of Commissioner Pegram, he can see no sufficient evidence of a wilful disregard of the interests of the State. The undersigned believes that the charges are sustained by the evidence as to Commissioner Pegram, but not as to the others."

All members of the committee, except McCrary, joined in recommending that the Attorney-General be instructed to institute proceedings against the commissioners for relocating the seat of government, for the recovery from them of any bonus they might have received for their votes or influence in making said location. On motion of W. H. Seevers, the House decided that the testimony taken by the Committee of Investigation be not printed in the House Journal. As the House adjourned early on the morning of the second day after this report was made, no further action was taken, and when the pamphlets containing all the evidence taken by the committee were published, by some mysterious process, they were quietly gathered up and disappeared.

No small portion of the attention of this session of the

General Assembly was given to a discussion of the vital issues now engaging the serious consideration of the thoughtful people of the country. The aggressions of the Missouri "Border Ruffians," who had deliberately invaded the Territory of Kansas, not for settlement as citizens, but as armed freebooters with the avowed purpose of forcing slavery upon bona fide settlers, against their earnest protest, aroused an intense feeling of indignation throughout the North. The promulgation of the doctrine lately enunciated by the United States Supreme Court, in the Dred Scott decision, that slavery was a national institution and, by virtue of the Constitution had a legal existence in the Territories of the Nation, was so abhorrent to the free people of the Union that public sentiment in the North and West was sending up solemn protests from every settlement in the free States. The "irrepressible conflict" between freedom and slavery foretold by that great statesman, William H. Seward, was now in active progress and people were arraying themselves on one side or the other. The administrations of Presidents Pierce and Buchanan had openly espoused the cause of slavery and now the highest court in the country had sustained the right of slavery to invade all of the free territory of the Nation.

Iowa, long under the control of the party which defended this institution, had at last revolted and retired that party from power. This vital issue was revolutionizing parties, dividing churches and even families; every neighborhood was aroused to earnest discussion of the absorbing topic. It was a war between free and slave labor and all thoughful men saw clearly that it must be fought out. either in legislative halls or on the field of battle. Every man in public life had to declare his position, for the intense earnestness of the aroused American citizens would tolerate no neutrality; and the old Whig party which endeavored to evade the issue was swept from existence.

It was in the midst of this gathering of the contending forces for the final struggle that the first General Assembly which convened at the new frontier Capitol met.

The dominant issues in National affairs could not be ignored. Governor Grimes was just retiring from the executive chair, which he had filled with commanding ability. He was a prominent candidate for United States Senator to be chosen by the Legislature; a radical of radicals, aggressive, courageous, able and born a leader of men. Time serving, timidity and neutrality were qualities foreign to the nature of this superb fighter. He was the man for the occasion and in his retiring message sounded the keynote for the rank and file of the young, conscientious Republican party, which he had helped to organize, for warfare against American slavery and which never in Iowa had an abler leader.

In this historic document he struck sturdy blows at the new edict promulgated in support of slavery by Chief Justice Roger B. Taney in the famous Dred Scott decisions, in which he says:

" I am aware that except upon the single question of the citizenship of Dred Scott, the opinions of the Judges are entirely extra-judicial, and entitled to no more weight than the opinions of any other citizens. But they are worthy of your consideration, because they foreshadow the opinion that will be authoritatively announced whenever the proper state of facts shall be presented that may seem to justify it. It is declared that the constitution plants slavery upon all the public domain, and there nurtures and protects it.

" It is no longer held under this decision that freedom is national and slavery local, confined to limits of the States that see fit to uphold it. It is fastened upon every foot of soil belonging to the Government, and there is no power in Congress, or in Territorial governments to expel it. Whatever territory may be acquired by the United States will instantly become slave soil. Wherever the flag of the country goes, there goes slavery with its chains and manacles.

" The logical result of this decision goes still farther; it carries slavery into every State in the Union.

" It needs no argument to show that this decision is unwarranted by the facts presented to the court; that it is revolutionary in its character; sub-

versive of the policy of the founders of the Republic, and violates the rights
of the States. Being wholly extra-judicial, so far as it relates to the power
of Congress and the States over slavery, it cannot bind the conscience, or
command the obedience of any man.

"I trust that as the representatives of the freedom loving citizens of
Iowa, you will explicitly declare that you will never consent that this State
shall become an integral part of a great slave republic, by assenting to the
abhorrent doctrines contained in the Dred Scott decision, let the couse-
quences be what they may.

"We cannot be indifferent to the efforts of the people of Kansas to
perpetuate freedom in that Territory. We ought not to be indifferent.
No people are deserving of freedom who do not sympathize with those who
are struggling to obtain it. The people of Kansas are the champions of
popular sovereignty everywhere. They are bringing to the test the great
principle enunciated by our Revolutionary fathers, that government derives
its powers from the cousent of the governed. The people of Iowa look with
alarm upon the constant aggressions of the slavery propagandists, but I
confess that I look with equal alarm upon the manifest tendency of our
Government to consolidation. The doctrine inherited from our ancestors,
that standing armies are dangerous to the liberties of the people, is repudiated by constant and strenuous efforts to increase the National army.
Sinecure offices are created for the purpose of influencing public opinion.
The army of office-holders scattered throughout the States, uttering the
sentiments, disbursing the money and obeying the commands of the central
authority, govern in a great degree the sentiment of the country. Thus
the Federal Government, instead of being as it was designed to be, the
mere creature and under the control of the States, is fast becoming their
master.

"The centralizing influence of the Government—the immense increase of
our National expenses—the history of the slavery propagandism in Kansas,
and the complicity of the Federal Government therewith; the attempts to
overthrow the clearest rights of self-government for the purpose of extending slavery; and the efforts to destroy the rights of the States by political
decisions of the Supreme Court, should remind the freemen of Iowa that
their great political rights are in danger.

"The liberties of the people can only be preserved by maintaining the
integrity of the State Governments against the corrupting influences of the
Federal patronage and power."

Thus spoke the fearless and incorruptible statesman
who never surrendered the freedom of speech and opinion
to any living power.

The Seventh General Assembly sustained the position
so firmly taken by the Governor, in choosing him for six

years to represent Iowa in the United States Senate, to take the place of George W. Jones, the last Democratic member of that body from Iowa.

State Senator Samuel J. Kirkwood, as Chairman of the Committee on Federal Relations, himself lately a Democrat, but also one of the founders of the Republican party, reported a series of resolutions, preceded by a lengthy preamble reciting the principal points made by the Governor and concluding with the following declarations:

> " *Resolved,* That we still recognize and sustain the time honored doctrines taught by the early fathers of our political faith, that freedom is the great cardinal principle which underlies, pervades and exalts our whole political system; that the Constitution of the United States does not in any way recognize the right of property in man; that slavery as a system is exceptional and purely local, deriving its existence and support wholly from local law.
>
> " *Resolved,* That the State of Iowa will not allow slavery within her borders, in any form or under any pretext, for any time, however short, be the consequences what they may."

Lincoln Clark, a distinguished ex-member of Congress, on behalf of the Democratic minority, made a lengthy report, from which the following extracts will show the position of his party in Iowa at this time on the slavery issue:

> " The power of Congress to govern the Territories is nowhere expressly given in the Constitution, neither can it be logically or fairly deduced from any power therein contained.
>
> " It is true that the General Government holds the Territories in trust for all States alike—-their interests are common—their rights are equal; and the General Government, as an impartial and honest trustee, is bound to see that those rights are not on one hand invaded, nor on the other monopolized. The Governor affirms that because the Court below had not jurisdiction, therefore the Superior Court had none to revise the case upon all that was embraced in the record.
>
> " The Court did not stumble from the question of jurisdiction in the Court below, to the consideration of the more substantial portion of the case. They carefully considered whether they had the power to investigate and adjudge the whole case after that point had been made and argued.

It may be a question whether good citizens, desirous of holding to the law, both for the sake of order and conscience, shall give the greater heed to what the law really is, to the well considered, solemn decision of the highest tribunal in the land, or to the opinion of a partisan Governor in his message; and this must be determined by everyone for himself.

"It is not denied that the Circuit Court had jurisdiction of the matter, though Scott had no right to sue because of personal disability. Was it therefore incompetent and wrong for the Court to declare the law in the cause before it, for the benefit of future litigants, and for the quiet of the whole country? We think not; and that no such grave charge lies against the decision as that it may be treated with contempt.

"The Governor concludes his message with these remarkable words: 'The decision cannot bind the conscience, or command the obedience of any man'

The undersigned hardly think that language of reprobation so strong against any department of the Government, by any official of a State Government, can be found since the War of 1812, and the times of the Hartford Convention. We do not say that such language is treasonable, but if there is such a thing as moral treason, this is believed to be that thing. It is not resistance to the Government in the shape of an overt act; but it is encouragement to resistance; it breathes the spirit of it, and would result in it when moved to corresponding action. It is the very last thing which the poorest patriot ought to do, an attempt to pull down the Superior Court of the United States. Freedom is certainly National, because it prevails in all the States as fully as it did at the adoption of the Constitution, and slavery prevails no more than under the Constitution it has a right to do.

"The decision admits that a Territory shall be erected into a State, the State has full power to legislate on the subject of slavery, as well as on others not given by some power in the Constitution to Congress. The decision in no sense invades the sovereignty of the States, nor in the slightest degree curtails their power.

"The undersigned take occasion to say that in their opinion it is not competent for the Executive or the Legislature of a State to review the decisions of the Supreme Court of the United States. It is in substance an infringement of that part of the Constitution which requires the respective departments of the Government not to invade each other."

This report was signed by Lincoln Clark, of Dubuque, and W. H. Clune, of Burlington, on behalf of the Democratic members.

The debate which followed in the two branches of the General Assembly lasted several days. The Republicans in the Senate were represented in the discussion by Kirk-

wood, Loughridge and Rankin; while the Democrats were
led by Trimble, Neal and Pusey. In the House, James F.
Wilson, E. E. Cooley, Thomas Drummond, T. W. Jackson
and George W. McCrary made aggressive war on the en-
croachments of slavery, while the courtly Lincoln Clark,
D. A. Mahoney, M. B. V. Bennett and I. C. Curtis appeared as defenders of Pierce, Buchanan and the Dred
Scott decision.

The Kirkwood resolutions were passed by a strict party
vote. Other resolutions on the subject of slavery brought
out long and exciting political debates; partisan feeling
was often intense and the discussions heated and bitter.
Protests and counter protests were entered upon the jour-
nals. It is a notable fact that the average age of the members of this Legislature was under forty; there were some
venerable men and experienced legislators, but the large
majority were in the vigorous fighting years of youth
and inclined to be impulsive; but their acts in the inauguration of a new State policy, comformable to the radical
changes made by the new Constitution, have stood the severe tests of nearly half a century of trial, under which
great progress in material, educational and intellectual development has been attained.

Lathrop's " Life of Governor Kirkwood " says:

" Never in the history of the State has there been an abler General Assembly than the Seventh, which was the first one to meet at Des Moines,
the new Capital, when the State was leaving its youthful condition and
entering upon that of incipient manhood. It was the first to assemble under
the new constitution, adapting laws to its new provisions, enacting them
for the creation of banks, passing upon measures for the relief of the people from great financial embarrassment—reorganization of our system of
popular education in which it had the assistance of such eminent educators
as Horace Mann and Amos Dean—remodeling the judiciary system, settling
the problem of the Des Moines River Improvement enterprise—rescuing our
magnificent school fund from waste caused by an unfaithful public officer—
providing for a more prompt collection of taxes, and building up our re-
formatory, charitable and higher educational institutions. To perform these
labors there were in the Senate such men as Rankin, Brigham, Coolbaugh,

Trimble, Saunders, Pusey, Anderson, Patterson, Kirkwood, Cattell, Grinnell and their associates; in the House such men of age and experience as Lincoln Clark, Shelledy, Ayers and Streeter, with men younger in years but equal in ability, like Casady, Seevers, Edwards and Bradley, while it contained a galaxy of sixteen young men the equal of whom are rarely found in any legislative body. They were Belknap, McCrary, Wilson, Gue, Wright, Bates, Carpenter, Drummond, Jackson, Curtis, Clune, Sprague, Woodward, Beal, Bennett and Casady, of Woodbury. Some were but a few years out of their "teens," McCrary being but twenty-two, and all were in "twenties," but there were giants among them. Of these Belknap afterwards became Secretary of War; McCrary, Secretary of War and afterwards a Judge of the United States Circuit Court; Wilson a United States Senator; Carpenter, Governor of the State; Gue, Lieutenant-Governor; Wright, a Brigadier General, while others of them attained high and responsible positions. Few brighter stars have shone in the intellectual firmament than Tom Drummond and T. Walter Jackson. It is a noteworthy fact that two of these youngsters, Gue and Wright, fought through and procured the passage of a bill establishing the Agricultural College in the face of an adverse report upon it from the committee of ways and means. Eight years later these same two youngsters, as presiding officers of the two branches of the Eleventh General Assembly, one as Lieutenant-Governor and the other as Speaker of the House, certified to the election to the United States Senate of Samuel J. Kirkwood, one of their co-lawmakers at this session."

A spirited contest was waged for some time before the Legislature assembled among the Republicans, who had elected a majority in both branches, over the choice of a candidate for United States Senator to succeed George W. Jones. After the Legislature convened the contest became warmer and a strong effort was made to unite the members from the northern part of the State upon a candidate in opposition to ex-Governor Grimes. It was not successful and in the Republican caucus, called to select a candidate, the ballot stood as follows: James W. Grimes, thirty-nine; James Thorington, thirteen; Wm. Smyth, eight; Timothy Davis, three; giving the nomination to Governor Grimes by a clear majority. The Democrats nominated Ben M. Samuels, and in the election which took place on the 26th of January, Grimes received sixty-four votes, and Samuels forty-one. James W. Grimes

was declared elected United States Senator for six years
from March 4, 1859.

Under the authority granted by the Legislature, a company of mounted men was organized for the protection of
the frontier from Indians, of which Henry B. Martin was
made captain. During the fall of 1858 several bands of
Sioux Indians came into northwestern Iowa, causing great
alarm among the frontier settlements. The " Frontier
Guards " were called out and remained in service several
months, holding the Indians in check. Congress made an
appropriation of $20,000, to pay the expenses incurred by
citizens of the States of Iowa and Minnesota in the campaigns against the Sioux who committed the massacres at
Okoboji and Springfield in the spring of 1857. Of this
sum $3,612.43 was paid to the command under Major Wil-
liams, which marched to the relief of the settlers after the
massacre.

The season of 1858 will long be remembered as one of
the most disastrous to farmers of any experienced up to
that time. Cold rains began early in April and continued
through the month. Wheat and oats were sown late but
the frequent rains of May caused them to make a rank
growth and delayed corn planting. Much of the seed corn
rotted in the ground. The wet weather continued in June
with cold nights, which forced the weeds until much of the
corn was smothered. To add to the general disaster
there was frost in a large portion of the State during
every month of the year. Wheat, oats and barley made
rank growth and fell down. Potatoes were ruined
by the rain. Early in July there were alternate heavy
rains and intensely hot days. A few days before harvest
time it was observed that the wheat heads were suddenly
turning white. Upon examination they were found to be
blasted. The grain was shriveled, shrunken, soft and worthless and farmers slowly realized that the one crop, then
so largely relied upon to bring in money for the year,
was ruined. Oats and barley were lodged on the ground,

the straw rusted and the grain was shriveled, chaffy and nearly worthless. Thousands of acres of grain were never harvested. The wheat that was cut and threshed was unfit for bread but many tried to use the chocolate-colored stuff which was tasteless and destitute of nutriment. The best of it served for seed of a very poor quality the next spring in the general inability of the farmers to raise money to import good seed. More than half of the corn which had been planted late, owing to the continuous cold rains, had failed to germinate; water and weeds everywhere smothered the growth of the scattering stalks that survived. Thousands of fields were plowed up and sowed with buckwheat. To crown the general misfortunes a heavy frost came unusually early and ruined the buckwheat and left the corn soft and unripe, so that it rotted in the cribs. The hay crop was badly damaged by continuous rains. All farm crops were so poor as to be unsalable for shipping and such as were sold for home use brought very low prices.

This crop failure extended over two-thirds of the area of the State, being most disastrous in the southeastern portion. The currency was of doubtful value, much of it being utterly worthless. The distress and destitution which prevailed among the farmers during this period can never be realized by those who were not among the sufferers.

The armed resistance of the Free State men of Kansas against the brutal attempts of the Border Ruffians of Missouri to force slavery into that Territory and make it a slave State—and the attempt to abolish the slave trade at the National Capital—had so intensified the conflict that no further compromises seemed possible that could restore harmonious relations between the North and the South. In the South, all parties were being rapidly absorbed by the Democrats, while in the North the Republican party was growing into formidable proportions. Slavery restriction was its chief purpose, and upon that issue it was absorbing the united antislavery strength of the nation.

The Republican State Convention met at Des Moines on the 22d of June, 1859, where Samuel J. Kirkwood was nominated for Governor by acclamation; Nicholas J. Rusch was nominated for Lieutenant-Governor and Ralph P. Lowe, Caleb Baldwin and Lacon D. Stockton were nominated for Supreme Judges. The resolutions indorsed the Republican National platform of 1856 and opposed the extension of slavery in the Territories. The convention also approved the granting of free homesteads to actual settlers of the public lands and opposed the abridgment of the privilege of naturalization to emigrants.

The Democratic Convention assembled at Des Moines on the 23d of June and placed the following candidates in nomination: for Governor, General A. C. Dodge; Lieutenant-Governor, L. W. Babbitt; Supreme Judges, Charles Mason, Thomas S. Wilson and Chester C. Cole. The resolutions were very lengthy and favored remanding the subject of slavery to the Territorial Legislatures, the exclusion of free negroes from Iowa, favored the acquisition of Cuba and the repeal of the prohibitory liquor law. The campaign which followed was one of the most notable in the history of the State. A series of joint discussions was arranged in which the rival candidates for Governor appeared before immense gatherings of the voters at various towns and divided the time in presenting their views of the issues involved.

General Dodge was one of the ablest men of his party, had served thirteen years in Congress and had been four years the American Minister to Spain. Kirkwood had been less prominent. But as the campaign progressed he proved fully the equal of General Dodge in debate. Plain in dress, direct, earnest and sincere in speech, candid and logical in discussion of the issues between the parties, he became one of the most effective and popular political speakers in the West. In this campaign he laid the founda-

MILL ON THE IOWA RIVER FROM WHICH KIRKWOOD WAS CALLED TO BE GOVERNOR

tion for that career which, for nearly a quarter of a century, led the State to trust him in the most exalted positions of the public service. The election resulted in the success of the Republican candidates, Kirkwood's majority over Dodge being 3,200. The Republicans also elected a majority of each branch of the Legislature.

CHAPTER XXIX

SOON after the enactment of the Fugitive Slave Law, with its barbarous penalties, many humane persons in Iowa, who could not resist the impulse to assist slaves from Missouri, escaping from bondage, organized lines of stations across the State by which they could coöperate in affording shelter, aid and transportation to fugitives. Beginning at Tabor, in Fremont County, near the State line, the Abolitionists had stations known only to trusted friends, extending by way of Des Moines, Grinnell, Iowa City and Springdale to Davenport. When the escaping slaves reached any station on this line (which was called the " Underground Railroad ") the keeper of that station would secrete the fugitives, furnish them food, clothing, money and transportation to the next station. The train usually consisted of a well equipped canvas-covered lumber wagon and a good team of horses, driven by a cool, courageous man, well armed. The colored passengers were concealed beneath the cover and traveling was in the shelter of night. Arriving at a station, the slaves were concealed and kindly cared for until night when they were again conveyed on their journey. The trains were run with such secrecy that their coming and going was very seldom discovered by the slave catchers in pursuit of their human chattels. Hundreds of slaves from Missouri found paths to freedom over the Iowa prairies, from 1850 to 1860, by the various lines of the " Underground Railroad." The men and women, who from feelings of humanity and without compensation kept the stations, well knew the risk of ruinous fines and imprisonment they were taking, but with the true John Brown spirit that moved them to aid men, women and children to freedom, they never shrunk from danger.

After the long time that has elapsed, no full history can now be written of these perilous journeys from slavery to freedom, as no records were kept and most of the conductors have passed away. Among the Iowa men who were actively engaged in aiding slaves who were fleeing from bondage were Rev. John Todd, James C. Jordan, John Teesdale, Isaac Brandt, Dr. Edwin James, Thomas Mitchell, J. B. Grinnell, John R. Price, H. G. Cummings, Wm. Penn Clarke, Jesse Bowen, S. C. Trowbridge, Dr. H. G. Gill, John H. Painter, James Townsend and R. H. Randall. There were scores of others in various parts of the State whose names were not made public. The armed invasion of Kansas, in 1855-6, by Missouri slaveholders, for the purpose of forcing slavery into that new Territory, brought into prominence several Iowa men who became famous in the long conflict between freedom and slavery which led to bloodshed on its soil. Hundreds of young men from Iowa went to Kansas to help fight the battles for freedom. John Brown first became known to the public as one of the most fearless leaders of the Free State men in that conflict. He passed through Iowa in September, 1855, on his way to Kansas with a son and son-in-law to join four sons who had already settled there. He anticipated trouble on the prairies of Kansas, over the attempt to force slavery into the Territory, and went there for the avowed purpose of helping to resist its enlargement by arms. He soon became a recognized leader of the Free State men and among his followers were several young men from Iowa.

At the Battle of Black Jack his little army, in which five of his sons were serving, after a severe conflict, defeated and captured a force nearly twice the size of his own, under the famous Captain Pate. This was the first battle in the Kansas War; yet few, if any, besides John Brown then realized its mighty significance. His mission was to liberate slaves, and never, during the few remaining years of his life, did he for a moment waver from his

JOHN BROWN
In 1855, When He First Passed Through Iowa

inflexible purpose. Every energy of this remarkable man
was henceforth concentrated upon the work that he re-
ligiously believed he was ordained to accomplish. During his career in Kansas Brown made the acquaintance
of many courageous young men, who recognized in him a
leader, able, tireless and fearless. Some of them served
with him in the Kansas War and several of them enlisted
in his desperate raid at Harper's Ferry. John Brown
made five trips through Iowa while he was engaged in the
Kansas conflict. He learned the location of many of the
stations on the " Underground Railroad," and met many
Iowa men who were aiding fugitive slaves on the way to
freedom.

In 1856, Richard J. Hinton (author of " John Brown
and His Men "), with a band of young men on their way to
Kansas, marched from Iowa City. They took with them
from the arsenal 1,500 muskets. The key had been
left on Governor Grimes's desk, where Hinton found
and " borrowed " it to open the arsenal door. When
they reached Kansas, Rev. Pardee Butler took charge
of the muskets and delivered them to the Free State
leaders. Mr. Butler was a well-known Christian minister
from Posten's Grove, Iowa, who had settled in Kansas in
1854. He was an active and influential Free State leader
and had lately been seized by a band of forty armed "Border Ruffians " at Atchison, placed upon a rude raft made
of three logs and sent adrift on the Missouri River. His
face was painted black and he was warned that if he ever
returned he would be killed. But Pardee Butler was not
to be intimidated and, managing to reach the shore some
miles down the river, he returned home and never ceased
his work of making Kansas a free State. George B. Gill,
Barclay Coppoc, Jeremiah G. Anderson and Charles P.
Moffett, all young men from Iowa, took an active part in
the Kansas War. Some of them served under John
Brown, in Kansas, and all enlisted in his Harper's Ferry
expedition.

In August, 1856, a large force of " Border Ruffians "
came to Hickory Point, robbing houses and stores, and
committing other depredations. Colonel Harvey hastily
gathered together a hundred Free State men to drive the
desperadoes from the country. He found them intrenched
in three houses and at once opened fire upon them with a
twelve-pound field piece. After a battle of six hours the
Ruffians surrendered and were permitted to leave the
country. But the little army, under Colonel Harvey, was
overtaken by a detachment of United States troops and
made prisoners. The President was in sympathy with
the slave power and the army of the United States was
used in Kansas to suppress the defenders of freedom.
Colonel Harvey and his men were taken before a pro-
slavery judge, prosecuted by a " Border Ruffian " attorney and tried for murder. A large number of them were
convicted and sentenced to prison for terms ranging from
five to ten years for protecting their neighbors in their
lives and property. Among those thus imprisoned were
the following Iowa volunteers: G. O. Eberhart of Muscatine; M. Rincle and Oliver C. Lewis, Davenport; Ed.
Jacobs, Mahaska County; Oliver Langworthy, Poweshiek
County; Jacob Fisher of Jefferson; E. R. Moffett, Bris-
tolville; Wm. Kern, Washington; and Wm. Rayman,
Cooper, Iowa. They had fought bravely and endured
unjust imprisonment and hard fare, in the consciousness
of having done their duty, until released when the Free
State cause finally triumphed.

In 1856, James Townsend, a member of the Society of
Friends, kept a public house in the little village of West
Branch, in Cedar County, Iowa. In October, John Brown,
on his way from Kansas on horseback, reached the "Travelers' Rest " in the evening and stopped over night.
Learning that the landlord was a Quaker, Brown made
known to him that he was " Osawatomie Brown," of
Kansas and at once received a most cordial welcome. He
was told of the strong antislavery views of the Quaker

THE MAXSON HOUSE NEAR SPRINGDALE

settlement at Springdale, four miles east, which also gave him a cordial reception. As the years passed a warm friendship grew up between John Brown, James Townsend and many of the citizens of Springdale. This Quaker settlement became one of his favorite stopping places on his numerous journeys to Kansas during his war on slavery. He could here find safe shelter and generous assistance for the slaves he frequently piloted from Missouri to freedom in Canada.

For several years John Brown had contemplated striking a blow at slavery in the mountain region of Virginia and, in 1857, he began to mature plans for the hazardous enterprise. He believed that a body of fearless men could make a safe lodgment in the mountains and liberate slaves who would join them. His plan was to arm the escaped slaves with pikes, organize and drill them under experienced officers selected from young men who had seen service in the Kansas War. He expected thousands of slaves to flock to his standard when his purpose became known to them and believed that he could soon establish a powerful force in the mountains, pledged to the liberation of slaves. He employed Hugh Forbes, who had seen service in Europe, to open a school of military instruction at Tabor, Iowa, for the purpose of drilling men for this expedition. Tabor was near the Missouri line but was an antislavery settlement, where he had warm friends. It had been an important point on the route of Free State men to Kansas and was in full sympathy with their cause. But Brown and Forbes did not agree in the work; Forbes was dismissed and returned to the east. Brown then went to Kansas to enlist a number of his old followers. He was joined by his son, Owen, John C. Cook, A. D. Stevens, Richard Realf, J. H. Kagi, C. P. Tidd, W. H. Leeman, Luke F. Parsons, C. W. Moffett and Richard Richardson, most of whom had served in the Kansas War.

They proceeded to Springdale, where they were quartered on the farm of William Maxson, three miles from the village. The Springdale settlement was remote from railroads or any public thoroughfare and was a peaceful community of thrifty, prosperous farmers, most of whom were Abolitionists. A school for military instruction was opened on the Maxson farm, in which A. D. Stevens, who had served in the regular army, was instructor. John Brown and the young men of his party were a remarkable group. Several of them were orators; others were poets, accomplished writers and scholars. They had served in the Kansas War, endured hardships of frontier life and proved their courage in numerous conflicts with "Border Ruffians." They were now drilling for the most daring and desperate enterprise in the annals of border warfare. They possessed the qualities of heroes and readily won the warm friendship and admiration of the intelligent and refined people of the quiet rural village and surrounding country, often assembling at the hospitable homes to spend the long winter evenings with the young people. The stories of their perils, escapes and battles in Kansas were told. Their rescue of slaves from bondage and the horrors of that national crime they had witnessed were recounted and thus they won the sympathy and enduring good-will of the liberty-loving people of Springdale. While the Quakers were from principle opposed to war, so warm were their sympathies for the oppressed, that they found a way to hold in high esteem and admiration these fearless young men who had risked their lives in striking sturdy blows for freedom in Kansas. The fame of John Brown, as one of the most daring leaders of the Free State men, had reached every part of the country and the peaceful people of the Quaker settlement saw in him a leader so devoted to emancipation that his life would be freely given to secure freedom to the slaves.

Stevens was an expert drill-master and on a meadow east of the Maxson house the daily military exercises took place under his instruction. Aaron D. Stevens had been a member of Company F, First United States Dragoons. In May, 1855, he and three comrades had been court-martialed for assaulting Major Longstreet, who was afterward General Lee's famous Lieutenant-General in the War of the Rebellion. They were sentenced to be shot, but the President commuted the punishment to three years in the penitentiary. Stevens made his escape, changed his name to Whipple and became a famous colonel in the Free State army during the Kansas War. John Henri Kagi was an accomplished writer and stenographer, a correspondent of the *New York Post* and an eloquent public speaker. Richard Realf was a young Englishman of rare talents, a poet and orator and had been a protegé of Lady Byron. John E. Cook was a young man, brave and chivalrous, a fine writer and poet. His young wife was a sister of the wife of Governor Willard of Indiana. Such were some of the young men enlisted in the Harper's Ferry plan for liberating slaves. John Brown made his home with John H. Painter and won the warm friendship of William Maxson, Dr. H. G. Gill, Griffith Lewis, Moses Varney and other good citizens of Springdale.

During the winter he revealed to some of his friends his plans for the future and the purpose for which he was drilling his followers. Not one of these looked with favor upon his desperate enterprise and all tried to dissuade him from such a hazardous and hopeless undertaking. They saw clearly that he would find the whole power of the Federal Government arrayed against the forcible liberation of slaves and that his attempt must end in the death or imprisonment of all engaged in it. But nothing could shake the resolve of the fearless old emancipator. He firmly believed that he could strike a blow at slavery that would eventually result in its overthrow. His faith was so firm and confidence in success so great, that several young men from Springdale and vicinity enlisted, among whom were George B. Gill, Edwin and Barclay Coppoc and Steward Taylor.

Before going east Brown revealed his plans to Dr. H.
G. Gill. He proposed to take fifty or a hundred men, well
armed, into the mountains near Harper's Ferry, collect
slaves in the vicinity, seize conveyances and transport
them to Canada. After the excitement had subsided he
would make a raid in some other locality and thus continue until slavery ceased to exist. Dr. Gill assured him
that he could not succeed in such plans and that he and
his men would soon be killed or captured. He replied that
for himself he was willing to give his life for the emancipation of slaves. He repeatedly said that he firmly believed that he was an instrument of God through which
slavery was to be abolished. The doctor said to him:
" You and your handful of men cannot cope with the
whole South." His reply was: " I tell you, doctor, it will
be the beginning of the end of slavery."

As improbable as it seemed to all but Brown and his
devoted band, he and they were not mistaken; the great
sacrifice at Harper's Ferry was the beginning of the end of
slavery. Therefore every incident relating to that desperate enterprise becomes of absorbing historic interest.
It is now known that nearly all of John Brown's intimate
friends to whom he divulged his plans, saw that they must
end in disaster and tried in vain to dissuade him from
embarking upon so hopeless an undertaking.

In the East, Gerrit Smith, F. B. Sanborn, Wendell Phil-
lips and Theodore Parker remonstrated with him in vain.
To all he replied that it was his mission to aid in the overthrow of slavery and every one of his followers was willing to risk his life in the attempt.

On the 27th of April, 1858, John Brown returned to
Springdale and ordered his men to move east. There was
a sorrowful leave-taking between their good friends at
Springdale and the young men who were starting upon
an expedition so dangerous and daring. Warm friend-
ships had grown up and all realized that it might be the
last farewell, as it proved to be. The party assembled at

Chatham, Canada, where a convention was held to organize a provisional government. John Brown was elected Commander-in-chief; J. H. Kagi, Secretary of War; Richard Realf, Secretary of State; and George B. Gill, Secretary of the Treasury. In the meantime Forbes had, in letters to prominent men and public officials, divulged some information as to Brown's plans and it was decided to postpone the enterprise for a time. The men separated, some going to Kansas, while Cook went to Harper's Ferry and carefully made observations that would be of service when the time came for action. John Brown again went to Kansas, where he was joined by Stevens, Kagi, Tidd, Gill, Jeremiah G. Anderson and Albert Hazlett.

In December, under the leadership of Brown, they crossed into Missouri to liberate slaves who were to be sold and their families separated. They took twelve slaves, horses, wagons, cattle and other property to which Brown claimed the slaves were entitled, for years of unpaid labor. One slaveholder who resisted was killed by Stevens. Large rewards were offered by the Governor of Missouri for the arrest of Brown and his men and the recovery of the slaves. Early in January, Brown and several members of his party began the journey with the slaves in wagons, by way of Nebraska and Iowa, to Canada. They reached Tabor, in Iowa, on the 5th of February, 1859, where they remained until the 11th. The citizens of Tabor had become alarmed at Brown's invasion of Missouri and forcible liberation of slaves, fearing retaliation from the Missourians, as they were near the State line. To relieve themselves from the charge of complicity with Brown, the citizens held a public meeting and passed resolutions, condemning the acts of him and his followers but no attempt was made to arrest them. On the eleventh the slaves were conveyed on their journey, guarded by their well armed liberators, along the line of the "Underground Railroad." On the Thirteenth they stayed with Lewis Mills, on the Fifteenth with Mr. Murray, on the

Seventeenth with James C. Jordan and on the Eighteenth
they passed through Des Moines, John Teesdale, of the
State Register, paying their ferriage across the Des Moines
River.   On the Twentieth the party reached Grinnell
and were warmly welcomed by Senator J. B. Grinnell and
the citizens generally.   They had now been on the way
more than a month and no one had attempted to earn the
large rewards offered for their arrest.   The slave hunters
seemed to have no relish for a conflict with the famous
commander of the Free State Army at the Battle of Black
Jack.   On the Twenty-fifth they passed through Iowa City
where Samuel Workman, the postmaster and Captain Kel-
ley, proposed to raise a party to earn the large rewards
offered, by making a night march to Springdale and capturing Brown and his party.   But they were unable to
find enough volunteers anxious for a fight with the Kansas
veterans, who were known to be well armed and among
friends.   After resting at Springdale some days, arrange-
ments were made by Wm. Penn Clark and others at Iowa
City, to procure a box car on the Rock Island Railroad
to convey the fugitives and their escort to Chicago.   Laurel Summers, United States Marshal at Davenport, was
quietly organizing a posse to arrest them when the train
reached that city.   But Clark had outwitted the officers by
arranging for a box car to be side-tracked at West Liberty.   Brown and Kagi slept at Dr. Bowen's at Iowa City
on the night fixed for departure.   Workman's spies were
watching for Brown, intending to arrest the leader while
his party was absent and then seize the slaves.   But the
slave catchers were hunting men who were on the alert
and not easily trapped.   At four o'clock, long before daylight, Brown and Kagi, mounted on fast horses, and piloted by Colonel Trowbridge, eluded the spies on watch
and were on their way to West Liberty, where the slaves
had been secreted in a mill, guarded by Stevens and others.
A box car stood on the side track waiting for its human
freight.   As soon as Brown arrived the slaves were quick-

ly transferred to the car, while Stevens and Kagi, leaning on their Sharp's rifles, their belts filled with revolvers, kept guard. Soon the train arrived from the West. It was a thrilling moment, as the guards with rifle in hand, anxiously watched the passengers alighting, to discover indication of officers coming to arrest them. The train backed down the side track, the car with locked doors was attached, the guards stepped into one of the passenger coaches, the train started and John Brown and his companions were leaving Iowa for the last time. At Davenport the marshal and aids walked through the cars in search of the twelve slaves, but no negroes were found, and no suspicion was aroused by the freight car in the rear. At Chicago, Allen Pinkerton, the famous detective, conducted the slaves to a waiting car, which took them safely to Canada.

CHAPTER XXX

A S the pioneer period began to give way to the advancing tide of immigration coming into the Mississippi Valley with the progress of railroad extension, Iowa experienced many of the advantages of incoming capital and gladly welcomed the luxuries brought by material progress.

But among the new settlers there were regrets over the innovations which banished in some degree the universal hospitality of the early days of common poverty, when every cabin was a house of entertainment for the white-top wagon loaded with " new comers," men, women, and bright-eyed, bare-footed children seeking new homes.

Before turning to the dark days of the Civil War, which even then was beginning to seem slowly gathering in the not distant future, we may take a backward glance at the log-cabin era which will linger in the memory of the gray-haired few who were of that generation.

The early settlements in Iowa were largely made by men and women with little of worldly possessions beyond youth, health, industrious habits and a determination to better their condition in a new country where most of the people were similarly situated.

It was not from the well-to-do classes that the pioneers set forth on their westward journeys, to explore new and unknown countries. The middle-aged man with a family, who from some misfortune had found it a hard struggle in the East to accumulate any surplus over bare subsistence could not endure the thought that his sons must be left with only an inheritance of industry; that his daughters must serve as servants in the families of strangers; that the long years of toil for a frugal living must go on among his descendants through the succeeding generations.

He looked around among his neighbors and saw boys no
brighter and girls no worthier than his own, enjoying
the advantages of education, the best society and all that
wealth could bring. His sons and daughters were as dear
to him as those who were highly favored by fortune were
to their parents. There were no class divisions in America
to exclude his children from aspiring to higher positions;
no exclusive social circles which they might not enter; the
field was open to all. Misfortune or poverty alone kept
the ambitious from participation in the luxuries of life.
There were great unsettled regions in the far West where
industry, perseverance and privations for this generation
would give all of these advantages to the children of the
poor. It was hard to sever all social and kindred ties and
seek among unsettled regions a place to make new homes;
endure the stern privations, slavish toil and long, slow
waiting for the coming in late years of life of the advantages that the children might some distant day enjoy.
The whole West of fifty years ago was dotted over with
log cabins, where, amid hardships, sickness, want and un-
ending toil, the best years of the lives of brave self-sacri-
ficing men and women were given to the building up of a
new civilization from little more than nature had provided.

The younger generation of the closing years of the
Nineteenth Century can know little of the slow progress
of evolution which has transformed the bleak prairies of
fifty years ago into beautiful farms of unsurpassed fertility, adorned with shady groves, fruitful orchards, large
barns, modern homes and generous equipments of the best
labor-saving implements. They cannot realize that our
network of railroads, telegraphs and telephones has so
recently displaced the stage coach, the emigrant wagon
drawn by oxen, the weekly horseback mail carrier. That
our cities and thriving villages with their modern homes,
imposing business blocks and public buildings, with factories, banks, elegant churches and stately school-houses

WILD TURKEYS WERE FINE GAME IN PIONEER TIMES IN IOWA

BUFFALO HUNT ON IOWA PRAIRIES IN 1834

have, within the memory of the older citizens, crowded out the Indian's wigwam and the pioneer's log cabin and sod house.

Looking back upon a picture of pioneer life as it was in the years beginning with the early " 30s," " 40s " and " 50s," we find a land where the Indians, buffalo, deer and elk were reluctantly retiring before the invasion of the hunter, trapper and pioneer farmer. The well-worn paths of these early inhabitants of the wild groves and boundless prairies were found along the wooded banks of the rivers and creeks.

Before the deadly rifle of the hunters and the snares of the stealthy trappers the red men and wild animals rapidly but most reluctantly retreated. Next came the resounding echoes of the wood-chopper's axe as the lofty walnut, oak and hickory trees were converted into cabins and fences for new homes of the pioneer and his family.

Toil had no terrors for the early settlers; all were workers. There was a charm in choosing a home in the wild, unsettled country, as the family journeyed on day after day in the solitude of the vast rolling prairies, fording the streams, winding along the trackless ridges, exploring the fringe of woodland that bordered the creeks and rivers; passing beautiful groves that in the distance slowly loomed up like islands in the ocean, where earlier immigrants had camped and staked off their claims. The finding of a spring in an unoccupied grove and taking possession for a home; getting acquainted with the neighbors who had preceded them; exploring the thickets for wild plums, grapes, crab-apples, hazel and hickory nuts. Choosing the site for the cabin, cutting the logs which the neighbors helped to raise into a rude house, hunting the deer, elk, wild turkeys, prairie chickens, ducks and geese for subsistence until sod corn could be raised; going two or three days' journey to mill or market and camping out nights on the way; constructing tables, bedsteads, stools and shelves; breaking the prairie with five or six yoke of oxen and the huge breaking plow and planting the sod corn. The women of the household were among the constant toilers. In addition to the ordinary housework of later times, living remote from towns, stores or factories, they were artisans and manufacturers as well as housekeepers. They had to spin, weave, cut and make clothing for the family, and often were the teachers of their children. There were compensations for the privations and hard toil. Hospitality was nowhere more general and genuine than among the early settlers. Entertainment of " new comers " was generally free and cordial. The one room of the cabin was never too full to furnish shelter and food for the traveler. Neighbors gathered together for miles around at corn huskings, which ended with a frolic for the youngsters in the evening. Shooting matches were made where the winners went home loaded with turkeys won; camp meetings were held by the light of blazing log piles where old and young assembled to listen to the rude eloquence of the uncultured preacher, lurid with fire and brimstone and endless wrath for sinners, which suited the sturdy pioneers. All joined in singing the grand old hymns with a fervor that raised enthusiasm to the highest pitch.

The annual Fourth of July celebration appealed to the patriotism of every citizen, old and young. The oration of the young lawyer from a distant town was listened to with rapt attention and the national songs resounded through the grove. A picnic dinner spread beneath the sheltering trees, and a country ball in the evening, made up a day of general enjoyment for the entire population.

Wolf hunts in the winter were occasions of wild excitement and political meetings in the country school-house at long intervals brought the widely separated settlers together and served to vary the monotony of their lives of rugged toil.

The malaria generated from decaying vegetation brought fevers and ague and when sickness came, often

THE PIONEER LOG CABIN
" Always Room for One More "

no doctor was within reach, neighborly help and kindness were never lacking, good-will and sympathy were the substitutes for skilled physicians. When death cast its shadow over the home, willing hands and warm hearts ministered to the stricken family and tenderly performed the last sad offices for the dead. A rude box inclosed the lifeless form borne by neighbors to the lonely grave. Often there was no minister, music or flowers. No carved marble or granite shaft told the name of the dead; the sturdy oak or lofty elm cast a grateful shadow over the grassy mound that alone marked the last resting place of the departed pioneer.

This period in northwestern Iowa lingered along well into the " 60s," as that portion of the State was the last to be settled, owing to the general absence of forests. The prairies were vast in extent, generally inclined to be level and in many places defective in surface drainage, with frequent ponds and marshes, the home of the muskrat. It was not until the homestead law was enacted by Congress that people began to venture out upon the great bleak prairies of northwestern Iowa to make homes. Mostly destitute of timber for cabins and fencing, with few deep ravines for shelter from the fierce blizzards that swept over them in winter, they long remained unoccupied after other portions of the State were fairly well settled. But when the time came in which the head of the family could secure a hundred and sixty acres of government land, as a home, for fourteen dollars, the hardy pioneers began to venture out upon the treeless plains and devise ways to live without timber. Then it was that sod houses and stables were invented. They were made by running a broad-shire breaking-plow over the wet prairie where the tough fiber of the sod of generations had accumulated, cutting it into long strips and turning them over. These strips of sod were then cut up with the spades into lengths suitable to handle and laid up like brick into walls for houses and stables. A few poles brought from the nearest timber supported a roof of slough hay, skillfully placed on like thatching, and a comfortable shelter was made for man and beast. The ground was smoothed off for a floor and until boards could be procured for doors, the skins of deer and wolves shut out the wind and snow. Then it was that the swarms of muskrats which inhabited every pond were utilized to supply the family with groceries. Muskrat pelts were always salable for cash at the nearest town, where buyers had agents to gather up all kinds of furs and hides of wild animals. During the first year of life on the prairie, before crops could be raised for market, thousands of homestead families were dependent upon trapping muskrats for the cash they must have to buy bacon and coffee. The homestead was exempt from taxes; deer and prairie chickens furnished meat for portions of the year; with industrious mending and the skins of wild animals the clothing was made to do long service; but some money was indispensable for fuel and such scant groceries as were indulged in.

Most of the homestead settlers were many miles from timber or coal. Their teams were usually oxen, which could live on prairie grass and wild hay, and break up the sod for cultivation. It was always a perilous journey in the winter to the nearest town or timber, or coal bank, for fuel or other supplies. It must be made generally by one man alone, over a trackless prairie covered with deep snow. No human foresight could guard against danger from the fearful blizzards of flinty snow driven with an ever-increasing wind and an ever-falling temperature that were so common in early days. With the sun obscured, nothing was left to guide the bewildered driver toward his destination, as the changing wind often misled him and many were the victims who perished in all of the early years of settling the great prairies.

Another danger that was encountered by the first settlers on the prairies came from the annual fires. Early

CAUGHT IN A BLIZZARD

STAGE COACH ENCOUNTERS A PRAIRIE FIRE

in the fall frosts killed the wild grass and in a few weeks
it became dry and would readily burn. Many of the
recent settlers were not aware of the danger and neglected to take the proper precaution for safety of their
buildings, stacks and even the families. Emigrants
crossing the great prairies and camping at night where
water could be found, late in the autumn, were often
the victims of carelessness or ignorance of danger. There
can be no more fearful sight or situation than the approach of a prairie fire before a strong wind in the night.
The horizon is lighted up in the distance with a vivid
glow, and dense columns of black smoke ascend in darken-
ing clouds as the long line of fire circles far to the right
and left. At first the sight is grand beyond description
as the rays of the glowing red rise higher and higher and
the smoke rolls upward in increasing density. But soon
an ominous roar is heard in the distance as the hurricane
of fire is driven with an ever-increasing wind, exceeding
the speed of a race horse, and the stifling atmosphere
glows with the smothering heat of a sirocco from a
parched desert. Escape for man or beast is impossible
unless a back fire has been started in time to meet the advancing tornado of resistless heat that can only be staid by
a counter-fire. Houses, barns, stacks, fences, bridges and
all animal life are quickly destroyed as the hot blasts
strike them and in a moment the ground is left a blackened, blistering waste of desolation. The ruin of the camp
or farm is as complete as the wreck of a burning town, or
the track of a tornado. Scores of people and hundreds of
homes were annual victims of these fires in the early years
of scattered farms on the great prairies, before experience brought to emigrants and settlers the wisdom to protect their lives and property by timely back-fires as soon
as the frost had killed the grass.

It was during these years of hard winters when the
homestead settlers ventured far out on the wild prairies
at great distances from timber and before railroads had

penetrated the great plains, that they began to use corn
and slough hay for fuel. There was no market for corn
within one or two days' travel and when the market was
reached, eight or ten cents a bushel was all that a farmer
could get for his load. A large load would sometimes
bring him from four to five dollars.

This was the pay for raising forty bushels of corn on an
acre of his farm, husking it and transporting the load a
journey of two or three days with his team. The proceeds
of his load would pay for about a ton of coal which he
must draw back to his home and which would furnish
about as much heat as the load of corn sold. It did not
take the settler long to see that he might far better burn
the corn at home and save a perilous journey in mid-
winter over the bleak prairies, often at the risk of his life.
He learned to twist the long coarse slough hay into ropes
with which to start his corn fire and utilized a home grown
vegetable production to furnish heat in place of the expensive foreign mineral production of the same earth
upon which he lived. Persons of the luxurious homes of
distant countries and states read of the burning of corn,
in the morning paper by a comfortable grate fire, and were
horrified at the reckless destruction of food by the western prairie farmers.

As the railroads were slowly extended westward in
Iowa settlements were made along the projected lines far
out on the wild prairies in anticipation of their coming.
Towns were laid out along the lines of survey and a new
impetus was given to all branches of business.

The public school system of Iowa had been a gradual
evolution from the First Territorial Legislature which,
in 1839, took the incipient steps toward its organization,
by the passage of an act which provided that:

" There shall be established a common school or schools in each of the
counties of the Territory, which shall be open and free for every class of
white citizens between the ages of five and twenty-one. The county board

is directed to organize districts in their respective counties whenever a petition may be presented for the purpose by a majority of the voters resident within such contemplated district."

The districts were in charge of trustees who were required to maintain a school at least three months of each year. This was before many of the older States had provided for a public school system supported by taxation and made free to the pupils. The first act providing for taxation to meet the expenses of such schools required that a portion of the funds for their support should be assessed against the parents of the pupils in attendance.

From time to time more liberal taxes were authorized until the schools were finally sustained from the proceeds of the lands granted by the general government, and taxes 'evied upon the property of the district or townships. In addition to these sources of income the State received five per cent. of the net proceeds of the sale of all public lands lying within its limits. During the pioneer period this amounted to a large sum annually as the lands found purchasers.

The first State Constitution also provided that the estates of deceased persons who died without leaving a will, or heirs, should inure to the public school fund. That the money paid by persons as an equivalent for exemption from military duty, and the clear proceeds of all fines collected in the several counties for any breach of penal laws, should go to the school fund. This provision was also incorporated in the Constitution of 1857. When the State was admitted into the Union in 1846, there were 20,000 children of school age and something more than four hundred school districts had been organized. In 1857 the number of districts had increased to 3,275. The State in 1858 authorized the holding of Teachers' Institutes, lasting not less than six days, when not less than thirty teachers should desire them; and an appropriation of $1,000 was made to defray the expenses.

While great progress had been made in the character of
the district school buildings the report of the Secretary
of the State Board of Education shows there were eight
hundred and ninety-three log school-houses still in use in
the State at the close of the year 1859. The total number
of schools at this time was 4,927. The average attendance
of pupils was 77,113 while the number entitled to attend
was 127,517. There were employed 6,374 teachers of which
3,155 were women. The average compensation for men
teachers was $5.94 per week, for women $3.82, for the year
1859. The aggregate amount paid the teachers of the entire State was $445,467.88; and the value of the school-
houses was $1,206,840.24, while the number of volumes in
the school libraries was 2,325. The permanent school fund
was now estimated at more than $2,000,000 and yearly in-
creasing.

The report of the State University at this date shows a
total fund arising from the sale of lands amounting to
$110,982.11, while the land unsold is estimated to be worth
$61,996. The University at this time had a Preparatory
Department, a Normal Department and a Model School.
The number of students in all of the departments for the
year was one hundred and eighty-two, and the number
of professors, including the president, was six. The only
building at this time was the old Capitol, but a boarding
hall was in process of erection. The library contained
1,410 volumes. The salary of the president was $2,000,
but in 1860 was reduced to $1,500. The five professors re-
ceived salaries of $1,000 each.

The annual appropriation of interest on the permanent
school fund was in 1849, in round numbers, $6,137, and in
1859 it amounted to $145,034.

The Agricultural College was not yet organized, but a
farm of six hundred and forty-seven acres had been purchased in Story County, where the location had been made,
and a farm house had been erected. An office was kept in
the Capitol under charge of the secretary for the collec-

tion and distribution of new and promising seeds and
plants sent out among the farmers of the State for experi-
mental' purposes.

The amount of improved lands in the farms of the State
at this time was reported at nearly 4,000,000 of acres out
of a total acreage in the State of 33,000,000. It is estimated that there was unimproved land entered at this
date and taxable amounting to nearly 24,000,000 of acres
of which nearly 16,000,000 belonged to non-residents. The
assessed value of unimproved land averaged $2.75 per
acre. The average price of wheat was forty cents per
bushel; corn, twelve cents; oats, fifteen cents; potatoes,
twenty-five cents; and hay, $1.50 per ton. There were
produced 3,000,000 gallons of sorghum syrup, valued at
thirty-three cents per gallon.

Barbed wire fencing had not then come into use and the
farmers were experimenting with hedge plants of osage
orange, hawthorn, willow and honey locust. Others were
making fences by ditching. But the common fence was of
rails or boards and was the great expense in making
farms, costing more than all other improvements combined.

Stage lines conveyed passengers, mail and express pack-
ages in various directions from the terminus of the railroad. Freight lines were established to transport goods,
lumber and coal to the chief towns of the interior and
western portions of the State and bring back farm produce for the eastern markets.

The population of the State had now reached 674,913,
showing an increase in ten years of 482,700. The aggregate value of the farms had reached, in round numbers, nearly $120,000,000; while the total value of farm
implements and machinery was more than $6,000,000.
The value of live stock was more than $22,000,000; the
corn crop made a yield of more than 42,000,000 of bushels;
wheat, 8,500,000 bushels; oats, 5,887,000 bushels; potatoes, 2,800,000 bushels. The dairy products were, in

round numbers, 12,000,000 pounds of butter, and 918,000 pounds of cheese. Of hay there were 813,000 tons, largely made from prairie grass.

The earlier settlers were building frame houses and barns. Pretentious business blocks, substantial churches, better school-houses and tasteful private dwellings were beginning to take the place in village and city of the log structures which everywhere prevailed in earlier years. Factories were relieving the overworked women in making cloth for the family clothing. Farmers were buying reapers to displace the grain cradles and mowers were taking the place of the scythe. Pine lumber was coming down the Mississippi River in huge rafts, supplying boards to relieve the slavish toil of rail-making for fencing, and lumber for farm buildings in place of logs. Improved cattle and swine were driving out the scrubs, while spring wagons and carriages were slowly coming into use in place of the saddle horse and lumber wagon. The young men in many localties wore factory made clothing in place of the home made butternut or linsey-woolsey, and the women dressed themselves in calico and muslin, which was a desirable and comfortable substitute for the home-woven fabrics of pioneer times. This relief from spinning and weaving gave the women and girls a little rest from the never ending drudgery of the household and leisure in evenings to read. Many ambitious girls now found time to study and prepare for teaching the country schools.

High schools and colleges were affording facilities for better education and the bright farm girls began to crowd out the ancient men teachers who had long ruled with the birch rod.

Boys from the farm were beginning to turn their eyes to the learned professions where social advantages were within their reach and visions of public offices in the future spurred them to acquire knowledge of the world in broader fields than those of the father's acres.

PIONEER WOMAN SPINNING

PIONEER WOMEN OF IOWA WOVE THE CLOTH FOR THE
GARMENTS OF THE FAMILY

The slow but sure accumulation of property on the fertile prairie farms had brought a degree of prosperity to all classes and there was gradual relief from continuous toil and rigid economy that was unavoidable in the pioneer years.

The new system of banks had for the first time furnished a safe currency for the transaction of business and eastern capital was now seeking investment in the State, facilitating the building of railroads and thus furnishing better markets. The liberal grants of public lands for railroad building attracted the attention of outside capitalists and far-seeing men realized that these fertile millions of acres must become valuable as they were made accessible to markets by the extension of railroads.

The hard times beginning with 1857 were passing away, and a steady and heavy immigration was annually coming into the State in search of cheap homes. Thousands of eastern men of wealth were sending money where the legal rate of interest was ten per cent. and the security as fertile lands as any in the world.

The reports of the discovery of rich gold deposits in the eastern range of the Rocky Mountains, near Pike's Peak in 1859, attracted thousands of Iowa people to that region, and it is likely that these departures in search of gold nearly equaled the immigration from eastern States into Iowa. But the tide soon turned back and most of the gold seekers returned to the prairies of Iowa again, better content to rely upon the steady gains derived with certainty from the fertile soil of well-tilled farms.